## More praise from across the nation for t⟍ JobBank series:

"One of the better publishers of employment almanacs is Adams Media Corporation ... publisher of *The Metropolitan New York JobBank* and similarly named directories of employers in Texas, Boston, Chicago, Northern and Southern California, and Washington DC. A good buy...."

> *-Wall Street Journal's*
> *National Business Employment Weekly*

"*JobBank* books are all devoted to specific job markets. This is helpful if you are thinking about working in cities like San Antonio, Washington, Boston, or states such as Tennessee or the Carolinas. You can use them for research, and a particularly useful feature is the inclusion of the type of positions that are commonly offered at the companies listed."

> **-Karen Ronald, Library Director**
> **Wilton Library, Wilton, CT**

"If you are looking for a job ... before you go to the newspapers and the help-wanted ads, listen to Bob Adams, publisher *of The Metropolitan New York JobBank.*"

> **-Tom Brokaw, NBC**

"Since 1985 the Adams *JobBank Series* has proven to be the consummate tool for the efficient job search."

> **-Mel Rappleyea, Human Resources Director**
> **Starbucks Coffee Company**

"Having worked in the Career Services field for 10 years, I know the quality of Adams publications."

> **-Philip Meade, Director of Graduate Career Services**
> **Baruch School of Business (New York NY)**

"I read through the 'Basics of Job Winning' and 'Resumes' sections [in *The Dallas-Fort Worth JobBank*] and found them to be very informative, with some positive tips for the job searcher. I believe the strategies outlined will bring success to any determined candidate."

> **-Camilla Norder, Professional Recruiter**
> **Presbyterian Hospital of Dallas**

"The ultimate in a superior series of job hunt directories."

> **-Cornell University Career Center's**
> *Where to Start*

"Help on the job hunt … Anyone who is job-hunting in the New York area can find a lot of useful ideas in a new paperback called *The Metropolitan New York JobBank*…."

**-Angela Taylor, *New York Times***

"A timely book for Chicago job hunters follows books from the same publisher that were well received in New York and Boston … [*The Chicago JobBank* is] a fine tool for job hunters…."

**-Clarence Peterson, *Chicago Tribune***

"Because our listing is seen by people across the nation, it generates lots for resumes for us. We encourage unsolicited resumes. We'll always be listed [in *The Chicago JobBank*] as long as I'm in this career."

**-Tom Fitzpatrick, Director of Human Resources Merchandise Mart Properties, Inc.**

"Job hunting is never fun, but this book can ease the ordeal …*[The Los Angeles JobBank*] will help allay fears, build confidence, and avoid wheel-spinning."

**-Robert W. Ross, *Los Angeles Times***

"*The Seattle JobBank* is an essential resource for job hunters."

**-Gil Lopez, Staffing Team Manager Battelle Pacific Northwest Laboratories**

"*The Phoenix JobBank* is a first-class publication. The information provided is useful and current."

**-Lyndon Denton Director of Human Resources and Materials Management Apache Nitrogen Products, Inc.**

"*The Florida JobBank* is an invaluable job-search reference tool. It provides the most up-to-date information and contact names available for companies in Florida. I should know – it worked for me!"

**-Rhonda Cody, Human Resources Consultant Aetna Life and Casualty**

"I read through the 'Basics of Job Winning' and 'Resumes' sections [in *The Dallas-Fort Worth JobBank*] and found them to be very informative, with some positive tips for the job searcher. I believe the strategies outlined will bring success to any determined candidate."

**-Camilla Norder, Professional Recruiter Presbyterian Hospital of Dallas**

"Through *The Dallas-Fort Worth JobBank,* we've been able to attract high-quality candidates for several positions."

**-Rob Bertino, Southern States Sales Manager CompuServe**

# What makes the
# JobBank series
# the nation's premier
# line of employment guides?

With vital employment information on thousands of employers across the nation, the JobBank series is the most comprehensive and authoritative set of career directories available today.

Each book in the series provides information on **dozens of different industries** in a given city or area, with the primary employer listings providing contact information, telephone and fax numbers, e-mail addresses, Websites, a summary of the firm's business, internships, and in many cases descriptions of the firm's typical professional job categories.

All of the reference information in the JobBank series is as up-to-date and accurate as possible. Every year, the entire database is thoroughly researched and verified by mail and by telephone. Adams Media Corporation publishes **more local employment guides more often** than any other publisher of career directories.

The JobBank series offers **20 regional titles**, from Boston to San Francisco. All of the information is organized geographically, because most people look for jobs in specific areas of the country.

A condensed, but thorough, review of the entire job search process is presented in the chapter **The Basics of Job Winning**, a feature that has received many compliments from career counselors. In addition, each JobBank directory includes a section on **resumes and cover letters** the *New York Times* has acclaimed as "excellent."

The JobBank series gives job hunters the most comprehensive, timely, and accurate career information, organized and indexed to facilitate your job search. An entire career reference library, JobBank books are designed to help you find optimal employment in any market.

# Top career publications from Adams Media

# 19th Edition
## THE Chicago
# JobBank

adams
media

Published by Adams Media, an F+W Publications Company
57 Littlefield Street, Avon, MA 02322 U.S.A.
www.adamsmedia.com

ISBN: 1-59337-444-5
ISSN: 1072-575X
Manufactured in USA

Because addresses and telephone numbers of smaller companies change rapidly, we recommend you call each company and verify the information before mailing to the employers listed in this book. Mass mailings are not recommended.

While the publisher has made every reasonable effort to obtain and verify accurate information, occasional errors are possible due to the magnitude of the data. Should you discover an error, or if a company is missing, please write the editors at the above address so that we may update future editions.

"This publication is designed to provide accurate and authoritative information with regard to the subject matter covered. It is sold with the understanding that the publisher is not engaged in rendering legal, accounting, or other professional advice. If legal advice or other expert assistance is required, the services of a competent professional person should be sought."
--From a Declaration of Principles jointly adopted by a Committee of the American Bar Association and a Committee of Publishers and Associations

This book is available on standing order and at quantity discounts for bulk purchases. For information, call 800/872-5627 (in Massachusetts, 508/427-7100).

# TABLE OF CONTENTS

- Physical Fitness Facilities
- Professional Sports Clubs; Sporting and Recreational Camps
- Public Golf Courses and Racing and Track Operations
- Theatrical Producers and Services

**Automotive/77**
- Automotive Repair Shops
- Automotive Stampings
- Industrial Vehicles and Moving Equipment
- Motor Vehicles and Equipment
- Travel Trailers and Campers

**Banking, Savings and Loans, & Other Depository Institutions/81**
- Banks
- Bank Holding Companies and Associations
- Lending Firms/Financial Services Institutions

**Biotechnology, Pharmaceuticals, and Scientific R&D/88**
- Clinical Labs
- Lab Equipment Manufacturers
- Pharmaceutical Manufacturers and Distributors

**Business Services and Non-Scientific Research/94**
- Adjustment and Collection Services
- Cleaning, Maintenance, and Pest Control Services
- Credit Reporting Services
- Detective, Guard, and Armored Car Services/Security Systems Services
- Miscellaneous Equipment Rental and Leasing
- Secretarial and Court Reporting Services

**Charities and Social Services/99**
- Social and Human Service Agencies
- Job Training and Vocational Rehabilitation Services
- Nonprofit Organizations

**Chemicals, Rubber, and Plastics/102**
- Adhesives, Detergents, Inks, Paints, Soaps, Varnishes
- Agricultural Chemicals and Fertilizers
- Carbon and Graphite Products
- Chemical Engineering Firms
- Industrial Gases

**Communications: Telecommunications and Broadcasting/109**
- Cable/Pay Television Services
- Communications Equipment
- Radio and Television Broadcasting Stations
- Telephone, Telegraph, and Other Message Communications

**Computer Hardware, Software, and Services/114**
- Computer Components and Hardware Manufacturers
- Consultants and Computer Training Companies
- Internet and Online Service Providers
- Networking and Systems Services
- Repair Services/Rental and Leasing
- Resellers, Wholesalers, and Distributors
- Software Developers/Programming Services

**Educational Services/125**
- Business/Secretarial/Data Processing Schools

# HOW TO USE THIS BOOK

Right now, you hold in your hands one of the most effective job-hunting tools available anywhere. In *The Chicago JobBank*, you will find valuable information to help you launch or continue a rewarding career. But before you open to the book's employer listings and start calling about current job openings, take a few minutes to learn how best to use the resources presented in *The Chicago JobBank*.

*The Chicago JobBank* will help you to stand out from other jobseekers. While many people looking for a new job rely solely on newspaper help-wanted ads, this book offers you a much more effective job-search method -- direct contact. The direct contact method has been proven twice as effective as scanning the help-wanted ads. Instead of waiting for employers to come looking for you, you'll be far more effective going to them. While many of your competitors will use trial and error methods in trying to set up interviews, you'll learn not only how to get interviews, but what to expect once you've got them.

In the next few pages, we'll take you through each section of the book so you'll be prepared to get a jump-start on your competition.

## Basics of Job Winning

Preparation. Strategy. Time management. These are three of the most important elements of a successful job search. *Basics of Job Winning* helps you address these and all the other elements needed to find the right job.

One of your first priorities should be to define your personal career objectives. What qualities make a job desirable to you? Creativity? High pay? Prestige? Use *Basics of Job Winning* to weigh these questions. Then use the rest of the chapter to design a strategy to find a job that matches your criteria.

In *Basics of Job Winning,* you'll learn which job-hunting techniques work, and which don't. We've reviewed the pros and cons of mass mailings, help-wanted ads, and direct contact. We'll show you how to develop and approach contacts in your field; how to research a prospective employer; and how to use that information to get an interview and the job.

Also included in *Basics of Job Winning*: interview dress code and etiquette, the "do's and don'ts" of interviewing, sample interview questions, and more. We also deal with some of the unique problems faced by those jobseekers who are currently employed, those who have lost a job, and college students conducting their first job search.

## Resumes and Cover Letters

The approach you take to writing your resume and cover letter can often mean the difference between getting an interview and never being noticed. In this section, we discuss different formats, as well as what to put on (and what to leave off) your resume. We review the benefits and drawbacks of professional resume writers, and the importance of a follow-up letter. Also included in this section are sample resumes and cover letters which you can use as models.

## The Employer Listings

Employers are listed alphabetically by industry. When a company does business under a person's name, like "John Smith & Co.," the company is usually listed by the surname's spelling (in this case "S"). Exceptions occur when a company's name is widely recognized, like "JCPenney" or "Howard Johnson Motor Lodge." In those cases, the company's first name is the key ("J" and "H" respectively).

The Chicago JobBank covers a very wide range of industries. Each company profile is assigned to one of the industry chapters listed below.

Accounting and Management Consulting
Advertising, Marketing, and Public
    Relations
Aerospace
Apparel, Fashion, and Textiles
Architecture, Construction, and Engineering
Arts, Entertainment, Sports, and Recreation
Automotive
Banking/Savings and Loans
Biotechnology, Pharmaceuticals, and
    Scientific R&D
Business Services and Non-Scientific
    Research
Charities and Social Services
Chemicals/Rubber and Plastics
Communications: Telecommunications and
    Broadcasting
Computer Hardware, Software, and
    Services
Educational Services
Electronic/Industrial Electrical Equipment
    and Components

Environmental and Waste Management
    Services
Fabricated/Primary Metals and Products
Financial Services
Food and Beverages/Agriculture
Government
Health Care: Services, Equipment, and
    Products
Hotels and Restaurants
Insurance
Legal Services
Manufacturing: Miscellaneous Consumer
Manufacturing: Miscellaneous Industrial
Mining/Gas/Petroleum/Energy Related
Paper and Wood Products
Printing and Publishing
Real Estate
Retail
Stone, Clay, Glass, and Concrete Products
Transportation/Travel
Utilities: Electric/Gas/Water
Miscellaneous Wholesaling

Many of the company listings offer detailed company profiles. In addition to company names, addresses, and phone numbers, these listings also include contact names or hiring departments, and descriptions of each company's products and/or services. Many of those listings also feature a variety of additional information including:

**Positions advertised** - A list of open positions the company was advertising at the time our research was conducted. Note: Keep in mind that The Chicago JobBank is a directory of major employers in the area, not a directory of openings currently available. Positions listed in this book that were advertised at the time research was conducted may no longer be open. Many of the companies listed will be hiring, others will not. However, since most professional job openings are filled without the placement of help-wanted ads, contacting the employers in this book directly is still a more effective method than browsing the Sunday papers.

**Special programs** - Does the company offer training programs, internships, or apprenticeships? These programs can be important to first time jobseekers and college students looking for practical work experience. Many employer profiles will include information on these programs.

**Parent company** - If an employer is a subsidiary of a larger company, the name of that parent company will often be listed here. Use this information to supplement your company research before contacting the employer.

**Number of employees** - The number of workers a company employs.

Company listings may also include information on other U.S. locations and any stock exchanges the firm may be listed on.

A note on all employer listings that appear in The Chicago JobBank: This book is intended as a starting point. It is not intended to replace any effort that you, the jobseeker, should devote to your job hunt. Keep in mind that while a great deal of effort has been put into collecting and verifying the company profiles provided in this book, addresses and contact names change regularly. Inevitably, some contact names listed herein have changed even before you read this. We recommend you contact a company before mailing your resume to ensure nothing has changed.

## Industry Associations

This section includes a select list of professional and trade associations organized by industry. Many of these associations can provide employment advice and job-search help, offer magazines that cover the industry, and provide additional information or directories that may supplement the employer listings in this book.

## Index of Primary Employers

*The Chicago JobBank* index is listed alphabetically by company name.

# THE JOB SEARCH

# THE BASICS OF JOB WINNING: A CONDENSED REVIEW

This chapter is divided into four sections. The first section explains the fundamentals that every jobseeker should know, especially first-time jobseekers. The next three sections deal with special situations faced by specific types of jobseekers: those who are currently employed, those who have lost a job, and college students.

## THE BASICS:
### Things Everyone Needs to Know

### Career Planning

The first step to finding your ideal job is to clearly define your objectives. This is better known as career planning (or life planning if you wish to emphasize the importance of combining the two). Career planning has become a field of study in and of itself.

If you are thinking of choosing or switching careers, we particularly emphasize two things. First, choose a career where you will enjoy most of the day-to-day tasks. This sounds obvious, but most of us have at some point found the idea of a glamour industry or prestigious job title attractive without thinking of the key consideration: Would we enjoy performing the *everyday* tasks the position entails?

The second key consideration is that you are not merely choosing a career, but also a lifestyle. Career counselors indicate that one of the most common problems people encounter in jobseeking is that they fail to consider how well-suited they are for a particular position or career. For example, some people, attracted to management consulting by good salaries, early responsibility, and high-level corporate exposure, do not adapt well to the long hours, heavy travel demands, and constant pressure to produce. Be sure to ask yourself how you might adapt to the day-to-day duties and working environment that a specific position entails. Then ask yourself how you might adapt to the demands of that career or industry as a whole.

### Choosing Your Strategy

Assuming that you've established your career objectives, the next step of the job search is to develop a strategy. If you don't take the time to develop a plan, you may find yourself going in circles after several weeks of randomly searching for opportunities that always seem just beyond your reach.

The most common jobseeking techniques are:

- following up on help-wanted advertisements (in the newspaper or online)
- using employment services
- relying on personal contacts
- contacting employers directly (the Direct Contact method)

Each of these approaches can lead to better jobs. However, the Direct Contact method boasts twice the success rate of the others. So unless you have specific reasons to employ other strategies, Direct Contact should form the foundation of your job search.

If you choose to use other methods as well, try to expend at least half your energy on Direct Contact. Millions of other jobseekers have already proven that Direct Contact has been twice as effective in obtaining employment, so why not follow in their footsteps?

## Setting Your Schedule

Okay, so now that you've targeted a strategy it's time to work out the details of your job search. The most important detail is setting up a schedule. Of course, since job searches aren't something most people do regularly, it may be hard to estimate how long each step will take. Nonetheless, it is important to have a plan so that you can monitor your progress.

When outlining your job search schedule, have a realistic time frame in mind. If you will be job-searching full-time, your search could take at least two months or more. If you can only devote part-time effort, it will probably take at least four months.

You probably know a few people who seem to spend their whole lives searching for a better job in their spare time. Don't be one of them. If you are presently working and don't feel like devoting a lot of energy to jobseeking right now, then wait. Focus on enjoying your present position, performing your best on the job, and storing up energy for when you are really ready to begin your job search.

> **The first step in beginning your job search is to clearly define your objectives.**

Those of you who are currently unemployed should remember that *job-hunting is tough work, both physically and emotionally*. It is also intellectually demanding work that requires you to be at your best. So don't tire yourself out by working on your job campaign around the clock. At the same time, be sure to discipline yourself. The most logical way to manage your time while looking for a job is to keep your regular working hours.

If you are searching full-time and have decided to choose several different strategies, we recommend that you divide up each week, designating some time for each method. By trying several approaches at once, you can evaluate how promising each seems and alter your schedule accordingly. Keep in mind that the *majority of openings are filled without being advertised*. Remember also that positions advertised on the Internet are just as likely to already be filled as those found in the newspaper!

If you are searching part-time and decide to try several different contact methods, we recommend that you try them sequentially. You simply won't have enough time to put a meaningful amount of effort into more than one method at once. Estimate the length of your job search, and then allocate so many weeks or months for each contact method, beginning with Direct Contact. The purpose of setting this schedule is not to rush you to your goal but to help you periodically evaluate your progress.

## The Direct Contact Method

Once you have scheduled your time, you are ready to begin your search in earnest. Beginning with the Direct Contact method, the first step is to develop a checklist for categorizing the types of firms for which you'd like to work. You might categorize firms by product line, size, customer type (such as industrial or consumer), growth prospects, or geographical location. Keep in mind, the shorter the list the easier it will be to locate a company that is right for you.

Next you will want to use this *JobBank* book to assemble your list of potential employers. Choose firms where *you* are most likely to be able to find a job. Try matching your skills with those that a specific job demands. Consider where your skills might be in demand, the degree of competition for employment, and the employment outlook at each company.

Separate your prospect list into three groups. The first 25 percent will be your primary target group, the next 25 percent will be your secondary group, and the remaining names will be your reserve group.

After you form your prospect list, begin working on your resume. Refer to the Resumes and Cover Letters section following this chapter for more information.

Once your resume is complete, begin researching your first batch of prospective employers. You will want to determine whether you would be happy working at the firms you are researching and to get a better idea of what their employment needs might be. You also need to obtain enough information to sound highly informed about the company during phone conversations and in mail correspondence. But don't go all out on your research yet! You probably won't be able to arrange interviews with some of these firms, so save your big research effort until you start to arrange interviews. Nevertheless, you should plan to spend several hours researching each firm. Do your research in batches to save time and energy. Start with this book, and find out what you can about each of the firms in your primary target group. For answers to specific questions, contact any pertinent professional associations that may be able to help you learn more about an employer. Read industry publications looking for articles on the firm. (Addresses of associations and names of important publications are listed after each section of employer listings in this book.) Then look up the company on the Internet or try additional resources at your local library. Keep organized, and maintain a folder on each firm.

**The more you know about a company, the more likely you are to catch an interviewer's eye. (You'll also face fewer surprises once you get the job!)**

Information to look for includes: company size; president, CEO, or owner's name; when the company was established; what each division does; and benefits that are important to you. An abundance of company information can now be found electronically, through the World Wide Web or commercial online services. Researching companies online is a convenient means of obtaining information quickly and easily. If you have access to the Internet, you can search from your home at any time of day.

You may search a particular company's Website for current information that may be otherwise unavailable in print. In fact, many companies that maintain a site update their information daily. In addition, you may also search articles written about the company online. Today, most of the nation's largest newspapers, magazines, trade publications, and regional business periodicals have online versions of their publications. To find additional resources, use a search engine like Yahoo! or Alta Vista and type in the keyword "companies" or "employers."

If you discover something that really disturbs you about the firm (they are about to close their only local office), or if you discover that your chances of getting a job there are practically nil (they have just instituted a hiring freeze), then cross them off your prospect list. If possible, supplement your research efforts by contacting individuals who know the firm well. Ideally you should make an informal contact with someone at that particular firm, but often a direct competitor or a major customer will be able to supply you with just as much information. At the very least, try to obtain whatever printed information the company has available -- not just annual reports, but product brochures, company profiles, or catalogs. This information is often available on the Internet.

## Getting the Interview

Now it is time to make Direct Contact with the goal of arranging interviews. If you have read any books on job-searching, you may have noticed that most of these books tell you to avoid the human resources office like the plague. It is said that the human resources office never hires people; they screen candidates. Unfortunately, this is often the case. If you can identify the appropriate manager with the authority to hire you, you should try to contact that person directly.

The obvious means of initiating Direct Contact are:

- Mail (postal or electronic)
- Phone calls

Mail contact is a good choice if you have not been in the job market for a while. You can take your time to prepare a letter, say exactly what you want, and of course include your resume. Remember that employers receive many resumes every day. Don't be surprised if you do not get a response to your inquiry, *and don't spend weeks waiting for responses that may never come.* If you do send a letter, follow it up (or precede it) with a phone call. This will increase your impact, and because of the initial research you did, will underscore both your familiarity with and your interest in the firm. Bear in mind that your goal is to make your name a familiar one with prospective employers, so that when a position becomes available, your resume will be one of the first the hiring manager seeks out.

---

### DEVELOPING YOUR CONTACTS: NETWORKING

Some career counselors feel that the best route to a better job is through somebody you already know or through somebody to whom you can be introduced. These counselors recommend that you build your contact base beyond your current acquaintances by asking each one to introduce you, or refer you, to additional people in your field of interest.

The theory goes like this: You might start with 15 personal contacts, each of whom introduces you to three additional people, for a total of 45 additional contacts. Then each of these people introduces you to three additional people, which adds 135 additional contacts. Theoretically, you will soon know every person in the industry.

Of course, developing your personal contacts does not work quite as smoothly as the theory suggests because some people will not be able to introduce you to anyone. The further you stray from your initial contact base, the weaker your references may be. So, if you do try developing your own contacts, try to begin with as many people that you know personally as you can. Dig into your personal phone book and your holiday greeting card list and locate old classmates from school. Be particularly sure to approach people who perform your personal business such as your lawyer, accountant, banker, doctor, stockbroker, and insurance agent. These people develop a very broad contact base due to the nature of their professions.

If you send a fax, always follow with a hard copy of your resume and cover letter in the mail. Often, through no fault of your own, a fax will come through illegibly and employers do not often have time to let candidates know.

Another alternative is to make a "cover call." Your cover call should be just like your cover letter: concise. Your first statement should interest the employer in you. Then try to subtly mention your familiarity with the firm. Don't be overbearing; keep your introduction to three sentences or less. Be pleasant, self-confident, and relaxed. This will greatly increase the chances of the person at the other end of the line developing the conversation. But don't press. If you are asked to follow up with "something in the mail," this signals the conversation's natural end. Don't try to prolong the conversation once it has ended, and don't ask what they want to receive in the mail. Always send your resume and a highly personalized follow-up letter, reminding the addressee of the phone conversation. *Always* include a cover letter if you are asked to send a resume, and treat your resume and cover letter as a total package. Gear your letter toward the specific position you are applying for and prove why you would be a "good match" for the position.

> **Always include a cover letter if you are asked to send a resume.**

Unless you are in telephone sales, making smooth and relaxed cover calls will probably not come easily. Practice them on your own, and then with your friends or relatives.

## DON'T BOTHER WITH MASS MAILINGS OR BARRAGES OF PHONE CALLS

Direct Contact does not mean burying every firm within a hundred miles with mail and phone calls. Mass mailings rarely work in the job hunt. This also applies to those letters that are personalized -- but dehumanized -- on an automatic typewriter or computer. Don't waste your time or money on such a project; you will fool no one but yourself.

The worst part of sending out mass mailings, or making unplanned phone calls to companies you have not researched, is that you are likely to be remembered as someone with little genuine interest in the firm, who lacks sincerity -- somebody that nobody wants to hire.

If you obtain an interview as a result of a telephone conversation, be sure to send a thank-you note reiterating the points you made during the conversation. You will appear more professional and increase your impact. However, unless specifically requested, don't mail your resume once an interview has been arranged. Take it with you to the interview instead.

You should never show up to seek a professional position without an appointment. Even if you are somehow lucky enough to obtain an interview, you will appear so unprofessional that you will not be seriously considered.

## HELP WANTED ADVERTISEMENTS

Only a small fraction of professional job openings are advertised. Yet the majority of jobseekers -- and quite a few people not in the job market -- spend a lot of time studying the help wanted ads. As a result, the competition for advertised openings is often very severe.

A moderate-sized employer told us about their experience advertising in the help wanted section of a major Sunday newspaper:

*It was a disaster. We had over 500 responses from this relatively small ad in just one week. We have only two phone lines in this office and one was totally knocked out. We'll never advertise for professional help again.*

If you insist on following up on help wanted ads, then research a firm before you reply to an ad. Preliminary research might help to separate you from all of the other professionals responding to that ad, many of whom will have only a passing interest in the opportunity. It will also give you insight about a particular firm, to help you determine if it is potentially a good match. That said, your chances of obtaining a job through the want ads are still much smaller than they are with the Direct Contact method.

## Preparing for the Interview

As each interview is arranged, begin your in-depth research. You should arrive at an interview knowing the company upside-down and inside-out. You need to know the company's products, types of customers, subsidiaries, parent company, principal locations, rank in the industry, sales and profit trends, type of ownership, size, current plans, and much more. By this time you have probably narrowed your job search to one industry. Even if you haven't, you should still be familiar with common industry terms, the trends in the firm's industry, the firm's principal competitors and their relative performance, and the direction in which the industry leaders are headed.

Dig into every resource you can! Surf the Internet. Read the company literature, the trade press, the business press, and if the company is public, call your stockbroker (if you have one) and ask for additional information. If possible, speak to someone at the firm before the

> **You should arrive at an interview knowing the company upside-down and inside-out.**

interview, or if not, speak to someone at a competing firm. The more time you spend, the better. Even if you feel extremely pressed for time, you should set aside several hours for pre-interview research.

If you have been out of the job market for some time, don't be surprised if you find yourself tense during your first few interviews. It will probably happen every time you re-enter the market, not just when you seek your first job after getting out of school.

Tension is natural during an interview, but knowing you have done a thorough research job should put you more at ease. Make a list of questions that you think might be asked in each interview. Think out your answers carefully and practice them with a friend. Tape record your responses to the problem questions. (*See also in this chapter: Informational Interviews.*) If you feel particularly unsure of your interviewing skills, arrange your first interviews at firms you are not as interested in. (But remember it is common courtesy to seem enthusiastic about the possibility of working for any firm at which you interview.) Practice again on your own after these first few interviews. Go over the difficult questions that you were asked.

Take some time to really think about how you will convey your work history. Present "bad experiences" as "learning experiences." Instead of saying "I hated my position as a salesperson because I had to bother people on the phone," say "I realized that cold-calling was not my strong suit. Though I love working with people, I decided my talents would be best used in a more face-to-face atmosphere." Always find some sort of lesson from previous jobs, as they all have one.

## Interview Attire

How important is the proper dress for a job interview? Buying a complete wardrobe, donning new shoes, and having your hair styled every morning are not enough to guarantee you a career position as an investment banker. But on the other hand, if you can't find a clean, conservative suit or won't take the time to wash your hair, then you are just wasting your time by interviewing at all.

Personal grooming is as important as finding appropriate clothes for a job interview. Careful grooming indicates both a sense of thoroughness and self-confidence. This is not the time to make a statement -- take out the extra earrings and avoid any garish hair colors not found in nature. Women should not wear excessive makeup, and both men and women should refrain from wearing any perfume or cologne (it only takes a small spritz to leave an allergic interviewer with a fit of sneezing and a bad impression of your meeting). Men should be freshly shaven, even if the interview is late in the day, and men with long hair should have it pulled back and neat.

Men applying for any professional position should wear a suit, preferably in a conservative color such as navy or charcoal gray. It is easy to get away with wearing the same dark suit to consecutive interviews at the same company; just be sure to wear a different shirt and tie for each interview.

Women should also wear a business suit. Professionalism still dictates a suit with a skirt, rather than slacks, as proper interview garb for women. This is usually true even at companies where pants are acceptable attire for female employees. As much as you may disagree with this guideline, the more prudent time to fight this standard is after you land the job.

The final selection of candidates for a job opening won't be determined by dress, of course. However, inappropriate dress can quickly eliminate a first-round candidate. So while you shouldn't spend a fortune on a new wardrobe, you should be sure that your clothes are appropriate. The key is to dress at least as or slightly more formally and conservatively than the position would suggest.

## What to Bring

Be complete. Everyone needs a watch, a pen, and a notepad. Finally, a briefcase or a leather-bound folder (containing extra, *unfolded*, copies of your resume) will help complete the look of professionalism.

Sometimes the interviewer will be running behind schedule. Don't be upset, be sympathetic. There is often pressure to interview a lot of candidates and to quickly fill a demanding position. So be sure to come to your interview with good reading material to keep yourself occupied and relaxed.

## The Interview

The very beginning of the interview is the most important part because it determines the tone for the rest of it. Those first few moments are especially crucial. Do you smile when you meet? Do you establish enough eye contact, but not too much? Do you walk into the office with a self-assured and confident stride? Do you shake hands firmly? Do you make small talk easily without being garrulous? It is human nature to judge people by that first impression, so make sure it is a good one. But most of all, try to be yourself.

---

### BE PREPARED:
### Some Common Interview Questions

Tell me about yourself.

Why did you leave your last job?

What excites you in your current job?

Where would you like to be in five years?

How much overtime are you willing to work?

What would your previous/present employer tell me about you?

Tell me about a difficult situation that you
faced at your previous/present job.

What are your greatest strengths?

What are your weaknesses?

Describe a work situation where you took initiative
and went beyond your normal responsibilities.

Why should we hire you?

---

Often the interviewer will begin, after the small talk, by telling you about the company, the division, the department, or perhaps, the position. Because of your detailed research, the information about the company should be repetitive for you, and the interviewer would probably like nothing better than to avoid this regurgitation of the company biography. So if you can do so tactfully, indicate to the interviewer that you are very familiar with the firm. If he or she seems intent on providing you with background information, despite your hints, then acquiesce.

But be sure to remain attentive. If you can manage to generate a brief discussion of the company or the industry at this point, without being forceful, great. It will help to further build rapport, underscore your interest, and increase your impact.

> ## The interviewer's job is to find a reason to turn you down; your job is to not provide that reason.
>
> -John L. LaFevre, author,
> *How You Really Get Hired*
>
> Reprinted from the 1989/90 *CPC Annual*, with permission of the National Association of Colleges and Employers (formerly College Placement Council, Inc.), copyright holder.

Soon (if it didn't begin that way) the interviewer will begin the questions, many of which you will have already practiced. This period of the interview usually falls into one of two categories (or somewhere in between): either a structured interview, where the interviewer has a prescribed set of questions to ask; or an unstructured interview, where the interviewer will ask only leading questions to get you to talk about yourself, your experiences, and your goals. Try to sense as quickly as possible in which direction the interviewer wishes to proceed. This will make the interviewer feel more relaxed and in control of the situation.

Remember to keep attuned to the interviewer and make the length of your answers appropriate to the situation. If you are really unsure as to how detailed a response the interviewer is seeking, then ask.

As the interview progresses, the interviewer will probably mention some of the most important responsibilities of the position. If applicable, draw parallels between your experience and the demands of the position as detailed by the interviewer. Describe your past experience in the same manner that you do on your resume: emphasizing results and achievements and not merely describing activities. But don't exaggerate. Be on the level about your abilities.

The first interview is often the toughest, where many candidates are screened out. If you are interviewing for a very competitive position, you will have to make an impression that will last. Focus on a few of your greatest strengths that are relevant to the position. Develop these points carefully, state them again in different words, and then try to summarize them briefly at the end of the interview.

Often the interviewer will pause toward the end and ask if you have any questions. Particularly in a structured interview, this might be the one chance to really show your knowledge of and interest in the firm. Have a list prepared of specific questions that are of real interest to you. Let your questions subtly show your research and your knowledge of the firm's activities. It is wise to have an extensive list of questions, as several of them may be answered during the interview.

Do not turn your opportunity to ask questions into an interrogation. Avoid reading directly from your list of questions, and ask questions that you are fairly certain the interviewer can answer (remember how you feel when you cannot answer a question during an interview).

Even if you are unable to determine the salary range beforehand, do not ask about it during the first interview. You can always ask later. Above all, don't ask about fringe benefits until you have been offered a position. (Then be sure to get all the details.)

Try not to be negative about anything during the interview, particularly any past employer or any previous job. Be cheerful. Everyone likes to work with someone who seems to be happy. Even if you detest your current/former job or manager, do not make disparaging comments. The interviewer may construe this as a sign of a potential attitude problem and not consider you a strong candidate.

Don't let a tough question throw you off base. If you don't know the answer to a question, simply say so -- do not apologize. Just smile. Nobody can answer every question -- particularly some of the questions that are asked in job interviews.

Before your first interview, you may be able to determine how many rounds of interviews there usually are for positions at your level. (Of course it may differ quite a bit even within the different levels of one firm.) Usually you can count on attending at least two or three interviews, although some firms are known to give a minimum of six interviews for all professional positions. While you should be more relaxed as you return for subsequent interviews, the pressure will be on. The more prepared you are, the better.

Depending on what information you are able to obtain, you might want to vary your strategy quite a bit from interview to interview. For instance, if the first interview is a screening interview, then be sure a few of your strengths really stand out. On the other hand, if later interviews are primarily with people who are in a position to veto your hiring, but not to push it forward, then you should primarily focus on building rapport as opposed to reiterating and developing your key strengths.

If it looks as though your skills and background do not match the position the interviewer was hoping to fill, ask him or her if there is another division or subsidiary that perhaps could profit from your talents.

### After the Interview

Write a follow-up letter immediately after the interview, while it is still fresh in the interviewer's mind (see the sample follow-up letter format found in the Resumes and Cover Letters chapter). Not only is this a thank-you, but it also gives you the chance to provide the interviewer with any details you may have forgotten (as long as they can be tactfully added in). If you haven't heard back from the interviewer within a week of sending your thank-you letter, call to stress your continued interest in the firm and the position. If you lost any points during the interview for any reason, this letter can help you regain footing. Be polite and make sure to stress your continued interest and competency to fill the position. Just don't forget to proofread it thoroughly. If you are unsure of the spelling of the interviewer's name, call the receptionist and ask.

# THE BALANCING ACT:
## Looking for a New Job While Currently Employed

For those of you who are still employed, job-searching will be particularly tiring because it must be done in addition to your normal work responsibilities. So don't overwork yourself to the point where you show up to interviews looking exhausted or start to slip behind at your current job. On the other hand, don't be tempted to quit your present job! The long hours are worth it. Searching for a job while you have one puts you in a position of strength.

## Making Contact

If you must be at your office during the business day, then you have additional problems to deal with. How can you work interviews into the business day? And if you work in an open office, how can you even call to set up interviews? Obviously, you should keep up the effort and the appearances on your present job. So maximize your use of the lunch hour, early mornings, and late afternoons for calling. If you keep trying, you'll be surprised how often you will be able to reach the executive you are trying to contact during your out-of-office hours. You can catch people as early as 8 a.m. and as late as 6 p.m. on frequent occasions.

## Scheduling Interviews

Your inability to interview at any time other than lunch just might work to your advantage. If you can, try to set up as many interviews as possible for your lunch hour. This will go a long way to creating a relaxed atmosphere. But be sure the interviews don't stray too far from the agenda on hand.

Lunchtime interviews are much easier to obtain if you have substantial career experience. People with less experience will often find no alternative to taking time off for interviews. If you have to take time off, you have to take time off. But try to do this as little as possible. Try to take the whole day off in order to avoid being blatantly obvious about your job search, and try to schedule two to three interviews for the same day. (It is very difficult to maintain an optimum level of energy at more than three interviews in one day.) Explain to the interviewer why you might have to juggle your interview schedule; he/she should honor the respect you're showing your current employer by minimizing your days off and will probably appreciate the fact that another prospective employer is interested in you.

> Try calling as early as 8 a.m. and as late as 6 p.m. You'll be surprised how often you will be able to reach the executive you want during these times of the day.

## References

What do you tell an interviewer who asks for references from your current employer? Just say that while you are happy to have your former employers contacted, you are trying to keep your job search confidential and would rather that your current employer not be contacted until you have been given a firm offer.

# IF YOU'RE FIRED OR LAID OFF:
## Picking Yourself Up and Dusting Yourself Off

If you've been fired or laid off, you are not the first and will not be the last to go through this traumatic experience. In today's changing economy, thousands of professionals lose their jobs every year. Even if you were terminated with just cause, do not lose heart. Remember, being fired is not a reflection on you as a person. It is usually a reflection of your company's staffing needs and its perception of your recent job performance and attitude. And if you were not performing up to par or enjoying your work, then you will probably be better off at another company anyway.

> **Be prepared for the question "Why were you fired?" during job interviews.**

A thorough job search could take months, so be sure to negotiate a reasonable severance package, if possible, and determine to what benefits, such as health insurance, you are still legally entitled. Also, register for unemployment compensation immediately. Don't be surprised to find other professionals collecting unemployment compensation -- it is for everyone who has lost their job.

Don't start your job search with a flurry of unplanned activity. Start by choosing a strategy and working out a plan. Now is not the time for major changes in your life. If possible, remain in the same career and in the same geographical location, at least until you have been working again for a while. On the other hand, if the only industry for which you are trained is leaving, or is severely depressed in your area, then you should give prompt consideration to moving or switching careers.

Avoid mentioning you were fired when arranging interviews, but be prepared for the question "Why were you fired?" during an interview. If you were laid off as a result of downsizing, briefly explain, being sure to reinforce that your job loss was not due to performance. If you were in fact fired, be honest, but try to detail the reason as favorably as possible and portray what you have learned from your mistakes. If you are confident one of your past managers will give you a good reference, tell the interviewer to contact that person. Do not to speak negatively of your past employer and try not to sound particularly worried about your status of being temporarily unemployed.

Finally, don't spend too much time reflecting on why you were let go or how you might have avoided It. Think positively, look to the future, and be sure to follow a careful plan during your job search.

## THE COLLEGE STUDENT:
### Conducting Your First Job Search

While you will be able to apply many of the basics covered earlier in this chapter to your job search, there are some situations unique to the college student's job search.

---

### THE GPA QUESTION

You are interviewing for the job of your dreams. Everything is going well: You've established a good rapport, the interviewer seems impressed with your qualifications, and you're almost positive the job is yours. Then you're asked about your GPA, which is pitifully low. Do you tell the truth and watch your dream job fly out the window?

*Never* lie about your GPA (they may request your transcript, and no company will hire a liar). You can, however, explain if there is a reason you don't feel your grades reflect your abilities, and mention any other impressive statistics. For example, if you have a high GPA in your major, or in the last few semesters (as opposed to your cumulative college career), you can use that fact to your advantage.

Perhaps the biggest problem college students face is lack of experience. Many schools have internship programs designed to give students exposure to the field of their choice, as well as the opportunity to make valuable contacts. Check out your school's career services department to see what internships are available. If your school does not have a formal internship program, or if there are no available internships that appeal to you, try contacting local businesses and offering your services. Often, businesses will be more than willing to have an extra pair of hands (especially if those hands are unpaid!) for a day or two each week. Or try contacting school alumni to see if you can "shadow" them for a few days, and see what their daily duties are like.

## Informational Interviews

Although many jobseekers do not do this, it can be extremely helpful to arrange an informational interview with a college alumnus or someone else who works in your desired industry. You interview them about their job, their company, and their industry with questions you have prepared in advance. This can be done over the phone but is usually done in person. This will provide you with a contact in the industry who may give you more valuable information -- or perhaps even a job opportunity -- in the future. Always follow up with a thank you letter that includes your contact information.

*The goal is to try to begin building experience and establishing contacts as early as possible in your college career.*

What do you do if, for whatever reason, you weren't able to get experience directly related to your desired career? First, look at your previous jobs and see if there's anything you can highlight. Did you supervise or train other employees? Did you reorganize the accounting system, or boost productivity in some way? Accomplishments like these demonstrate leadership, responsibility, and innovation -- qualities that most companies look for in employees. And don't forget volunteer activities and school clubs, which can also showcase these traits.

## On-Campus Recruiting

Companies will often send recruiters to interview on-site at various colleges. This gives students a chance to interview with companies that may not have interviewed them otherwise. This is particularly true if a company schedules "open" interviews, in which the only screening process is who is first in line at the sign-ups. Of course, since many more applicants gain interviews in this format, this also means that many more people are rejected. The on-campus interview is generally a screening interview, to see if it is worth the company's time to invite you in for a second interview. So do everything possible to make yourself stand out from the crowd.

The first step, of course, is to check out any and all information your school's career center has on the company. If the information seems out of date, check out the company on the Internet or call the company's headquarters and ask for any printed information.

Many companies will host an informational meeting for interviewees, often the evening before interviews are scheduled to take place. DO NOT MISS THIS MEETING. The recruiter will almost certainly ask if you attended. Make an effort to stay after the meeting and talk with the company's representatives. Not only does this give you an opportunity to find out more information about both the company and the position, it also makes you stand out in the recruiter's mind. If there's a particular company that you had your heart set on, but you weren't able to get an interview with them, attend the information session anyway. You may be able to persuade the recruiter to squeeze you into the schedule. (Or you may discover that the company really isn't the right fit for you after all.)

Try to check out the interview site beforehand. Some colleges may conduct "mock" interviews that take place in one of the standard interview rooms. Or you may be able to convince a career counselor (or even a custodian) to let you sneak a peek during off-hours. Either way, having an idea of the room's setup will help you to mentally prepare.

Arrive at least 15 minutes early to the interview. The recruiter may be ahead of schedule, and might meet you early. But don't be surprised if previous interviews have run over, resulting in your 30-minute slot being reduced to 20 minutes (or less). Don't complain or appear anxious; just use the time you do have as efficiently as possible to showcase the reasons *you* are the ideal candidate. Staying calm and composed in these situations will work to your advantage.

## LAST WORDS

A parting word of advice. Again and again during your job search you will face rejection. You will be rejected when you apply for interviews. You will be rejected after interviews. For every job offer you finally receive, you probably will have been rejected many times. Don't let rejections slow you down. Keep reminding yourself that the sooner you go out, start your job search, and get those rejections flowing in, the closer you will be to obtaining the job you want.

# RESUMES AND COVER LETTERS

When filling a position, an employer will often have 100-plus applicants, but time to interview only a handful of the most promising ones. As a result, he or she will reject most applicants after only briefly skimming their resumes.

Unless you have phoned and talked to the employer -- which you should do whenever you can -- you will be chosen or rejected for an interview entirely on the basis of your resume and cover letter. *Your cover letter must catch the employer's attention, and your resume must hold it.* (But remember -- a resume is no substitute for a job search campaign. *You* must seek a job. Your resume is only one tool, albeit a critical one.)

## RESUME FORMAT:
### Mechanics of a First Impression

### The Basics

Employers dislike long resumes, so unless you have an unusually strong background with many years of experience and a diversity of outstanding achievements, keep your resume length to one page. If you must squeeze in more information than would otherwise fit, try using a smaller typeface or changing the margins. Watch also for "widows" at the end of paragraphs. You can often free up some space if you can shorten the information enough to get rid of those single words taking up an entire line. Another tactic that works with some word processing programs is to decrease the font size of your paragraph returns and changing the spacing between lines.

Print your resume on standard 8 1/2" x 11" paper. Since recruiters often get resumes in batches of hundreds, a smaller-sized resume may be lost in the pile. Oversized resumes are likely to get crumpled at the edges, and won't fit easily in their files.

*First impressions matter, so make sure the recruiter's first impression of your resume is a good one.* Never hand-write your resume (or cover letter)! Print your resume on quality paper that has weight and texture, in a conservative color such as white, ivory, or pale gray. Good resume paper is easy to find at many stores that sell stationery or office products. It is even available at some drug stores. Use *matching* paper and envelopes for both your resume and cover letter. One hiring manager at a major magazine throws out all resumes that arrive on paper that differs in color from the envelope!

Do not buy paper with images of clouds and rainbows in the background or anything that looks like casual stationery that you would send to your favorite aunt. Do not spray perfume or cologne on your resume. Do not include your picture with your resume unless you have a specific and appropriate reason to do so.

Another tip: Do a test print of your resume (and cover letter), to make sure the watermark is on the same side as the text so that you can read it. Also make sure it is right-side up. As trivial as this may sound, some recruiters check for this! One recruiter at a law firm in New Hampshire sheepishly admitted this is the first thing he checks. *"I open each envelope and check the watermarks on the resume and cover letter. Those candidates that have it wrong go into a different pile."*

## Getting it on Paper

Modern photocomposition typesetting gives you the clearest, sharpest image, a wide variety of type styles, and effects such as italics, bold-facing, and book-like justified margins. It is also too expensive for many jobseekers. The quality of today's laser printers means that a computer-generated resume can look just as impressive as one that has been professionally typeset.

A computer with a word processing or desktop publishing program is the most common way to generate your resume. This allows you the flexibility to make changes almost instantly and to store different drafts on disk. Word processing and desktop publishing programs also offer many different fonts to choose from, each taking up different amounts of space. (It is generally best to stay between 9-point and 12-point font size.) Many other options are also available, such as bold-facing or italicizing for emphasis and the ability to change and manipulate spacing. It is generally recommended to leave the right-hand margin unjustified as this keeps the spacing between the text even and therefore easier to read. It is not wrong to justify both margins of text, but if possible try it both ways before you decide.

For a resume on paper, the end result will be largely determined by the quality of the printer you use. Laser printers will generally provide the best quality. Do not use a dot matrix printer.

Many companies now use scanning equipment to screen the resumes they receive, and certain paper, fonts, and other features are more compatible with this technology. White paper is preferable, as well as a standard font such as Courier or Helvetica. You should use at least a 10-point font, and avoid bolding, italics, underlining, borders, boxes, or graphics.

Household typewriters and office typewriters with nylon or other cloth ribbons are *not* good enough for typing your resume. If you don't have access to a quality word processing program, hire a professional with the resources to prepare your resume for you. Keep in mind that businesses such as Kinko's (open 24 hours) provide access to computers with quality printers.

*Don't* make your copies on an office photocopier. Only the human resources office may see the resume you mail. Everyone else may see only a copy of it, and copies of copies quickly become unreadable. Furthermore, sending photocopies of your resume or cover letter is completely unprofessional. Either print out each copy individually, or take your resume to a professional copy shop, which will generally offer professionally-maintained, extra-high-quality photocopiers and charge fairly reasonable prices. You want your resume to represent <u>you</u> with the look of polished quality.

## Proof with Care

Whether you typed it or paid to have it produced professionally, mistakes on resumes are not only embarrassing, but will usually remove you from consideration (particularly if something obvious such as your name is misspelled). No matter how much you paid someone else to type, write, or typeset your resume, *you* lose if there is a mistake. So proofread it as carefully as possible. Get a friend to help you. Read your draft aloud as your friend checks the proof copy. Then have your friend read aloud while you check. Next, read it letter by letter to check spelling and punctuation.

If you are having it typed or typeset by a resume service or a printer, and you don't have time to proof it, pay for it and take it home. Proof it there and bring it back later to get it corrected and printed.

If you wrote your resume with a word processing program, use the built-in spell checker to double-check for spelling errors. Keep in mind that a spell checker will not find errors such as "to" for "two" or "wok" for "work." Many spell check programs do not recognize missing or misused punctuation, nor are they set to check the spelling of capitalized words. It's important that you still proofread your resume to check for grammatical mistakes and other problems, even _after_ it has been spellchecked. If you find mistakes, do not make edits in pen or pencil or use white-out to fix them on the final copy!

## Electronic Resumes

As companies rely increasingly on emerging technologies to find qualified candidates for job openings, you may opt to create an electronic resume in order to remain competitive in today's job market. Why is this important? Companies today sometimes request that resumes be submitted by e-mail, and many hiring managers regularly check online resume databases for candidates to fill unadvertised job openings. Other companies enlist the services of electronic employment database services, which charge jobseekers a nominal fee to have their resumes posted to the database to be viewed by potential employers. Still other companies use their own automated applicant tracking systems, in which case your resume is fed through a scanner that sends the image to a computer that "reads" your resume, looking for keywords, and files it accordingly in its database.

Whether you're posting your resume online, e-mailing it directly to an employer, sending it to an electronic employment database, or sending it to a company you suspect uses an automated applicant tracking system, you must create some form of electronic resume to take advantage of the technology. Don't panic! An electronic resume is simply a modified version of your conventional resume. An electronic resume is one that is sparsely formatted, but filled with keywords and important facts.

In order to post your resume to the Internet -- either to an online resume database or through direct e-mail to an employer -- you will need to change the way your resume is formatted. Instead of a Word, WordPerfect, or other word processing document, save your resume as a plain text, DOS, or ASCII file. These three terms are basically interchangeable, and describe text at its simplest, most basic level, without the formatting such as boldface or italics that most jobseekers use to make their resumes look more interesting. If you use e-mail, you'll notice that all of your messages are written and received in this format. First, you should remove all formatting from your resume including boldface, italics, underlining, bullets, differing font sizes, and graphics. Then, convert and save your resume as a plain text file. Most word processing programs have a "save as" feature that allows you to save files in different formats. Here, you should choose "text only" or "plain text."

Another option is to create a resume in HTML (hypertext markup language), the text formatting language used to publish information on the World Wide Web. However, the real usefulness of HTML resumes is still being explored. Most of the major online databases do not accept HTML resumes, and the vast majority of companies only accept plain text resumes through their e-mail.

Finally, if you simply wish to send your resume to an electronic employment database or a company that uses an automated applicant tracking system, there is no need to convert your resume to a plain text file. The only change you need to make is to organize the information in your resume by keywords. Employers are likely to do keyword searches for information, such as degree held or knowledge of particular types of software. Therefore, using the right keywords or key phrases in your resume is critical to its ultimate success. Keywords are usually nouns or short phrases that the computer searches for which refer to experience, training, skills, and abilities. For example, let's say an employer searches an employment database for a sales representative with the following criteria:

BS/BA
exceeded quota
cold calls
high energy
willing to travel

Even if you have the right qualifications, neglecting to use these keywords would result in the computer passing over your resume. Although there is no way to know for sure which keywords employers are most likely to search for, you can make educated guesses by checking the help-wanted ads or online job postings for your type of job. You should also arrange keywords in a keyword summary, a paragraph listing your qualifications that immediately follows your name and address (see sample letter in this chapter). In addition, choose a nondecorative font with clear, distinct characters, such as Helvetica or Times. It is more difficult for a scanner to accurately pick up the more unusual fonts. Boldface and all capital letters are best used only for major section headings, such as "Experience" and "Education." It is also best to avoid using italics or underlining, since this can cause the letters to bleed into one another.

## Types of Resumes

The most common resume formats are the functional resume, the chronological resume, and the combination resume. (Examples can be found at the end of this chapter.) A functional resume focuses on skills and de-emphasizes job titles, employers, etc. A functional resume is best if you have been out of the work force for a long time or are changing careers. It is also good if you want to highlight specific skills and strengths, especially if all of your work experience has been at one company. This format can also be a good choice if you are just out of school or have no experience in your desired field.

Choose a chronological format if you are currently working or were working recently, and if your most recent experiences relate to your desired field. Use reverse chronological order and include dates. To a recruiter your last job and your latest schooling are the most important, so put the last first and list the rest going back in time.

A combination resume is perhaps the most common. This resume simply combines elements of the functional and chronological resume formats. This is used by many jobseekers with a solid track record who find elements of both types useful.

## Organization

Your name, phone number, e-mail address (if you have one), and a complete mailing address should be at the top of your resume. Try to make your name stand out by using a slightly larger font size or all capital letters. Be sure to spell out everything. Never abbreviate St. for Street or Rd. for Road. If you are a college student, you should also put your home address and phone number at the top. Change your message on your answering machine if necessary – RUSH blaring in the background or your sorority sisters screaming may not come across well to all recruiters. If you think you may be moving within six months then include a second address and phone number of a trusted friend or relative who can reach you no matter where you are.

*Remember that employers will keep your resume on file and may contact you months later if a position opens that fits your qualifications. All too often, candidates are unreachable because they have moved and had not previously provided enough contact options on their resume.*

Next, list your experience, then your education. If you are a recent graduate, list your education first, unless your experience is more important than your education. (For example, if you have just graduated from a teaching school, have some business experience, and are applying for a job in business, you would list your business experience first.)

Keep everything easy to find. Put the dates of your employment and education on the left of the page. Put the names of the companies you worked for and the schools you attended a few spaces to the right of the dates. Put the city and state, or the city and country, where you studied or worked to the right of the page.

The important thing is simply to break up the text in some logical way that makes your resume visually attractive and easy to scan, so experiment to see which layout works best for your resume. However you set it up, *stay consistent*. Inconsistencies in fonts, spacing, or tenses will make your resume look sloppy. Also, be sure to use tabs to keep your information vertically lined up, rather than the less precise space bar.

# RESUME CONTENT:
## Say it with Style
### Sell Yourself

You are selling your skills and accomplishments in your resume, so it is important to inventory yourself and know yourself. If you have achieved something, say so. Put it in the best possible light, but avoid subjective statements, such as "I am a hard worker" or "I get along well with my coworkers." Just stick to the facts.

While you shouldn't hold back or be modest, don't exaggerate your achievements to the point of misrepresentation. <u>Be honest</u>. Many companies will immediately drop an applicant from consideration (or fire a current employee) upon discovering inaccurate or untrue information on a resume or other application material.

Write down the important (and pertinent) things you have done, but do it in as few words as possible. Your resume will be scanned, not read, and short, concise phrases are much more effective than long-winded sentences. Avoid the use of "I" when emphasizing your accomplishments. Instead, use brief phrases beginning with action verbs.

While some technical terms will be unavoidable, you should try to avoid excessive "technicalese." Keep in mind that the first person to see your resume may be a human resources person who won't necessarily know all the jargon -- and how can they be impressed by something they don't understand?

### Keep it Brief

Also, try to hold your paragraphs to six lines or less. If you have more than six lines of information about one job or school, put it in two or more paragraphs.

A short resume will be examined more carefully. Remember: Your resume usually has between eight and 45 seconds to catch an employer's eye. So make every second count.

## Job Objective

A functional resume may require a job objective to give it focus. One or two sentences describing the job you are seeking can clarify in what capacity your skills will be best put to use. Be sure that your stated objective is in line with the position you're applying for.

*Examples:*

> An entry-level editorial assistant position in the publishing industry.
> A senior management position with a telecommunications firm.

Don't include a job objective on a chronological resume unless your previous work experiences are <u>completely</u> unrelated to the position for which you're applying. The presence of an overly specific job objective might eliminate you from consideration for other positions that a recruiter feels are a better match for your qualifications. But even if you don't put an objective on paper, having a career goal in mind as you write can help give your resume a solid sense of direction.

---

### USE ACTION VERBS

*How* you write your resume is just as important as *what* you write. In describing previous work experiences, the strongest resumes use short phrases beginning with action verbs. Below are a few you may want to use. (This list is not all-inclusive.)

| | | | |
|---|---|---|---|
| achieved | developed | integrated | purchased |
| administered | devised | interpreted | reduced |
| advised | directed | interviewed | regulated |
| arranged | distributed | launched | represented |
| assisted | established | managed | resolved |
| attained | evaluated | marketed | restored |
| budgeted | examined | mediated | restructured |
| built | executed | monitored | revised |
| calculated | expanded | negotiated | scheduled |
| collaborated | expedited | obtained | selected |
| collected | facilitated | operated | served |
| compiled | formulated | ordered | sold |
| completed | founded | organized | solved |
| computed | generated | participated | streamlined |
| conducted | headed | performed | studied |
| consolidated | identified | planned | supervised |
| constructed | implemented | prepared | supplied |
| consulted | improved | presented | supported |
| controlled | increased | processed | tested |
| coordinated | initiated | produced | trained |
| created | installed | proposed | updated |
| determined | instructed | published | wrote |

---

Some jobseekers may choose to include both "Relevant Experience" and "Additional Experience" sections. This can be useful, as it allows the jobseeker to place more emphasis on certain experiences and to de-emphasize others.

Emphasize continued experience in a particular job area or continued interest in a particular industry. De-emphasize irrelevant positions. It is okay to include one opening line providing a general description of each company you've worked at. Delete positions that you held for less than four months (unless you are a very recent college grad or still in school). Stress your <u>results</u> and your achievements, elaborating on how you contributed in your previous jobs. Did you increase sales, reduce costs, improve a product, implement a new program? Were you promoted? Use specific numbers (i.e., quantities, percentages, dollar amounts) whenever possible.

## Education

Keep it brief if you have more than two years of career experience. Elaborate more if you have less experience. If you are a recent college graduate, you may choose to include any high school activities that are directly relevant to your career. If you've been out of school for a while you don't need to list your education prior to college.

Mention degrees received and any honors or special awards. Note individual courses or projects you participated in that might be relevant for employers. For example, if you are an English major applying for a position as a business writer, be sure to mention any business or economics courses. Previous experience such as Editor-in-Chief of the school newspaper would be relevant as well.

If you are uploading your resume to an online job hunting site such as CareerCity.com, action verbs are still important, but the key words or key nouns that a computer would search for become more important. For example, if you're seeking an accounting position, key nouns that a computer would search for such as "Lotus 1-2-3" or "CPA" or "payroll" become very important.

## Highlight Impressive Skills

Be sure to mention any computer skills you may have. You may wish to include a section entitled "Additional Skills" or "Computer Skills," in which you list any software programs you know. An additional skills section is also an ideal place to mention fluency in a foreign language.

## Personal Data

This section is optional, but if you choose to include it, keep it brief. A one-word mention of hobbies such as fishing, chess, baseball, cooking, etc., can give the person who will interview you a good way to open up the conversation.

Team sports experience is looked at favorably. It doesn't hurt to include activities that are somewhat unusual (fencing, Akido, '70s music) or that somehow relate to the position or the company to which you're applying. For instance, it would be worth noting if you are a member of a professional organization in your industry of interest. Never include information about your age, alias, date of birth, health, physical characteristics, marital status, religious affiliation, or political/moral beliefs.

## References

The most that is needed is the sentence "References available upon request" at the bottom of your resume. If you choose to leave it out, that's fine. This line is not really necessary. It is understood that references will most likely be asked for and provided by you later on in the interviewing process. Do not actually send references with your resume and cover letter unless specifically requested.

# HIRING A RESUME WRITER:
## Is it the Right Choice for You?

If you write reasonably well, it is to your advantage to write your own resume. Writing your resume forces you to review your experiences and figure out how to explain your accomplishments in clear, brief phrases. This will help you when you explain your work to interviewers. It is also easier to tailor your resume to each position you're applying for when you have put it together yourself.

If you write your resume, everything will be in your own words; it will sound like you. It will say what you want it to say. If you are a good writer, know yourself well, and have a good idea of which parts of your background employers are looking for, you should be able to write your own resume better than someone else. If you decide to write your resume yourself, have as many people as possible review and proofread it. Welcome objective opinions and other perspectives.

## When to Get Help

If you have difficulty writing in "resume style" (which is quite unlike normal written language), if you are unsure which parts of your background to emphasize, or if you think your resume would make your case better if it did not follow one of the standard forms outlined either here or in a book on resumes, then you should consider having it professionally written.

Even some professional resume writers we know have had their resumes written with the help of fellow professionals. They sought the help of someone who could be objective about their background, as well as provide an experienced sounding board to help focus their thoughts.

## If You Hire a Pro

The best way to choose a writer is by reputation: the recommendation of a friend, a personnel director, your school placement officer, or someone else knowledgeable in the field.

*Important questions:*
- "How long have you been writing resumes?"
- "If I'm not satisfied with what you write, will you go over it with me and change it?"
- "Do you charge by the hour or a flat rate?"

There is no sure relation between price and quality, except that you are unlikely to get a good writer for less than $50 for an uncomplicated resume and you shouldn't have to pay more than $300 unless your experience is very extensive or complicated. There will be additional charges for printing. Assume nothing no matter how much you pay. It is your career at stake if there are mistakes on your resume!

Few resume services will give you a firm price over the phone, simply because some resumes are too complicated and take too long to do for a predetermined price. Some services will quote you a price that applies to almost all of their customers. Once you decide to use a specific writer, you should insist on a firm price quote *before* engaging their services. Also, find out how expensive minor changes will be.

# COVER LETTERS:
## Quick, Clear, and Concise

*Always* mail a cover letter with your resume. In a cover letter you can show an interest in the company that you can't show in a resume. You can also point out one or two of your skills or accomplishments the company can put to good use.

## Make it Personal

The more personal you can get, the better, so long as you keep it professional. If someone known to the person you are writing has recommended that you contact the company, get permission to include his/her name in the letter. If you can get the name of a person to send the letter to, address it directly to that person (after first calling the company to verify the spelling of the person's name, correct title, and mailing address). Be sure to put the person's name and title on both the letter and the envelope. This will ensure that your letter will get through to the proper person, even if a new person now occupies this position. It will not always be possible to get the name of a person. Always strive to get at least a title.

Be sure to mention something about why you have an interest in the company -- *so many candidates apply for jobs with no apparent knowledge of what the company does!* This conveys the message that they just want any job.

Type cover letters in full. Don't try the cheap and easy ways, like using a computer mail merge program or photocopying the body of your letter and typing in the inside address and salutation. You will give the impression that you are mailing to a host of companies and have no particular interest in any one.

Print your cover letter on the same color and same high-quality paper as your resume.

## Cover letter basic format

<u>Paragraph 1:</u> State what the position is that you are seeking. It is not always necessary to state how you found out about the position -- often you will apply without knowing that a position is open.

<u>Paragraph 2:</u> Include what you know about the company and why you are interested in working there. Mention any prior contact with the company or someone known to the hiring person if relevant. Briefly state your qualifications and what you can offer. (Do not talk about what you cannot do).

<u>Paragraph 3:</u> Close with your phone number and where/when you can be reached. Make a request for an interview. State when you will follow up by phone (or mail or e-mail if the ad requests no phone calls). Do not wait long -- generally five working days. If you say you're going to follow up, then actually do it! This phone call can get your resume noticed when it might otherwise sit in a stack of 225 other resumes.

## Cover letter do's and don'ts

- *Do* keep your cover letter brief and to the point.
- *Do* be sure it is error-free.
- *Do* accentuate what you can offer the company, not what you hope to gain.

- *Do* be sure your phone number and address is on your cover letter just in case it gets separated from your resume (this happens!).
- *Do* check the watermark by holding the paper up to a light -- be sure it is facing forward so it is readable -- on the same side as the text, and right-side up.
- *Do* sign your cover letter (or type your name if you are sending it electronically). Blue or black ink are both fine. Do not use red ink.
- *Don't* just repeat information verbatim from your resume.
- *Don't* overuse the personal pronoun "I."
- *Don't* send a generic cover letter -- show your personal knowledge of and interest in that particular company.

# THANK YOU LETTERS:
## Another Way to Stand Out

As mentioned earlier, *always* send a thank you letter after an interview (see the sample later in this section). So few candidates do this and it is yet another way for you to stand out. Be sure to mention something specific from the interview and restate your interest in the company and the position.

It is generally acceptable to handwrite your thank you letter on a generic thank you card (but *never* a postcard). Make sure handwritten notes are neat and legible. However, if you are in doubt, typing your letter is always the safe bet. If you met with several people it is fine to send them each an individual thank you letter. Call the company if you need to check on the correct spelling of their names.

**Remember to:**
- Keep it short.
- Proofread it carefully.
- Send it *promptly*.

# FUNCTIONAL RESUME

## C.J. RAVENCLAW
129 Pennsylvania Avenue
Washington DC 20500
202/555-6652
e-mail: ravenclaw@dcpress.net

### Objective
A position as a graphic designer commensurate with my acquired skills and expertise.

### Summary
Extensive experience in plate making, separations, color matching, background definition, printing, mechanicals, color corrections, and personnel supervision. A highly motivated manager and effective communicator. Proven ability to:

- **Create Commercial Graphics**
- **Produce Embossed Drawings**
- **Color Separate**
- **Control Quality**
- **Resolve Printing Problems**
- **Analyze Customer Satisfaction**

### Qualifications
**Printing:**
Knowledgeable in black and white as well as color printing. Excellent judgment in determining acceptability of color reproduction through comparison with original. Proficient at producing four- or five-color corrections on all media, as well as restyling previously reproduced four-color artwork.

**Customer Relations:**
Routinely work closely with customers to ensure specifications are met. Capable of striking a balance between technical printing capabilities and need for customer satisfaction through entire production process.

**Specialties:**
Practiced at creating silk screen overlays for a multitude of processes including velo bind, GBC bind, and perfect bind. Creative design and timely preparation of posters, flyers, and personalized stationery.

**Personnel Supervision:**
Skillful at fostering atmosphere that encourages highly talented artists to balance high-level creativity with maximum production. Consistently beat production deadlines. Instruct new employees, apprentices, and students in both artistry and technical operations.

### Experience
Graphic Arts Professor, Ohio State University, Columbus OH (1998-2002).
Manager, Design Graphics, Washington DC (2003-present).

### Education
Massachusetts Conservatory of Art, Ph.D. 1996
University of Massachusetts, B.A. 1994

# CHRONOLOGICAL RESUME

**HARRY SEABORN**
**557 Shoreline Drive**
**Seattle, WA 98404**
**(206) 555-6584**
**e-mail: hseaborn@centco.com**

## EXPERIENCE

THE CENTER COMPANY                                      Seattle, WA
*Systems Programmer*                                    2002-present
  • Develop and maintain customer accounting and order tracking
  database using a Visual Basic front end and SQL server.
  • Plan and implement migration of company wide transition from
  mainframe-based dumb terminals to a true client server environment
  using Windows NT Workstation and Server.
  • Oversee general local and wide area network administration
  including the development of a variety of intranet modules to
  improve internal company communication and planning across
  divisions.

INFO TECH, INC.                                         Seattle, WA
*Technical Manager*                                     1996-2002
  • Designed and managed the implementation of a network providing
  the legal community with a direct line to Supreme Court cases
  across the Internet using SQL  Server and a variety of Internet tools.
  • Developed a system to make the entire library catalog available on
  line using PERL scripts and SQL.
  • Used Visual Basic and Microsoft Access to create a registration
  system for university registrar.

## EDUCATION

SALEM STATE UNIVERSITY                                  Salem, OR
      M.S. in Computer Science.                         1999
      B.S. in Computer Science.                         1997

## COMPUTER SKILLS

  • Programming Languages: Visual Basic, Java, C++, SQL, PERL
  • Software: SQL Server, Internet Information Server, Oracle
  • Operating Systems: Windows NT, UNIX, Linux

# FUNCTIONAL RESUME

**Donna Hermione Moss**
703 Wizard's Way
Chicago, IL 60601
(312) 555-8841
e-mail: donna@cowfire.com

**OBJECTIVE:**
To contribute over five years of experience in promotion, communications, and administration to an entry-level position in advertising.

**SUMMARY OF QUALIFICATIONS:**
- Performed advertising duties for small business.
- Experience in business writing and communications skills.
- General knowledge of office management.
- Demonstrated ability to work well with others, in both supervisory and support staff roles.
- Type 75 words per minute.

**SELECTED ACHIEVEMENTS AND RESULTS:** •
Promotion:
Composing, editing, and proofreading correspondence and public relations materials for own catering service. Large-scale mailings.

Communication:
Instruction; curriculum and lesson planning; student evaluation; parent-teacher conferences; development of educational materials. Training and supervising clerks.

Computer Skills:
Proficient in MS Word, Lotus 1-2-3, Excel, and Filemaker Pro.

Administration:
Record-keeping and file maintenance. Data processing and computer operations, accounts receivable, accounts payable, inventory control, and customer relations. Scheduling, office management, and telephone reception.

**PROFESSIONAL HISTORY:**
Teacher; Self-Employed (owner of catering service); Floor Manager; Administrative Assistant; Accounting Clerk.

**EDUCATION:**
Beloit College, Beloit, WI, BA in Education, 1997

# CHRONOLOGICAL RESUME

**PERCY ZIEGLER**
16 Josiah Court
Marlborough CT  06447
203/555-9641 (h)
203/555-8176, x14 (w)

**EDUCATION**

Keene State College, Keene NH
Bachelor of Arts in Elementary Education, 2003
• Graduated *magna cum laude*
• English minor
• Kappa Delta Pi member, inducted 2001

**EXPERIENCE**
September 2003-
Present

Elmer T. Thienes Elementary School, Marlborough CT
*Part-time Kindergarten Teacher*
• Instruct kindergartners in reading, spelling, language  arts, and
  music.
• Participate in the selection of textbooks and learning aids.
• Organize and supervise class field trips and coordinate in-class
  presentations.

Summers
2000-2002

Keene YMCA, Youth Division, Keene NH
*Child-care Counselor*
• Oversaw summer program for low-income youth.
• Budgeted and coordinated special events and field trips,
  working with Program Director to initiate variations in the
  program.
• Served as Youth Advocate in cooperation with social worker to
  address the social needs and problems of participants.

Spring 2002

Wheelock Elementary School, Keene NH
*Student Teacher*
• Taught third-grade class in all elementary subjects.
• Designed and implemented a two-week unit on Native
  Americans.
• Assisted in revision of third-grade curriculum.

Fall 2001

Child Development Center, Keene NH
*Daycare Worker*
• Supervised preschool children on the playground and during art
  activities.
• Created a "Wishbone Corner," where children could quietly
  look at books or take a voluntary "time-out."

**ADDITIONAL INTERESTS**
Martial arts, Pokemon, politics, reading, skiing, writing.

# ELECTRONIC RESUME

## GRIFFIN DORE
69 Dursley Drive
Cambridge, MA 02138
(617) 555-5555

### KEYWORD SUMMARY

Senior financial manager with over ten years experience in Accounting and Systems Management, Budgeting, Forecasting, Cost Containment, Financial Reporting, and International Accounting. MBA in Management. Proficient in Lotus, Excel, Solomon, and Windows.

### EXPERIENCE

COLWELL CORPORATION, Wellesley, MA
Director of Accounting and Budgets, 1995 to present
    Direct staff of twenty in General Ledger, Accounts Payable, Accounts Receivable, and International Accounting.
    Facilitate month-end closing process with parent company and auditors.
    Implemented team-oriented cross-training program within accounting group, resulting in timely month-end closings and increased productivity of key accounting staff.
    Developed and implemented a strategy for Sales and Use Tax Compliance in all fifty states.
    Prepare monthly financial statements and analyses.

FRANKLIN AND DELANEY COMPANY, Melrose, MA
Senior Accountant, 1993-1996
    Managed Accounts Payable, General Ledger, transaction processing, and financial reporting. Supervised staff of five.

Staff Accountant, 1991-1993
    Managed Accounts Payable, including vouchering, cash disbursements, and bank reconciliation.
    Wrote and issued policies.
    Maintained supporting schedules used during year-end audits.
    Trained new employees.

### EDUCATION

MBA in Management, Northeastern University, Boston, MA, 1995
BS in Accounting, Boston College, Boston, MA, 1991

### ASSOCIATIONS

National Association of Accountants

# GENERAL MODEL
# FOR A COVER LETTER

Your mailing address
Date

Contact's name
Contact's title
Company
Company's mailing address

Dear Mr./Ms. _____:

Immediately explain why your background makes you the best candidate for the position that you are applying for. Describe what prompted you to write (want ad, article you read about the company, networking contact, etc.). Keep the first paragraph short and hard-hitting.

Detail what you could contribute to this company. Show how your qualifications will benefit this firm. Describe your interest in the corporation. Subtly emphasizing your knowledge about this firm and your familiarity with the industry will set you apart from other candidates. Remember to keep this letter short; few recruiters will read a cover letter longer than half a page.

If possible, your closing paragraph should request specific action on the part of the reader. Include your phone number and the hours when you can be reached. Mention that if you do not hear from the reader by a specific date, you will follow up with a phone call. Lastly, thank the reader for their time, consideration, etc.

Sincerely,

(signature)

Your full name (typed)

Enclosure (use this if there are other materials, such as your resume, that are included in the same envelope)

# SAMPLE COVER LETTER

16 Josiah Court
Marlborough CT  06447
January 16, 2006

Ms. Leona Malfoy
Assistant Principal
Laningham Elementary School
43 Mayflower Drive
Keene NH  03431

Dear Ms. Malfoy:

Toby Potter recently informed me of a possible opening for a third grade teacher at Laningham Elementary School. With my experience instructing third-graders, both in schools and in summer programs, I feel I would be an ideal candidate for the position. Please accept this letter and the enclosed resume as my application.

Laningham's educational philosophy that every child can learn and succeed interests me, since it mirrors my own. My current position at Elmer T. Thienes Elementary has reinforced this philosophy, heightening my awareness of the different styles and paces of learning and increasing my sensitivity toward special needs children. Furthermore, as a direct result of my student teaching experience at Wheelock Elementary School, I am comfortable, confident, and knowledgeable working with third-graders.

I look forward to discussing the position and my qualifications for it in more detail. I can be reached at 203/555-9641 evenings or 203/555-8176, x14 weekdays. If I do not hear from you before Tuesday of next week, I will call to see if we can schedule a time to meet. Thank you for your time and consideration.

Sincerely,

Percy Ziegler

Percy Ziegler

Enclosure

# GENERAL MODEL FOR A
# THANK YOU/FOLLOW-UP LETTER

Your mailing address
Date

Contact's name
Contact's title
Company
Company's mailing address

Dear Mr./Ms._____:

Remind the interviewer of the reason (i.e., a specific opening, an informational interview, etc.) you were interviewed, as well as the date. Thank him/her for the interview, and try to personalize your thanks by mentioning some specific aspect of the interview.

Confirm your interest in the organization (and in the opening, if you were interviewing for a particular position). Use specifics to re-emphasize that you have researched the firm in detail and have considered how you would fit into the company and the position. This is a good time to say anything you wish you had said in the initial meeting. Be sure to keep this letter brief; a half page is plenty.

If appropriate, close with a suggestion for further action, such as a desire to have an additional interview, if possible. Mention your phone number and the hours you can be reached. Alternatively, you may prefer to mention that you will follow up with a phone call in several days. Once again, thank the person for meeting with you, and state that you would be happy to provide any additional information about your qualifications.

Sincerely,

(signature)

Your full name (typed)

# PRIMARY EMPLOYERS

## ACCOUNTING & MANAGEMENT CONSULTING

### You can expect to find the following types of companies in this section:
Consulting and Research Firms • Industrial Accounting Firms • Management Services • Public Accounting Firms • Tax Preparation Companies

---

**BDO SEIDMAN, LLP**
130 East Randolph Drive, Suite 2800, Chicago IL 60601. 312/240-1236. **Fax:** 312/540-1750. **Contact:** Human Resources. **E-mail address:** r7@bdo.com. **World Wide Web address:** http://www.bdo.com. **Description:** A public accounting and consulting firm. **NOTE:** This company has other Illinois locations. See website for addresses. Apply online. **Positions advertised include:** Business Development Manager; Valuation Manager; Administrative Assistant. **Corporate headquarters location:** This location. **Other U.S. locations:** Boston MA.

**BDO SEIDMAN, LLP**
233 North Michigan Avenue, Suite 2500, Chicago IL 60601. 312/856-9100. **Fax:** 312/856-1379. **Contact:** Human Resources. **World Wide Web address:** http://www.bdo.com. **Description:** A location of the public accounting and consulting firm. **NOTE:** Apply online at the company's website. **Special programs:** Internships. **Operations at this facility include:** Sales. **Other U.S. locations:** Boston MA.

**BANSLEY & KIENER**
8745 West Higgins Road, Suite 200, Chicago IL 60631. 312/263-2700. **Fax:** 312/263-6935. **Contact:** Human Resources. **E-mail address:** humanresources@bk-cpa.com. **World Wide Web address:** http://www.bk-cpa.com. **Description:** A certified public accounting firm. **NOTE:** Fax or e-mail resumes. **Positions advertised include:** Senior In-Charge Auditors; Staff Assistants; Payroll Compliance Auditor; Paraprofessionals. **Special programs:** Internships. **Corporate headquarters location:** This location. **Operations at this facility include:** Service.

**THE CHICAGO GROUP, INC.**
744 North Wells Street, Chicago IL 60610. 312/751-0303. **Fax:** 312/751-0470. **Contact:** Human Resources. **World Wide Web address:** http://www.thechicagogroup.com. **Description:** A management consulting firm specializing in strategic marketing for utility, telecommunications, industrial, technology, and service businesses. **Positions advertised include:** Analyst; Consultant; Director; Manager. **Corporate headquarters location:** This location. **Listed on:** Privately held.

**CLIFTON GUNDERSON L.L.C.**
P.O. Box 1835, Peoria IL 61656-1835. 309/671-4500. **Physical address:** 301 Southwest Adams Street, Peoria IL 61656-1835. **Fax:** 309/671-4508. **Contact:** Human Resources. **World Wide Web address:** http://www.cliftoncpa.com. **Description:** A certified public accounting and consulting firm. **NOTE:** Send resumes to: Clifton Gunderson L.L.C., Human Resources, 2323 North Mayfair

Road, Milwaukee WI 53226. **Positions advertised include:** Accountant; Human Resources Professional; Statistical Typist; Accounting Software Sales; Network Infrastructure Sales Consultant. **Corporate headquarters location:** This location.

## HEWITT ASSOCIATES
100 Half Day Road, Lincolnshire IL 60069. 847/295-5000. **Contact:** Human Resources. **World Wide Web address:** http://www.hewitt.com. **Description:** Hewitt Associates is an international firm of consultants and actuaries specializing in the design, financing, communication, and administration of employee benefit and compensation programs. **Positions advertised include:** Programmer Analyst; WM Analyst; Compliance Specialist; Financial Consultant; Client Coordinator. **Corporate headquarters location:** This location.

## KPMG
303 East Wacker Drive, Chicago IL 60601. 312/665-1000. **Fax:** 312/665-6000. **Contact:** Human Resources. **World Wide Web address:** http://www.kpmgcareers.com. **Description:** KPMG delivers a wide range of value-added assurance, tax, and consulting services. **NOTE:** KPMG prefers job candidates to apply online at its website; however, it possible to fax a scannable resume. See website and job listings for additional information. Positions advertised include: Senior Associate; Senior Actuarial Manager; Public Sector Audit; Internal Audit Manager; Senior Writer. **Corporate headquarters location:** Montvale NJ. **Parent company:** KPMG International is a leader among professional services firms engaged in capturing, managing, assessing, and delivering information to create knowledge that will help its clients maximize shareholder value.

## A.T. KEARNEY PROCUREMENT SOLUTIONS
222 West Adams Street, Suite 2500, Chicago IL 60606. 312/648-0111. **Toll-free phone:** 888/327-3842. **Fax:** 312/223-7070. **Contact:** Human Resources. **E-mail services:** atkps_careers@atkearney.com. **World Wide Web address:** http://www.atkearney.com. **Description:** A general management consulting firm. **NOTE:** E-mail resumes. **Positions advertised include:** eSourcing Manager.

## GEORGE S. MAY INTERNATIONAL COMPANY
303 South Northwest Highway, Park Ridge IL 60068. 847/825-8806. **Toll-free phone:** 800/999-3020. Fax: 847/825-2951. **Contact:** Human Resources. **World Wide Web address:** http://www.georgesmay.com. **Description:** One of the world's largest and oldest management consulting firms. George S. May International focuses on consulting for small businesses. **NOTE:** Visit the website to submit a resume or download the online application and fax it. **Positions advertised include:** Field Service Representative; Executive Analyst; Staff Executive; Marketing Assistant. **Listed on:** Privately held. **President:** Israel Kushnir.

## McGLADREY & PULLEN, LLP
20 North Martingale Road, Schaumburg IL 60173. 847/517-7070. **Contact:** Human Resources. **E-mail address:** careers@rsmi.com. **World Wide Web address:** http://www.mcgladrey.com. **Description:** A certified public accounting firm providing audit, tax, management, data processing, and cost systems services. **NOTE:** Entry-level positions are offered. **Positions advertised include:** Audit Manager **Special programs:** Internships. **Corporate**

**headquarters location:** Bloomington MN. **Other U.S. locations:** Nationwide. **Operations at this facility include:** Administration; Service.

**PRICEWATERHOUSECOOPERS**
One North Wacker Drive, Chicago IL 60606. 312/298-2000. **Contact:** Human Resources. **World Wide Web address:** http://www.pwcglobal.com. **Description:** A location of one of the largest certified public accounting firms in the world. PricewaterhouseCoopers provides public accounting, business advisory, management consulting, and taxation services. **NOTE:** Apply online. **Corporate headquarters location:** New York NY. **Other U.S. locations:** Nationwide.

**PRICEWATERHOUSECOOPERS**
411 Hamilton Boulevard, Suite 1110, Peoria IL 61602-1135. 309/676-8557. **Contact:** Human Resources. **World Wide Web address:** http://www.pwcglobal.com. **Description:** A location of one of the largest certified public accounting firms in the world. PricewaterhouseCoopers provides public accounting, business advisory, management consulting, and taxation services. **NOTE:** Apply online. **Corporate headquarters location:** New York NY. **Other U.S. locations:** Nationwide.

**RSM MCGLADREY, INC.**
191 North Wacker Drive, Suite 1400, Chicago IL 60606. 312/207-2124. **Contact:** Human Resources. **World Wide Web address:** http://www.rsmmcgladrey.com. **Description:** An accounting firm. **NOTE:** Apply online. **Positions advertised include:** Consulting Actuary; Programmer Analyst; Actuarial Analyst; Audit Senior Associate; Audit Manager.

# ADVERTISING, MARKETING, AND PUBLIC RELATIONS

**You can expect to find the following types of companies in this section:**
Advertising Agencies • Direct Mail Marketers • Market Research Firms • Public Relations Firms

---

**ACNIELSEN**
150 North Martingale Road, Schaumburg IL 60173-2076. 847/605-5000. **Fax:** 847/605-2559. **Contact:** Human Resources. **World Wide Web address:** http://www.acnielsen.com. **Description:** Provides demographic and related information such as television audience rating services and consumer polling for the consumer goods industry. **NOTE:** AC Nielsen has additional locations in Illinois. See its website for locations and job listings and apply online. **Positions advertised include:** Associate Database Specialist; Business Analyst; Operations Director; Consumer Insight Director; Order Conversion Specialist. **Corporate headquarters location:** New York NY. **Parent company:** VNU. **Operations at this facility include:** Administration; Regional Headquarters; Research and Development; Sales; Service. **Number of employees worldwide:** 21,000.

**AMD INDUSTRIES, INC.**
4620 West 19th Street, Cicero IL 60804. 708/863-8900. **Toll-free phone:** 800/367-9999. **Fax:** 708/863-2065. **Contact:** Human Resources Director. **World Wide Web address:** http://www.amdpop.com. **Description:** Manufactures and sells point-of-purchase (P.O.P.) displays. **Corporate headquarters location:** This location. **Other U.S. locations:** OH; WI. **Listed on:** Privately held.

**BBDO CHICAGO INC.**
410 North Michigan Avenue, Chicago IL 60611. 312/337-7860. **Contact:** Human Resources. **World Wide Web address:** http://www.bbdo.com. **Description:** A worldwide advertising agency with related businesses in public relations, direct marketing, sales promotion, graphic arts, and printing. **NOTE:** Apply online. **Special programs:** Internships. **Corporate headquarters location:** New York NY. **Other U.S. locations:** Los Angeles CA; San Francisco CA; Miami FL; Atlanta GA; Wellesley MA; Southfield MI. **Parent company:** BBDO Worldwide operates 156 offices in 42 countries and 96 cities. The company also operates 83 subsidiaries, affiliates, and associates engaged solely in advertising and related operations. **Operations at this facility include:** Administration; Service.

**THE BRADFORD GROUP**
9333 North Milwaukee Avenue, Niles IL 60714. 847/966-2770. **Fax:** 847/581-8630. **Contact:** Recruiter. **E-mail address:** jobs@collectiblestoday.com. **World Wide Web address:** http://www.collectiblestoday.com. **Description:** An international direct marketing company specializing in fine arts and collectibles. **NOTE:** Entry-level positions are offered. **Positions advertised include:** Marketing Professional; Product Manager; Product Designer; Product Development Associate. **Special programs:** Internships. **Corporate headquarters location:** This location. **Listed on:** Privately held.

**LEO BURNETT USA**
35 West Wacker Drive, Chicago IL 60601. 312/220-5959. **Contact:** Human Resources. **World Wide Web address:** http://www.leoburnett.com. **Description:** One of the world's largest advertising agencies, with 200 operating units worldwide. Leo Burnett USA also provides direct marketing, promotional, interactive, and public relations services. Founded in 1935. **NOTE:** Apply online at the company's website. **Positions advertised include:** Digital Studio Artist; Creative Director; Database Analyst. **Special programs:** Internships. **Number of employees worldwide:** 8,000.

**CAMPBELL MITHUN**
101 East Erie, 10th Floor, Chicago IL 60611. 312/278-6000. Fax: 312/278-6210. **Contact:** Human Resources. **E-mail address:** careers@campbell-mithun.com. **World Wide Web address:** http://www.campbellmithun.com. **Description:** A full-service advertising agency. Campbell Mithun also offers public relations services including corporate relations, marketing support, employee relations, financial relations, government affairs, and community relations.

**CHICAGO DISPLAY MARKETING CORPORATION**
1999 North Ruby Street, Melrose Park IL 60160. 708/681-4340. **Fax:** 708/681-5852. **Contact:** Human Resources. **World Wide Web address:** http://www.chicagodisplay.com. **Description:** Designs and markets advertising display materials for merchandisers and manufacturers.

**CORMARK, INC.**
1701 S. Winthrop Drive, Des Plaines IL 60018. 847/364-5900. **Toll-free phone:** 800/211-9646. **Contact:** Human Resources. **E-mail address:** recruit2@cormarkinc.com. **World Wide Web address:** http://www.cormarkinc.com. **Description:** A merchandising company. **Positions advertised include:** Business Unit Manager, Graphic Designer, Industrial Designer, Project Engineers, Project Manager. **Corporate headquarters location:** This location.

**CUSHMAN/AMBERG COMMUNICATIONS INC.**
180 North Michigan Avenue, Suite 1600, Chicago IL 60601. 312/263-2500. **Contact:** Thomas Amberg. **World Wide Web address:** http://www.cushmanamberg.com. **Description:** A public relations agency. Founded in 1952. **Corporate headquarters location:** This location.

**DDB CHICAGO, INC.**
200 East Randolph Drive, Chicago IL 60601. 312/552-6000. **Contact:** Human Resources. **World Wide Web address:** http://www.ddbjobs.com. **Description:** A full-service, international advertising agency. **NOTE:** Apply online. **Corporate headquarters location:** New York NY. **Other U.S. locations:** Los Angeles CA. **Parent company:** Omnicom. **Operations at this facility include:** Administration; Marketing; Research and Development; Service.

**EDELMAN WORLDWIDE**
200 East Randolph Drive, Suite 6300, Chicago IL 60601. 312/240-3000. **Fax:** 312/240-2900. **Contact:** Human Resources. **World Wide Web address:** http://www.edelman.com. **Description:** A public relations firm. Founded in 1952. **NOTE:** Apply online at the company's website. **Positions advertised include:** Editorial Supervisor; Senior Account Executive; Administrative Assistant; Print Production Coordinator.

**EURO RSCG TATHAM**
36 East Grand Avenue, Chicago IL 60611. 312/337-4400. **Contact:** Teresa Mogush, Director of Talent Development. **E-mail address:** TathamHR@eurorscg.com. **World Wide Web address:** http://www.eurorscgchicago.com. **Description:** An advertising agency. **Corporate headquarters location:** New York NY. **Operations at this facility include:** Administration; Research and Development; Sales. **Listed on:** Privately held.

**FOOTE CONE & BELDING**
101 East Erie Street, Chicago IL 60611. 312/425-5000. **Fax:** 312/425-5010. **Contact:** Human Resources. **E-mail address:** CareersChi@fcb.com. **World Wide Web address:** http://www.fcb.com. **Description:** One of the largest advertising agencies in the world. Foote Cone & Belding analyzes the advertising needs of clients, plans and creates advertising for their products and services, and places advertising in various mass-market media. The firm offers additional services such as the design and production of merchandising and promotional programs, product research, and package design. **Corporate headquarters location:** New York NY. **Other U.S. locations:** Nationwide.

**GE FINANCIAL ASSURANCE PARTNERSHIP MARKETING**
200 North Martingale Road, Schaumburg IL 60173. 847/605-3000. **Contact:** Human Resources. **World Wide Web address:** http://www.gecareers.com. **Description:** One of the nation's largest telemarketing and direct mail companies. GE Financial Assurance offers retail, wholesale, enhancement, and employee assistance and benefit programs. The company also markets several of the country's largest auto, dental, and legal services plans. Founded in 1966. **Corporate headquarters location:** This location. **Other U.S. locations:** Nationwide. **Parent company:** General Electric Company. **Listed on:** New York Stock Exchange. **Stock exchange symbol:** GE.

**BERNARD HODES ADVERTISING**
430 North Michigan Avenue, Suite 1101, Chicago IL 60611. 312/288-2550. **Contact:** Human Resources. **World Wide Web address:** http://www.hodes.com. **Description:** An advertising agency specializing in recruitment and employee communications. **Positions advertised include:** Client Services Account Executive. **Special programs:** Internships. **Corporate headquarters location:** New York NY. **Other U.S. locations:** Phoenix AZ; Cambridge MA; Dallas TX. **Parent company:** Omnicom.

**KETCHUM**
200 East Randolph Street, Chicago IL 60601. 312/228-6800. **Contact:** Human Resources. **World Wide Web address:** http://www.ketchum.com. **Description:** A communications agency specializing in advertising, public relations, and directory advertising. **NOTE:** Apply online for open positions. **Positions advertised include:** Office Manager/Human Resources Coordinator; Financial Analyst; Corporate Vice President. **Special programs:** Internships. **Corporate headquarters location:** New York NY. **Other U.S. locations:** Nationwide. **International locations:** United Kingdom. **Parent company:** Omnicom.

**SCOTT LAUDER ASSOCIATES**
1580 South Milwaukee, Suite 207, Libertyville IL 60048. 847/549-6262. **Contact:** Sandra White, Office Manager. **E-mail address:** swhite@v2gfk.com. **World**

**Wide Web address:** http://www.scottlauderassociates.com. **Description:** Engaged in a variety of business services including custom market research. **NOTE:** Send resumes via e-mail, fax or mail to Ms. White at V2 GfK, 587 Skippack Pike, Blue Bell PA 19422. Fax: 215/283-3201. **Parent company:** V2 GfK (Blue Bell PA).

## MARSHALL ASSOCIATES, INC.

680 N. Lake Shore Drive, Chicago IL 60611. 312/266-8500. **Fax:** 312/266-7925. **Contact:** Human Resources. **E-mail address:** jobs@marshassoc.com. **World Wide Web address:** http://www.marshassoc.com. **Description:** Marshall Associates is a sales and merchandising company that sells consumer products to retailers across the country. They act on behalf of specific manufacturers to serve as their direct sales force. Marshall Associates' primary product categories include lawn & garden, toys, sporting goods and furniture. **Positions advertised include:** Inside Sales Representative; In-Store Sales Merchandiser; Receptionist. **Corporate headquarters location:** This location. **Other U.S. locations:** Nationwide.

## OGILVY & MATHER

111 East Wacker Drive, Chicago IL 60601. 312/856-8200.**Fax:** 312/856-8420. **Recorded jobline:** 212/237-5627. **Contact:** Human Resources. **World Wide Web address:** http://www.ogilvy.com. **Description:** An advertising agency. **Other U.S. locations:** New York NY. **Parent company:** WWP.

## RAPID DISPLAYS

4300 West 47th Street, Chicago IL 60632. 800/356-5775. **Fax:** 773/927-1091. **Contact:** Human Resources. **World Wide Web address:** http://www.rapiddisplays.com. **Description:** Manufactures signs and advertising displays. Founded in 1938. **NOTE:** See website for job listings. Mail or fax resumes. **Positions advertised include:** Estimator; Design Technician; Illustrator; Account Executive; Customer Service. **Operations at this facility include:** This is a sales and production office.

## SYNOVATE

222 South Riverside Plaza, Chicago IL 60606. 312/526-4000. **Contact:** Human Resources. **E-mail address:** HR.Resumes@synovate.com. **World Wide Web address:** http://www.synovate.com. **Description:** A market research firm that provides services to the government as well as to national and international companies. **NOTE:** Apply online. **Positions advertised include:** Account Director; Account Group Manager; Associate Data Director; Business Systems Analyst; Executive Assistant. . **Other U.S. locations:** Nationwide. **International locations:** Worldwide. **Parent company:** Aegis.

## WAGSTAFF WORLDWIDE

615 West Randolph Street, 2nd Floor, Chicago IL 60661. 312/902-6900. Fax: 312/902-6982. **Contact:** Human Resources. **World Wide Web address:** http://www.wagstaffworldwide.com. **Description:** A travel and hospitality public relations company. **Corporate headquarters location:** Los Angeles CA.

## J. WALTER THOMPSON COMPANY

900 North Michigan Avenue, Chicago IL 60611. 312/951-4000. **Contact:** Human Resources. **World Wide Web address:** http://www.jwtworld.com. **Description:** An advertising agency. **NOTE:** Apply online. **Other U.S. locations:** Nationwide.

**WILLARD & JAMES**
900 North Shore, Suite 225, Lake Bluff IL 60044. 847/295-6300. **Fax:** 847/295-6333.   **Contact:**   Human   Resources.   **E-mail**   **address:** willardandjames@mindspring.com.   **World   Wide   Web   address:** http://www.willardandjames.com. **Description:** An advertising agency that provides creative advertising, strategic marketing, campaign development, and Internet web page design and technology. Founded in 1986. **Managing Principal:** James P. Graziano.

**YOUNG & RUBICAM, INC./CHICAGO**
233 North Michigan Avenue, Suite 1600, Chicago IL 60601. 312/596-3000. **Contact:** Human Resources. **World Wide Web address:** http://www.yandr.com. **Description:** An international advertising agency. The company operates through three divisions: Young & Rubicam International; Marsteller Inc., a worldwide leader in business-to-business and consumer advertising; and Young & Rubicam USA, with 14 consumer advertising agencies operating through four regional groups, and five specialized advertising and marketing agencies. **Corporate headquarters location:** New York NY. **Other U.S. locations:** Nationwide. **International locations:** Worldwide. **Subsidiaries include:** Burson-Marsteller provides public relations services throughout the world.

**ZIMENT ASSOCIATES**
7016 North Overhill Avenue, Chicago IL 60631. 773/594-6390. **Contact:** Human Resources. **World Wide Web address:** http://www.ziment.com. **Description:** Provides healthcare marketing research. **Parent company:** The Kantar Group.

## AEROSPACE

### You can expect to find the following types of companies in this section:
Aerospace Products and Services • Aircraft Equipment and Parts

---

**AAR**
One AAR Place, 1100 North Wood Dale Road, Wood Dale IL 60191. 630/227-2000. **Fax:** 630/227-2019. **Contact:** Human Resources. **World Wide Web address:** http://www.aarcorp.com. **Description:** Provides trading, overhaul, and manufacturing services, primarily to aviation-related customers including commercial airlines, the government, original equipment manufacturers, and aviation service companies. In trading, AAR buys, sells, and leases aircraft, engines, and airframe components and distributes factory-new airframe and engine hardware. The company also customizes programs for airlines seeking inventory management. Overhaul includes the maintenance of aircraft and components including instruments; hydraulic, pneumatic, and electrical systems; landing gear; and engine parts. AAR also designs and manufactures a variety of aviation products with an emphasis on air cargo transport systems and related materials. Founded in 1951. **Corporate headquarters location:** Wood Dale, IL. **Listed on:** New York Stock Exchange. **Stock exchange symbol:** AIR.

**ARMOLOY OF ILLINOIS**
118 Simonds Avenue, DeKalb IL 60115. 815/758-6691. **Toll-free phone:** 800/654-1157. **Fax:** 815/758-6640. **Contact:** Human Resources. **E-mail address:** info@armoloy-il.com. **World Wide Web address:** http://www.armoloyil.com. **Description:** Manufactures coatings used on ferrous and non-ferrous metals, including all grades of stainless steel, for the aerospace and other industries.

**DANVILLE METAL STAMPING COMPANY, INC.**
20 Oakwood Avenue, Danville IL 61832. 217/446-0647. **Contact:** Human Resources. **World Wide Web address:** http://www.danvillemetal.com. **Description:** Develops and produces fabricated metal components for the aerospace and gas turbine industries. Founded in 1946. This company has another facility in Danville IL at 1100 Martin Street.

**FRASCA INTERNATIONAL, INC.**
906 East Airport Road, Urbana IL 61802-7407. 217/344-9200. **Fax:** 217/344-9207. **Contact:** Human Resources. **E-mail address:**personnel@frasca.com. **World Wide Web address:** http://www.frasca.com. **Description:** Manufactures certified full-flight simulators, flight training devices, cockpit procedures trainers, and noncertified ab-initio trainers for the airline, military, and general aviation industries. Modifications and upgrades of flight simulation and training equipment are available. Frasca also offers engineering and consulting services. Founded in 1958. **Office hours:** Monday - Friday, 8:00 a.m. - 5:00 p.m.

## GENERAL ELECTRIC COMPANY (GE)
## AIRCRAFT ENGINES DIVISION
1543 South 54th Avenue, Cicero IL 60804. 708/780-2600. **Contact:** Human Resources. **World Wide Web address:** http://www.ge.com. **Description:** GE operates in the following areas: aircraft engines (jet engines, replacement parts, and repair services for commercial, military, executive, and commuter aircraft); appliances; broadcasting (NBC); industrial (lighting products, electrical distribution and control equipment, transportation systems products, electric motors and related products, a broad range of electrical and electronic industrial automation products, and a network of electrical supply houses); materials (plastics, ABS resins, silicones, superabrasives, and laminates); power systems (products for the generation, transmission, and distribution of electricity); technical products and systems (medical systems and equipment, as well as a full range of computer-based information and data interchange services for both internal use and external commercial and industrial customers); and capital services (consumer services, financing, and specialty insurance). **NOTE:** Apply online at http://www.gecareers.com. **Company slogan:** We bring good things to life. **Corporate headquarters location:** Fairfield CT. **Operations at this facility include:** This location manufactures aircraft engines and engine parts. **Listed on:** New York Stock Exchange. **Stock exchange symbol:** GE.

## HAMILTON SUNDSTRAND CORPORATION
4747 Harrison Avenue, P.O. Box 7002, Rockford IL 61125-7002. 815/226-6000. **Contact:** Human Resources. **World Wide Web address:** http://www.hamiltonsundstrandcorp.com. **Description:** Manufactures a wide range of aircraft components, systems, and subsystems. **NOTE:** This company provides job listings for this location and its other U.S. facilities. See its website and apply online.

## MPC PRODUCTS CORPORATION
7426 North Linder Avenue, Skokie IL 60077. 847/673-8300. **Fax:** 847/673-7144. **Contact:** Human Resources. **E-mail address:** human_resources@mpcproducts.com. **World Wide Web address:** http://www.mpcproducts.com. **Description:** Engineers and manufactures electromechanical equipment including motors, gears, and electronics for the government and aerospace companies. **NOTE:** See website for job listings and apply online.

## NORTHROP GRUMMAN CORPORATION
600 Hicks Road, Rolling Meadows IL 60008. 847/259-9600. **Contact:** Human Resources. **World Wide Web address:** http://www.es.northropgrumman.com. **Description:** Electronic Systems division of Northrop Grumman provides airborne radar systems, secondary surveillance systems, inertial navigation systems and sensors, electronic warfare systems, precision weapons, air traffic control systems, air defense systems, communications systems, space systems, marine systems, oceanic and naval systems, integrated avionics systems, logistics systems, and government systems. **Positions advertised include:** Manufacturing Supervisor; Program Manager; Mechanical Technician; Mechanical Engineer; Electronics Engineer; Industrial Security; CAD/CAM Engineer.

**NORTHSTAR AEROSPACE**
**WINDSOR DIVISION**
6006 West 73rd Street, Bedford Park IL 60638. 708/728-2000. **Fax:** 708/728-2009. **Contact:** Human Resources. **World Wide Web address:** http://www.windsor.northstar-aerospace.com. **Description:** Manufactures parts for helicopters including transmissions, gear boxes, and flap drives.

**UNISON INDUSTRIES**
530 Blackhawk Park Avenue, Rockford IL 61104. 815/965-4700. **Contact:** Human Resources. **World Wide Web address:** http://www.unisonindustries.com. **Description:** Manufactures aircraft equipment including ignition parts, digital engine control systems, sensors, and power generation equipment.

## APPAREL, FASHION, AND TEXTILES

**You can expect to find the following types of companies in this section:**
Broadwoven Fabric Mills • Knitting Mills • Yarn and Thread Mills • Curtains and Draperies • Footwear • Nonwoven Fabrics • Textile Goods and Finishing

---

### CINTAS
5600 West 73rd Street, Chicago IL 60638. 708/563-4913. **Fax:** 708/563-4360. **Contact:** Human Resources. **World Wide Web address:** http://www.cintas.com. **Description:** Designs, manufactures, and markets specialty apparel for the hospitality, restaurant, and entertainment industries. **Corporate headquarters location:** This location. **International locations:** Canada; Mexico; Puerto Rico. **Operations at this facility include:** Administration; Regional Headquarters; Research and Development; Sales; Service. **Listed on:** NASDAQ. **Stock exchange symbol:** CTAS.

### HARTMARX CORPORATION
101 North Wacker Drive, Chicago IL 60606. 312/372-6300. **Fax:** 312/444-2679. **Contact:** Susan Klawitter, Director of Human Resources Administration. **World Wide Web address:** http://www.hartmarx.com. **Description:** A manufacturer of men's tailored clothing under the labels Hart Schaffner & Marx, Austin Reed, Tommy Hilfiger, and Krizia. Hartmarx Corporation also manufactures women's clothing and sportswear under the brand names Hart Schaffner & Marx, Pierre Cardin, Austin Reed, and Hickey-Freeman. The company conducts direct marketing and catalog sales operations worldwide. **Corporate headquarters location:** This location. **Other U.S. locations:** Winchester KY; Cape Girardeau MO; New York NY. **Operations at this facility include:** Administration; Manufacturing; Sales; Service.

### HUMPHREYS, INC.
2009 West Hastings Street, Chicago IL 60608. 312/997-2358. **Toll-free phone:** 800/843-8455. **Fax:** 312/997-2147. **Contact:** Marilyn Bly, Office Manager. **E-mail address:** blym@randacorp.com. **World Wide Web address:** http://www.humphreysinc.com. **Description:** Manufactures belts, wallets, and other leather accessories. **NOTE:** Fax or e-mail resumes to Ms. Bly.

### O'BRYAN BROTHERS
4220 West Belmont Avenue, Chicago IL 60641. 773/283-3000. **Contact:** Eva Vollrath, Human Resources Director. **Description:** Manufactures ladies' loungewear and lingerie. **Corporate headquarters location:** This location.

### OXXFORD CLOTHES
1220 West Van Buren Street, Chicago IL 60607. 312/829-3600. **Toll-free phone:** 800/525-4727. **Fax:** 312/829-6075. **Contact:** Human Resources. **World Wide Web address:** http://www.oxxfordclothes.com. **Description:** A manufacturer of hand-sewn suits and coats for men. **NOTE:** Entry-level positions are offered. **Parent company:** Tom James Company. **Operations at this facility include:** Administration; Manufacturing; Sales.

**WHITE SWAN META UNIFORM COMPANY**
13975 Polo Trail, Suite 101, Lake Forest IL 60045. 847/247-0380. **Contact:** Human Resources. **Description:** White Swan Meta Uniform Company manufactures uniforms. **Operations at this facility include:** This location is the sales and service office

## ARCHITECTURE, CONSTRUCTION, AND ENGINEERING

**You can expect to find the following types of companies in this section:**
Architectural and Engineering Services • Civil and Mechanical Engineering Firms • Construction Products, Manufacturers, and Wholesalers • General Contractors/Specialized Trade Contractors

---

**ADVANCE MECHANICAL SYSTEMS INC.**
2080 South Carboy, Mount Prospect IL 60056-5750. 847/593-2510. **Contact:** Human Resources. **World Wide Web address:** http://www.advmech.com. **Description:** An engineering firm specializing in mechanical and HVAC contracting.

**AMBITECH ENGINEERING CORPORATION**
1333 Butterfield Road, Suite 200, Downers Grove IL 60515. 630/963-5800. **Fax:** 630/963-8099. **Contact:** Carrie Koenig, Human Resources Manager. **E-mail address:** ckoenig@ambitech.com. **World Wide Web address:** http://www.ambitech.com. **Description:** A consulting and engineering firm engaged in the engineering and design of petroleum refineries, chemical plants, and petrochemical plants including. **NOTE:** See website for application. **Positions advertised include:** Instrumentation and Controls Programmer; Mechanical Engineer; Senior Piping Engineer; Senior Process Engineer. **Corporate headquarters location:** This location. **Listed on:** Privately held.

**ANNING-JOHNSON COMPANY**
1959 Anson Drive, Melrose Park IL 60160. 708/681-1300. **Fax:** 708/681-1386. **Contact:** Human Resources. **World Wide Web address:** http://www.anningjohnson.com. **Description:** Engaged in a variety of areas including acoustical ceiling, drywall, fireproofing, metal floor decks, metal siding, roofing, and geotechnical fill. Founded in 1940. **Corporate headquarters location:** This location. **Parent company:** Anson Industries Inc.

**AXIS INC.**
2201 West Townline Road, Peoria IL 61615. 309/691-3988. **Fax:** 309/691-4172. **Contact:** Human Resources. **E-mail address:** careers@axis-inc.com. **World Wide Web address:** http://www.axis-inc.com. **Description:** Engaged in civil and mechanical engineering, information technology, and client-site technical services. Founded in 1987. **NOTE:** See list of job openings at the company's website. **Other U.S. locations:** Indianapolis IN. **International locations:** Australia; United Kingdom. **Subsidiaries include:** Axis Software, Inc. (Indianapolis IN); Axis Computers Ltd. (New Delhi, India); Axis EU Ltd. (London, England).

**BELCAN CORPORATION**
Woodland Courte Office Center, 3130 Finley Road, Suite 520, Downers Grove IL 60515. 630/786-9900. **Contact:** Human Resources. **World Wide Web address:** http://www.belcan.com. **Description:** An engineering and consulting firm offering long-term, client-site consulting services in the Midwest. **NOTE:** Entry-level positions are offered. This company has many locations throughout Illinois. See

website for additional offices and apply online. **Positions advertised include:** Civil Project Engineer; Design Engineer; Electrical Engineer; Physical-Electrical Designer. **Corporate headquarters location:** Ann Arbor MI. **International locations:** England. **Listed on:** Privately held.

**BRICKKICKER**
849 North Ellsworth, Naperville IL 60563. 630/420-9900. **Toll-free phone:** 800/821-1820. **Fax:** 630/420-2270.**Contact:** Human Resources. **World Wide Web address:** http://www.brickkicker.com. **Description:** Performs home and building inspections.

**BURNSIDE CONSTRUCTION COMPANY**
2400 Wisconsin Avenue, Downers Grove IL 60515-4019. 630/515-9999. **Contact:** Human Resources. **World Wide Web address:** http://www.burnsidehomes.com. **Description:** A residential construction company. Founded in 1911.

**CAPITOL CONSTRUCTION GROUP**
220 North Smith Street, Suite 210, Palatine Il 60067. 847/654-4700. Fax: 847/358-7331. **Contact:** Human Resources. **E-mail address:** info@capitol.com. **World Wide Web address:** http://www.capitolconstruction.com. **Description:** A general contractor. **NOTE:** Interested jobseekers should fax or e-mail their resumes. **Positions advertised include:** Project Manager; Construction Superintendent. **Other U.S. locations:** Phoenix AZ; Tampa FL; St. Louis MO.

**THE CHICAGO FAUCET COMPANY**
2100 South Clearwater Drive, Des Plaines IL 60018. 847/803-5000. **Fax:** 847/803-44995454. **Contact:** Human Resources. **World Wide Web address:** http://www.chicagofaucets.com. **Description:** Manufactures brass products including plumbing fittings.

**COMMERCIAL LIGHT COMPANY**
245 Fencl Lane, Hillside IL 60162. 708/449-6900. **Fax:** 708/449-6942. **Contact:** Human Resources. **World Wide Web address:** http://www.clcats.com. **Description:** An electrical contractor. Founded in 1915.

**CONSOER TOWNSEND ENVIRODYNE ENGINEERS, INC.**
303 East Wacker Drive, Suite 600, Chicago IL 60601. 312/938-0300. **Fax:** 312/938-1109. **Contact:** Director of Human Resources. **E-mail address:** jobs@cte-eng.com. **World Wide Web address:** http://www.cte-eng.com. **Description:** Provides engineering consulting for highways, airports, and waste management projects. **NOTE:** Apply online at the company's website or e-mail resumes.

**CONTRACTING & MATERIAL COMPANY**
9550 West 55th Street, Suite B, McCook IL 60525. 708/588-6000. **Contact:** Human Resources. **World Wide Web address:** http://www.candmcompany.com. **Description:** Provides contract construction services for electrical, pipeline, highway, and heavy construction projects. **NOTE:** Garages are located at 5401 West Harrison Street, Chicago IL 60644-5030.

**ELKAY MANUFACTURING COMPANY**
2222 Camden Court, Oak Brook IL 60523. 630/574-8484. **Fax:** 630/574-5012. **Contact:** Human Resources. **World Wide Web address:** http://www.elkay.com.

**Description:** Manufactures stainless steel sinks, faucets, water coolers, and kitchen cabinets. **NOTE:** Entry-level positions are offered. Apply online for all positions. **Corporate headquarters location:** This location. **Listed on:** Privately held.

**ENERFAB**
1913 South Briggs Street, Joliet IL 60433. 815/727-4624. **Fax:** 815/727-0776. **Contact:** Human Resources. **World Wide Web address:** http://www.enerfab.com. **Description:** A mechanical engineering company that provides a variety of services including HVAC, power piping, fabrication, and plumbing. **Corporate headquarters location:** Cincinnati OH.

**GANNETT FLEMING**
222 South Riverside Plaza, Suite 1860, Chicago IL 60606. 312/454-9494. **Fax:** 312/454-1277. **Contact:** Human Resources. **E-mail address:** employment@gfnet.com. **World Wide Web address:** http://www.gannettfleming.com. **Description:** Provides civil and structural engineering consulting services.

**GERBER PLUMBING FIXTURES CORPORATION**
4600 West Touhy Avenue, Lincolnwood IL 60712. 847/675-6570. **Fax:** 847/675-5192. **Contact:** Human Resources. **World Wide Web address:** http://www.gerberonline.com. **Description:** Manufactures a variety of bathroom and kitchen plumbing products including faucets, valves, lavatories, toilets, and vanities. **Corporate headquarters location:** This location.

**HANSON ENGINEERS**
1525 South Sixth Street, Springfield IL 62703. 217/788-2450. **Fax:** 217/788-2503. **Contact:** Human Resources. **World Wide Web address:** http://www.hansonengineers.com. **Description:** A consulting firm that provides a variety of architectural, engineering, and scientific services. Founded in 1954. **Corporate headquarters location:** This location. **Other U.S. locations:** Nationwide.

**HONEYWELL**
1500 West Dundee Road, Arlington Heights IL 60004. 847/797-4000. **Contact:** Human Resources. **World Wide Web address:** http://www.honeywell.com. **Description:** Honeywell is engaged in the research, development, manufacture, and sale of advanced technology products and services in the fields of chemicals, electronics, automation, and controls. The company's major businesses are home and building automation and control, performance polymers and chemicals, industrial automation and control, space and aviation systems, and defense and marine systems. **NOTE:** See job listings on Honeywell's website and apply online. **Operation at this facility include:** This location manufactures home heating and air-conditioning controls. **Listed on:** New York Stock Exchange. **Stock exchange symbol:** HON.

**KENNY CONSTRUCTION COMPANY**
250 Northgate Parkway, Wheeling IL 60090. 847/541- 8200. **Fax:** 847/541-8358. **Contact:** Human Resources. **World Wide Web address:** http://www.kennyconstruction.com. **Description:** A construction company that handles various large scale projects such as subways, tunnels, airports, stadiums, buildings, hotels, power plants, mass transit, bridges, highways and all manner of Infrastructure projects. Kenny Construction operates primarily in five

operating groups: Tunnels, Transportation, Underground, Building, and Power. **Positions advertised include:** Accounts Payable Clerk, Construction Superintendent, Cost Control Engineer, Office Assistant, Project Engineer, Project Manager. **Corporate headquarters location:** This location.

## M+W ZANDER
549 West Randolph Street, Chicago IL 60661. 312/577-3200. **Contact:** Human Resources. **World Wide Web address:** http://www.mw-zander.com. **Description:** An architectural and engineering firm. Founded in 1945.

## MACKIE CONSULTANTS, INC.
9575 West Higgins Road, Suite 500, Rosemont IL 60018. 847/696-1400. **Contact:** Human Resources. **Description:** An engineering consulting firm providing a variety of engineering services as well as land surveying and grading.

## MOHN CUSTOM INTERIORS
601 South MacArthur Boulevard, Springfield IL 62704. 217/787-6251. **Contact:** Manager. **World Wide Web address:** http://www.mohninteriors.com. **Description:** Provides professional interior design and furniture upholstering services. Founded in 1968. **Office hours:** Monday – Friday, 9:00 a.m. – 5:00 p.m.; Saturday – 10:00 a.m. – 12:00 p.m.

## F.E. MORAN
2265 Carlson Drive, Northbrook IL 60062. 847/498-4800. **Contact:** Human Resources. **World Wide Web address:** http://www.femoran.com. **Description:** An international mechanical contracting company specializing in fire detection, heating, air conditioning, plumbing, and ventilation systems. **NOTE:** See website for job listings and contact information. **Corporate headquarters location:** This location.

## W.E. O'NEIL CONSTRUCTION COMPANY
2751 North Clybourn Avenue, Chicago IL 60614. 773/755-1611. **Fax:** 773/327-4806. **Contact:** Pat McGowan, Organizational Development Director. **E-mail address:** chicago.careers@oneilind.com. **World Wide Web address:** http://www.oneilind.com. **Description:** A general construction company specializing in construction management, general contracting, design/build, and preconstruction. **NOTE:** Jobseekers should indicate the department in which they are interested in a cover letter. **Corporate headquarters location:** This location. **Parent company:** O'Neil Industries, Inc. (also at this location).

## PACKER ENGINEERING INC.
1950 North Washington Street, Naperville IL 60563. 630/505-5722. **Toll-free phone:** 800/323-0114. **Fax:** 630/505-3010. **Contact:** Human Resources. **E-mail address:** pejobs@packereng.com. **World Wide Web address:** http://www.packereng.com. **Description:** A multidisciplinary engineering, consulting, and technical services company. The practice includes failure analysis; accident investigation and reconstruction; fire/explosion cause and origin studies; product design evaluations; process design assessments; customized and routine testing; applied research; commercial product development; and litigation support. **NOTE:** Apply online for all positions. Entry-level positions are offered. **Special programs:** Internships. **Internship information:** Paid summer internships are available through The Packer Foundation. For additional information, visit the Foundation's website at http://www.packerfoundation.com/internships. **Corporate headquarters**

**location:** This location. **Other U.S. locations:** Nationwide. **Parent company:** The Packer Group.

## PARSONS TRANSPORTATION GROUP
10 South Riverside, Suite 400, Chicago IL 60606. 312/930-5100. **Fax:** 312/930-0018. **Contact:** Technical Recruiter. **World Wide Web address:** http://www.parsons.com. **Description:** Designs and builds roads, bridges, highways, and other transportation infrastructure. **NOTE:** Apply online. **Positions advertised include:** Project Manager; Associate Engineer; Principal Designer. **Corporate headquarters location:** Washington DC.

## PATRICK ENGINEERING
4970 Varsity Drive, Lisle IL 60532. 630/790-7200. **Fax:** 630/790-1681. **Contact:** Human Resources. **E-mail address:** hr_jobs@patrickengineering.com. **World Wide Web address:** http://www.patrickengineering.com. **Description:** Offers solid waste planning, architecture, surveying, and engineering services in the civil, transportation, environmental, geotechnical, hydraulic, water resources, structural, and electrical sectors. Founded in 1979. **Other area locations:** Chicago IL; Springfield IL. **Other U.S. locations:** MI: WI; PA.

## PERKINS & WILL
330 North Wabash Avenue, Suite 3600, Chicago IL 60611. 312/755-0770. **Toll-free phone:** 800/837-9455. **Fax:** 312/755-4788. **Contact:** Human Resources. **E-mail address:** hr@perkinswill.com. **World Wide Web address:** http://www.perkinswill.com. **Description:** An architectural, interior design and planning firm that serves both commercial and industrial companies. The company also provides an IDP/IDEP program for unlicensed designers. This location also hires seasonally. Founded in 1935. **NOTE:** Mail, fax or e-mail resumes. Entry-level positions and part-time jobs are offered. **Positions advertised include:** Environmental Graphics Designer; Marketing Coordinator. **Corporate headquarters location:** This location. **Other U.S. locations:** Los Angeles CA; Miami FL; Atlanta GA; Minneapolis MN; Charlotte NC; New York NY. **International locations:** Paris, France. **Subsidiaries include:** TY Lin, Inc. **Parent company:** Dar Al Handesah. **Listed on:** Privately held.

## RAGNAR BENSON INC.
250 South Northwest Highway, Park Ridge IL 60068-4252. 847/698-4900. **Fax:** 847/692-9320. **Contact:** Human Resources. **World Wide Web address:** http://www.ragnarbenson.com. **Description:** An engineering and construction firm that specializes in design-build, construction management, and general contracting. Founded in 1922. **Positions advertised include:** Project Superintendent.

## RAYMOND PROFESSIONAL GROUP, INC.
550 West Van Buren Street, Suite 400, Chicago IL 60607. 312/935-3200. **Fax:** 312/935-3201. **Contact:** Human Resources. **World Wide Web address:** http://www.raymondgroup.com. **Description:** A multidisciplinary engineering consulting firm. Services include electrical, mechanical, and structural engineering.

## ROBERTS & SCHAEFER COMPANY
120 South Riverside Plaza, Suite 400, Chicago IL 60606. 312/236-7292. **Contact:** Human Resources. **World Wide Web address:** http://www.r-s.com. **Description:** A multidisciplinary engineering firm. Founded in 1903.

**SARGENT & LUNDY**
55 East Monroe Street, Chicago IL 60603. 312/269-2000. **Fax:** 312/269-1960. **Contact:** Kathleen A. Lynch, Human Resources. **E-mail address:** kathleen.a.lynch@sargentlundy.com. **World Wide Web address:** http://www.sargentlundy.com. **Description:** Provides a broad range of engineering services. Founded in 1891. **NOTE:** See website for job listings and contact information. Entry-level and temporary positions are offered. **Corporate headquarters location:** This location. **Other U.S. locations:** Nationwide. **International locations:** Worldwide. **Listed on:** Privately held.

**SMITHFIELD CONSTRUCTION GROUP, INC.**
400 W. Huron, Chicago IL 60610. 312/266-9800. **Fax:** 312/2669530. **Contact:** Adrienne Pearlman, Human Resources. **E-mail address:** apearlman@smith-field.com. **World Wide Web address:** http://www.smith-field.com. **Description:** Residential, commercial, and industrial construction company. **Positions advertised include:** Safety Director.

**GEORGE SOLLITT CONSTRUCTION COMPANY**
790 North Central, Wood Dale IL 60191. 630/860-7333. **Fax:** 630/860-7347. **Contact:** Howard Strong, Vice President of Operations. **World Wide Web address:** http://www.sollitt.com. **Description:** A leading general contractor/construction management firm. Clients include hospitals, schools, and major corporations. Founded in 1838. **NOTE:** Entry-level positions are offered. **Special programs:** Training. **Corporate headquarters location:** This location. **Listed on:** Privately held.

**STERLING PLUMBING GROUP, INC.**
2900 Golf Road, Rolling Meadows IL 60008. 847/734-1777. **Contact:** Human Resources. **World Wide Web address:** http://www.sterlingplumbing.com. **Description:** Manufactures sinks, faucets, tubs, and toilets as well as other plumbing supplies for kitchens and bathrooms. **NOTE:** For job listings, visit Kohler's website at http://www.hr.kohler.com/careers. Parent company: Kohler.

**R&D THIEL INC.**
2340 Newburg Road, Belvidere IL 61008. 815/544-1699. **Contact:** Human Resources. **E-mail address:** HumanResources@rdthiel.com. **World Wide Web address:** http://www.rdthiel.com. **Description:** Provides a variety of construction services ranging from carpentry labor to completed residential housing. **NOTE:** See website for job listings and contact information. **Positions advertised include:** Wall Panel Designer; Truss Designers; Carpenter Helpers; Carpenters; Lead Carpenters; Jobsite Foreman. **Corporate headquarters location:** This location.

**UNDERWRITERS LABORATORIES INC.**
333 Pfingsten Road, Northbrook IL 60062. 847/272-8800. **Fax:** 847/509-6300. **Contact:** Human Resources **E-mail address:** northbrook@us.ul.com. **World Wide Web address:** http://www.ul.com. **Description:** An independent, nonprofit corporation established to help reduce or prevent bodily injury, loss of life, and property damage. Engineering functions are divided between six departments: Electrical Department; Burglary Protection and Signaling Department; Casualty and Chemical Hazards Department; Fire Protection Department; Heating, Air Conditioning, and Refrigeration Department; and Marine Department. The company also provides factory inspection services through offices in the United

States and 54 other countries. **Corporate headquarters location:** This location. **Other U.S. locations:** CA; NC; NY; WA. **Operations at this facility include:** Administration; Service.

**THE WALSH GROUP**
929 West Adams, Chicago IL 60607. 312/563-5400. **Fax:** 312/563-5453. **Contact:** Human Resources. **E-mail address:** agonzalez@walshgroup.com. **World Wide Web address:** http://www.walshgroup.com. **Description:** A construction contracting company. **Positions advertised include:** Payroll Data Entry Clerk; Field Secretary; Project Engineer.

**WICKES INC.**
706 Deerpath Drive, Vernon Hills IL 60061. 847/367-3400. **Fax:** 847/3673767. **Contact:** Human Resources. **E-mail address:** humanresources@wickes.com. **World Wide Web address:** http://www.wickes.com. **Description:** One of the largest suppliers of building materials in the United States. Wickes's manufacturing facilities produce prehung door units, window assemblies, roof and floor trusses, and framed wall panels. **Corporate headquarters location:** This location. **Other U.S. locations:** Denver CO; Elwood IN; Ocean Springs MS; Lomira WI. **Listed on:** NASDAQ. **Stock exchange symbol:** WIKS.

## ARTS, ENTERTAINMENT, SPORTS, AND RECREATION

**You can expect to find the following types of companies
in this section:**
Botanical and Zoological Gardens • Entertainment Groups • Motion
Picture and Video Tape Production and Distribution • Museums and Art
Galleries • Physical Fitness Facilities • Professional Sports Clubs;
Sporting and Recreational Camps • Public Golf Courses and Racing and
Track Operations • Theatrical Producers and Services

---

**ADLER PLANETARIUM & ASTRONOMY MUSEUM**
1300 South Lake Shore Drive, Chicago IL 60605. 312/322-0591. **Fax:** 312/322-9909. **Contact:** Marguerite E. Dawson, Human Resources Manager. **E-mail address:** mdawson@adlernet.org. **World Wide Web address:** http://www.adlerplanetarium.org. **Description:** A planetarium and science museum focusing on astronomy. Founded in 1930. **NOTE:** Entry-level and part-time positions are offered. **Positions advertised include:** Distance Learning Educator; Museum Service Staff. **Special programs:** Internships; Training; Volunteer. **Corporate headquarters location:** This location. **Operations at this facility include:** Administration.

**ALLIED VAUGHN**
1200 Thorndale Avenue, Elk Grove Village IL 60007. 847/595-2900. **Toll-free phone:** 800/759-4087. **Fax:** 847/595-8677. **Contact:** Human Resources. **World Wide Web address:** http://www.alliedvaughn.com. **Description:** One of the nation's leading independent multimedia manufacturing companies offering CD-audio and CD-ROM mastering and replication, videocassette and audiocassette duplication, off-line and online video editing, motion picture film processing, film-to-tape and tape-to-film transfers, and complete finishing, packaging, warehousing, and fulfillment services. **Positions advertised include:** Sales Executive. **Corporate headquarters location:** Minneapolis MN.

**ART INSTITUTE OF CHICAGO**
111 South Michigan Avenue, Chicago IL 60603. 312/443-3600. **Fax:** 312/857-0141. **Contact:** Human Resources. **E-mail address:** aic.jobs@artic.edu. **World Wide Web address:** http://www.artic.edu. **Description:** An art museum that provides educational programs, family workshops, artist demonstrations, and lectures. Exhibits include African and Ancient American Art, Architecture, Arms and Armor, Impressionism and Post-Impressionism, Modern Art, and Textiles. **NOTE:** Part-time and temporary positions available. E-mail or fax resumes and cover letters. An application is available also online. It can be downloaded and e-mailed or faxed. **Positions advertised include:** Auxiliary Board Assistant Director; Evening Associates Assistant Director; Membership Associate Director; Coordinator; Day Security Officer; Housekeeper; Information Systems Assistant. **Special programs:** Volunteer; Internship. **Office hours:** Monday - Friday, 9:00 a.m. - 5:00 p.m.

**BALLY TOTAL FITNESS CORPORATION**
8700 West Bryn Mawr Avenue, Chicago IL 60631. 773/399-1300. **Contact:** Personnel Director. **World Wide Web address:** http://www.ballyfitness.com. **Description:** Bally Total Fitness operates 360 fitness centers located in 27

states with approximately 4.2 million members. The fitness centers operate under the Bally name in conjunction with various others including Holiday Health, Jack LaLanne, Holiday Spa, Chicago Health Clubs, Scandinavian, President's First Lady, Vic Tanny and Aerobics Plus, and The Vertical Clubs. In addition, the company operates four fitness centers in Canada. **NOTE:** Bally has offices throughout the United States. Their website provides job listings and contact information for each location. See website. **Positions advertised include:** Staff Accountant; Senior Auditor; Financial Reporting Manager. **Special programs:** Internships. **Corporate headquarters location:** This location. **Other U.S. locations:** Nationwide. **Listed on:** New York Stock Exchange. **Stock exchange symbol:** BFT.

### BROADVIEW MEDIA
142 East Ontario, 3rd Floor, Chicago IL 60611. 312/337-6000. **Contact:** Human Resources. **World Wide Web address:** http://www.broadviewmedia.com. **Description:** A full-service film and video production company involved in production, editing, audio, consumer graphics, and distribution, servicing broadcast and cable networks, corporate advertising agencies, and business to business markets. **NOTE:** Entry-level positions are offered.

### CHICAGO ACADEMY OF SCIENCES
### PEGGY NOTEBAERT NATURE MUSEUM
2340 North Cannon Drive, Chicago IL 60614. 773/755-5100. **Fax:** 773/549-5199. **Contact:** Human Resources. **World Wide Web address:** http://www.chias.org. **Description:** A natural history museum. The Nature Museum, located on the North Pier, offers hands-on exhibits and also runs week-long summer nature camps June through August each year. Founded in 1857. **NOTE:** See website for job listings and specific contact information.

### CHICAGO BOTANIC GARDEN
1000 Lake Cook Road, Glencoe IL 60022. 847/835-8300. **Fax:** 847/835-4263. **Contact:** Human Resources. **E-mail address:** employment@chicagobotanic.org. **World Wide Web address:** http://www.chicago-botanic.org. **Description:** Contains horticultural displays used to promote the understanding of plants, gardening, and natural resource conservation. Founded in 1965. **NOTE:** See website for job listings and e-mail resumes and cover letters. **Positions advertised include:** College First Instructor; Curriculum Development Coordinator; Coordinator Retail Events Floor Supervisor. **Special programs:** Internships.

### CHICAGO CUBS
Wrigley Field, 1060 West Addison Street, Chicago IL 60613. 773/404-2827. **Contact:** Director of Human Resources. **World Wide Web address:** http://www.cubs.com. **Description:** The administrative offices for the professional baseball team. **NOTE:** See website.

### CHICAGO SYMPHONY ORCHESTRA
220 South Michigan Avenue, Chicago IL 60604. 312/294-3333. **Fax:** 312/294-3838. **Recorded jobline:** 312/294-3326. **Contact:** Human Resources. **E-mail address:** hr@cso.org. **World Wide Web address:** http://www.chicagosymphony.org. **Description:** One of the nation's most prestigious orchestras. **Positions advertised include:** Director of Research; Ticket Sales and Service Associate. **Special programs:** Internship. **Corporate headquarters location:** This location.

**CHICAGO TOUR GUIDES INSTITUTE, INC.**
**EUROPEAN LANGUAGE CENTER INC.**
60 East Chestnut, Suite 381, Chicago IL 60611. 773/276-6683. **Fax:** 773/252-3729. **Contact:** Human Resources Department. **World Wide Web address:** http://www.chicagoguide.net. **Description:** Offers tours of Chicago. The European Language Center (also at this location) hires part-time and full-time foreign language interpreters for U.S. and foreign companies. **NOTE:** Guides earn $15 to $25 per hour and need to have comprehensive knowledge of the city including local museums, architecture, art, and city history. **Positions advertised include:** Tour Guide. **Corporate headquarters location:** This location. **Operations at this facility include:** Administration; Service.

**CIRCA '21 DINNER PLAYHOUSE**
1828 Third Avenue, Rock Island IL 61201. 309/786-2667. **Fax:** 309/786-4119. **Contact:** Dennis Hitchcock, Producer. **E-mail address:** dlaake@circa21.com. **World Wide Web address:** http://www.circa21.com. **Description:** Produces musicals and modern comedies, as well as a series of children's plays and concerts year-round. Circa '21 Dinner Playhouse has produced numerous national tours. Founded in 1977. **NOTE:** Part-time jobs are offered. Interested jobseekers may fill out an application in person at the office or e-mail their resumes. **Positions advertised include:** Housekeeper; Cook; Dishwasher; Maintenance Worker. **Special programs:** Internships. **Listed on:** Privately held.

**THE FIELD MUSEUM OF NATURAL HISTORY**
1400 South Lake Shore Drive, Chicago IL 60605. 312/922-9410. **Fax:** 312/665-7272. **Contact:** Human Resource. **E-mail address:** hr@fieldmuseum.org. **World Wide Web address:** http://www.fmnh.org. **Description:** A natural history museum. The museum provides both formal and informal educational opportunities for the public and conducts its own research in the fields of anthropology, geology, zoology, and biology. Founded in 1893. **NOTE:** The museum only accepts online applications via its website. Entry-level positions are offered. **Positions advertised include:** Annual Giving Manager; Campaign Manager; Enterprise Application and Project Manager; Major Gifts Office, Prospect Research Coordinator. **Special programs:** Internships; Volunteer. **Corporate headquarters location:** This location. **Operations at this facility include:** Administration; Research and Development; Service. **Listed on:** Privately held.

**GOODMAN THEATRE**
170 North Dearborn Street, Chicago IL 60601. 312/443-3811. **Contact:** Human Resources. **World Wide Web address:** http://www.goodman-theatre.org. **Description:** A nonprofit theater producing both classic and contemporary works. Founded in 1925. **NOTE:** See the theatre's website for job listings and contact information.

**HARPO INC.**
110 North Carpenter Street, Chicago IL 60607. 312/633-1000. **Contact:** Human Resources. **World Wide Web address:** http://www.oprah.com. **Description:** Engaged in film and television production. **Corporate headquarters location:** This location. **President:** Oprah Winfrey.

## JOHN DEERE HISTORIC SITE

8393 South Main, Grand Detour, Dixon IL 61021. 815/652-4551. **Contact:** Human Resources. **World Wide Web address:** http://www.deere.com. **Description:** The historic site of John Deere, who founded one of the country's largest agricultural manufacturing companies. This location houses a museum and a blacksmith shop.

## KNIGHT'S ACTION PARK & CARIBBEAN WATER ADVENTURE

1700 Recreation Drive, Springfield IL 62707. 217/546-8881. **Contact:** Human Resources. **E-mail address:** knightsap@aol.com. **World Wide Web address:** http://www.knightsactionpark.com. **Description:** An action and water park offering bumper boats, batting cages, miniature golf, a driving range, laser tag, and other activities. **NOTE:** E-mail resumes or drop by the park to fill out an application. **Positions advertised include:** Office; Cashier; Maintenance; Ride Operator; Lifeguard; Food Service; Housekeeping; Parking Attendant; Guest Greeter; Landscaping.

## KOHL CHILDREN'S MUSEUM

165 Green Bay Road, Wilmette IL 60091. 847/256-6056. **Fax:** 847/853-9154. **Contact:** Human Resources. **World Wide Web address:** http://www.kohlchildrensmuseum.org. **Description:** A children's museum with multisensory exhibits and programs intended to enhance children's understanding of themselves and the world around them. **Positions advertised include:** Exhibit Guide. **Special programs:** Internships; Volunteers. **Corporate headquarters location:** This location.

## LINCOLN PARK ZOO

P.O. Box 14903, 2001 North Clark Street, Chicago IL 60614. 312/742-2000. **Fax:** 312/742-2299. **Contact:** Human Resources. **World Wide Web address:** http://www.lpzoo.com. **Description:** The Greater Chicago area's zoological exhibit, including amusement rides, a train and restaurants. **NOTE:** A completed application must be submitted for any position. . See website for job listings, application and submission procedures. Part-time and seasonal positions are offered. **Positions advertised include:** Education Interpreter; Retail Greeter; Production Manager; Curator; Guest Services Attendant. **Special programs:** Volunteer.

## LYRIC OPERA OF CHICAGO

20 North Wacker Drive, Chicago IL 60606. 312/332-2244. **Fax:** 312/419-1082. **Contact:** Human Resources. **E-mail address:** jobs@lyricopera.org. **World Wide Web address:** http://www.lyricopera.org. **Description:** Engaged in the study of opera, music, and the fine arts. Lyric Opera is a nonprofit organization that sponsors, produces, and encourages opera and musical performances in Chicago and the surrounding areas. Founded in 1954. **NOTE:** Part-time, seasonal and entry-level positions are offered. See website for job listings. Fax, mail or e-mail resumes. **Special programs:** Internships. **Corporate headquarters location:** This location.

## McCORMICK PLACE

2301 South Lake Shore Drive, Chicago IL 60616. 312/791-7000. **Fax:** 312/791-6001. **Recorded jobline:** 312/791-6090. **Contact:** Human Resources Director. **World Wide Web address:** http://www.mccormickplace.com. **Description:** A convention center that features three theaters, 114 meeting rooms, a ballroom, and over 2 million square feet of exhibition space. **NOTE:** An application is required for any position. See website for application. **Positions advertised include:** Production Coordinator.

## MUSEUM OF CONTEMPORARY ART
220 East Chicago Avenue, Chicago IL 60611. 312/280-2660. **Toll-free phone:** 800/MCA-7858. **Fax:** 312/397-4095. **Recorded jobline:** 312/397-4050. **Contact:** Susan Kieffer, Human Resources Manager. **E-mail address:** skieffer@mcachicago.org. **World Wide Web address:** http://www.mcachicago.org. **Description:** A nonprofit, contemporary art museum offering exhibitions of international works from 1945 to the present, with a permanent collection of over 1,500 works. **NOTE:** See website for job listings. Submit resumes and cover letters by mail or fax. An application may also be completed in person at the Human Resources Office. Entry-level positions, part-time jobs, and second and third shifts are offered. **Positions advertised include:** Accounts Payable/Payroll Accountant; Coordinator of Interpretive Training; Accounting Assistant; Marketing Coordinator; Media Relations Coordinator; Box Office Associate; Free-Lance Preparators; Gallery Officers; Visitor Services Associate; Coatroom Attendants. **Special programs:** Internships; Summer Jobs. **Office hours:** Monday - Friday, 10:00 a.m. - 5:00 p.m.

## MUSEUM OF SCIENCE & INDUSTRY
57th Street & Lake Shore Drive, Chicago IL 60637. 773/684-1414. **Fax:** 773/684-0019. **Contact:** Human Resources. **E-mail address:** Human.Resources@msichicago.org. **World Wide Web address:** http://www.msichicago.org. **Description:** One of the largest science museums in the world. Museum of Science & Industry offers over 800 exhibits. Founded In 1933. **NOTE:** Interested jobseekers may fax, mail or e-mail resumes. Walk-in applicants are also accepted in the Human Resources Office. Part-time and temporary positions are offered. **Positions advertised include:** Demonstrator; Public Programs; Internal Auditor; Program Interpreters; Administration Assistant; Retail Businesses and Technology Services; Director of Marketing; Maintenance Technician; Manager of Program Development. **Special programs:** Internships; Volunteers. **Office hours:** Monday, Tuesday and Wednesday – 10:00 a.m. – 3:00 p.m. **Corporate headquarters location:** This location.

## SHEDD AQUARIUM
1200 South Lake Shore Drive, Chicago IL 60605. 312/939-2426. **Contact:** Tina Ausley, Human Resources Recruiter. **E-mail address:** jobs@sheddaquarium.org. **World Wide Web address:** http://www.shedd.org. **Description:** An aquarium and oceanarium offering a wide range of exhibits, outreach programs, and educational workshops. **NOTE:** See website for job listings. Part-time positions offered. Mail or e-mail resumes for all positions. **Positions advertised include:** Admissions Associate; Aquarist; Interpretive Naturalist; Membership Associate; Audio-Visual Operator; Multimedia Manager. **Corporate headquarters location:** This location.

## SIX FLAGS GREAT AMERICA
P.O. Box 1776, Gurnee IL 60031. 847/249-2133. **Contact:** Human Resources. **World Wide Web address:** http://www.sixflags.com. **Description:** A theme park. **NOTE:** Apply in person at the company's Human Resources Office. **Special programs:** Internships. **Office hours:** Monday – Friday, 1:00 p.m. – 5:00 p.m.; Saturday, 11:00 a.m. – 3:00 p.m. **Other U.S. locations:** CA; GA; NJ; TX. **International locations:** Toronto, Canada. **Parent company:** Premier Parks

(OK) owns and operates 35 theme parks nationwide. **Operations at this facility include:** Administration; Sales.

## STEPPENWOLF THEATRE COMPANY
758 West North Avenue, 4th Floor, Chicago IL 60610. 312/335-1888. **Fax:** 312/335-0808. **Contact:** Human Resources. **World Wide Web address:** http://www.steppenwolf.org. **Description:** A Tony Award-winning theater company. **NOTE:** See website for job listings and contact information. **Positions advertised include:** Technical Director; Fundraising; Theatre Sales. **Special programs:** Internships; Volunteers.

## THE UNITED CENTER
1901 West Madison Street, Chicago IL 60612. 312/455-4500. **Fax:** 312/455-4750. **Contact:** Human Resources. **World Wide Web address:** http://www.united-center.com. **Description:** A state-of-the-art stadium and entertainment facility. The United Center is home to the Chicago Bulls basketball team and the Chicago Blackhawks ice hockey team. **Operations at this facility include:** Administration; Sales; Service.

## WMS INDUSTRIES, INC.
3401 North California Avenue, Chicago IL 60618. 773/961-1620. **Fax:** 773/961-1025. **Contact:** Human Resources. **E-mail address:** hr@wmsgaming.com. **World Wide Web address:** http://www.wmsgaming.com. **Description:** WMS Industries operates in three divisions: the gaming division designs and manufactures slot machines; the pinball and cabinets division; and the contract manufacturing division produces coin-operated video games for Midway Games. **Positions advertised include:** BOM Analyst; Electrical Lab Assistant; Lead Artist; Manufacturing Engineer; Planner; Principal Engineer; Software Engineer. **Subsidiaries include:** WMS Gaming Inc. **Listed on:** New York Stock Exchange. **Stock exchange symbol:** WMS.

# AUTOMOTIVE

**You can expect to find the following types of companies in this section:**
Automotive Repair Shops • Automotive Stampings • Industrial Vehicles and Moving Equipment • Motor Vehicles and Equipment • Travel Trailers and Campers

---

**AMERIDRIVES INTERNATIONAL**
**MARLAND CLUTCH PRODUCTS**
650 East Elm Avenue, La Grange IL 60525. 708/352-3330. **Contact:** Human Resources. **World Wide Web address:** http://www.ameridrives.com. **Description:** Manufactures couplings, backstops, and RINGSPANN freewheel clutches.

**BORG-WARNER AUTOMOTIVE**
700 25th Avenue, Bellwood IL 60104. 708/547-2600. **Contact:** Director of Human Resources. **World Wide Web address:** http://www.bwauto.com. **Description:** Manufactures powertrain components for original equipment manufacturers and original equipment suppliers in the automobile industry. **Corporate headquarters location:** Chicago IL. Operations at this facility include: This location is a powertrain engine manufacturing facility. **Listed on:** New York Stock Exchange. **Stock exchange symbol:** BWA.

**BORG-WARNER AUTOMOTIVE**
200 South Michigan Avenue, Chicago IL 60604. 312/322-8500. **Fax:** 312/322-8500. **Contact:** Director of Human Resources. **World Wide Web address:** http://www.bwauto.com. **Description:** Manufactures powertrain components for original equipment manufacturers and original equipment suppliers in the automobile industry. Operations include powertrain assembly and the manufacture of automatic transmission systems, and chain and control systems. **Corporate headquarters location:** This location. **Operations at this facility include:** Administration. **Listed on:** New York Stock Exchange. **Stock exchange symbol:** BWA.

**ROBERT BOSCH CORPORATION**
P.O. Box 4601, Carol Stream IL 60197. 708/865-5200. **Physical address:** 2800 South 25th Avenue, Broadview IL 60155. **Fax:** 708/865-6430. **Contact:** Human Resources. **World Wide Web address:** http://www.bosch.com. **Description:** Robert Bosch Corporation operates through three groups: Automotive Equipment, Industrial Technology, and Consumer Goods and Building Technology. The largest segment of the company's business is the Automotive Equipment group, which includes products such as antilock braking systems, airbag electronics, fuel injectors, and oxygen sensors. The Industrial Technology group consists of the Packaging Technology Division, which sells high-tech packaging equipment, primarily to the food processing and pharmaceutical industries; the Bosch Rexroth Division, which creates products that control motors and motion equipment; and Metal Technology Division, which manufactures water pipes for various industries. The Consumer Goods and Building Technology group has five divisions: Power Tools (sold in many hardware stores); Thermotechnology (residential and industrial heating systems); Household Appliances; and Broadband Networks. **NOTE:** This company

provides job listings for all its locations on its website. Apply online. **Corporate headquarters location:** This location.

**BRAKE PARTS INC.**
4400 Prime Parkway, McHenry IL 60050. 815/363-9000. **Fax:** 815/363-9303. **Contact:** Human Resources. **World Wide Web address:** http://www.raybestos.com. **Description:** Manufactures and distributes a variety of automotive brake products. **NOTE:** Mail resume or apply online in persona at this location's Human Resources office. **Parent company:** Dana Corporation. **Operations at this facility include:** Administration; Manufacturing; Sales; Service.

**DANA BRAKE PARTS INC.**
1600 North Industrial Drive, McHenry IL 60050. 815/385-7000. **Contact:** Employment Relations Manager. **World Wide Web address:** http://www.dana.com. **Description:** Manufactures and distributes a variety of automotive brake products. **NOTE:** Mail resume or apply online in persona at this location's Human Resources office.

**DANA CORPORATION**
1945 Ohio Street, Lisle IL 60532. 630/960-4200. **Contact:** Human Resources. **World Wide Web address:** http://www.dana.com. **Description:** Dana Corporation is a global leader in engineering, manufacturing, and marketing products and systems for the worldwide vehicular, industrial, and mobile off-highway original equipment markets and is a major supplier to the related aftermarkets. Dana Corporation also provides lease financing services in selected markets. The company's products include drivetrain components such as axles, driveshafts, clutches, and transmissions; engine parts such as gaskets, piston rings, seals, pistons, and filters; chassis products such as vehicular frames and cradles and heavy-duty side rails; fluid power components such as pumps, motors, and control valves; and industrial products such as electrical and mechanical brakes and clutches, drives, and motion control devices. Dana's vehicular components and parts are used on automobiles, pickup trucks, vans, minivans, sport utility vehicles, medium and heavy trucks, and off-highway vehicles. The company's industrial products include mobile off-highway and stationary equipment. **Corporate headquarters location:** Toledo OH. **Operations at this facility include:** This location manufactures gaskets for automobiles and tractors.

**FORD MOTOR COMPANY**
12600 South Torrance Avenue, Chicago IL 60633. 773/646-3100. **Contact:** Human Resources. **World Wide Web address:** http://www.ford.com. **Description:** Ford Motor Company is engaged in the design, development, manufacture, and sale of cars, trucks, tractors, and related components and accessories. Ford is also one of the largest providers of financial services in the United States. Ford's two core businesses are the Automotive Group and the Financial Services Group (Ford Credit, The Associates, USL Capital, and First Nationwide). Ford is also engaged in a number of other businesses including electronics, glass, electrical and fuel-handling products, plastics, climate-control systems, automotive service and replacement parts, vehicle leasing and rental, and land development. **NOTE:** For hourly positions, contact the plant or the nearest state employment center office. For managerial positions, see the company's website for job listings and application procedures. **Corporate**

**headquarters location:** Dearborn MI. **Operations at this facility include:** This location is an assembly plant.

**GNB TECHNOLOGIES, INC.**
2475 West Station Street, Kankakee IL 60901. 815/937-6925. **Contact:** Human Resources. **World Wide Web address:** http://www.gnb.com. **Description:** Manufactures and recycles lead-acid batteries for a wide range of consumer and industrial uses. **Corporate headquarters location:** Princeton NJ.

**HENDRICKSON INTERNATIONAL**
800 South Frontage Road, Woodridge IL 60517. 630/910-2800. **Fax:** 630/910-2899. **Contact:** Beth Bretz, Human Resources. **World Wide Web address:** http://www.hendrickson-intl.com. **Description:** A worldwide supplier of engineered products for the truck and automotive industries. Hendrickson International designs, develops, and manufactures suspension systems, leaf springs, and heavy stampings primarily for heavy-duty trucks. **NOTE:** See website for contact information. **Corporate headquarters location:** This location. **Parent company:** The Boler Company. **Listed on:** Privately held.

**JOHNSON CONTROLS, INC.**
300 South Glengarry Drive, Geneva IL 60134. 630/232-4270. **Contact:** Human Resources. **World Wide Web address:** http://www.jci.com. **Description:** Johnson Controls, Inc. provides air conditioning services, air filters, automatic temperature control, chiller services, coil cleaning, lighting services, energy management, facilities management systems, fire alarm systems, heating service, maintenance contracts, refrigeration service, and security systems. **NOTE:** Apply online. **Corporate headquarters location:** Milwaukee WI. **Operations at this facility include:** This location manufactures automobile batteries. **Listed on:** New York Stock Exchange. **Stock exchange symbol:** JCI.

**ROCKFORD POWERTRAIN, INC.**
1200 Windsor Road, Loves Park IL 61111. 815/633-7460. **Contact:** Human Resources. **World Wide Web address:** http://www.rockfordpowertrain.com. **Description:** Manufactures clutch and driveline equipment for off-road vehicles.

**S&S AUTOMOTIVE, INC.**
740 North Larch Avenue, Elmhurst IL 60126. 630/279-1600. **Contact:** Human Resources. **Description:** A wholesaler of janitorial products and automotive accessories to car dealerships.

**TENNECO AUTOMOTIVE**
500 North Field Drive, Lake Forest IL 60045. 847/482-5000. **Contact:** Human Resources. **World Wide Web address:** http://www.tenneco-automotive.com. **Description:** Develops and manufactures suspension systems and engine mounting systems providing noise, shock, and vibration control for the transportation industry. **NOTE:** Submit resume online at the company's website. **Corporate headquarters location:** This location. **Parent company:** Tenneco (Greenwich CT). **Listed on:** New York Stock Exchange. **Stock exchange symbol:** TEN.

**TRAILMOBILE, INC.**
1101 Skokie Boulevard, Suite 350, Northbrook IL 60062. 847/504-2000. **Toll-free phone:** 800/877-4990. **Fax:** 847/480-9262. 1000 North 14th Street, Charleston IL 60921. 217/348-8181. **Contact:** Human Resources. **World Wide Web**

**address:** http://www.trailmobile.com. **Description:** Trailmobile manufactures over-the-road semitrailers. **Operations at this facility include:** Administration; Sales; Manufacturing.

## BANKING, SAVINGS & LOANS, AND OTHER DEPOSITORY INSTITUTIONS

**You can expect to find the following types of companies in this section:**
Banks • Bank Holding Companies and Associations • Lending Firms/Financial Services Institutions

---

### ALBANY BANK & TRUST COMPANY N.A.
3400 West Lawrence Avenue, Chicago IL 60625. 773/267-7300. **Contact:** Human Resources. **World Wide Web address:** http://www.albanybank.com. **Description:** A full-service bank with three locations throughout the Chicago metropolitan area. **Parent company:** Albank Corporation.

### AMCORE BANK ROCKFORD
501 Seventh Street, P.O. Box 1537, Rockford IL 61104. 815/968-2241. **Contact:** Human Resources. **World Wide Web address:** http://www.amcore.com. **Description:** A chain of banks with more than 65 locations in Illinois, Wisconsin and Iowa. Founded in 1910. **NOTE:** This company's website includes job listings and contact information for all its locations. See website for specific contact information. **Listed on:** NASDAQ. **Stock exchange symbol:** AMFI.

### BANCO POPULAR BANK & TRUST COMPANY
4000 West North Avenue, Chicago IL 60639. 773/772-8600. **Contact:** Human Resources. **World Wide Web address:** http://www.bancopopular.com. **Description:** A bank. **NOTE:** This bank has branches throughout Illinois. See its website for additional locations. Apply online.

### BANK OF AMERICA
601 North Dearborn Street, Chicago IL 60610. 312/274-9450. **Contact:** Human Resources. **World Wide Web address:** http://www.bankofamerica.com. **Description:** Bank of America is a full-service banking and financial institution. The company operates through four business segments: Global Corporate and Investment Banking, Principal Investing and Asset Management, Commercial Banking, and Consumer Banking. **Corporate headquarters location:** Charlotte NC. **Other U.S. locations:** Nationwide. **Listed on:** New York Stock Exchange. **Stock exchange symbol:** BAC.

### BANK ONE
120 North Scott Street, Joliet IL 60432. 815/727-2601. **Contact:** Human Resources. **World Wide Web address:** http://www.bankone.com. **Description:** Bank One is a bank holding company that provides a broad range of commercial and investment banking, trust services, and financial and other services on a worldwide basis to individuals, businesses, and governmental units. **Corporate headquarters location:** Chicago IL. **Operations at this facility include:** This locations is a bank. **Listed on:** New York Stock Exchange. **Stock exchange symbol:** ONE. **Number of employees nationwide:** 73,500.

## BANK ONE

8001 Lincoln Avenue, Skokie IL 60077. 847/673-2500. **Contact:** Human Resources. **World Wide Web address:** http://www.bankone.com. **Description:** Bank One is a bank holding company that provides a broad range of commercial and investment banking, trust services, and financial and other services on a worldwide basis to individuals, businesses, and governmental units. **Corporate headquarters location:** Chicago IL. **Operations at this facility include:** This locations is a bank. **Listed on:** New York Stock Exchange. **Stock exchange symbol:** ONE. **Number of employees nationwide:** 73,500.

## BANK ONE CORPORATION

One Bank One Plaza, Chicago IL 60670. 312/732-4000. **Contact:** Human Resources. **World Wide Web address:** http://www.bankone.com. **Description:** A bank holding company that provides a broad range of commercial and investment banking, trust services, and financial and other services on a worldwide basis to individuals, businesses, and governmental units. **Corporate headquarters location:** This location. **Listed on:** New York Stock Exchange. **Stock exchange symbol:** ONE. **Number of employees nationwide:** 73,500.

## BANK ONE LA GRANGE, N.A.

14 South La Grange Road, La Grange IL 60525. 708/579-4400. **Contact:** Human Resources. **World Wide Web address:** http://www.bankone.com. **Description:** A full-service bank. **Corporate headquarters location:** Chicago IL. **Other U.S. locations:** Nationwide. **Parent company:** Bank One Corporation is one of the nation's largest bank holding companies. Bank One has an affiliate network of over 75 banks with more than 1,500 banking locations. In addition, Bank One operates corporations involved in data processing, venture capital, investment and merchant banking, trust, brokerage, investment management, leasing, mortgage banking, consumer finance, and insurance. **Listed on:** New York Stock Exchange. **Stock exchange symbol:** ONE. **Number of employees nationwide:** 73,500.

## BANK ONE SPRINGFIELD, N.A.

One East Old State Capital Plaza, Springfield IL 62701. 217/525-9733. **Contact:** Human Resources. **World Wide Web address:** http://www.bankone.com. **Description:** A bank. **Parent company:** Bank One Corporation is one of the nation's largest bank holding companies. Bank One has an affiliate network of over 75 banks with more than 1,500 banking locations. In addition, Bank One operates corporations involved in data processing, venture capital, investment and merchant banking, trust, brokerage, investment management, leasing, mortgage banking, consumer finance, and insurance. **Listed on:** New York Stock Exchange. **Stock exchange symbol:** ONE. **Number of employees nationwide:** 73,500.

## CHARTER ONE BANK

6700 West North Avenue, Chicago IL 60707. 773/622-5000. **Contact:** Human Resources. **World Wide Web address:** http://www.charteronebank.com. **Description:** A federally chartered savings and loan bank. **NOTE:** Part-time shifts offered. Apply online or at the nearest branch location for all positions. **Positions advertised include:** Assistant Sales. **Corporate headquarters location:** This location. **Operations at this facility include:** Administration; Sales; Service.

**CITIBANK**
500 West Madison Street, 5th Floor, Chicago IL 60661. 312/627-5231. **Fax:** 312/627-5235. **Recorded jobline:** 312/627-5299. **Contact:** Strategic Staffing. **World Wide Web address:** http://www.citibank.com. **Description:** Citibank operates a global, full-service consumer franchise encompassing branch banking, credit and charge cards, and private banking. In branch banking, Citibank services almost 20 million accounts in 41 countries and territories. In global card products, Citibank is one of the world's largest bankcard and charge card issuers, with almost 50 million cards in force (34 million bankcards in the United States, 9 million in other countries, and almost 7 million Diners Club cards). In addition, Citibank issues and services approximately 5 million private-label cards for department stores and retail outlets. Citibank Private Bank's offices in 31 countries and territories provide a full-range of wealth management services and give clients access to the full range of Citibank's global capabilities. **NOTE:** This company lists all its open positions in its Chicago area, Illinois and United States locations. See website and apply online. **Special programs:** Internships. **Corporate headquarters location:** New York NY. **Other U.S. locations:** Nationwide. **Parent company:** Citigroup. **Operations at this facility include:** Divisional Headquarters. **Listed on:** New York Stock Exchange. **Stock exchange symbol:** C.

**COLE TAYLOR BANK**
9550 West Higgins Road, Rosemont IL 60018. 847/653-7978.x350. East Dundee Road, Wheeling IL 60090. 847/459-6666. **Contact:** Human Resources. **World Wide Web address:** http://www.ctbnk.com. **Description:** A full-service bank with multiple locations throughout the Greater Chicago area. **Positions advertised include:** Chief Financial Officer; Consumer Loan Specialist; Systems Project Manager; Vice President of Product Development.

**CORUS BANK, N.A.**
3959 North Lincoln Avenue, Chicago IL 60613. 773/880-7900. **Fax:** 773/832-5262. **Contact:** Human Resources. **World Wide Web address:** http://www.corusbank.com. **Description:** A full-service banking institution. **NOTE:** Entry-level and part-time positions are offered. This bank has several branches throughout the Chicago area. See website for additional locations and job listings. Apply online. **Parent company:** Corus Bankshares. **Listed on:** NASDAQ. **Stock exchange symbol:** CORS.

**FIFTH THIRD BANK**
105 South York Street, Elmhurst IL 60126. 630/941-5200. **Contact:** Human Resources. **World Wide Web address:** http://www.53.com. **Description:** A single branch of a bank that provides commercial and personal banking and trust services. **NOTE:** Fifth Third Bank has locations throughout Chicago and the midwestern part of the United States. See its website for job listings at specific branch locations. **Positions advertised include:** Lockbox Extractor; Lockbox Processor; Proof Operator. **Parent company:** Fifth Third Bancorp.

**FIRST MIDWEST BANK**
300 Park Boulevard, Suite 405, Itasca, IL 60143. 630/875-7450. **Fax:** 630/875-7369. **Recorded jobline:** 866/562-7362. **Contact:** Human Resources. **World Wide Web address:** http://www.firstmidwest.com. **Description:** A full-service bank with approximately 70 offices throughout northern Illinois and eastern Iowa. **NOTE:** This bank provides job listings for all its branch locations. See its website and apply online. **Listed on:** NASDAQ. **Stock exchange symbol:** FMBI.

**HARRIS BANK**
P.O. Box 755, Chicago IL 60690. 312/461-2121. **Physical address:** 111 West Monroe Street, Chicago IL 60603. **Contact:** Human Resources. **World Wide Web address:** http://www.harrisbank.com. **Description:** Provides a wide range of banking, trust, and investment services to individuals and small businesses. Harris Bank has 140 locations in the greater Chicago area. **NOTE:** Apply online at the company's website. **Parent company:** Bank of Montreal.

**LASALLE BANK N.A.**
5250 North Harlem Avenue, Chicago IL 60656. 773/775-6800. **Fax:** 877/619-2005. **Recorded jobline:** 312/904-5627. **Contact:** Human Resources. **World Wide Web address:** http://www.lasallebanks.com. **Description:** A full-service savings and loan bank. **NOTE:** Apply online at ABN ARMO's website: http://www.abnamro.com. **Parent company:** ABN ARMO Bank N.V. is one of the world's largest banking institutions, with more than 1,900 locations in 71 countries.

**LASALLE BANK N.A.**
5200 West Fullerton Avenue, Chicago IL 60639. 773/889-1000. **Fax:** 877/619-2005. **Recorded jobline:** 312/904-5627. **Contact:** Human Resources. **World Wide Web address:** http://www.lasallebanks.com. **Description:** A location of the largest savings bank in Illinois. **NOTE:** Apply online at ABN ARMO's website: http://www.abnamro.com. **Parent company:** ABN ARMO Bank N.V. is one of the world's largest banking institutions, with more than 1,900 locations in 71 countries.

**LASALLE BANK N.A.**
135 South LaSalle Street, Suite 3300, Chicago IL 60603. 312/904-2000. **Fax:** 877/619-2005. **Recorded jobline:** 312/904-5627. **Contact:** Human Resources. **World Wide Web address:** http://www.lasallebanks.com. **Description:** A divisional headquarters of the bank chain. **NOTE:** Apply online at ABN ARMO's website: http://www.abnamro.com. **Parent company:** ABN ARMO Bank N.V. is one of the world's largest banking institutions, with more than 1,900 locations in 71 countries.

**LASALLE BANK N.A.**
5501 South Kedzie Avenue, Chicago IL 60629. 773/434-3322. **Fax:** 877/619-2005. **Recorded jobline:** 312/904-5627. **Contact:** Human Resources. **World Wide Web address:** http://www.lasallebanks.com. **Description:** This is the regional headquarters for LaSalle Bank. **NOTE:** Apply online at ABN ARMO's website: http://www.abnamro.com. **Parent company:** ABN ARMO Bank N.V. is one of the world's largest banking institutions, with more than 1,900 locations in 71 countries. **Operations at this facility include:** Administration.

**LASALLE BANK N.A.**
4747 West Irving Park Road, Chicago IL 60641. 773/777-7700. **Fax:** 877/619-2005. **Recorded jobline:** 312/904-5627. **Contact:** Human Resources. **World Wide Web address:** http://www.lasallebanks.com. **Description:** A location of the largest savings bank in Illinois. **NOTE:** Apply online at ABN ARMO's website: http://www.abnamro.com. **Parent company:** ABN ARMO Bank N.V. is one of the world's largest banking institutions, with more than 1,900 locations in 71 countries.

**MB FINANCIAL BANK**
2 South LaSalle Street, Chicago IL 60602. 312/782-6200. **Contact:** Human Resources Director. **World Wide Web address:** http://www.mbfinancial.com. **Description:** A bank. **NOTE:** See website for job listings and resume submission procedures. Part-time positions offered. **Special program:** Internships. **Listed on:** NASDAQ. **Stock exchange symbol:** MBFI.

**MIDAMERICA BANK**
55th Street & Holmes Avenue, Clarendon Hills IL 60514. 630/325-7300. **Contact:** Teresa Colson, Human Resources Manager. **World Wide Web address:** http://www.midamerica-bank.com. **Description:** A full-service bank. **NOTE:** See website for job listings and apply online. **Corporate headquarters location:** Westchester IL. **Other area locations:** Cicero IL; La Grange Park IL; Naperville IL; Riverside IL; St. Charles IL; Wheaton IL. **Parent company:** MAF Bancorp, Inc. **Listed on:** NASDAQ. **Stock exchange symbol:** MAFB.

**NATIONAL CITY BANK**
120 West State Street, Rockford IL 61101. 815/987-2000. **Fax:** 815/987-2185. **Contact:** Human Resources. · **World Wide Web address:** http://www.nationalcity.com. **Description:** One of the largest banks in the Midwest. National City offers a wide variety of financial services including mortgages, checking accounts, and mutual funds. **NOTE:** Apply online at the corporate website. **Special programs:** Internships. **Corporate headquarters location:** Cleveland OH. **Other U.S. locations:** AZ; FL; IN; MI; MO; NC; SC. **Listed on:** New York Stock Exchange. **Stock exchange symbol:** NCC. **Number of employees worldwide:** 32,300.

**NATIONAL CITY BANK**
One Old Capital Plaza North, Springfield IL 62701. 217/753-7100. **Contact:** Human Resources. **World Wide Web address:** http://www.nationalcity.com. **Description:** One of the largest banks in the Midwest. **NOTE:** Apply online at the corporate website.

**NATIONAL CITY BANK**
325 North Milwaukee Avenue, Libertyville IL 60048. 847/362-3000. **Fax:** 847/816-5798. **Contact:** Human Resources. **World Wide Web address:** http://www.nationalcity.com. **Description:** The regional headquarters for this chain of banks. **NOTE:** Apply online at the corporate website. **Operations at this facility include:** Administration; Sales; Service.

**NATIONAL CITY BANK**
301 SW Adams Street, Peoria IL 61602. 309/655-5000. **Contact:** Human Resources. **World Wide Web address:** http://www.nationalcity.com. **Description:** A branch of the largest banks in the Midwest. Founded in 1845. **NOTE:** Apply online at the corporate website. **Operations at this facility include:** Private Client Group and NatCity Investments.

**THE NORTHERN TRUST COMPANY**
50 South LaSalle Street, Chicago IL 60675. 312/630-6000. **Contact:** Human Resources. **World Wide Web address:** http://www.ntrs.com. **Description:** A full-service bank engaged in commercial lending services, trust services, financial services, bond services, financial management, and other related services. **NOTE:** This company has branches throughout Illinois. See its website for jobs listings and location information. Apply online for open positions. **Positions**

**advertised include:** Private Banker; Marketing Representative; Broker; Process Manager; Teller Services Team Leader. **Special programs:** Internships. **Corporate headquarters location:** This location.

**OLD SECOND NATIONAL BANK**
37 South River Street, Aurora IL 60506. 630/892-0202. **Contact:** Bob Dicosola, Director of Human Resources. **World Wide Web address:** http://www.o2bancorp.com. **E-mail address:** rdicosola@o2bancorp.com. **Description:** A full-service bank whose services include savings bonds; investment services; large commercial, business, personal, student, parent PLUS, and automobile loans; and wire transfer services. **NOTE:** See website for job listings and contact information. For general resume submissions, e-mail or write to Mr. Dicosola. **Positions advertised include:** Credit Analyst.

**TCF BANK**
4192 South Archer Avenue, Chicago IL 60632. 773/847-1140. **Contact:** Human Resources. **World Wide Web address:** http://www.tcfbank.com. **Description:** A full-service bank with more than 300 branch offices in five states. **NOTE:** See website for job listings and apply online. \ **Corporate headquarters location:** Minneapolis MN. **Other U.S. locations:** CO, MI, MN, WI.

**U.S. FEDERAL RESERVE BANK OF CHICAGO**
230 South LaSalle Street, Chicago IL 60604. 312/322-5490. **Fax:** 312/322-5332. **Contact:** Staffing Division. **World Wide Web address:** http://www.chicagofed.org. **Description:** One of 12 regional Federal Reserve banks that, along with the Federal Reserve Board of Governors in Washington DC and the Federal Open Market Committee, comprise the Federal Reserve System (the nation's central bank). As the nation's central bank, Federal Reserve is charged with three major responsibilities: setting monetary policy, banking supervision and regulation, and payment processing. **Office hours:** Monday - Friday, 8:15 a.m. - 5:00 p.m. **Corporate headquarters location:** Washington DC.

**WACHOVIA SECURITIES, INC.**
77 West Wacker Drive, 25th Floor, Chicago IL 60601. 312/574-6000. **Contact:** Human Resources Department. **World Wide Web address:** http://www.wachoviasec.com. **Description:** A full-service brokerage firm with more than 300 offices serving 1.5 million clients. **Office hours:** Monday - Friday, 8:00 a.m. - 5:00 p.m. **Other U.S. locations:** Nationwide. **Parent company:** Wachovia Corporation. **Listed on:** New York Stock Exchange. **Stock exchange symbol:** WB.

**WELLS FARGO**
225 West Wacker Drive, Suite 2550, Chicago IL 60606-2228. 312/592-5600. **Fax:** 312/782-0969. **Contact:** Human Resources. **World Wide Web address:** http://www.wellsfargo.com. **Description:** Wells Fargo is a diversified financial institution with over $234 billion in assets. Wells Fargo serves over 17 million customers through 5,300 independent locations worldwide. The company also maintains several stand-alone ATMs and branches within retail outlets. Services include community banking, credit and debit cards, home equity and mortgage loans, online banking, student loans, and insurance. Wells Fargo also offers a complete line of commercial and institutional financial services. Founded in 1852. **Corporate headquarters location:** San Francisco CA. **Other U.S. locations:**

Nationwide. **International locations:** Worldwide. **Listed on:** New York Stock Exchange. **Stock exchange symbol:** WFC.

## WEST SUBURBAN BANK
711 South Meyers Road, Lombard IL 60148. 630/629-4200. **Contact:** Human Resources. **World Wide Web address:** http://www.westsuburbanbank.com. **Description:** A full-service bank. **Positions advertised include:** Branch Manager; Teller; Loan Servicer; Shift Leader; Personal Banker; Administrative Assistant.

## BIOTECHNOLOGY, PHARMACEUTICALS, AND SCIENTIFIC R&D

**You can expect to find the following types of companies in this section:**
Clinical Labs • Lab Equipment Manufacturers • Pharmaceutical Manufacturers and Distributors

### ABBOTT LABORATORIES
100 Abbott Park Road, Abbott Park IL 60064-3500. 847/937-6100. **Fax:** 847/937-1511. **Contact:** Human Resources. **World Wide Web address:** http://www.abbott.com. **Description:** Manufactures pharmaceuticals and liquid nutrition products including Similac, Pedialyte, and Ensure. The company also manufactures anesthetics, blood pressure monitors, and intravenous systems. **NOTE:** Apply online at this company's website. **Positions advertised include:** Secretary; Senior Financial Analyst; Manager of Strategy and Development; Contract Coordinator; Project Engineer; Secretary; Technical Project Leader/Architect; Project Engineer. **Corporate headquarters location:** This location. **Other U.S. locations:** AZ; CA; GA; MA; MI; NJ; OH; TX; UT; VA. **Operations at this facility include:** Administration; Manufacturing; Research and Development; Sales; Service. **Listed on:** New York Stock Exchange. **Stock exchange symbol:** ABT. **Number of employees worldwide:** 52,000.

### ADVANCED LIFE SCIENCES
1440 Davey Road, Woodridge IL 60517. 630/739-6744. **Fax:** 630/739-6754. **Contact:** Human Resources. **E-mail address:** careers@advancedlifesciences.com. **World Wide Web address:** http://www.advancedlifesciences.com. **Description:** A biopharmaceutical company focused on the discovery, development and commercialization of drugs in the areas of infectious disease, inflammation and oncology. **Positions advertised include:** Vice President of Clinical Research; Director of Regulatory Affairs.

### ALRA LABORATORIES, INC.
3850 Clearview Court, Gurnee IL 60031. 847/244-9440. **Toll-free phone:** 800/248-ARLA. **Fax:** 847/244-9464. **Contact:** Human Resources. **Description:** Researches, develops, and manufactures generic pharmaceuticals. Products include eryzole, gelpirin, multivitamins, and methalgen cream. Founded in 1982. **Corporate headquarters location:** This location.

### AMERICAN PHARMACEUTICAL SERVICES
1717 Park Street, Naperville IL 60563. 630/305-8000. **Contact:** Human Resources. **Description:** A pharmaceutical delivery service whose primary customers are nursing homes.

### ARGONNE NATIONAL LABORATORY
9700 South Cass Avenue, Argonne IL 60439. 630/252-2000. **Contact:** Human Resources. **World Wide Web address:** http://www.anl.gov. **Description:** One of the Department of Energy's largest research centers. Argonne National Laboratory's research falls into three broad categories: engineering research

including research on meltdown-proof nuclear reactors, advanced batteries, and fuel cells; physical research including materials science, physics, chemistry, mathematics, and computer science; and energy, environmental, and biological research including research into the causes and cures of cancer, alternate energy systems, and environmental and economic impact assessments. The laboratory is operated by the University of Chicago for the U.S. Department of Energy. **NOTE:** Apply online at the laboratory's website. **Positions advertised include:** Assistant Electrical Engineer; Contract Specialist; STA Lifeguard; Senior Secretary; Supervisor of Subcontracts.

**COLE-PARMER INSTRUMENT COMPANY**
625 East Bunker Court, Vernon Hills IL 60061. 847/549-7600. **Toll-free phone:** 800/323-4340. **Fax:** 847/549-1515. **Contact:** Human Resources. **E-mail address:** hr@coleparmer.com. **World Wide Web address:** http://www.coleparmer.com. **Description:** An international exporter and distributor of scientific instruments for laboratories. **NOTE:** See website for job listings. Apply online or e-mail resumes. **Positions advertised include:** Application Specialist; Desktop Publishing Specialist; Financial Analyst.

**DSM DESOTECH INC.**
1122 St. Charles Street, Elgin IL 60120. 847/697-0400. **Toll-free phone:** 800/223-7191. **Fax:** 847/468-7795. **Contact:** Human Resources Department. **World Wide Web address:** http://www.dsmdesotech.com. **Description:** A researcher, formulator, and manufacturer of ultraviolet and electron beam curable materials and technology. **NOTE:** Apply online to open positions. **Corporate headquarters location:** This location.

**DADE BEHRING, INC.**
1717 Deerfield Road, Deerfield IL 60015-0778. 847/267-5300. **Fax:** 847/267-5408. **Contact:** Human Resources. **World Wide Web address:** http://www.dadebehring.com. **Description:** Manufactures and distributes diagnostic instrument systems and other labware that serve clinical and research laboratories worldwide. Dade Behring also offers its customers support services. **Positions advertised include:** Bilingual Customer Satisfaction Representative; Office Services Clerk; Systems Analyst. **Corporate headquarters location:** This location. **International locations:** Worldwide.

**THE FEMALE HEALTH COMPANY**
515 North State Street, Suite 2225, Chicago IL 60610. 312/595-9123. **Fax:** 312/595-9122. **Contact:** Human Resources. **World Wide Web address:** http://www.femalehealth.com. **Description:** Markets and distributes a proprietary female barrier contraceptive product known as the Reality female condom. **Corporate headquarters location:** This location. **Parent company:** Wisconsin Pharmacal Company, Inc. (Jackson WI).

**FERMALOGIC, INC.**
2201 West Campbell Park Drive, Chicago IL 60612. 312/738-0050. Fax: 312/738-0963. **Contact:** Human Resources. **World Wide Web address:** http://www.fermalogic.com. **Description:** A research-driven biotechnology company that develops and implements strain improvement technology for fermentation-based products to lower the cost of drugs and improve the profitability of pharmaceutical manufacturing. The company's research focus is in industrial microbiology as it applies to strain and process improvement for the production of antibiotics and other natural products.

**FERMI NATIONAL ACCELERATOR LABORATORY**
P.O. Box 500, MS 116, Batavia IL 60510. 630/840-3324. **Fax:** 630/840-2306.
**Contact:** Employment Manager. **World Wide Web address:**
http://www.fnal.gov. **Description:** A federally funded, nonprofit organization
dedicated to basic research in the field of high-energy physics. **NOTE:** See
website for job listings and contact information. **Special programs:** Internships.
**Corporate headquarters location:** Washington DC. **Parent company:**
Universities Research Association. **Operations at this facility include:**
Research and Development.

**FERRO PFANSTIEHL LABORATORIES, INC.**
1219 Glen Rock Avenue, Waukegan IL 60085. 847/623-0370. **Fax:** 847/623-
9173. **Contact:** Human Resources. **E-mail address:** resume@ferro.com. **World
Wide Web address:** http://www.ferro.com. **Description:** A chemical laboratory
specializing in the production of carbohydrates and biological chemicals. Clients
are primarily pharmaceutical companies. **NOTE:** See website for job
requirements and e-mail resumes. **Corporate headquarters location:**
Cleveland, OH. **Listed on:** New York Stock Exchange. **Stock exchange
symbol:** FOE.

**FUJISAWA HEALTHCARE, INC.**
Three Parkway North, Deerfield IL 60015. 847/317-8800. **Fax:** 847/317-1245.
**Contact:** Human Resources. **E-mail address:** employment@fujisawa.com.
**World Wide Web address:** http://www.fujisawausa.com. **Description:** A
pharmaceutical company that markets products in the area of anti-infectives,
cardiovasculars, transplantation, and dermatology. **NOTE:** Apply online at the
company's website for specific job openings. Resumes may also be e-mailed for
specific job openings. **Positions advertised include:** Assistant/Associate
Director Regulatory Affairs; Senior Corporate Records Assistant; Senior Medical
Writer; Project Assistant. **Corporate headquarters location:** This location.
**Parent company:** Fujisawa Company Ltd.

**GE HEALTH**
3350 North Ridge Avenue, Arlington Heights IL 60004. 847/398-8400. **Fax:**
847/818-6629. **Contact:** Human Resources. **World Wide Web address:**
http://www.gehealthcare.com. **Description:** Researches, develops, and
manufactures nuclear medicine and radiopharmaceuticals. **NOTE:** For a list of
job openings, visit the website. To apply, either fax or e-mail resumes and cover
letters, stating desired position. **Operations at this facility include:**
Manufacturing; Research and Development.

**IMMTECH INTERNATIONAL, INC.**
150 Fairway Drive, Suite 150, Vernon Hills IL 60061. 847/573-0033. Fax:
847/573-9805. **Contact:** Helen Reese. **E-mail address:** hreese@immtech.biz.
**World Wide Web address:** http://www.immtech-international.com. **Description:**
A pharmaceutical company advancing the development and commercialization of
oral drugs to treat infectious diseases, neoplastic (cancer), and metabolic
(diabetes) disorders. Immtech is developing treatments for diseases such as
malaria, Pneumocystis pneumonia, fungal infections, tuberculosis and hepatitis,
and tropical diseases such as African sleeping sickness and leishmaniasis.
**NOTE:** No telephone calls concerning positions. **Positions advertised include:**
Director, Commercial Development; Director of Clinical Operations.

## LEICA NORTH AMERICA
2345 Waukegan Road, Bannockburn IL 60015. 847/405-0123. **Contact:** Human Resources. **World Wide Web address:** http://www.leica.com. **Description:** Manufactures and sells microscopes and other scientific instruments.

## NANOSPHERE
4088 Commercial Avenue, Northbrook IL 60062. 847/400-9000. Fax: 847/400-9199. **Contact:** Human Resources. **World Wide Web address:** http://www.nanosphere-inc.com. **Description:** A nanotechnology-based life sciences company that applies proprietary nanotechnology to provide a unique chemistry for simplified molecular testing. Nanosphere is advancing the development of assays for genomic and proteomic research, clinical laboratories, and point-of-care markets. **Positions advertised include:** Quality Assurance Product Release Leader; Quality Assurance Specialist; Production Associate; Quality Control Analyst; Application Development Scientist; Application Development Technician.

## NEIGHBORCARE
1250 East Diehl Road, Suite 208, Naperville IL 60563. 630/245-4800. **Fax:** 630/505-1319. **Contact:** Human Resources. **World Wide Web address:** http://www.neighborcare.com. **Description:** An institutional pharmacy provider that offers services such as infusion therapy, drug distribution, patient management, educational services, and consulting services for managing health care costs. **Corporate headquarters location:** Baltimore MD.

## NEWNEURAL, LLC.
8S070 Greene Road, Naperville IL 60540. 630/297-7492. **Fax:** 630/839-2936. **E-mail address:** hr@newneural.com. **Contact:** Human Resources. **World Wide Web address:** http://www.newneural.com. **Description:** An emerging biotechnology company in the pre-clinical stage that intends to develop products to treat diseases of and injuries to the central nervous system such as stroke, ALS, Parkinson's and spinal cord injury. **Positions advertised include:** Research Scientist, Neurobiology. **Other area locations:** Lisle IL.

## NORTHFIELD LABORATORIES, INC.
1560 Sherman Avenue, Suite 1000, Evanston IL 60201-4422. 847/864-3500. **Fax:** 847/864-0353. **Contact:** Human Resources. **World Wide Web address:** http://www.northfieldlabs.com. **Description:** Develops chemically altered human hemoglobin as an alternative for blood transfusion where acute blood loss has occurred. The company markets PolyHeme, a blood substitute product that carries as much oxygen and loads and unloads oxygen in the same manner as transfused blood. **Listed on:** NASDAQ. **Stock exchange symbol:** NFLD.

## OVATION PHARMACEUTICALS, INC.
Four Parkway North, Deerfield IL 60015. 847/282-1000. **Fax:** 847/282-1001. **Contact:** Human Resources. **Email address:** jobs@ovationpharma.com. **World Wide Web address:** http://www.ovationpharma.com. **Description:** A specialty pharmaceutical company that acquires underpromoted branded pharmaceutical products and promising late-stage development products. **Positions advertised include:** Clinical Project Manager; Drug Safety Associate; Manager, Global Pharmacovigilance; Senior Clinical Safety Associate; Senior Sales & Market Research Analyst. **Other U.S. locations:** Lebanon NJ.

**PYXIS GENOMICS, INC.**
2201 West Campbell Park Drive, Chicago IL 60612. 312/455-0602. **Fax:**312/455-0723. **Contact:** Human Resources. **E-mail address:** info@pyxisgenomics.com. **World Wide Web address:** http://www.pyxisgenomics.com. **Description:** The company discovers, develops, and commercializes proprietary, genomics-based products and solutions that enhance animal health and performance. Pyxis is developing products in three sectors of the agribusiness and health industries: meat traceability, performance traits, and health products. **Positions advertised include:** Senior Scientist/Scientist; Associate/Assistant Scientist.

**QUEST DIAGNOSTICS INCORPORATED**
1614 W. Central Road, Arlington Heights IL 60005. 847/342-0344. **Contact:** Human Resources. **World Wide Web address:** http://www.questdiagnostics.com. **Description:** Quest Diagnostics is one of the largest clinical laboratories in North America, providing a broad range of clinical laboratory services to health care clients that include physicians, hospitals, clinics, dialysis centers, pharmaceutical companies, and corporations. The company offers and performs tests on blood, urine, and other bodily fluids and tissues to provide information for health and well-being. **NOTE:** This company has locations throughout Illinois and the United States. See website for locations and job listings. **Operations at this facility include:** This location is a testing laboratory. **Listed on:** New York Stock Exchange. **Stock exchange symbol:** DGX.

**SARGENT-WELCH SCIENTIFIC COMPANY**
911 Commerce Court, Buffalo Grove IL 60089. 800/727-4368. **Contact:** Human Resources. **E-mail address:** sarwel@sargentwelch.com. **World Wide Web address:** http://www.sargentwelch.com. **Description:** Sargent-Welch Scientific Company is a distributor and manufacturer of a wide range of analytical instruments, scientific apparatus, lab equipment, supplies, chemicals, and furniture. **Corporate headquarters location:** West Chester PA. **Parent company:** VWR Corporation. **Operations at this facility include:** This location houses customer service offices.

**SILLIKER LABORATORIES GROUP, INC.**
900 Maple Road, Homewood IL 60430. 708/957-7878. **Fax:** 708/957-3798. **Contact:** Margo Neetz, Human Resources Generalist. **E-mail address:** human.resources@silliker.com. **World Wide Web address:** http://www.silliker.com. **Description:** Operates a network of food testing laboratories. The labs test for pathogens and microbes and serve to verify the accuracy of nutritional labeling. Founded in 1967. **NOTE:** See website for job listings. Apply online or e-mail or mail resumes. Entry-level positions and part-time jobs are offered. **Special programs:** Summer Jobs. **Corporate headquarters location:** This location. **International locations:** Worldwide. **Listed on:** Privately held.

**UNITED THERAPEUTICS**
2225 West Harrison Street, Chicago IL 60612. 312/421-1819. **Fax:** 312/421-8177. **Contact:** Human Resources. **Description:** A biotechnology company focused on developing chronic therapies for life threatening conditions in three therapeutic areas: cardiovascular, oncology, and infectious diseases. **Positions advertised include:** Director, Quality Assurance; Quality Control Manager. **Corporate headquarters location:** Silver Spring MD. **Operations at this facility include:** Manufacturing.

**VASSOL INC.**
833 West Jackson, 8th Floor, Chicago IL 60607-3544. 312/601-4431. **Contact:** Human Resources. **E-mail address:** jobs@vassolinc.com. **World Wide Web address:** http://www.vassolinc.com. **Description:** Developers of a product that quantifies blood flow in vessels using standard MRI scanning.

**ZELLERX CORPORATION**
400 North Noble, Suite 100, Chicago IL 60622. 312/243-5200. **Fax:** 312/275-7364. **Contact:** Human Resources. **E-mail address:** hr@zellerx.com. **World Wide Web address:** http://www.zellerx.com. **Description:** A biopharmaceutical company developing cancer treatment products based on its proprietary natural killer cell line.

# BUSINESS SERVICES & NON-SCIENTIFIC RESEARCH

### You can expect to find the following types of companies in this section:

Adjustment and Collection Services • Cleaning, Maintenance, and Pest Control Services • Credit Reporting Services • Detective, Guard, and Armored Car Services • Security Systems Services • Miscellaneous Equipment Rental and Leasing • Secretarial and Court Reporting Services

---

### ACXIOM CORPORATION

1501 Opus Place, Downers Grove IL 60515. 630/964-1501. **Contact:** Human Resources. **World Wide Web address:** http://www.acxiom.com. **Description:** Provides a variety of services including data integration services, data products, and information technology outsourcing. **NOTE:** Entry-level positions offered. Apply online for all positions. **Positions advertised include:** Client Executive; Client Representative; Decision Support Analyst. **Special programs:** Internships. **Corporate headquarters location:** Little Rock AR. **Listed on:** NASDAQ. **Stock exchange symbol:** ACXM.

### ARTHUR ANDERSEN

33 West Monroe Street, Chicago IL 60603. 312/580-0033. **Fax:** 312/507-6748. **Contact:** Human Resources. **World Wide Web address:** http://www.arthurandersen.com. **Description:** One of the largest certified public accounting firms in the world. Andersen's four key practice areas are Audit and Business Advisory, Tax and Business Advisory, Business Consulting, and Economic and Financial Consulting. **NOTE:** This firm does not accept unsolicited resumes. Please check its website for available positions. **Corporate headquarters location:** This location.

### AUDIT BUREAU OF CIRCULATIONS (ABC)

900 North Meacham Road, Schaumburg IL 60173. 847/605-0909. **Toll-free phone:** 800/285-2220. **Fax:** 847/605-9771. **Contact:** Manager of Human Resources. **World Wide Web address:** http://www.accessabc.com. **Description:** A nonprofit membership organization created by advertisers and publishers to ensure that circulating facts and statistics are compliant with industry bylaws and rules. Founded in 1914. **NOTE:** Entry-level positions are offered. **Positions advertised include:** Field Auditor. **Special programs:** Training. **Office hours:** Monday - Friday, 7:30 a.m. - 5:00 p.m. **Corporate headquarters location:** This location. **Other U.S. locations:** Nationwide. **Operations at this facility include:** Administration; Regional Headquarters.

### AUTOMATIC DATA PROCESSING, INC. (ADP)

100 Northwest Point Boulevard, Elk Grove Village IL 60007. 847/718-2000. **Contact:** Senior Employment Specialist. **World Wide Web address:** http://www.adp.com. **Description:** Automatic Data Processing (ADP) helps over 300,000 clients improve their business performance by providing computerized transaction processing, data communications, and information services. The company's services include payroll, payroll tax, and human resource information management; brokerage industry market data; back-office and proxy services;

industry-specific services to auto and truck dealers; and computerized auto repair and replacement estimating for auto insurance companies and body repair shops. **Positions advertised include:** Help Desk Coordinator; Express Representative; Product Manager; Teledata Representative; Staffing Specialist; Program Manager; Billing Specialist; CVR Regional Director; Tax Data Representative. **Corporate headquarters location:** Roseland NJ. **Operations at this facility include:** Administration; Regional Headquarters; Sales; Service. **Listed on:** New York Stock Exchange. **Stock exchange symbol:** ADP.

## BOISE OFFICE SOLUTIONS
150 East Pierce Road, Itasca IL 60143. **Toll-Free phone:** 800-47BOISE. **Fax:** 800/57BOISE. **Contact:** Human Resources. **World Wide Web address:** http://www.bcop.com. **Description:** A business-to-business distributor of office and computer supplies, furniture, paper products, and promotional products. Founded in 1964. **NOTE:** Apply online. **International locations:** Australia; Canada; England; France; Germany; Spain. **Subsidiaries include:** Boise Marketing Services, Inc.; Grande Toy; JPG; Neat Ideas; Reliable. **Parent company:** Boise Cascade Corporation. **Listed on:** New York Stock Exchange. **Stock exchange symbol:** BCC.

## CANON BUSINESS SOLUTIONS
425 North Martingale Road, Schaumburg IL 60173. 847/706-3480. **Fax:** 847/706-3419. **Contact:** Recruiter. **World Wide Web address:** http://www.solutions.canon.com. **Description:** Offers customized solutions for business offices. Canon Business Solutions markets the full line of Canon office equipment including copiers, laser printers, fax machines, and scanners. Founded in 1974. **NOTE:** Entry-level positions are offered. **NOTE:** Apply online at this website for open positions. **Positions advertised include:** Sales Manager; Field Service Technician. **Corporate headquarters location:** This location. **Parent company:** Canon USA. **Listed on:** New York Stock Exchange. **Stock exchange symbol:** CAJ.

## DIAMONDCLUSTER INTERNATIONAL
875 North Michigan Avenue, Suite 3000, John Hancock Center, Chicago IL 60611. 312/255-5000. **Fax:** 312/255-6000. **Contact:** Aneeta Muradali, Human Resources. **World Wide Web address:** http://www.diamondcluster.com. **Description:** Develops e-commerce solutions for companies. Founded in 1994. **NOTE**: Apply online at this company's website. **Special programs:** Internships. **Corporate headquarters location:** This location. **Other U.S. locations:** San Francisco CA. **International locations:** London, England. **Listed on:** NASDAQ. **Stock exchange symbol:** DTPI.

## ELECTRO RENT CORPORATION
200 West Mark Street, Woodale IL 60191. 630/860-3991. **Contact:** Human Resources. **World Wide Web address:** http://www.electrorent.com. **Description:** Rents and leases electronic equipment including test and measurement instruments, workstations, personal computers, and data communication products. **Corporate headquarters location:** Van Nuys CA. **Other U.S. locations:** Nationwide.

## EXPERIAN
955 American Lane, Schaumburg IL 60173. 847/517-5600. **Contact:** Human Resources. **World Wide Web address:** http://www.experian.com. **Description:** Maintains credit reports and provides information services for the real estate

industry. **NOTE:** Send resumes to: Experian, Human Resources Department, 475 Anton Boulevard, Building D, Costa Mesa CA 92626. Resumes may also be faxed. **Positions advertised include:** Administrative Assistant; Channel Manager; Inside Sales; Account Executive; Data Quality Analyst; Client Services Analyst. **Other U.S. locations:** Nationwide.

**FRY, INC.**
740 Pasquinelli Drive, Suite 100, Westmont IL 60559. 630/850-9144. **Toll-free phone:** 800/FRY-6858. **Fax:** 630/850-8043. **Contact:** Human Resources. **World Wide Web address:** http://www.fry.com. **Description:** Fry, Inc. designs, develops, and manages high scale ebusiness brands, applications, and systems. Fry was one of the first companies to offer ecommerce, branding sites, and extranets to its clients. **Positions advertised include:** Account Director; Director of Business Development; E-commerce Project Manager; Office Manager; Proposal Writer. **Corporate headquarters location:** Ann Arbor MI. **Other U.S. locations:** New York NY.

**GREAT LAKES MAINTENANCE & SECURITY CORPORATION**
8734 South Cottage Grove, Suite 200, Chicago IL 60619-6924. 773/994-1899. **Contact:** Human Resources. **Description:** Provides maintenance, cleaning, and security guard services.

**LANTER DELIVERY SYSTEMS**
1636 New Milford School Road, Rockford IL 61109. 815/874-0401. **Contact:** Human Resources. **Description:** One location of a chain the Lanter Delivery Systems courier company.

**LEXIS DOCUMENT SERVICES**
801 Adlai Stevenson Drive, Springfield IL 62703. 217/529-5599. **Contact:** Human Resources. **E-mail address:** Employment.HR@lexisnexis.com. **World Wide Web address:** http://www.lexisnexis.com. **Description:** Offers searching, filing, and retrieval services for law firms and financial organizations. This facility provides document service and storage for the Midwest region. **NOTE:** Apply online.

**McCOY SECURITY, INC.**
404 South Wells, 4th Floor, Chicago IL 60607. 312/322-4900. **Fax:** 312/322-0078. **Contact:** Personnel Manager. **E-mail address:** jobs@mccoysecurity.com. **World Wide Web address:** http://www.mccoysecurity.com. **Description:** A security firm providing primarily unarmed guards and patrolmen in the greater Chicago area. **NOTE:** Call or an appointment, e-mail resume or complete the online application.

**MERRILL LYNCH**
33 West Monroe Street, Suite 2200, Chicago IL 60603. 312/269-5100. **Fax:** 312/269-5092. **Contact:** Human Resources. **World Wide Web address:** http://www.ml.com. **Description:** One of the largest securities brokerage firms in the world, Merrill Lynch provides financial services in securities, financial planning, insurance, estate planning, mortgages, and related areas. The company also brokers commodity futures and options, is a major underwriter of new securities issues, and is a dealer in corporate and municipal securities. **NOTE:** This company has other locations throughout Chicago, Illinois and the United States. See website for additional locations and job listings. Apply online.

**Special programs:** Internships. **Corporate headquarters location:** New York NY. **Operations at this facility include:** Sales; Service.

## MERRILL LYNCH/HOWARD JOHNSON & COMPANY
300 South Wacker Drive, Suite 2600, Chicago IL 60606. 312/697-1040. **Contact:** Human Resources. **World Wide Web address:** http://www.ml.com. **Description:** As a subsidiary of Merrill Lynch, Howard Johnson & Co. has been specializing in employee benefits consulting on a national basis for over 30 years. **NOTE:** See website for job listings and apply online. . **Corporate headquarters location:** New York NY. **Other U.S. locations:** San Francisco CA; Seattle WA. **Operations at this facility include:** Divisional Headquarters.

## NORTH CENTRAL REGIONAL EDUCATIONAL LAB INC.
1120 East Diehl Road, Suite 200, Naperville IL 60563. 630/649-6500. **Contact:** Human Resources. **E-mail address:** jobs@learningpt.org. **World Wide Web address:** http://www.ncrel.org. **Description:** A nonprofit organization that promotes education by providing information access through research-based resources to teachers, parents, students, and policymakers. Founded in 1984. **NOTE:** For job listings, visit http://www.learningpt.org/employ/. **Positions advertised include:** Applied Research and Development Director; Program Specialist; Senior Research Associate; Program Associate.

## SCOTTISH DEVELOPMENT INTERNATIONAL
1020 31st Street, Lower Level 20, Downers Grove IL. 60515. 630/968-6555. **Contact:** Human Resources Department. **World Wide Web address:** http://www.scottishdevelopmentinternational.com. **Description:** A nonprofit, economic development agency for the British government engaged in attracting new business to Scotland.

## SERVICEMASTER COMPANY
3250 Lacey Road, Suite 600, Downers Grove IL 60515. 630/663-2000. **Fax:** 901/766-1157. **Contact:** Gina DePompei, People Services Director. **E-mail address:** careers@servicemaster.com. **World Wide Web address:** http://www.servicemaster.com. **Description:** A housekeeping, maintenance, and management company that provides services to residential, commercial, educational, industrial, and health care facilities in 50 states, Washington DC, and 15 foreign countries. Other services include lawn care (through TruGreen and ChemLawn), cleaning and restoration, pest control, radon testing, and child care. **NOTE:** E-mail or fax resumes to the attention of Corporate People Services – Careers. Resumes may also be mailed to the Corporate People Services – Careers' office at ServiceMaster Consumer Services, 860 Ridge Lake Boulevard, Suite AL-1099, Memphis TN 38120. **Corporate headquarters location:** This location. **Listed on:** New York Stock Exchange. **Stock exchange symbol:** SVM.

## SIEMENS BUSINESS SERVICES
3041 Woodcreek Drive, Suite 100, Downers Grove IL 60515. 630/724-8000. **Fax:** 630/336-1222. **Contact:** Recruiter. **E-mail address:** careers@sbs.siemens.com. **World Wide Web address:** http://www.sbs-usa.siemens.com. **Description:** Provides systems integration services and resells software. **NOTE:** See website for job listings.

## SMITH, BUCKLIN AND ASSOCIATES
401 North Michigan Avenue, Suite 2200, Chicago IL 60611. 312/644-6610. **Fax:** 312/673-6580. **Contact:** Human Resources. **E-mail address:**

ChicagoHR@smithbucklin.com. **World Wide Web address:** http://www.sba.com. **Description:** Provides daily management services for nonprofit organizations worldwide and for full-service and contract clients.

## STRATOS LIGHTWAVE, INC.
7444 West Wilson Avenue, Harwood Heights IL 60706. 708/867-9600. **Contact:** Human Resources. **World Wide Web address:** http://www.stratoslightwave.com. **Description:** Stratos Lightwave develops, manufactures, and sells optical subsystems and components for high data rate networking, data storage, and telecommunications applications. **NOTE:** Apply online. **Corporate headquarters location:** This location. **Other area locations:** Carthage IL; Rolling Meadows IL; Warsaw IL. **International locations:** Singapore; United Kingdom. **Listed on:** NASDAQ. **Stock exchange symbol:** STLW.

## TOPCO ASSOCIATES, INC.
7711 Gross Point Road, Skokie IL 60077. 847/676-3030. **Fax:** 847/329-3621. **Contact:** Dennis Pieper, Human Resources Manager. **E-mail address:** dpieper@topco.com. **World Wide Web address:** http://www.topco.com. **Description:** A leader in private label procurement and brand management for the supermarket and food service industries. The company specializes in procuring, packaging, and distributing corporate brands, perishables, and pharmaceutical products. **NOTE:** Fax or e-mail resumes to Mr. Pieper. **Corporate headquarters location:** This location. **Other U.S. locations:** Visalia CA; Lakeland FL. **Listed on:** Privately held.

## WUNDERMAN
233 North Michigan Avenue, Suite 1500, Chicago IL 60601-5519. 312/596-2500. **Contact:** Human Resources. **World Wide Web address:** http://www.wunderman.com. **Description:** An advertising agency.

## CHARITIES AND SOCIAL SERVICES

### You can expect to find the following types of companies in this section:
Social and Human Service Agencies • Job Training and Vocational Rehabilitation Services • Nonprofit Organizations

---

**AMERICAN RED CROSS OF GREATER CHICAGO**
2200 W. Harrison Street, Chicago IL 60612. 312/729-6100. **Fax:** 312/729-6306. **Contact:** Human Resources. **E-mail address:** chicagohr@usa.redcross.org. **World Wide Web address:** http://www.chicagoredcross.org. **Description:** A humanitarian organization that aids disaster victims, gathers blood for crisis distribution, trains individuals to respond to emergencies, educates individuals on various diseases, and raises funds for other charitable establishments. **Positions advertised include:** Training Specialist (Per Diem). **Special programs:** Internships. **Corporate headquarters location:** Washington DC. **Other U.S. locations:** Nationwide.

**ANIXTER CENTER**
6610 Clark Street, Chicago IL 60626-4062. 773/973-7900. **Fax:** 773/973-2180. **Contact:** Debbie Thom, Human Resources Director. **World Wide Web address:** http://www.anixter.org. **Description:** A nonprofit job training and rehabilitation organization for people with developmental disabilities. **NOTE:** Part-time positions offered. **Positions advertised include:** Advocate; Certified Nursing Assistant; Certified Occupational Therapist; Certified Special Educators; Child Care Worker; Mental Health Professional; Occupational Therapy Consultant; Substance Abuse Counselor; Teaching Assistant/Substitute Teacher.

**ASPIRE**
9901 Derby Lane, Westchester IL 60154. 708/547-3550x3577. **Fax:** 708/547-4067. **Contact:** Human Resources Administrator. **E-mail address:** chrishunt@aspireofillinois.org **World Wide Web address:** http://www.aspireofillinois.org. **Description:** A private, nonprofit agency serving the developmental, residential, and vocational needs of adults and children with developmental and mental disabilities. **NOTE:** Apply in person at the Human Resources Office. **Special programs:** Internships; Volunteers. **Office hours:** Monday – Friday, 9:00 a.m. – 3:00 p.m. **Corporate headquarters location:** This location. **Listed on:** Privately held.

**CATHOLIC CHARITIES OF THE ARCHDIOCESE OF CHICAGO**
126 North Desplaines Street, Chicago IL 60661. 312/655-7000. **Fax:** 312/831-1321. **Recorded jobline:** 312/655-7118. **Contact:** Employment Services. **World Wide Web address:** http://www.catholiccharities.net. **Description:** A network of private social service organizations that provides food, shelter, and clothing to more than 10 million poor and homeless people each year. **NOTE:** This organization provides a complete list of open positions and contact information on its website. See website. **Positions advertised include:** Intake/Marketing Specialist; Supervisor; Bi-Lingual Receptionist/Clerk; Social Work/Coordinator.

## CHICAGO YOUTH CENTERS
104 South Michigan Avenue, 14th Floor, Chicago IL 60603-5902. 312/648-1550. **Fax:** 312/795-3520. **Contact:** Human Resources. **World Wide Web address:** http://www.chicagoyouthcenters.org. **Description:** Provides recreational and educational opportunities for children.

## RAY GRAHAM ASSOCIATION
2801 Finley Road, Downers Grove IL 60515. 630/620-2222. **Fax:** 630/628-2351. **Contact:** Human Resources. **E-mail address:** rgajobs@yahoo.com. **World Wide Web address:** http://www.ray-graham.org. **Description:** A consumer-driven organization that responds to the needs of people with disabilities and their families. **NOTE:** An application is required for any position and must be completed in person at the Human Resources office. **Positions advertised include:** Dietary Technician; Lab Technician; Community Support Specialist; ADT/AM Aide. **Corporate headquarters location:** This location. **Operations at this facility include:** Administration.

## JANE ADDAMS HULL HOUSE ASSOCIATION
10 South Riverside Plaza, Suite 1700, Chicago IL 60606. 312/906-8600. **Contact:** Staffing Coordinator. **World Wide Web address:** http://www.hullhouse.org. **Description:** A nonprofit, multiservice social agency dedicated to helping people build better lives for themselves and their families. Jane Addams Hull House Association has 6 community centers and 35 satellite locations throughout metropolitan Chicago. The organization serves approximately 225,000 people from geographically, culturally, and economically diverse backgrounds each year. **NOTE:** See website for job listings and contact information. **Positions advertised include:** Literacy Aide; Case Management Supervisor; Program Supervisor; Caseworker; Administrative Assistant. **Corporate headquarters location:** This location.

## KNOX COUNTY COUNCIL FOR DEVELOPMENTAL DISABILITIES
2015 Windish Drive, Galesburg IL 61401. 309/344-2600. **Contact:** Deputy Executive Director. **World Wide Web address:** http://www.kccdd.com. **Description:** A nonprofit agency serving people with developmental disabilities. **Special programs:** Volunteers. **Corporate headquarters location:** This location. **Operations at this facility include:** Administration; Manufacturing; Service.

## KREIDER CENTER
P.O. Box 366, Dixon IL 61021. 815/288-6691. **Physical address:** 500 Anchor Road, Dixon IL. **Contact:** Human Resources. **World Wide Web address:** http://www.kreiderservices.org. **Description:** Provides residential and day services for adults with mental disabilities.

## LIONS CLUBS INTERNATIONAL
300 West 22nd Street, Oak Brook IL 60523-8842. 630/571-5466. **Contact:** Human Resources. **World Wide Web address:** http://www.lionsclubs.org. **Description:** An international service organization. This location is the headquarters for the International Activities and Program Planning Division. **NOTE:** See website for job listings.

## MARYVILLE CITY OF YOUTH
1150 North River Road, Des Plaines IL 60016. 847/824-6126. **Fax:** 847/824-7190. **Contact:** Human Resources Department. **World Wide Web address:**

http://www.maryvilleacademy.org. **Description:** A residential home for orphaned and homeless children. Founded in 1882. **Positions advertised include:** Family Educator. **Special programs:** Volunteers. **Corporate headquarters location:** This location.

## METROPOLITAN FAMILY SERVICES

14 East Jackson Boulevard, 14th Floor, Chicago IL 60604. 312/986-4000. **Fax:** 312/986-4347. **Contact:** Human Resources. **E-mail address:** resumes@metrofamily.org. **World Wide Web address:** http://www.metrofamily.org. **Description:** A nonprofit, social services agency that provides counseling and support services to low-income families and individuals. The agency operates 23 other locations in the Chicago area. Positions advertised include: Bi-lingual Social Worker; Program Supervisor; Social Worker or Counselor. **Special programs:** Internships. **Corporate headquarters location:** This location. **Operations at this facility include:** Administration; Service.

## ROTARY INTERNATIONAL

One Rotary Center, 1560 Sherman Avenue, Evanston IL 60201. 847/866-3000. **Fax:** 847/866-5766. **Contact:** Human Resources. **World Wide Web address:** http://www.rotary.org. **Description:** Rotary International is one of the largest international, nonprofit, service organizations in the world. Founded in 1905. **Special programs:** Internships. **Corporate headquarters location:** This location. **Operations at this facility include:** This location provides administrative services to Rotary clubs including publicity and the administration of humanitarian and scholarship programs funded by the Rotary Foundation.

## THE WOODLAWN ORGANIZATION

6040 South Harper Avenue, Chicago IL 60637. 773/288-5840. **Contact:** Human Resources. **Description:** Provides social services including a detoxification center, a child abuse treatment center, mental health facilities, two early childhood development programs, secretarial and word-processing training programs, a youth try-out employment project, and HUD real estate management services. **Corporate headquarters location:** This location. **Operations at this facility include:** Administration.

## YMCA OF METROPOLITAN CHICAGO

801 North Dearborn, Chicago IL 60610. 312/932-1200. **Contact:** Human Resources. **World Wide Web address:** http://www.ymcachgo.org. **Description:** One of the nation's largest and most comprehensive service organizations. The YMCA provides health and fitness; social and personal development; sports and recreation; education and career development; and camps and conferences to children, youths, adults, the elderly, families, the disabled, refugees and foreign nationals, YMCA residents, and community residents, through a broad range of specific programs. **Special programs:** Internships.

## CHEMICALS, RUBBER, AND PLASTICS

**You can expect to find the following types of companies in this section:**
Adhesives, Detergents, Inks, Paints, Soaps, Varnishes • Agricultural Chemicals and Fertilizers • Carbon and Graphite Products • Chemical Engineering Firms • Industrial Gases

---

**ACE HARDWARE CORPORATION**
2200 Kensington Court, Oak Brook IL 60523. 630/990-6600. **Fax:** 630/990-6838. **Contact:** Director of Human Resources. **World Wide Web address:** http://www.acehardware.com. **Description:** A worldwide dealer-owned cooperative operating through 5,100 hardware retailers in 62 countries. Ace Hardware Corporation also produces a line of hand and power tools, plumbing products, lawn and garden products, cleaning supplies, and manufactures a line of paint. **NOTE:** Apply online at the company's website. **Positions advertised include:** Advertising Distribution Analyst; Financial Analyst; Senior Audit Consultant; POR Operator; Network Administrator; Assistant Buyer. **Corporate headquarters location:** This location.

**AKZO NOBEL, INC.**
525 West Van Buren Street, Suite 1600, Chicago IL 6067-3823. 312/544-7153. **Fax:** 312/544-7073. **Contact:** Human Resources. **World Wide Web address:** http://www.akzonobelusa.com. **Description:** Produces salt and chemicals, coatings, health care products, and fibers. Business activities are conducted in four units: Chemicals, Coatings, Pharma, and Fibers. The Chemicals Group produces polymer chemicals, rubber chemicals, catalysts, detergents, surfactants, functional chemicals, salt, chlor-alkali, and industrial chemicals. The Coatings Group produces decorative coatings, car refinishes, industrial coatings, industrial wood finishes, aerospace finishes, automotive finishes, and resins. The Pharma Group includes the production of ethical drugs, hospital supplies, nonprescription products, raw materials for the pharmaceutical industry, generics, and veterinary products. The Fibers Group produces textile, industrial, and high-performance fibers; industrial nonwovens; and membranes for medical, technical, and industrial uses. **Corporate headquarters location:** This location. **International locations:** Worldwide. **Operations at this location include:** This location is the headquarters for Azko Nobel, Inc.'s Risk Management Department. **Listed on:** NASDAQ. **Stock exchange symbol:** AKZOY.

**AKZO NOBEL CHEMICALS, INC.**
525 West Van Buren Street, Chicago IL 60607. 312/544-7000. **Contact:** Human Resources. **World Wide Web address:** http://www.akzonobelusa.com. **Description:** Akzo Nobel is a diverse manufacturing company whose primary products include chemical and medical products. The company is involved in molecular biology research as well as electronic, automotive, food packaging, and aerospace products. **NOTE:** There are several Akzo Nobel divisions at this location: Akzo Nobel Functional Chemicals (Chelates and Micronutrients); Akzo Nobel Polymer Chemicals and Akzo Nobel Surface Chemistry. The website provides job listings for all divisions. Apply online. **Operations at this facility include:** This location researches, develops, and manufactures industrial coatings and finishes. **Listed on:** NASDAQ. **Stock exchange symbol:** AKZOY.

## APPLIED COMPOSITES
333 North Sixth Street, St. Charles IL 60174. 877/653-9577x122. Fax: 630/584-5365. **Contact:** Human Resources. **E-mail address:** lstritzel@appliedcompositecorp.com. **World Wide Web address:** http://www.appliedcompositescorp.com. **Description:** Manufactures fiber-reinforced plastic. **Positions advertised include:** Outside Sales Engineer; Customer Relations Manager; Plant Manager; Production Supervisor; Quality Manager; Human Resources Manager. **Corporate headquarters location:** This location. **Operations at this facility include:** Administration; Manufacturing; Research and Development; Sales; Service.

## BP CHEMICAL
28100 Torch Park Way, Warrenville IL 60555. 877/701-2726. **Contact:** Human Resources. **World Wide Web address:** http://www.bp.com/chemicals. **Description:** Manufactures industrial intermediate petrochemicals. Overall, BP is a major supplier of fuel for transportation, energy for heat and light, solar power, and petrochemicals for plastics, fabrics, and fibers. The company is also one of the world's largest marketers of aviation fuels, and a major supplier of fuels and lubricants to the global market. **Special programs:** Internships. **NOTE:** This company provides job listings for all its Illinois, United States and international locations. See website and apply online. **Corporate headquarters location:** This location. **Parent company:** BP (United Kingdom). **Operations at this facility include:** Administration.

## BAGCRAFT PACKAGING LLC
3900 West 43rd Street, Chicago IL 60632. 773/254-8000. **Toll-free phone:** 800/621-8468. **Fax:** 773/254-8204. **Contact:** Human Resources. **E-mail address:** hr@bagcraft.com. **World Wide Web address:** http://www.bagcraft.com. **Description:** Manufactures flexible packaging and laminating materials. **Parent company:** Packaging Dynamics.

## CF INDUSTRIES, INC.
One Salem Lake Drive, Long Grove IL 60047-8402. 847/438-9500. **Fax:** 847/438-0211. **Contact:** Human Resources. **World Wide Web address:** http://www.cfindustries.com. **Description:** One of North America's largest manufacturers and distributors of fertilizer products. Founded in 1946. **NOTE:** Entry-level positions are offered. **Corporate headquarters location:** This location. **Listed on:** Privately held.

## CABOT CORPORATION
## CAB-O-SIL DIVISION
700 East U.S. Highway 36, Tuscola IL 61953-9643. 217/253-3370. **Fax:** 217/253-4334. **Contact:** Human Resources. **World Wide Web address:** http://www.cabot-corp.com/cabosil. **Description:** Cabot Corporation's operations are in specialty chemicals, materials, and energy. The company produces carbon black, an essential reinforcing agent in tires and rubber products and a pigment in inks, coatings, and plastics. The company also produces fumed silica, electronic materials, and refractory metals. Cabot Corporation is a European producer of plastic concentrates and compounds. Cabot Corporation also makes eyewear, hearing protection, and industrial noise control products. **NOTE:** Apply online or mail resumes. **Corporate headquarters location:** Boston. **Listed on:** New York Stock Exchange. Stock exchange symbol: CBT.

## CONTINENTAL PLASTIC CONTAINERS

2727 East Higgins, Elk Grove IL 60007. 847/364-3800. **Contact:** Human Resources. **Description:** A leading developer, manufacturer, and marketer of custom extrusion, blow-molded plastic containers. Founded in 1904. **Other U.S. locations:** Nationwide. **Parent company:** Continental Can Company, Inc. is an international packaging company with several subsidiaries in Europe. **Operations at this facility include:** This location is a technical center. **Listed on:** New York Stock Exchange. **Stock exchange symbol:** CAN.

## DESOTO, INC.

P.O. Box 609, Joliet IL 60433. 815/727-4931. **Contact:** Anita Jackson, Director of Human Resources. **Description:** A diversified manufacturer of consumer paints, industrial coatings, and specialty products.

## ECOLAB INC.

3001 Channahon Road, Joliet IL 60436. 815/729-4900. **Fax:** 815/729-7303. **Contact:** Human Resources. **World Wide Web address:** http://www.ecolab.com. **Description:** Manufactures industrial-strength surface cleaners and disinfectants for use in hospitals, restaurants, schools, dairy farms, and other industrial facilities. **NOTE:** Apply online. **Positions advertised include:** Water Care Specialist; Route Manager; Account Sales Executive; Service Technician; Warehouse Supervisor; Corporate Account Manager.

## ENTHONE-OMI INC.

9809 Industrial Drive, Bridgeview IL 60455. 708/598-3210. **Fax:** 708/598-1719. **Contact:** Human Resources. **World Wide Web address:** http://www.enthone-omi.com. **Description:** A wholesale manufacturer and distributor of plating equipment and supplies.

## EQUISTAR CHEMICALS LLP

8805 North Tabler Road, Morris IL 60450. 815/942-7011. **Fax:** 815/942-7331. **Contact:** Human Resources Department. **World Wide Web address:** http://www.equistarchem.com. **Description:** A leading producer of ethylene, propylene, and polyethylene. **Parent company:** Lyondell Chemical Company (Houston TX). **Listed on:** New York Stock Exchange. **Stock exchange symbol:** LYO.

## FMC TECHNOLOGIES
## FMC FOODTECH

200 East Randolph Drive, Chicago IL 60601. 312/861-6000. **Contact:** Human Resources. **World Wide Web address:** http://www.fmctechnologies.com. **Description:** FMC Technologies is a diversified manufacturer of specialty, industrial, and agricultural chemicals; defense-related systems; industrial machinery. FMC, a subsidiary, creates computerized systems for the food industry. **Corporate headquarters location:** This location is the corporate office for the parent company, FMC Technologies and its subsidiary FMC Foodtech. **Subsidiaries include:** FMC Energy Systems; FMC Airport Systems; FMC Technologies A.G.

## FUCHS LUBRICANTS COMPANY

17050 Lathrop Avenue, Harvey IL 60426. 708/333-8900. **Contact:** Human Resources. **E-mail address:** jobs@fuchs.com. **World Wide Web address:** http://www.fuchs.com. **Description:** Manufactures and markets specialty lubricants primarily for the metalworking and mining industries. Founded in 1924. **Parent company:** Fuchs Worldwide Group.

## HOFFER PLASTICS CORPORATION
500 North Collins Street, South Elgin IL 60177-1195. 847/741-5740. **Fax:** 847/741-2675. **Contact:** Human Resources. **World Wide Web address:** http://www.hofferplastics.com. **Description:** A custom injection molder of thermoplastics products. **NOTE:** Fax resumes or apply in person at the Human Resources Office. **Office hours:** Monday – Friday, 8:00 a.m. - 4:00 p.m.

## IVEX PACKAGING CORPORATION
100 Tri-State International, Suite 200, Lincolnshire IL 60069. 847/945-9100. **Contact:** Human Resources. **World Wide Web address:** http://www.ivexpackaging.com. **Description:** Manufactures paper and plastic packaging products including dessert trays, containers, and toilet tissue overwraps. **Corporate headquarters location:** This location. **Operations at this facility include:** Administration.

## IVEX PACKAGING CORPORATION
8100 South 77th Avenue, Bridgeview IL 60455. 708/458-8084. **Contact:** Shelly Dentzman, Human Resources. **World Wide Web address:** http://www.ivexpackaging.com. **Description:** Manufactures corrugated packaging and mailers. **Corporate headquarters location:** Lincolnshire IL.

## KELLY-SPRINGFIELD TIRE COMPANY
3769 U.S. Route 20 East, Freeport IL 61032-9653. 815/235-4185. **Contact:** Human Resources. **World Wide Web address:** http://www.kelly-springfield.com. **Description:** Manufactures tires. **Corporate headquarters location:** Cumberland MD. **Other U.S. locations:** Fayetteville NC; Tyler TX. **International locations:** Worldwide. **Parent company:** Goodyear Tire & Rubber Company's principal business is the development, manufacture, distribution, marketing, and sale of tires for most applications worldwide. The company also manufactures and sells a broad spectrum of rubber products and rubber-related chemicals for various industrial and consumer markets, and provides auto repair services. Goodyear operates 32 plants in the United States, 42 plants in 29 other countries, and more than 1,800 retail tire and service centers and other distribution facilities around the globe. **Listed on:** New York Stock Exchange. **Stock exchange symbol:** GT.

## MONSANTO CORPORATION
3100 Sycamore Road, De Kalb IL 60115. 815/758-3461. **Fax:** 815/756-2676. **Contact:** Human Resources. **World Wide Web address:** http://www.monsanto.com. **Description:** Manufactures and markets agricultural products, performance chemicals used in consumer products, prescription pharmaceuticals, and food ingredients. **NOTE:** See website for job listings and apply online. **Corporate headquarters location:** Peapack NJ. **Other U.S. locations:** Nationwide. **Operations at this facility include:** This is the DeKalb Genetics Corporation's main office.

## NALCO CHEMICAL COMPANY
1601 West Diehl Road, Naperville IL 60563-1198. 877/813-3523. **Fax:** 630/305-2900. **Contact:** Human Resources. **World Wide Web address:** http://www.nalco.com. **Description:** Engaged in the manufacture and sale of highly specialized service chemicals used in water treatment, pollution control,

energy conservation, oil production and refining, steel making, paper making, mining, and other industrial processes. Founded in 1928. **NOTE:** Apply online. **Positions advertised include:** Paper Industry Development Manager; Administrative Services Specialist. **Corporate headquarters location:** This location. **Operations at this facility include:** Administration; Research and Development; Sales. **Number of employees at this location:** 1,200. **Number of employees worldwide:** 6,500.

### PLASTOFILM INDUSTRIES, INC.
935 West Union Avenue, Wheaton IL 60187. 630/668-2838. **Contact:** Human Resources. **Description:** Manufactures plastic packaging for cosmetics, pharmaceuticals, toys, and small tools. **Corporate headquarters location:** Lincolnshire IL.

### ROHM & HAAS COMPANY
123 North Wacker Drive, Chicago IL 60606. 312/807-2000. **Contact:** Human Resources. **World Wide Web address:** http://www.rohmhaas.com. **Description:** A diverse manufacturer of industrial and consumer items including Morton brand salt. The company is also a large producer of inflatable air bags for the automotive industry, adhesives for the packaging industry, liquid plastic coatings for automobiles, electronic products used in printed circuit boards and semiconductor wafers, and dyes used by the printing industry. **International locations:** Bahamas; Canada; Europe; Mexico. **Listed on:** New York Stock Exchange. **Stock exchange symbol:** ROH.

### ROHM & HAAS COMPANY
5005 Barnard Mill Road, Ringwood IL 60072. 815/653-2411. **Contact:** Human Resources. **World Wide Web address:** http://www.rohmhaas.com. **Description:** A location of Rohm and Haas company.

### ROHM & HAAS COMPANY
2701 East 170th Street, Lansing IL 60438. 708/474-7000. **Fax:** 708/868-7490. **Contact:** Human Resources. **Description:** A location of Rohm & Haas Company.

### RUST-OLEUM CORPORATION
11 Hawthorne Parkway, Vernon Hills IL 60061. 847/367-7700. **Fax:** 847/816-2230. **Contact:** Human Resources. **E-mail address:** corporatejobs1@rustoleum.com. **World Wide Web address:** http://www.rustoleum.com. **Description:** Manufactures rust fighting, decorative, and roof repair paints for the commercial and industrial markets. **NOTE:** Apply online. **Corporate headquarters location:** This location. **Other U.S. locations:** Evanston IL.

### W.H. SALISBURY & COMPANY
7520 North Long Avenue, Skokie IL 60077. 847/679-6700. **Fax:** 847/679-2401.**Contact:** Rosa Martinez, Human Resources Manager. **World Wide Web address:** http://www.whsalisbury.com. **Description:** Manufactures a variety of insulating equipment that protects workers from electrical shock. The company also manufactures temporary grounding equipment, plastic covers, and insulated bypass jumpers. **Corporate headquarters location:** This location.

## SCHOLLE CORPORATION
200 West North Avenue, Northlake IL 60164. 708/562-7290. **Contact:** Human Resources. **World Wide Web address:** http://www.scholle.com. **Description:** A manufacturer and distributor of flexible film packaging for the food and beverage industries; specialty chemical solutions for coating and related industries; and bulk and packaged acid. Scholle also manufactures filling equipment for food and beverage packages. **NOTE:** See website for job listings and contact information. **Corporate headquarters location:** This location. **Operations at this facility include:** Administration; Manufacturing; Research and Development; Sales; Service. **Listed on:** Privately held.

## STEPAN COMPANY
22 West Frontage Road, Northfield IL 60093. 847/446-7500. **Fax:** 847/501-2100. **Contact:** Human Resources. **World Wide Web address:** http://www.stepan.com. **Description:** Develops, manufactures, and markets a wide range of chemical intermediates sold to producers of shampoos, toothpastes, household detergents, and other personal care items. Products are also used as ingredients in industrial detergents and cleansers, agricultural fertilizers, herbicides, and petroleum-based detergents. Stepan Company is a major producer of phthalic anhydride, an essential ingredient in plastics and polyesters, and also manufactures urethane foam systems and other specialty products. **NOTE:** Apply online. **Corporate headquarters location:** This location. **Operations at this facility include:** Administration; Research and Development; Sales. **Listed on:** New York Stock Exchange. **Stock exchange symbol:** SCL.

## SUN CHEMICAL
135 West Lake Street, Northlake IL 60164. 708/562-0550. **Fax:** 708/562-0580. **Contact:** Human Resources. **World Wide Web address:** http://www.sunchemicalink.com. **Description:** One of the world's largest producers of printing inks and organic pigments. Sun Chemical also designs and manufactures graphic arts equipment.

## SYMONS CORPORATION
200 East Touhy Avenue, Des Plaines IL 60018. 847/298-3200. **Fax:** 847/635-9287. **Contact:** Human Resources. **E-mail address:** jobs@symons.com. **World Wide Web address:** http://www.symons.com. **Description:** An international manufacturer of standard, custom, and fiberglass concrete-forming equipment. The company also manufactures chemical systems including acrylic sealers, bonding agents, construction grouts, and curing compounds. **NOTE:** See website for job listings. Fax resumes or apply online. **Positions advertised include:** Customer Service Coordinator; Senior Account Manager; Senior Form Designer; Administrative Assistant; Corporate Health and Safety Specialist. **Corporate headquarters location:** This location.

## TURTLE WAX, INC.
5655 West 73rd Street, Chicago IL 60638. 708/563-3600. **Fax:** 708/563-3559. **Contact:** Sean Speilman, Human Resources. **E-mail address:** Recruiting@turtlewax.com. **World Wide Web address:** http://www.turtlewax.com. **Description:** Manufactures Turtle Wax brand polishing products. **NOTE:** See website for job listings. Mail, fax e-mail resumes. **Corporate headquarters location:** This location.

**UOP, INC.**
25 East Algonquin Road, Des Plaines IL 60017. 847/391-2000. **Fax:** 847/391-2253. **Contact:** Human Resources. **World Wide Web address:** http://www.uop.com. **Description:** Provides research, development, engineering, and manufacturing services relating to process technology and products for the petroleum and petrochemical industries. **NOTE:** Apply online. Part-time positions offered. **Positions advertised include:** Project Engineer; MRO Buyer; Web Coordinator; Development Chemist; Research Technician; Field Technical Advisor. **Special programs:** Internships. **Corporate headquarters location:** This location. **Listed on:** Privately held.

**UOP, INC.**
P.O. Box 163, Riverside IL 60546. 708/442-7400. **Contact:** Human Resources. **World Wide Web address:** http://www.uop.com. **Description:** UOP provides research, development, engineering, and manufacturing services relating to process technology and products for the petroleum and petrochemical industries. **NOTE:** Apply online. **Operations at this facility include:** This location is a research center.

**UNIVAR USA INC.**
P.O. Box 446 Summit IL 60501-0446. 708/728-6740. **Physical address:** 8500 West 68th Street, Bedford Park IL 60501. **Contact:** Human Resources. **World Wide Web address:** http://www.univarusa.com. **Description:** Manufactures and wholesales chemical pesticides and industrial chemicals.

**VAN LEER CONTAINERS, INC.**
4300 West 130th Street, Alsip IL 60803. 708/371-4777. **Fax:** 708/371-2047. **Contact:** Human Resources. **World Wide Web address:** http://www.greif.com. **Description:** Manufactures plastic and fiber containers including intermediate bulk containers and closures. The consumer packaging business includes molded fiber products, flexible packaging such as metalized paper, strength films, folding cartons, tubs, and lids. **NOTE:** Current job openings are listed on http://www.hotjobs.com. The Human Resources address is: 425 Winter Road, Delaware OH 43015, Fax: 740/549-6100. **Positions advertised include:** Physical Therapist; CNC Operator; Lead Maintenance Technician. **Corporate headquarters location:** This location. **Other U.S. locations:** Atlanta GA; Florence KY; Canton MS; Greenville OH; Warminster PA. **Parent company:** Greif Brothers. **Operations at this facility include:** Administration; Divisional Headquarters; Manufacturing; Research and Development; Sales; Service.

**VISKASE CORPORATION**
625 Willowbrook Center Parkway, Willowbrook IL 60527. 630/789-4900. **Toll-free phone:** 800/323-8562. **Fax:** 630/455-2155. **Contact:** Human Resources. **World Wide Web address:** http://www.viskase.com. **Description:** Manufactures cellulose casings and flexible packaging used primarily in the food industry. **Special programs:** Internships. **Corporate headquarters location:** This location. **Parent company:** Envirodyne Industries.

## COMMUNICATIONS: TELECOMMUNICATIONS AND BROADCASTING

**You can expect to find the following types of companies in this section:**
Cable/Pay Television Services • Communications Equipment • Radio and Television Broadcasting Stations • Telephone, Telegraph, and Other Message Communications

---

**ANDREW CORPORATION**
10500 West 153rd Street, Orland Park IL 60462. 708/349-3300. **Fax:** 708/873-3640. **Contact:** Human Resources. **World Wide Web address:** http://www.andrew.com. **Description:** A manufacturer of telecommunications equipment including Earth Station Satellite, cellular, and microwave antennas, towers, shelters, cables, and associated equipment. **Positions advertised include:** Buyer; Compensation Analyst; Corporate Communications Writer; Cost Accounting Assistant; Customer Relationship Representative; Operations Supervisor; Project Manager; Senior Engineer Industrial. **Special programs:** Internships. **Corporate headquarters location:** This location. **Operations at this facility include:** Administration; Manufacturing; Research and Development; Sales; Service. **Listed on:** NASDAQ. **Stock exchange symbol:** ANDW.

**ANIXTER INC.**
2301 Patriot Boulevard, Glenview IL 60025-8020. Toll-free phone: 800/264-9837. **Contact:** Human Resources. **World Wide Web address:** http://www.anixter.com. **Description:** A value-added provider of industrial wire and cabling solutions that support voice and data applications. Solutions include customized pre- and post-sale services and products. **Positions advertised include:** Inventory Group Accountant; Staff Accountant. **Corporate headquarters location:** This location. **Other U.S. locations:** Nationwide. **Parent company:** Anixter International. **Operations at this facility include:** Administration; Marketing; Research and Development; Service. **Listed on:** New York Stock Exchange. **Stock exchange symbol:** AXE.

**CBS INC.**
630 North McClurg Court, Chicago IL 60611. 312/202-2222. **Contact:** Human Resources. **World Wide Web address:** http://www.cbs.com. **Description:** CBS Inc. is a broad-based entertainment and communications company that operates one of the country's four major commercial television networks and two nationwide radio networks, which include 8 AM and 13 FM stations. **NOTE:** Interested jobseekers should mail their resumes and indicate in their cover letters if they are applying for TV, AM or FM radio positions. **Operations at this facility include:** This location houses regional administrative offices.

**COMCAST**
5N301 Medinah Road, Addison IL 60101. 708/383-7280. **Contact:** Human Resources. **World Wide Web address:** http://www.comcast.com. **Description:** One of the nation's largest cable television and broadband services companies. **NOTE:** In addition to this location, Comcast has several locations in Illinois.

Jobseekers are encouraged to apply via the company's website. Positions advertised include: Recruiting Assistant; Collections Representative; Supervisor of Inbound Sales/Retention. **Corporate headquarters location:** Philadelphia PA. **Listed on:** NASDAQ. **Stock exchange symbol:** CMCSA. **Number of employees worldwide:** 150,000.

### GLENAYRE ELECTRONICS, INC.
One Glenayre Way, Quincy IL 62301. 217/223-3211. **Fax:** 217/221-6489. **Contact:** Ed Danielski, Human Resources Manager. **World Wide Web address:** http://www.glenayre.com. **Description:** Provides infrastructure equipment to providers of wireless communication services such as paging and voice messaging. **NOTE:** Send resumes to: Glenayre Electronics, Inc., 11360 Lakefield Drive, Duluth GA 30097. **Special programs:** Internships. **Corporate headquarters location:** Duluth GA. **Other U.S. locations:** Duluth GA. **Parent company:** Glenayre Technologies, Inc. provides paging products and systems including messaging pagers. Other services are for both mobile and fixed telecommunication systems and include voice mail, fax messaging, and debit/prepaid calling card platforms. **Operations at this facility include:** Administration; Manufacturing; Research and Development; Sales; Service. **Listed on:** NASDAQ. **Stock exchange symbol:** GEMS.

### LUCENT TECHNOLOGIES
2600 Warrenville Road, Lisle IL 60532. 630/224-4000. **Contact:** Human Resources. **World Wide Web address:** http://www.lucent.com. **Description:** Designs and delivers systems, software, silicon, and services for next-generation communications networks for service providers and enterprises. Lucent focuses on areas such as broadband and mobile Internet infrastructure; communications software; communications semiconductors and optoelectronics; Web-based enterprise solutions that link private and public networks; and professional network design and consulting services. **NOTE:** Search and apply for positions online. **Positions advertised include:** Packet Data Call Processing Developer; Network Security Implementation Engineer; LAN Design and Engineer; Voice Design Engineer; Wireless Standards Engineer; UMTS Data Systems Engineer/Developer. **Corporate headquarters location:** Murray Hill NJ.

### MCI
205 North Michigan Avenue, Suite 2600, Chicago IL 60601. 312/470-2121. **Contact:** Human Resources. **World Wide Web address:** http://www.mci.com. **Description:** One of the world's largest suppliers of local, long distance, and international telecommunications services, and a global Internet service provider. Founded in 1968. MCI services more than 150 countries and places. **Corporate headquarters location:** Ashburn VA. **Other U.S. locations:** Nationwide. **Parent company:** MCI Communications Corporation. **Listed on:** NASDAQ. **Stock exchange symbol:** MCIP. Number of employees worldwide: 50,000.

### MIDWEST TELEVISION, INC.
### WCIA-CHANNEL 3
P.O. Box 20, Champaign IL 61824-0020. 217/356-8333. **Contact:** Human Resources. **World Wide Web address:** http://www.wcia.com. **Description:** A television and radio broadcasting company. **NOTE:** See website for contact information. **Positions advertised include:** Traffic Assistant; News Photographer/Sports Reporter.

## MITEL TELECOMMUNICATIONS SYSTEMS
241 South Furnace Road, Suite 37, Burr Ridge IL 60527. 630/850-2170. **Contact:** Human Resources. **World Wide Web address:** http://www.mitel.com. **Description:** Sells and services a variety of business telephone systems including voicemail. **NOTE:** Send resumes to the corporate headquarters' Human Resources Office – Mitel Networks, 350 Legget Drive, Kanata, Ontario, Canada, K2K 2W7. Or phone: 613/592-2122 for additional employment information. **Operations at this facility include:** This is a sales office.

## MOTOROLA, INC.
1303 East Algonquin Road, Schaumburg IL 60196. 847/576-5000. **Contact:** Human Resources. **World Wide Web address:** http://www.motorola.com. **Description:** Motorola manufactures communications equipment and electronic products including car radios, cellular phones, semiconductors, computer systems, cellular infrastructure equipment, pagers, cordless phones, and LANs. **NOTE:** Apply online for open positions. **Corporate headquarters location:** This location. **Other U.S. locations:** Nationwide. **International locations:** Worldwide. **Listed on:** New York Stock Exchange. **Stock exchange symbol:** MOT.

## NETWORK CHICAGO
5400 North St. Louis Avenue, Chicago IL 60625-4698. 773/583-5000. **Fax:** 773/583-5300. **Recorded jobline:** 773/509-5333. **Contact:** Laura Backus, Vice President, Human Resources. **E-mail address:** job@networkchicago.com. **World Wide Web address:** http://www.networkchicago.com. **Description:** Owns and operates WTTW Channel 11, The Chicago Production Center, and WFMT & The Radio Networks. **NOTE:** E-mail or fax resumes to Ms. Backus. Resumes may also be mailed to her at Window To the World Communications, Inc., 5400 North St. Louis Avenue, Chicago IL 60625. **Special programs:** Internships. **Corporate headquarters location:** This location.

## PANDUIT CORPORATION
17301 South Ridgeland Avenue, Tinley Park IL 60477. 708/532-1800. **Toll-free phone:** 888/506-5400. **Fax:** 708/532-1811. **Contact:** Cheryl Lewis, Supervisor of Corporate Recruiting. **World Wide Web address:** http://www.panduit.com. **Description:** Manufactures electrical wiring components, electrical accessories, and communications products. **NOTE:** See website for job listings and to submit resume. Entry-level positions are offered. **Special programs:** Internships. **Corporate headquarters location:** This location. **Other U.S. locations:** Nationwide. **International locations:** Worldwide. **Listed on:** Privately held.

## TALK-A-PHONE COMPANY
5013 North Kedzie Avenue, Chicago IL 60625. 773/539-1100. **Contact:** Human Resources. **World Wide Web address:** http://www.talkaphone.com. **Description:** Manufactures emergency phones and intercom units.

## TELEPHONE AND DATA SYSTEMS, INC. (TDS)
30 North LaSalle Street, Suite 4000, Chicago IL 60602. 312/630-1900. **Fax:** 312/630-1908. **Contact:** Human Resources. **E-mail address:** careers@teldta.com. **World Wide Web address:** http://www.teldta.com. **Description:** Provides local telecommunications services including cellular, landline telephone, and paging to customers nationwide. TDS's strategic business units include United States Cellular Corporation, which manages and invests in cellular systems throughout the nation; TDS Telecommunications Corporation, which provides local telephone and access service to rural and

suburban areas across the nation and acquires operating telephone companies; American Paging, Inc., which operates paging and voicemail systems; and Aerial Communications, Inc., which is one of the largest licensees of personal communications services in the United States. Founded in 1968. **NOTE:** See website for job listings. E-mail resumes. **Positions advertised include:** Accountant; Support Analyst; Distribution Clerk; Machine Operator; Senior Credit Analyst; Communications Manager. **Special programs:** Internships. **Corporate headquarters location:** This location. **Other U.S. locations:** Nationwide. **Subsidiaries include:** Suttle Press, Inc. is a commercial printing subsidiary; TDS Computing Services, Inc. is an information systems subsidiary. **Operations at this facility include:** Administration.

### TELLABS
1415 West Diehl Road, Naperville IL 60563. 630/378-8800. **Fax:** 630/798-2000. **Contact:** Human Resources. **World Wide Web address:** http://www.tellabs.com. **Description:** Designs, manufactures, markets, and services voice and data transport systems and network access systems used worldwide by public telephone companies, long-distance carriers, alternate service providers, cellular and wireless service providers, cable operators, government agencies, and businesses. Founded in 1975. **NOTE:** See website for job listings and apply online. Entry-level positions are offered. **Special programs:** Internships. **Internship information:** Tellabs hires summer to work in software and hardware development and testing areas. See website for more information. **Corporate headquarters location:** This location. **Other U.S. locations:** Boston MA; Hawthorne NY; Round Rock TX; Ashburn VA. **International locations:** Helsinki, Finland; Shannon, Ireland. **Operations at this facility include:** Administration; Manufacturing; Research and Development; Sales; Service. **Listed on:** NASDAQ. **Stock exchange symbol:** TLAB.

### VERIZON COMMUNICATIONS
1312 East Empire Street, Bloomington IL 61701. 309/663-3311. **Contact:** Human Resources Director. **World Wide Web address:** http://www.verizon.com. **Description:** A full-service communications services provider. Verizon offers residential local and long distance telephone services and Internet access; wireless service plans, cellular phones, and data services; a full-line of business services including Internet access, data services, and telecommunications equipment and services; and government network solutions including Internet access, data services, telecommunications equipment and services, and enhanced communications services. **Corporate headquarters location:** New York NY. **Other U.S. locations:** Nationwide. **Operations at this facility include:** Engineering and Design; Payroll; Regional Headquarters; Sales. **Listed on:** New York Stock Exchange. **Stock exchange symbol:** VZ.

### WFLD FOX 32
205 North Michigan Avenue, Chicago IL 60601. 312/565-5532. **Recorded jobline:** 312/565-5555. **Contact:** Human Resources Department. **World Wide Web address:** http://www.foxchicago.com. **Description:** Owns WFLD-TV, a Fox affiliate. **Positions advertised include:** Stage Hand; Transmitter Supervisor; Local Account Executive; Engineering Manager. **Special programs:** Internships. **Corporate headquarters location:** Los Angeles CA.

**WMAY**
P.O. Box 460. Springfield IL 62705. 217/629-7077. **Fax:** 217/629-7952. **Contact:** Human Resources. **World Wide Web address:** http://www.wmay.com. **Description:** A talk radio station.

**WESTELL TECHNOLOGIES INC.**
750 North Commons Drive, Aurora IL 60504. 630/898-2500. **Fax:** 630/375-4148. **Contact:** Human Resources Department. **E-mail address:** employment@ westell.com. **World Wide Web address:** http://www.westell.com. **Description:** Manufactures telecommunications access products. The company's DSL products enable telephone companies to provide interactive media services through existing telephone lines. These products are used to provide faster Internet access as well as telecommuting opportunities. **Positions advertised include:** Account Manager; Account Representative. **Corporate headquarters location:** This location. **Subsidiaries include:** Westell, Inc. **Listed on:** NASDAQ. **Stock exchange symbol:** WSTL.

**WESTWOOD ONE INC.**
111 East Wacker Drive, Suite 955, Chicago IL 60601. 312/938-0222. **Fax:** 312/938-0353. **Contact:** Office Manager. **World Wide Web address:** http://www.westwoodone.com. **Description:** A broadcasting network serving over 7,500 radio stations. **Positions advertised include:** Account Representative; Sales Representative. **Office hours:** Monday - Friday, 9:00 a.m. - 5:00 p.m. **Other U.S. locations:** Culver City CA; Detroit MI; New York NY; Arlington VA. **International locations:** London, England; Tokyo, Japan. **Subsidiaries include:** Shadow Broadcast Service. **Listed on:** New York Sock Exchange. **Stock exchange symbol:** WON.

## COMPUTER HARDWARE, SOFTWARE, AND SERVICES

**You can expect to find the following types of companies in this section:**
Computer Components and Hardware Manufacturers • Consultants and Computer Training Companies • Internet and Online Service Providers • Networking and Systems Services • Repair Services/Rental and Leasing • Resellers, Wholesalers, and Distributors • Software Developers/Programming Services • Web Technologies

---

**ACCENTURE**
161 North Clark Street, 44th Floor, Chicago IL 60601. 312/693-0161. **Fax:** 312/693-0507. **Contact:** Human Resources. **World Wide Web address:** http://www.accenture.com. **Description:** A management and technology consulting firm. Accenture offers a wide range of services including business re-engineering; customer service system consulting; data system design and implementation; Internet sales systems research and design; and strategic planning. **NOTE:** This company provides job listings for all its Illinois, U.S. and global offices. Apply online. **Positions advertised include:** Entry-Level Programmers; Oracle PL; Tester; Cobol. **Corporate headquarters location:** This location. **Other U.S. locations:** Nationwide. **International locations:** Worldwide. **Listed on:** New York Stock Exchange. **Stock exchange symbol:** ACN. **Number of employees worldwide:** 75,000.

**ALERI**
Two Prudential Plaza, 41$^{st}$ Floor, Chicago IL 60601. 312/540-0100. **Fax:** 312/540-0717. **Contact:** Human Resources. **E-mail address:** careers@aleri.com. **World Wide Web address:** http://www.aleri.com. **Description:** Designs and develops solutions for financial institutions including the ATLAS software product line, a series of financial transaction processing systems that allow companies to increase productivity and reduce operating costs. Founded in 1981.

**ANALYSTS INTERNATIONAL CORPORATION (AIC)**
1101 Perimeter Drive, Suite 837, Schaumburg IL 60173-5060. 847/619-4673. **Fax:** 847/605-9489. **Contact:** Human Resources. **World Wide Web address:** http://www.analysts.com. **Description:** AIC is an international computer consulting firm. The company assists clients in developing systems in a variety of industries using different programming languages and software. **NOTE:** Apply online. **Corporate headquarters location:** Minneapolis MN. **Listed on:** NASDAQ. **Stock exchange symbol:** ANLY.

**APPLIED SYSTEMS, INC.**
200 Applied Parkway, University Park IL 60466. 708/534-5575. **Contact:** Director of Human Resources. **World Wide Web address:** http://www.appliedsystems.com. **Description:** Provides computer systems integration and design services to the insurance industry. **Positions advertised include:** Equipment Maintenance Technician; Web Development Engineer; Web Product Engineer.

## APROPOS TECHNOLOGY, INC.
One Tower Lane, 28th Floor, Oakbrook Terrace IL 60181. 630/472-9600. **Toll-free phone:** 877/277-6767. **Fax:** 630/472-9745. **Contact:** Human Resources. **E-mail address:** hr@apropos.com. **World Wide Web address:** http://www.apropos.com. **Description:** Apropos develops and markets a real-time, multi-channel interaction management application for managing customer interactions across a variety of communications media, including E-mail, Web and voice. **NOTE:** Search and apply for positions online. **Positions advertised include:** Programmer Analyst; Pre-Sales Solution Consultant; Senior Software Engineer; Financial Operations Supervisor.

## BITSPOINT, INC.
4118 West Lawrence Avenue, Suite 204, Chicago IL 60630-2848. 773/282-3565. **Contact:** Human Resources. **E-mail address:** careers@bitspoint.com. **World Wide Web address:** http://www.bitspoint.com. **Description:** Provides technology that enables wireless credit card processing, online automated vehicle location, remote vehicle management, courier and dispatch services, messaging and alerting, and location based services.

## CDW COMPUTER CENTERS, INC.
200 North Milwaukee Avenue, Vernon Hills IL 60061. 847/465-6000. **Fax:** 847/465-3858. **Contact:** Human Resources. **World Wide Web address:** http://www.cdw.com. **Description:** Resells name-brand computers and peripherals to small and medium-sized businesses through catalog, phone, and online sales. **NOTE:** Apply online. **Corporate headquarters location:** This location. **Listed on:** NASDAQ. **Stock exchange symbol:** CDWC. **Annual sales/revenues:** More than $100 million.

## CATERPILLAR INC.
## CATERPILLAR LOGISTICS
500 North Morton Avenue, Morton IL 61550-0474. **Toll-free phone:** 800/240-2126. **Contact:** Human Resources. **World Wide Web address:** http://www.cat.com. **Description:** Caterpillar Logistics Division provides products and services that help businesses and government agencies manage their supply chains. **NOTE:** Caterpillar Logistics has another location in Aurora IL. See website for street address. Apply online at the corporate website for all open positions in Caterpillar and Caterpillar Logistics. **Corporate headquarters location:** Peoria IL. **Operations at this facility include:** Administration. This location is the headquarters for Caterpillar Logistics. **Listed on:** New York Stock Exchange. **Stock exchange symbol:** CAT. **Number of employees worldwide:** 72,000.

## CHICAGO MICROSYSTEMS, INC.
1825 Elmdale Avenue, Glenview IL 60026-1297. 847/998-9970. **Fax:** 847/998-9975. **Contact:** Human Resources. **World Wide Web address:** http://www.chimicro.com. **Description:** A computer reseller and an Internet service provider.

## COMPUTER ASSOCIATES INTERNATIONAL, INC.
2400 Cabot Drive, Lisle IL 60532. 630/505-6000. **Contact:** Human Resources. **World Wide Web address:** http://www.cai.com. **Description:** Computer Associates International is one of the world's leading developers of client/server and distributed computing software. The company develops, markets, and supports enterprise management, database and applications development,

business applications, and consumer software products for a broad range of mainframe, midrange, and desktop computers. Computer Associates International serves major business, government, research, and educational organizations. Founded in 1976. **NOTE:** Apply online at the website or send resumes for open positions to the company's headquarters: One Computer Associates Plaza, Islandia NY 11749, Attention: Human Resources Recruitment. **Positions advertised include:** Technology Services Architect; Consultant; Customer Advocate; Sales. **Corporate headquarters location:** Islandia NY. **Other U.S. locations:** Nationwide. **Listed on:** New York Stock Exchange. **Stock exchange symbol:** CA. **Number of employees nationwide:** 16,000.

### COMPUTER HORIZONS CORPORATION
### RECRUITING CENTER, MIDWEST REGION
6400 Shafer Court, Suite 600, Rosemont IL 60018. 847/698-6800. **Toll-free phone:** 800/877-2421. **Fax:** 847/698-6823. **Contact:** Staffing Manager. **World Wide Web address:** http://www.computerhorizons.com. **Description:** Computer Horizons is a full-service technology solutions company offering contract staffing, outsourcing, re-engineering, migration, downsizing support, and network management. Founded in 1969. **NOTE:** Apply online at the company's website. **Corporate headquarters location:** Mountain Lakes NJ.

### COMPUTER SCIENCES CORPORATION (CSC)
935 Lakeview Parkway, Suite 190, Vernon Hills IL 60061. 847/573-4400. **Contact:** Human Resources. **World Wide Web address:** http://www.csc.com. **Description:** Develops software for the many industries and governments, and provides solutions to client/server, e-business, and mainframe applications. Founded in 1959. **Listed on:** New York Stock Exchange. **Stock exchange symbol:** CSC. **Number of employees worldwide:** 90,000.

### COMPUWARE CORPORATION
2 Pierce Place, Suite 1900, Itasca IL 60143. 630/285-8560. **Contact:** Human Resources. **World Wide Web address:** http://www.compuware.com. **Description:** Develops, markets, and supports an integrated line of systems software products that improve the productivity of programmers and analysts in application program testing, test data preparation, error analysis, and maintenance. Compuware also provides a broad range of professional data processing services including business systems analysis, design, and programming, as well as systems planning and consulting. **NOTE:** Apply online to open positions. **Corporate headquarters location:** Farmington Hills MI.

### CONVERGYS
2 Pierce Place, Itasca IL 60143-3153. 630/775-1700. **Fax:** 630/775-8890. **Contact:** Human Resources. **World Wide Web address:** http://www.convergys.com. **Description:** Designs and markets information systems, and provides consulting and technical services for telecommunications companies. **NOTE:** Apply online at the website. **Positions advertised include:** Senior Manager of Professional Services; Engagement Director.

### CORPORATE DISK COMPANY
4610 Prime Parkway, McHenry IL 60050. 815/331-6000. **Toll-free phone:** 800/634-3475. **Fax:** 815/331-6030. **Contact:** Human Resources. **World Wide Web address:** http://www.disk.com. **Description:** Manufactures and develops software packages and provides related support services.

## CYBORG SYSTEMS INC.
120 South Riverside Plaza, 17th Floor, Chicago IL 60606. 312/279-7000. **Contact:** Human Resources. **E-mail address:** careers@cyborg.com. **World Wide Web address:** http://www.cyborg.com. **Description:** Designs software for human resources departments. **NOTE:** Entry-level positions are offered. **International locations:** Africa; Asia; Australia; Canada; Latin America; United Kingdom. **Parent company:** Hewitt Associates.

## DATA COMMUNICATION FOR BUSINESS INC.
2949 County Road, 1000 East, Dewey IL 61840. 217/897-6600. **Fax:** 217/897-1331. **Contact:** Human Resources. **World Wide Web address:** http://www.dcbnet.com. **Description:** Manufactures and markets data communications equipment. The company also aids in network installation by providing assistance with accessory equipment, communications lines and suppliers, site planning, and installation.

## DATALOGICS INC.
101 North Wacker Drive, Suite 1800, Chicago IL 60606. 312/853-8200. **Fax:** 312/853-8282. **Contact:** Human Resources. **World Wide Web address:** http://www.datalogics.com. **Description:** Develops and markets software for publishing companies. **Positions advertised include:** Marketing Manager; Sales Engineer/Web Developer. **Corporate headquarters location:** This location.

## EBIX.COM
1900 East Golf Street, Suite 1200, Schaumburg IL 60173. 847/789-3047. **Fax:** 847/619-4773. **Contact:** Human Resources. **World Wide Web address:** http://www.ebix.com. **Description:** Develops agency management applications software for insurance companies.

## EDGE SYSTEMS, INC.
1805 High Point Drive, Suite 103, Naperville IL 60563-9359. 630/810-9669. **Fax:** 630/810-9228. **Contact:** Human Resources Director. **World Wide Web address:** http://www.edge.com. **Description:** Engaged in systems integration and information resource management solutions. **Corporate headquarters location:** This location. **Other area locations:** Chicago IL (Sales).

## ELECTRO RENT CORPORATION
200 West Mark Street, Woodale IL 60191. 630/860-3991. **Contact:** Human Resources. **World Wide Web address:** http://www.electrorent.com. **Description:** Rents and leases electronic equipment including test and measurement instruments, workstations, personal computers, and data communication products. **Corporate headquarters location:** Van Nuys CA. **Other U.S. locations:** Nationwide.

## FUJITSU IT HOLDINGS, INC.
9399 West Higgins Road, Suite 1000, Rosemont IL 60018. 847/692-6940. **Contact:** Human Resources. **World Wide Web address:** http://www.amdahl.com. **Description:** Designs, develops, manufactures, markets, and services more than 470 large-scale, high-performance, general purpose computer systems. Customers are primarily large corporations, government agencies, and large universities with high-volume data processing requirements. **Corporate headquarters location:** Sunnyvale CA. Other area locations: Rosemont IL (Fujitsu Computer Systems). Operations at this facility

include: This is a office for Fujitsu Computer Systems. **Parent company:** Fujitsu Limited.

**FUTURESOURCE**
955 Parkview Boulevard, Lombard IL 60148. 630/620-8444. **Fax:** 630/792-2600. **Contact:** Human Resources. **World Wide Web address:** http://www.futuresource.com. **Description:** An online, real-time, financial news provider.

**GALILEO INTERNATIONAL**
9700 West Higgins Road, Suite 400, Rosemont IL 60018. 847/518-4000. **Contact:** Human Resources. **World Wide Web address:** http://www.galileo.com. **Description:** Designs and installs software for the travel industry that provides access to inventory, scheduling, and pricing information. **NOTE:** Apply online at this company's website. **Corporate headquarters location:** Parsippany NJ. **Other U.S. locations:** Centennial CO. **International locations:** UK; Saudi Arabia; India. **Operations at this facility include:** This office is a corporate regional office.

**GREENBRIER & RUSSEL, INC.**
1450 East American Lane, Suite 1700, Schaumburg IL 60173. 847/706-4000. **Toll-free phone:** 800/453-0347. **Fax:** 847/706-4020. **Contact:** Sherry Greer, Recruiter. **E-mail address:** recruiting@gr.com. **World Wide Web address:** http://www.gr.com. **Description:** A leader in providing strategic business solutions through technical services and software. The company offers technical and management consulting, information systems training, and a wide range of intranet and client/server software. The consulting division is a national practice that focuses on helping clients meet business goals through the use of technology. The company's training division offers instructor-led intranet, client/server, AS/400, and DB2 classes. **NOTE:** Entry-level positions are offered. **Positions advertised include:** Senior Business Objects Developer; Data Warehouse Architect; MS Analysis Services Consultant; Oracle Application DBA; Student Systems Functional Consultant; CRM Functional Consultant. **Corporate headquarters location:** This location. **Other U.S. locations:** Milwaukee WI; Appleton WI; Minneapolis MN; Atlanta GA; Dallas TX.

**HEALTH MANAGEMENT SYSTEMS**
820 West Jackson Boulevard, Chicago IL 60607. 312/962-6100. **Contact:** Laura Pontarelli, Human Resources Director. **World Wide Web address:** http://www.hmsy.com. **Description:** Develops software for the health insurance and health care industries. **NOTE:** Entry-level positions are offered. **Corporate headquarters location:** New York NY. **Other U.S. locations:** Nationwide. **Operations at this facility include:** Administration; Research and Development; Sales; Service. **Listed on:** Privately held.

**IBM CORPORATION**
One IBM Plaza, Chicago IL 60611. 312/245-6383. **Contact:** IBM Staffing Services. **World Wide Web address:** http://www.ibm.com. **Description:** IBM is a developer, manufacturer, and marketer of advanced information processing products including computers and microelectronic technology, software, networking systems, and information technology-related services. **Corporate headquarters location:** Armonk NY. **International locations:** Africa; Asia; Canada; Europe; Latin America; Middle East. **Operations at this facility**

**include:** This location is a marketing office. **Listed on:** New York Stock Exchange. **Stock exchange symbol:** IBM.

## IBM CORPORATION
6250 River Road, Suite 7050, Rosemont IL 60018. 877/683-6235. **Contact:** Human Resources. **World Wide Web address:** http://www.ibm.com. **Description:** IBM is a developer, manufacturer, and marketer of advanced information processing products including computers and microelectronic technology, software, networking systems, and information technology-related services. Founded in 1983. **Corporate headquarters location:** Beaverton OR. **International locations:** Worldwide. **Operations at this facility include:** This location is a sales office. **Subsidiaries include:** IBM Credit Corporation; IBM Instruments, Inc.; IBM World Trade Corporation. **Listed on:** New York Stock Exchange. **Stock exchange symbol:** IBM.

## INFORMATION RESOURCES, INC.
150 North Clinton Street, Chicago IL 60661. 312/726-1221. **Fax:** 312/726-5304. **Contact:** Human Resources. **World Wide Web address:** http://www.infores.com. **Description:** Develops and maintains computerized proprietary databases, decision support software, and analytical models to assist clients, primarily in the consumer packaged goods industry, in testing and evaluating their marketing plans for new products, media advertising, price, and sales promotions. **NOTE:** Apply online. **Corporate headquarters location:** This location. **Other U.S. locations:** Los Angeles CA; San Francisco CA; Darien CT; Waltham MA; Fairfield NJ; Cincinnati OH. **Operations at this facility include:** Administration.

## INGENIENT TECHNOLOGIES, INC.
1701 West Golf Road, Tower 1, Suite 300, Rolling Meadows IL 60008. 847/357-1980. **Fax:** 847/357-1981. **Contact:** Human Resources. **E-mail address:** hr@ingenient.com. **World Wide Web address:** http://www.ingenient.com. **Description:** A technology company that develops multimedia product solutions based upon embedded Digital Signal Processors (DSPs) and General Purpose Processors (GPPs). **NOTE:** Search for open positions on the company website. **Positions advertised include:** Business Development Manager; Design Verification and Testing Engineer; Firmware Engineers; Hardware Engineers; Senior DSP Engineer; WindowsCE Software Engineer. **Corporate headquarters location:** This location. **Other U.S. locations:** Baltimore MD.

## INRULE SOLUTIONS
224 North Des Plaines, Suite 601, Chicago IL 60661. 312/648-1800. **Fax:** 312/873-3851. **Contact:** Rick Chomko, Chief Product Officer. **E-mail address:** resume@inrule.com. **World Wide Web address:** http://www.inrule.com. **Description:** Manufacturer of software (InRuleSuite) that helps streamline the development of program coding. Primary clients are those in the insurance, finance, manufacturing and professional markets. **NOTE:** E-mail resumes. **Listed on:** Privately held.

## INSIGHT ENTERPRISES, INC.
444 Scott Drive, Bloomingdale IL 60108-3111. 630/924-6700. **Toll-free phone:** 800/723-2254. **Contact:** Human Resources. **World Wide Web address:** http://www.corp.insight.com. **Description:** Sells and distributes computer hardware, software and peripherals to *Fortune* 500 companies. Founded in 1988. **Positions advertised include:** Wireless Sales Engineer; Corporate Sales

Representative; Inside Sales Representative; Procurement Specialist; Software Sales Engineer. **Office hours:** Monday - Friday, 8:00 a.m. - 5:00 p.m. **Corporate headquarters location:** This location. **Other U.S. locations:** Nationwide. **Listed on:** NASDAQ. **Stock exchange symbol:** NSIT.

## KLEINSCHMIDT INC.
450 Lake Cook Road, Deerfield IL 60015. 847/945-1000. **Contact:** Human Resources. **World Wide Web address:** http://www.kleinschmidt.com. **Description:** Offers third-party computer networking services.

## LAKEVIEW TECHNOLOGY
1901 South Meyers Road, Suite 600, Oak Brook Terrace IL 60181. 630/282-8100. **Toll-free phone:** 800/573-8371. **Fax:** 630/282-8500. **Contact:** Human Resources. **E-mail address:** hr@lakeviewtech.com. **World Wide Web address:** http://www.lakeviewtech.com. **Description:** Resells IBM products and services. LAS also provides training, education, and software development services.

## McKESSON CORPORATION
1400 South Wolf Road, Wheeling IL 60090. 847/537-4800. **Toll-free phone:** 800/323-8154. **Fax:** 847/537-4866. **Contact:** Recruiter. **World Wide Web address:** http://www.mckesson.com. **Description:** Produces and sells software applications catering to the specific needs of medical facilities. Some of the programs include materials management, financial accounting, patient scheduling for operating rooms, and inventory control for health clinics. Founded in 1974. **NOTE:** See website for job listings and apply online. Entry-level positions are offered. **Positions advertised include:** VP Health Systems National Accounts; Sales Support Product Demonstrator; Staff Pharmacist; Director of National Accounts; Product Manager/Development Manager. **Special programs:** Internships. **Corporate headquarters location:** San Francisco CA. **Other U.S. locations:** Boulder CO. **Listed on:** New York Stock Exchange. **Stock exchange symbol:** MCK.

## MERCURY INTERACTIVE CORPORATION
10255 West Higgins Road, Suite 620, Rosemont IL 60018. 847/803-3176. **Fax:** 847/803-5686. **Contact:** Human Resources. **World Wide Web address:** http://www.mercuryinteractive.com. **Description:** Mercury Interactive is a developer of automated software quality (ASQ) tools for enterprise applications testing. The company's products are used to isolate software and system errors prior to application deployment. **NOTE:** See website for job listings and apply online. **Corporate headquarters location:** Sunnyvale CA. **Operations at this facility include:** This location is a sales office. **Listed on:** NASDAQ. **Stock exchange symbol:** MERQ.

## MICRO SOLUTIONS COMPUTER PRODUCTS INC.
132 West Lincoln Highway, DeKalb IL 60115. 815/756-3411. **Contact:** Human Resources. **World Wide Web address:** http://www.micro-solutions.com. **Description:** Manufactures parallel printer port computer drives.

## MIDWAY GAMES INC.
2704 West Roscoe Street, Chicago IL 60618. 773/961-1000. **Contact:** Human Resources. **World Wide Web address:** http://www.midway.com. **Description:** Develops a wide variety of coin-operated arcade and home video game entertainment and software products. Midway produces games for Sony, Nintendo, and Saga platforms. **Positions advertised include:** Executive

Producer; Financial Planning Analyst. **Special programs:** Internships. **Corporate headquarters location:** This location. **International locations:** Midway Games Limited, London England. **Listed on:** New York Stock Exchange. **Stock exchange symbol:** MWY.

## PC WHOLESALE
444 Scott Drive, Bloomingdale IL 60108. 630/307-1700. **Fax:** 630/307-2450. **Contact:** Human Resources. **World Wide Web address:** http://www.pcwholesale.com. **Description:** Distributes computer systems, peripherals, and supplies to an international client base. PC Wholesale also offers support services. Founded in 1989. **Corporate headquarters location:** This location. **Other U.S. locations:** MN; NJ: GA.

## PEOPLESOFT
233 South Wacker Drive, 45th Floor, Chicago IL 60606. 312/651-8000. **Contact:** Human Resources. **World Wide Web address:** http://www.peoplesoft.com. **Description:** PeopleSoft designs, markets, and supports a wide variety of business software applications. **Corporate headquarters location:** Pleasanton CA. **Other U.S. locations:** Nationwide. **International locations:** Worldwide. **Parent company:** Oracle. **Operations at this facility include:** This location serves as the Midwestern U.S. Regional Headquarters for the company. **Listed on:** NASDAQ. **Stock exchange symbol:** PSFT.

## PITNEY BOWES DOCUMENT MESSAGING TECHNOLOGIES
220 Western Court, Suite 100, Lisle IL 60532. 630/435-7500. **Contact:** Human Resources. **World Wide Web address:** http://www.pbdmt.com. **Description:** Develops information management software for customer service, marketing, and systems integration applications. **Parent company:** Pitney Bowes Inc.

## QUADRAMED
440 North Wells, Suite 505, Chicago IL 60610. 312/396-0700. **Toll-free phone:** 800/634-0800. **Fax:** 312/396-0800. **Contact:** Human Resources. **E-mail address:** resume@quadramed.com. **World Wide Web address:** http://www.quadramed.com. **Description:** Develops and markets specialized decision support software designed to improve the organizational and clinical effectiveness of hospitals, academic medical centers, managed care providers, large physician groups, and other health care providers. **NOTE:** See website for job listings. Apply online or e-mail resumes. Resumes may also be faxed to the company's corporate office in Santa Ana CA at 714/371-1700. **Positions advertised include:** Nurse Consultant; Support Analyst.

## RESOURCE INFORMATION MANAGEMENT SYSTEMS, INC.
500 Technology Drive, Naperville IL 60563. 630/369-5300. **Contact:** Human Resources. **E-mail address:** recruiting@rims.com. **World Wide Web address:** http://www.rims.com. **Description:** Develops software programs to help medical and dental insurance agencies manage their claim systems.

## S.I. TECH, INC.
P.O. Box 609, Geneva IL 60134. 630/761-3640. **Fax:** 630/761-3644. **Contact:** Ramesh Sheth, Human Resources Manager. **World Wide Web address:** http://www.sitech-bitdriver.com. **Description:** Manufactures and markets fiber-optic products such as modems, multiplexers, F.O. hubs, LAN/WAN products, short-haul modems, and cable assemblies for data communications use.

Founded in 1984. **Office hours:** Monday - Friday, 7:00 a.m. - 7:00 p.m. **Corporate headquarters location:** This location. **Listed on:** Privately held.

**SPSS INC.**
233 South Wacker Drive, Suite 1100, Chicago IL 60606. 312/651-3000. **Contact:** Human Resources. **World Wide Web address:** http://www.spss.com. **Description:** Develops, markets, and supports statistical software. **NOTE:** See this company's website for job listings. Apply online.

**SSA GLOBAL**
500 West Madison, Suite 1600, Chicago IL 60661. 312/258-6000. **Fax:** 312/474-7500. **Contact:** Human Resources. **E-mail address:** careersops@ssaglobal.com. **World Wide Web address:** http://www.ssagt.com. **Description:** System Software Associates develops, markets, and supports an integrated line of business application, computer-aided software engineering (CASE), and electronic data interchange (EDI) software, primarily for IBM minicomputers and workstations. **NOTE:** See website for job listings and mail or e-mail resumes. **Corporate headquarters:** This location. **Other U.S. locations:** Nationwide. **International locations:** Worldwide.

**SILVON SOFTWARE INC.**
900 Oakmont Lane, Suite 400, Westmont IL 60559. 630/655-3313. **Contact:** Human Resources. **World Wide Web address:** http://www.silvon.com. **Description:** Develops sales tracking software. **NOTE:** See website for job listings and contact information.

**SOLUCIENT**
1007 Church Street, Suite 700, Evanston IL 60201. 800/366-PLAN. **Contact:** Human Resources. **World Wide Web address:** http://www.solucient.com. **Description:** Solucient provides healthcare business intelligence to the healthcare industry. The company maintains the nation's largest healthcare database, comprised of more than 22.6 million hospital discharges per year. Serving a client base of more than 3,300 customers, Solucient provides information resources to more than 2,000 hospitals, as well as many of the largest pharmaceutical manufacturers in the United States. **Positions advertised include:** Desktop Services Supervisor; Director of Vendor Management; Senior Systems Database Administrator. **Corporate headquarters location:** This location.

**STARTSPOT MEDIAWORKS, INC.**
1840 Oak Avenue, Evanston IL 60201. 847/866-1830. **Fax:** 847/866-1880. **Contact:** Human Resources. **World Wide Web address:** http://www.startspot.com. **Description:** Develops a group of informational websites that work as search engines. StartSpot's sites include: LibrarySpot is library resource site; BookSpot offers book reviews and reading lists, along with lists of authors, publishers, and the latest news on happenings in the book world; GourmetSpot offers advice and links to some of the best recipes, restaurants, culinary equipment, and wine available; EmploymentSpot provides information and related links for jobseekers.

**TECHNIUM, INC.**
8745 West Higgins Road, Suite 350, Chicago IL 60631. 773/380-0555. **Fax:** 773/380-0568. **Contact:** Jim Archuleta, Human Resources. **E-mail address:** jarchuleta@technium.com. **World Wide Web address:**

http://www.technium.com. **Description:** Technium provides computer consulting services focusing on client/server technologies. The company's client base represents a variety of industries, from consumer products and health care to financial services and software. Technium provides a full range of services to deploy client/server applications including architecture planning, application analysis, visualization, and design; graphical user interface development, using Visual C++, Visual Basic, PowerBuilder, and Delphi; object-oriented development with C, C++, and Smalltalk; relational database development in SQL Server, Microsoft Access, Oracle, and Sybase; and decision support systems development using OLAP and Data Warehousing technologies. **NOTE:** E-mail resumes. Entry-level positions are offered. **Special programs:** Training. **Corporate headquarters location:** This location. **Other U.S. locations:** Dallas TX; Milwaukee WI. **Listed on:** Privately held.

## THOMAS ELECTRONICS
300 South LaLonde Avenue, Addison IL 60101. 630/543-6444. **Fax:** 630/543-0287. **Contact:** Human Resources. **World Wide Web address:** http://www.thomaselectronics.com. **Description:** Manufactures deflective yokes for CRTs. **NOTE:** Resumes should be mailed to Thomas Electronics Human Resources Department, 208 Davis Parkway, Clyde NY 14433.

## 3COM CORPORATION
3800 Golf Road, Rolling Meadows IL 60008. 847/262-5000. **Contact:** Human Resources. **World Wide Web address:** http://www.3com.com. **Description:** 3Com is a billion-dollar *Fortune* 500 company delivering global data networking solutions to organizations around the world. 3Com designs, manufactures, markets, and supports a broad range of ISO 9000-compliant global data networking solutions including routers, hubs, remote access servers, switches, and adapters for Ethernet, Token Ring, and high-speed networks. These products enable computers to communicate at high speeds and share resources including printers, disk drives, modems, and minicomputers. **NOTE:** Apply online. **Positions advertised include:** Customer Operations Representative; Program Manager; Software Engineer; Technical Voice Education Developer; Product Engineer.

## TIGER DIRECT
175 Ambassador Drive, Naperville IL 60540. 630/355-3000. **Contact:** Human Resources. **World Wide Web address:** http://www.tigerdirect.com. **Description:** Manufactures a wide variety of computer supplies including hardware, software, and computer office equipment. **Operations at this facility include:** This location is a distribution center.

## UNISYS CORPORATION
333 Butterfield Road, One Unisys Center, Lombard IL 60148. 630/810-8000. **Contact:** Human Resources. **World Wide Web address:** http://www.unisys.com. **Description:** Unisys Corporation provides information services, technology, and software. Unisys specializes in developing critical business solutions based on open information networks. The company's Enabling Software Team creates a variety of software projects that facilitate the building of user applications and the management of distributed systems. The company's Platforms Group is responsible for UNIX Operating Systems running across a wide range of multiple processor server platforms including all peripheral and communication drivers. The Unisys Commercial Parallel Processing Team develops microkernel-based operating systems, I/O device

drivers, ATM hardware, diagnostics, and system architectures. The System Management Group is in charge of the overall management of development programs for UNIX desktop and entry-server products. **Corporate headquarters location:** Blue Bell PA. **Other U.S. locations:** Nationwide. **Operations at this facility include:** This location is a sales office. **Listed on:** New York Stock Exchange. **Stock exchange symbol:** UIS.

**WOLFRAM RESEARCH, INC.**
100 Trade Center Drive, Champaign IL 61820. 217/398-0700. **Fax:** 217/398-0747. **Contact:** Human Resources. **E-mail address:** resumes@wolfram.com. **World Wide Web address:** http://www.wri.com. **Description:** Develops mathematical software and services including Mathematica. **Positions advertised include:** NKS Development Director; Project Assistant; Numerical Computation Developer; Analysis Developer; Symbolic Computation Developer; Software Quality Engineer; Academic Account Sales Executive; Commercial Sales Representative; Technical Product Manager.

# EDUCATIONAL SERVICES

**You can expect to find the following types of companies in this section:**
Business/Secretarial/Data Processing Schools • Colleges/Universities/Professional Schools • Community Colleges/Technical Schools/Vocational Schools • Elementary and Secondary Schools • Preschool and Child Daycare Services

## AURORA UNIVERSITY
347 South Gladstone Avenue, Aurora IL 60506. 630/844-5493. **Fax:** 630/844-5650. **Contact:** Human Resources. **E-mail address:** hr@aurora.edu. **World Wide Web address:** http://www.aurora.edu. **Description:** A private university with an enrollment of approximately 2,000 graduate and undergraduate students. Programs are offered through the School of Business and Professional Studies; the School of Education of George Williams College; the University College of Arts & Sciences; the New College (adult learning center); the School of Nursing; the School of Physical Education, Recreation, and Athletics of George Williams College; and the School of Social Work. **NOTE:** Resumes and cover letters may be faxed, e-mailed, or mailed. Interested jobseekers may also apply online at the university's website. **Positions advertised include:** Assistant Professor (Various); Adjunct Faculty; Assistant Dean of Campus Activities; Director of Publications; Director of Field Experiences; Program Secretary; La Aurora Program Secretary.

## BRADLEY UNIVERSITY
1501 West Bradley Avenue, Peoria IL 61625. 309/676-7611. **Fax:** 309/677-3223. **Contact:** Human Resources. **World Wide Web address:** http://www.bradley.edu. **Description:** A private, four-year university offering both undergraduate and graduate degrees. Programs are offered through the Slane College of Communications and Fine Arts; Engineering and Technology; Education and Health Sciences; Liberal Arts and Sciences; and the Foster College of Business Administration. Founded in 1897. **NOTE:** See website for job listings and contact information. **Office hours:** Monday – Friday, 8:00 a.m. – 5:00 p.m. (closed between noon and 1:00 p.m.) **Corporate headquarters location:** This location.

## CHICAGO STATE UNIVERSITY
9501 South King Drive, Chicago IL 60628. 773/995-2000. **Contact:** Human Resources. **World Wide Web address:** http://www.csu.edu. **Description:** A four-year, state university offering undergraduate and graduate degree programs through its colleges of Arts and Sciences, Business, Education, and Health Sciences. **NOTE:** See website for job listings and contact information. **Office hours:** Monday – Friday, 8:30 a.m. – 5:00 p.m.

## COLLEGE OF LAKE COUNTY
19351 West Washington Street, Grayslake IL 60030. 847/543-2065. **Fax:** 847/223-0824. 223-6601. **Contact:** Human Resources. **E-mail address:** personnel@clcillinois.edu. **World Wide Web address:** http://www.clcillinois.edu. **Description:** A two-year community college. College of Lake County offers a

variety of transfer and career preparation programs to over 14,000 students. The college is a nonresidential institution. **NOTE:** See website for job listings, contact information and application procedures. Positions advertised include: Dental Hygiene Instructor; Architectural Technology Instructor; Medical Imaging Instructor; Director of Nursing Education. **Office hours:** Monday – Friday, 8:00 a.m. – 4:30 p.m.

## COLUMBIA COLLEGE
600 South Michigan Avenue, Chicago IL 60605-1996. 312/663-1600. **Contact:** Human Resources. **World Wide Web address:** http://www.colum.edu. **Description:** A college offering bachelor's and master's degrees and specializing in communications, media, applied and fine arts, theatrical and performing arts, and management and marketing. Columbia College's enrollment is approximately 7,300 students. At the graduate level, Columbia offers the master of arts degree in seven disciplines: arts, entertainment, and media management; teaching of writing; dance/movement therapy; interdisciplinary arts; journalism; multicultural education; and photography. The master of fine arts degree is awarded in creative writing, film and video, and photography. **NOTE:** See website for job listings, contact information and application procedures. **Positions advertised include:** Attorney; Director of L.A. Semester; Coordinator of Sports Management; Professor (Various).

## DEVRY INSTITUTE OF TECHNOLOGY
3300 North Campbell Avenue, Chicago IL 60618. 773/929-8500. **Fax:** 773/348-1780. **Contact:** Peggy O'Brien, Human Resources Manager. **World Wide Web address:** http://www.chi.devry.edu. **Description:** A technical training institute that provides courses in electronics technology, computer information systems, business operations, telecommunications management, accounting, and technical management. Founded in 1931. **Corporate headquarters location:** Oakbrook Terrace IL. **International locations:** Canada. **Listed on:** New York Stock Exchange. **Stock exchange symbol:** DV.

## EASTERN ILLINOIS UNIVERSITY
600 West Lincoln Avenue, Charleston IL 61920. 217/581-3463. **Fax:** 217/581-7266. **Contact:** Human Resources. **World Wide Web address:** http://www.eiu.edu. **Description:** A four-year, state university offering a variety of degree programs to approximately 9,200 undergraduate and 1,400 graduate students. **NOTE:** An application must be completed for any open position. Interested jobseekers must apply in person at the Human Resources office on Tuesdays and Thursdays from 8:00 a.m. – 4:30 p.m.

## ELMHURST COLLEGE
190 Prospect Avenue, Elmhurst IL 60126. 630/617-3016. **Fax:** 630/617-3746. **Recorded jobline:** 630/617-3779. **Contact:** Kathryn Patera, Human Resources Secretary. **E-mail address:** kathyp@elmhurst.edu. **World Wide Web address:** http://www.elmhurst.edu. **Description:** A four-year, private, liberal arts college affiliated with the United Church of Christ. The college has 22 academic departments and offers 48 majors. Preprofessional studies in dentistry, medicine, law, engineering, and theology are also offered. Founded in 1871. **NOTE:** Entry-level positions and second and third shifts are offered. **Special programs:** Internships; Apprenticeships; Summer Jobs. **Office hours:** Monday - Friday, 8:30 a.m. - 5:00 p.m.

## GOVERNORS STATE UNIVERSITY
One University Parkway, University Park IL 60466. 708/534-5000. **Contact:** Human Resources. **World Wide Web address:** http://www.govst.edu. **Description:** A state university offering 42 degree programs to juniors, seniors, and master's candidates. **NOTE:** See website for job listings and contact and application information.

## HAROLD WASHINGTON COLLEGE
30 East Lake Street, Chicago IL 60601. 312/553-5600. **Contact:** Steve Crosby, Director of Personnel. **World Wide Web address:** http://www.hwashingtonccc.edu. **Description:** A four-year college operating as part of the City Colleges of Chicago system. The college offers associate's degrees and certificates to approximately 9,400 students. **NOTE:** Apply online at the college's website or visit the Human Resources Office during regular business hours. **Office hours:** Monday – Friday, 9:00 a.m. – 4:30 p.m.

## HARPER COLLEGE
1200 West Algonquin Road, Palatine IL 60067. 847/925-6000. **Contact:** Human Resources. **World Wide Web address:** http://www.harpercollege.edu. **Description:** A community college offering associate's degrees and certificates to approximately 23,000 students. **NOTE:** Harper College no longer will accept mailed or faxed resumes. Apply online at its website. **Positions advertised include:** Counselor; Instructors (Various); Professors (Various); Student Development Specialist; Coordinator of Accommodations; Secretary; Custodian; Career Mentor; Computer Support and Training.

## ILLINOIS INSTITUTE OF TECHNOLOGY
3300 South Federal Street, Main Building, Room 302, Chicago IL 60616. 312/567-3318. **Fax:** 312/567-3450. 000. **Contact:** Human Resources. **E-mail address:** hr@iit.edu. **World Wide Web address:** http://www.iit.edu. **Description:** A four-year college offering bachelor's, master's (including MBA), and doctoral degrees. Approximately 2,500 undergraduate and 2,500 graduate students attend Illinois Institute of Technology. **NOTE:** The Human Resources Office prefers resumes to be sent via e-mail. **Positions advertised include:** Assistant to the Director; Service Coordinator; Administrative Assistant; Career Specialist; International Student Advisor; Web Programmer; Help Desk Supervisor.

## ILLINOIS STATE UNIVERSITY
Campus Box 1300, Normal IL 61790. 309/438-8311. **Contact:** Human Resources. **World Wide Web address:** http://www.ilstu.edu. **Description:** A four-year, state university offering bachelor's, master's, and doctoral degrees to approximately 20,000 students. **NOTE:** To apply for administrative and professional positions, see website for job listings and contact information. To apply for civil service positions, an application is required and can be obtained on the website or in person at the Human Resources Office in the Nelson Smith Building, Room 101 Applications may also be faxed to Human Resources at 309/438-7421. **Office hours:** Monday – Friday, 7:30 a.m. – 4:30 p.m.

## JOLIET JUNIOR COLLEGE
1215 Houbolt Road, Joliet IL 60431-8938. 815/280-2266. **Fax:** 815/729-3331. **Contact:** Human Resources. **E-mail address:** hr@jjc.edu. **World Wide Web address:** http://www.jjc.cc.il.us. **Description:** A community college offering associate degrees and career and technical degrees and certificates. Founded in

1901. **NOTE:** An application is required. See website to download a copy or contact the Human Resources Office to have one mailed or faxed. Entry-level positions and second and third shifts are offered. **Positions advertised include:** Office Systems Instructor; Pastry and Baking Instructor; Adjunct Faculty (Various).

## KAPLAN UNIVERSITY
550 West Van Buren, 7th Floor, Chicago IL 60607. 312/777-6333. **Fax:** 312-777-6704. **Contact:** Human Resources. **E-mail address:** kaplaninc@trm.brassring.com. **World Wide Web address:** http://www.kaplan.edu. **Description:** Kaplan is an online university offering Associates, Bachelors, Masters, and Certificate programs to students who wish to learn over the Internet. **NOTE:** Search and apply for positions online. **Positions advertised include:** Editorial Assistant; Faculty; Advanced Website Design Technicians. **Corporate headquarters location:** Fort Lauderdale FL.

## LOYOLA UNIVERSITY OF CHICAGO
6525 North Sheridan Road, Chicago IL 60626. 773/274-3000. **Contact:** Human Resources. **World Wide Web address:** http://www.luc.edu. **Description:** A private university and medical center. Loyola University operates four additional campuses in the greater Chicago area including Loyola University Medical Center in Maywood, Lake Shore and Water Tower campuses in Chicago, and Mallinckrodt campus in Wilmette. **NOTE:** See website for staff and faculty job listings and application and resume submission procedures. The Human Resources Office is located at 820 North Michigan Avenue. **Corporate headquarters location:** This location.

## MILLIKIN UNIVERSITY
1184 West Main Street, Decatur IL 62522-2084. 217/362-6416. **Fax:** 217/424-6468. **Contact:** Human Resources. **World Wide Web address:** http://www.millikin.edu. **Description:** A liberal arts university affiliated with the Presbyterian Church. Approximately 2,000 students are enrolled at Millikin University. **NOTE:** See website for job listings and application. Interested jobseekers may apply to open positions by mailing or faxing resumes. Interested jobseekers may also apply in person at the Human Resources Office, Room 212 of Shilling Hall. **Office hours:** Monday – Friday, 8:00 a.m. – 5:00 p.m. **Positions advertised include:** Continuing Education Services Coordinator and Research/Instruction Librarian; Instructor of Nursing; Assistant Professor; Acting Department Chair; Hall Director; Database Analyst; Team Coach (Various); Executive Secretary. **Special programs:** Internships. **Corporate headquarters location:** This location. **Operations at this facility include:** Administration. **Listed on:** Privately held.

## MORAINE VALLEY COMMUNITY COLLEGE
10900 South 88th Avenue, Palos Hills IL 60465. 708/974-4300. **Contact:** Director of Human Resources. **World Wide Web address:** http://www.moraine.cc.il.us. **Description:** A community college offering programs for students who are planning to transfer to a four-year institution. Founded in 1967.

## NATIONAL EDUCATION TRAINING GROUP (NETG)
1751 West Diehl Road, Suite 200, Naperville IL 60563. 630/369-3000. **Toll-free phone:** 877/561-6384. **Fax:** 630/983-4877. **Contact:** Human Resources. **World Wide Web address:** http://www.netg.com. **Description:** A source of products

and services for training and education in the areas of advanced technologies. **NOTE:** Apply online. **Positions advertised include:** Corporate/Financial Analyst; Senior Systems Specialist; Lead Product Development Manager; Contract Analyst; Senior Software Engineer. **Corporate headquarters location:** This location. **Parent company:** Thomson Corporation.

**NATIONAL-LOUIS UNIVERSITY**
1000 Capitol Drive, Wheeling IL 60090. 847/465-0575. **Fax:** 847/465-5610. **Recorded jobline:** 847/465-5400. **Contact:** Human Resources. **World Wide Web address:** http://www.nl.edu. **Description:** A university offering undergraduate and graduate programs to approximately 1,600 students. **NOTE:** See website for job postings and contact information. Entry-level positions, part-time jobs, and second and third shifts are offered. **Positions advertised include:** Administrative Assistant; Enrollment Representative; Associate Director of Alumni Relations; Director of School-College Relations; Construction Manager. **Office hours:** Monday - Friday, 8:30 a.m. - 4:30 p.m. **Corporate headquarters location:** This location. **Other area locations:** Chicago IL; Evanston IL. **Other U.S. locations:** Washington DC; Orlando FL; Tampa FL; Atlanta GA; St. Louis MO; Milwaukee WI.

**NORTHEASTERN ILLINOIS UNIVERSITY**
5500 North St. Louis Avenue, Chicago IL 60625. 773/583-4050. **Contact:** Human Resources. **World Wide Web address:** http://www.neiu.edu. **Description:** A state university serving more than 10,000 commuter students with over 80 graduate and undergraduate programs. **NOTE:** See website for job listings and contact information and application requirements. **Positions advertised include:** Associate Director of Admissions; Clinical Psychologist of Counseling Office; Director of Public Safety; Professor (Various); Assistant Professor (Various); Secretary.

**NORTHERN ILLINOIS UNIVERSITY**
1515 West Lincoln Highway, De Kalb IL 60115. 815/753-6021. **Contact:** Human Resources. **World Wide Web address:** http://www.niu.edu. **Description:** A university comprised of seven colleges offering more than 100 graduate and undergraduate programs to approximately 23,000 students. **NOTE:** See web site for job listings, contact information and application procedures. **Positions advertised include:** Assistant Area Coordinator; Professor (Various); Assistant Professor (Various); Information Technology Associate; Route Driver; Secretary.

**NORTHWESTERN UNIVERSITY**
720 University Place, Evanston IL 60208. 847/491-7507. **Contact:** Human Resources. **E-mail address:** resume@northwestern.edu. **World Wide Web address:** http://www.nwu.edu. **Description:** One of the country's largest private research universities. The university offers academic specialties in 12 colleges to its 17,700 students. **NOTE:** See website for job listings and contact information. **Positions advertised include:** Administrative Secretary; Animal Care Technician; Group Leader; Library Assistant; Research Technologist; Program Assistant.

**OAKTON COMMUNITY COLLEGE**
1600 East Golf Road, Des Plaines IL 60016. 847/635-1675 **Fax:** 847/635-1764. **Contact:** Human Resources. **E-mail address:** hr@oakton.edu. **World Wide Web address:** http://www.oakton.edu. **Description:** A community college offering programs for students who are planning to transfer to a four-year

institution. The college also offers training courses and career programs. **NOTE:** See website for job listings, contact information and application form. **Positions advertised include:** Director of Resource Development; Admission Specialist; Health Services Manager; Learning Center Specialist; Faculty (Various); System Director.

### ROOSEVELT UNIVERSITY
430 South Michigan Avenue, Chicago IL 60605. 312/341-3500. **Contact:** Human Resources. **World Wide Web address:** http://www.roosevelt.edu. **Description:** A university offering graduate and undergraduate programs through its colleges of Arts and Sciences, Business, Education, and Performing Arts. **NOTE:** See website for job listings and application procedures.

### TRUMAN COLLEGE
1145 West Wilson Avenue, Chicago IL 60640. 773/878-1700. **Contact:** Human Resources. **World Wide Web address:** http://www.trumancollege.cc. **Description:** A community college offering automotive, cosmetology, ESL, and continuing education classes. **NOTE:** See website for job listings and contact information. Positions advertised include: Faculty (Various); Nursing Laboratory Coordinator.

### UNIVERSITY OF CHICAGO
956 East 58th Street, Chicago IL 60637. 773/702-8900. **Contact:** Human Resources. **World Wide Web address:** http://www.uchicago.edu. **Description:** A university with a total enrollment of over 12,000 students. Founded in 1892. **NOTE:** Apply online.

### UNIVERSITY OF ILLINOIS AT CHICAGO
715 South Wood Street, Mail Code 862, Chicago IL 60612. 312/996-0840. **Fax:** 312/413-1190. **Contact:** Associate Director of Employment. **World Wide Web address:** http://www.uic.edu. **Description:** One location of the state university offering graduate and undergraduate programs of study to approximately 25,000 students. **NOTE:** Applicants must apply online. **Operations at this facility include:** Administration; Research and Development; Service.

### UNIVERSITY OF ILLINOIS AT SPRINGFIELD
P.O. Box 19243, Springfield IL 62794-9243. 217/206-6600. **Contact:** Human Resources. **World Wide Web address:** http://www.uis.edu. **Description:** One location of the state university specializing in liberal arts and professional studies. The university offers undergraduate and graduate programs of study. Founded in 1969.

### UNIVERSITY OF ILLINOIS AT URBANA-CHAMPAIGN
52 East Gregory Drive, Champaign IL 61820. 217/333-2137. **Contact:** Human Resources. **World Wide Web address:** http://www.uiuc.edu. **Description:** The main campus of the state university. Graduate and undergraduate programs are offered through the colleges of Communications; Liberal Arts and Sciences; Fine and Applied Arts; Agriculture, Consumer, and Environmental Sciences; Commerce and Business Administration; Applied Life Sciences; Library and Information Science; Law; Social Work; Medicine; and Veterinary Medicine.

### WAUBONSEE COMMUNITY COLLEGE
Route 47 at Waubonsee Drive, Building A, Sugar Grove IL 60554. 630/466-4811. **Contact:** Michele Morey, Director of Human Resources. **World Wide Web**

**address:** http://www.wcc.cc.il.us. **Description:** A community college offering occupational programs and programs to students who are planning to transfer to a four-year institution. **Positions advertised include:** Adult Education Student Records Clerk; Bookstore Clerk; Child Care Center Aide; ESL Secretary; Public Safety Cadet; Fitness Center Technical Assistant; Site Manager.

**WESTERN ILLINOIS UNIVERSITY**
One University Circle, 105 Sherman Hall, Macomb IL 61455. 309/298-1971. **Fax:** 309/298-2300. **Contact:** Pam Bowman, Director Human Resources. **World Wide Web address:** http://www.wiu.edu. **Description:** A university offering over 80 graduate and undergraduate programs of study.

**WHEATON COLLEGE**
501 College Avenue, Wheaton IL 60187. 630/752-5060. **Contact:** Human Resources. **E-mail address:** hr@wheaton.edu. **World Wide Web address:** http://www.wheaton.edu. **Description:** A private, coeducational, Christian college with an undergraduate enrollment of 2,300.

# ELECTRONIC/INDUSTRIAL ELECTRICAL EQUIPMENT AND COMPONENTS

**You can expect to find the following types of companies in this section:**
Electronic Machines and Systems • Semiconductor Manufacturers

---

**ADVANCE TRANSFORMER COMPANY**
10275 West Higgins Road, Rosemont IL 60018. 847/390-5000. **Toll-free phone:** 800/322-2086. **Contact:** Human Resources. **World Wide Web address:** http://www.advancetransformer.com. **Description:** Manufactures magnetic and electronic fluorescent lamp ballasts. Advance Transformer Company also manufactures high-intensity discharge ballasts for the starting and regulating of fluorescent and high-intensity discharge lamps. The company focuses primarily in the fields of consumer electronics, consumer products, electrical and electronics components, and professional equipment.

**AMPHENOL CORPORATION**
**FIBER OPTICS DIVISION**
61925A Ohio Street, Lisle IL 60532. 630/960-1010. **Fax:** 630/810-5640. **Contact:** Human Resources. **World Wide Web address:** http://www.amphenol-fiberoptics.com. **Description:** Manufactures fiber optic products. **Parent company:** Amphenol (Wallingford CT).

**BODINE ELECTRIC COMPANY**
2500 West Bradley Place, Chicago IL 60618. 773/478-3515. **Fax:** 773/478-3232. **Contact:** Human Resources. **E-mail address:** careers@bodine-electric.com. **World Wide Web address:** http://www.bodine-electric.com. **Description:** Manufactures fractional horsepower electric motors, gear motors, and motor controls. Founded in 1905. **NOTE:** Entry-level positions and second and third shifts are offered. **Other U.S. locations:** Peosta IA. **Operations at this facility include:** Administration; Manufacturing; Research and Development; Sales; Service. **Listed on:** Privately held.

**CII TECHNOLOGIES**
844 East Rockland Road, Libertyville IL 60048-3375. 847/680-7400. **Fax:** 847/680-8169. **Contact:** Human Resources. **World Wide Web address:** http://www.cor.com. **Description:** One of the world's largest suppliers of radio frequency interference (RFI) filters. Products are used to control noise pollution in a wide variety of digital electronic devices. Founded in 1955. **Corporate headquarters location:** This location. **Parent company:** Tyco Electronics. **Listed on:** New York Stock Exchange. **Stock exchange symbol:** TYC.

**CABOT MICROELECTRONICS**
870 North Commons Drive, Aurora IL 60504. 630/375-6631. **Toll-free phone:** 800/811-2756. **Contact:** Human Resources. **E-mail address:** cmc_jobs@cabotcmp.com. **World Wide Web address:** http://www.cabotcmp.com. **Description:** The leading supplier of polishing compounds and a provider of polishing pads used in the manufacture of advanced semiconductors (chips) and rigid disks. **Positions advertised**

**include:** Facilities Operations Team Leader; Seafety, Health & Environmental Specialist; IT Engineer; Director of Investor Relations; Sr. Supply Manager; Assistant Treasurer; Patent Agent; Internal Audit Manager; Distribution Specialist.

**THE CHERRY ELECTRICAL CORPORATION**
3600 Sunset Avenue, Waukegan IL 60087. 847/662-9200. **Contact:** Human Resources. **World Wide Web address:** http://www.cherrycorp.com. **Description:** Manufactures and distributes a wide range of electrical components for the computer, automotive, consumer, and commercial markets worldwide. The principal segments are electromechanical devices including snap-action, selector, and special-use switches principally for use in automobiles, home appliances, office and industrial equipment, and vending machines; and electronic assemblies including keyboards, keyboard switches, gas discharge displays, and automotive electronics for use in data entry terminals, automobiles, industrial and commercial control devices, business machines, and amusement products. **Corporate headquarters location:** Pleasant Prairie WI. **Subsidiaries include:** Cherry Automotive Division; Cherry Electrical Products Division; Cherry de Mexico.

**CINCH CONNECTORS**
1700 Finley Road, Lombard IL 60148. 630/705-6000. **Toll-free phone:** 800/323-9612. **Fax:** 630/705-6054. **Contact:** Human Resources. **E-mail address:** careers@cinch.com. **World Wide Web address:** http://www.cinch.com. **Description:** Produces connectors, interconnection systems, IC sockets, relay sockets, tube sockets, terminal strips, barrier blocks, crimp terminals, communications cross-connect systems, harness assemblies, and adapters. Major markets served include military/aerospace, telecommunications, computer and instrumentation, and automotive. **Operations at this facility include:** Administration; Divisional Headquarters; Manufacturing; Research and Development; Sales; Service.

**CLINTON ELECTRONICS CORPORATION**
6701 Clinton Road, Loves Park IL 61111. 815/633-1444. **Toll-free phone:** 800/447-3306. **Fax:** 815/633-8712. **Contact:** Employee Relations Supervisor. **World Wide Web address:** http://www.cec-displays.com. **Description:** Manufactures cathode ray tubes for use in computer screens.

**COGNEX CORPORATION**
850 East Diehl Road, Suite 125, Naperville IL 60563. 630/505-9990. **Fax:** 630/505-9995. **Contact:** Human Resources. **World Wide Web address:** http://www.cognex.com. **Description:** Designs, develops, manufactures, and markets machine vision systems used to automate a wide range of manufacturing processes. Cognex machine vision systems are used in the electronics, semiconductor, pharmaceutical, health care, aerospace, automotive, packaging, and graphic arts industries to gauge, guide, inspect, and identify products in manufacturing operations. **NOTE:** Resumes should be sent to Human Resources, Cognex Corporation, One Vision Drive, Natick MA 01760-2059. Fax: 508/650-3340. **Corporate headquarters location:** Natick MA. **Other U.S. locations:** CA. **International locations:** France; Germany; Japan; Singapore; United Kingdom. **Operations at this facility include:** This location is the company's Midwest Regional Technology Center. **Listed on:** NASDAQ. **Stock exchange symbol:** CGNX.

## COOPER INDUSTRIES, INC.
1830 Howard Street, Suite B, Elk Grove Village IL 60007. 847/228-1199. **Contact:** Human Resources. **E-mail address:** egv.recrult@cooperlighting.corn. **World Wide Web address:** http://www.cooperlighting.com. **Description:** The Cooper Lighting Division of Cooper Industries produces lighting fixtures sold under the Lumark, McGraw-Edison, Sure-Lites, Iris, Optiance, Halo, and Metalux brand names. Products include indoor and outdoor lighting, recessed and track lighting, fluorescent lighting, and vandal-resistant lighting products. Overall, Cooper Industries manufactures electrical power equipment, tools and hardware, automotive products, and petroleum and industrial equipment. **NOTE:** Apply online. **Corporate headquarters location:** Peachtree City GA.

## DICKEY-JOHN CORPORATION
P.O. Box 10, Auburn IL 62615. 217/438-3371. **Toll-free phone:** 800/637-2952. 2243. **Fax:** 217/438-3623. **Contact:** Human Resources. **World Wide Web address:** http://www.dickey-john.com. **Description:** DICKEY-john Corporation is an electronic design and manufacturing company. Products include application control systems, grain moisture monitoring equipment, ice control systems, and hand-held analytical viscometers. The company's primary markets are the agriculture, public works, and construction industries. **NOTE:** See website for job listings and apply online. **Special programs:** Internships. **Corporate headquarters location:** This location. **Parent company:** Churchill Companies. **Operations at this facility include:** Administration; Manufacturing; Research and Development; Sales; Service.

## DUKANE CORPORATION
2900 Dukane Drive, St. Charles IL 60174. 630/584-2300. **Fax:** 630/584-2370. **Contact:** Human Resources. **E-mail address:** hr@dukane.com. **World Wide Web address:** http://www.dukane.com. **Description:** An electronics firm operating through four divisions: Communications; Audio/Visual; Ultrasonics; and Sea Com, which manufactures underwater locators for aircraft.

## EESCO, INC.
3939 South Karlov Avenue, Chicago IL 60632-3813. 773/376-8750. **Fax:** 773/376-8288. **Contact:** Paul Morris, Human Resources. **World Wide Web address:** http://www.eescodist.com. **Description:** A wholesale distributor of electrical, electronic, and communication systems products. **NOTE:** Interested jobseekers may also apply in person. **Corporate headquarters location:** This location. **Other U.S. locations:** FL; GA; IN; MI; MN; SC; WI. **Operations at this facility include:** Sales. **Listed on:** Privately held.

## EGS ELECTRICAL GROUP
9377 West Higgins Road, Rosemont Il 60018. 847/679-7800. **Fax:** 847/763-6011. **Contact:** Human Resources. **E-mail address:** recruiter@egseg.com. **World Wide Web address:** http://www.egseg.com. **Description:** Manufactures electronic components such as conduit bodies and boxes, plugs and receptacles, industrial lighting fixtures, cord reels, and junction bodies. **NOTE:** E-mail or fax resumes. **Positions advertised include:** Customer Service Representative; Quality Engineer; **Corporate headquarters location:** This location. **Parent company:** Emerson Electric Company and SPX Corporation

## ELECTRO SWITCH
60 Orland Square Drive, Suite 5, Orland Park IL 60462. 708/226-6982. **Contact:** Human Resources. **World Wide Web address:** http://www.electro-nc.com.

**Description:** Designs and manufactures electromechanical switches and controls. **Corporate headquarters location:** Raleigh NC. **Operations at this facility include:** Administration; Manufacturing; Research and Development; Sales; Service.

## FEDERAL SIGNAL CORPORATION
## SIGNAL DIVISION
2645 Federal Signal Drive, University Park IL 60466-3195. 708/534-4756. **Fax:** 708/534-4852. **Contact:** Peggy Szumski, Human Resources Representative. **World Wide Web address:** http://www.fedsig.com. **Description:** A manufacturer of audio and visual emergency warning equipment for vehicle and industrial applications. **NOTE:** See the corporate website, http://www.federalsignaljobs.com, for job listings and contact information. **Positions advertised include:** Customer Service Representative; Marketing Manager; Project Coordinator; Quality Manager; Regional Systems Sales Manager; Section Manager; Senior Mechanical Engineer. **Special programs:** Training. **Corporate headquarters location:** Oak Brook IL. **Operations at this facility include:** This location is manufactures signals.

## G&W ELECTRIC COMPANY
3500 West 127th Street, Blue Island IL 60406. 708/388-5010. **Contact:** Human Resources. **E-mail address:** hr@gwelec.com. **World Wide Web address:** http://www.gwelec.com. **Description:** Manufactures power cable terminals, switches, and splices. **Corporate headquarters location:** This location. **Operations at this facility include:** Administration; Manufacturing; Research and Development; Sales; Service. **Listed on:** Privately held.

## GRAYHILL, INC.
561 Hillgrove Avenue, LaGrange IL 60525. 708/354-1040. **Fax:** 708/354-2820. **Contact:** Human Resources. **E-mail address:** resumes@grayhill.com. **World Wide Web address:** http://www.grayhill.com. **Description:** Manufactures rotary, push-button, and DIP switches, keyboards and keypads, encoders, wireless products, I/O modules, and industrial control systems. **Corporate headquarters location:** This location. **Other U.S. locations:** Carpentersville IL; Fox River Grove IL; Iola WI. **Operations at this facility include:** Administration; Manufacturing; Research and Development; Sales. **Listed on:** Privately held.

## GUARDIAN ELECTRIC MANUFACTURING COMPANY
1425 Lake Avenue, Woodstock IL 60098. 815/337-0050. **Fax:** 815/337-0377. **Contact:** Human Resources. **World Wide Web address:** http://www.guardian-electric.com. **Description:** Manufactures electromechanical components and relays.

## ISCO INTERNATIONAL
1001 Cambridge Drive, Elk Grove Village IL 60007. 847/391-9400. **Fax:** 847/299-9609. **Contact:** Human Resources. **World Wide Web address:** http://www.iscointl.com. **Description:** A global supplier of RF management and interference-control solutions for the wireless telecommunications industry. **Positions advertised include:** Wireless Salesperson.

## INTERMATIC, INC.
7777 Winn Road, Intermatic Plaza, Spring Grove IL 60081. 815/675-2321. **Contact:** Human Resources. **World Wide Web address:** http://www.intermatic.com. **Description:** A manufacturer of electromechanical

and electronic timers and photo controls. **NOTE:** Apply online at this company's website.

### INVENSYS CLIMATE CONTROLS AMERICA
191 East North Avenue, Carol Stream IL 60188. 630/260-3402. **Contact:** Human Resources. **World Wide Web address:** http://www.icca.invensys.com. **Description:** Manufactures thermostats, smoke detectors, and carbon monoxide detectors. **NOTE:** See website for job listings.

### KINETICSYSTEMS COMPANY, LLC
900 North State Street, Lockport IL 60441. 815/838-0005. **Fax:** 815/838-0095. **Contact:** Human Resources. **World Wide Web address:** http://www.kscorp.com. **Description:** A manufacturer of high-performance data acquisition and control systems. Products include modules such as analog to digital converters; digital to analog converters; signal conditioners; timers; counters; buffer memories; computer interfaces; software packages and drivers; mainframes; and VXI slot-0 controllers. Founded in 1970.

### LITTELFUSE, INC.
800 East Northwest Highway, Des Plaines IL 60016. 847/824-1188. **Fax:** 847/391-0434. **Contact:** Human Resources. **World Wide Web address:** http://www.littelfuse.com. **Description:** Manufactures a wide variety of fuses. **Special programs:** Internships. **Corporate headquarters location:** This location. **Other area locations:** Arcola IL. **Other U.S. locations:** TX. **International locations:** Worldwide. **Operations at this facility include:** Administration; Manufacturing; Research and Development; Sales; Service.

### MOLEX INC.
2222 Wellington Court, Lisle IL 60532. 630/969-4550. **Contact:** Human Resources. **World Wide Web address:** http://www.molex.com. **Description:** Designs, manufactures, and distributes electrical and electronic devices such as terminals, connectors, switches, and related application tooling. Products are used by television, stereo, home computer, electronic game, audio, video, and other consumer manufacturing firms, as well as by the automotive and farm equipment industries. Founded in 1938. **NOTE:** Apply online for corporate positions. **Corporate headquarters location:** This location. **Other area locations:** Addison IL; Downers Grove IL; Schaumburg IL.

### NEWARK ELECTRONICS
4801 North Ravenswood Avenue, Chicago IL 60640. 773/784-5100. **Fax:** 773/907-5218. **Contact:** Human Resources. **World Wide Web address:** http://www.newark.com. **Description:** An electronics distributor with sales offices located throughout North America. **Positions advertised include:** Customer Database Specialist; Senior Financial Analyst; Director of Product Management; Government Associate Marketing Manager. **Corporate headquarters location:** Leeds, England. **Operations at this facility include:** Administration; Divisional Headquarters.

### NEWARK INONE
1919 South Highland Avenue, A320, Lombard IL 60148-6119. **Toll-free phone:** 800/263-9275. **Fax:** 630/424-8048. **Contact:** Human Resources. **E-mail address:** chicago@newarkinone.com. **World Wide Web address:** http://www.newark.com. **Description:** A sales office of the electronics distributor Newark Electronics. **Positions advertised include:** Account Representative.

## NORTHROP GRUMMAN CORPORATION
600 Hicks Road, Room U-3100, Rolling Meadows IL 60008. 847/259-9600. **Contact:** Human Resources. **E-mail address:** northgrum@rpc.webhire.com. **World Wide Web address:** http://www.northropgrumman.com. **Description:** Northrop Grumman makes military aircraft, commercial aircraft parts, and electronic systems. Northrop Grumman has developed the B-2 Spirit Stealth Bomber, as well as parts for the F/A-18 and the Boeing 747. Other operations include computer systems development for management and scientific applications and radar equipment. **NOTE:** This company provides job listings for all its locations on its website. See website for job listings and apply online. **Positions advertised include:** Rates and Budgets; Mechanical Technician; Business Planner; Electronics Engineer; Systems Engineer. **Special programs:** Internships. **Corporate headquarters location:** Los Angeles CA. **Operations at this facility include:** This location is engaged in the manufacturing of electronic countermeasures for military applications. **Listed on:** New York Stock Exchange. **Stock exchange symbol:** NOC.

## OPW FUEL MANAGEMENT SYSTEMS
6900 Santa Fe Drive, Hodgkins IL 60525. 708/485-4200. **Contact:** Human Resources. **World Wide Web address:** http://www.petrovend.com. **Description:** Develops automated fuel systems for oil companies. **NOTE:** Apply online. **Positions advertised include:** Service Technician.

## ONEAC CORPORATION
27944 North Bradley Road, Libertyville IL 60048. 847/816-6000. **Toll-free phone:** 800/327-801. **Fax:** 847/680-5124. **Contact:** Human Resources. **E-mail address:** hr@oneac.com. **World Wide Web address:** http://www.oneac.com. **Description:** Manufactures power conditioners that protect electrical systems from lightning and other electrical surges. **NOTE:** Mail resumes and cover letters. **Positions advertised include:** Manufacturing Engineer.

## PANDUIT CORPORATION
17301 South Ridgeland Avenue, Tinley Park IL 60477. 708/532-1800. **Toll-free phone:** 888/506-5400. **Fax:** 708/532-1811. **Contact:** Cheryl Lewis, Supervisor of Corporate Recruiting. **World Wide Web address:** http://www.panduit.com. **Description:** Manufactures electrical wiring components, electrical accessories, and communications products. **NOTE:** See website for job listings and to submit resume. Entry-level positions are offered. **Special programs:** Internships. **Corporate headquarters location:** This location. **Other U.S. locations:** Nationwide. **International locations:** Worldwide. **Listed on:** Privately held.

## RAULAND-BORG CORPORATION
3450 West Oakton Street, Skokie IL 60076. 847/679-0900. **Fax:** 847/679-0793. **Contact:** Human Resources. **E-mail address:** jobs@rauland.com. **World Wide Web address:** http://www.rauland.com. **Description:** Manufactures electronic communications and sound equipment. **Positions advertised include:** Regional Manager. **Corporate headquarters location:** This location. **Operations at this facility include:** Administration; Manufacturing; Research and Development.

## RICHARDSON ELECTRONICS, LTD.
P.O. Box 393, LaFox IL 60147-0393. 630/208-2200. **Fax:** 630/208-2550. **Contact:** Human Resources. **World Wide Web address:** http://www.rell.com. **Description:** An international distributor of electronic components such as

electron tubes, RF and microwave components, semiconductors, and security equipment. **NOTE:** See job listings and contact information on the website. **Positions advertised include:** EDI Programmer; Industrial Engineer; Glassblower; Mechanical Engineer. **Corporate headquarters location:** This location. **International locations:** Worldwide. **Operations at this facility include:** Administration; Sales; Service. **Listed on:** NASDAQ. **Stock exchange symbol:** RELL.

## S&C ELECTRIC COMPANY
6601 North Ridge Boulevard, Chicago IL 60626. 773/338-1000. **Contact:** Human Resources. **World Wide Web address:** http://www.sandc.com. **Description:** Manufactures switchgear and switchboard apparatus. **NOTE:** Apply online.

## SHURE INC.
5800 West Tilley Avenue, Niles IL 60714-4608. 847/600-2000. **Toll-free phone:** 800/2574873. **Fax:** 847/600-6303. **Contact:** Marcie Austen, Human Resources Manager. **E-mail address:** careers@shure.com. **World Wide Web address:** http://www.shure.com. **Description:** Manufactures a wide range of electronic equipment including microphones, mixers, audio processors, and wireless systems. **NOTE:** See website for job listings. Apply online or fax resume. **Corporate headquarters location:** This location. **Other U.S. locations:** Douglas AZ; El Paso TX. **Operations at this facility include:** Administration; Manufacturing; Research and Development; Sales; Service. **Listed on:** Privately held.

## SIEMENS BUILDING TECHNOLOGIES, INC.
1000 Deerfield Parkway, Buffalo Grove IL 60089. 847/215-1000. **Contact:** Human Resources. **World Wide Web address:** http://www.sbt.siemens.com. **Description:** A designer, manufacturer, and installer of computer-based heating and cooling controls for nonresidential buildings. The company's integrated building systems manage energy usage, HVAC, fire safety, and security. **NOTE:** Apply online at the parent company's website – http:/www.siemens.com. **Parent company:** Siemens.

## SIEMENS ENERGY & AUTOMATION, INC.
1000 McKee Street, Batavia IL 60510. 630/879-6000. **Contact:** Human Resources. **World Wide Web address:** http://www.sea.siemens.com. **Description:** Develops, manufactures, and markets an expanding line of electronic control products and systems for a wide variety of industrial applications. **NOTE:** Apply online. **Other U.S. locations:** Nationwide. **Operations at this facility include:** Administration; Manufacturing; Research and Development; Sales; Service.

## SIMPSON ELECTRIC COMPANY
853 Dundee Avenue, Elgin IL 60120. 847/697-2260. **Fax:** 847/697-2272. **Contact:** Human Resources. **World Wide Web address:** http://www.simpsonelectric.com. **Description:** Manufactures instruments and panel meters.

## SWITCHCRAFT, INC.
5555 North Elston Avenue, Chicago IL 60630. 773/792-2700. **Fax:** 773/792-8529. **Contact:** Debbie Zumsteg, Human Resources Director. **E-mail address:** dzumsteg@switchcraft.com. **World Wide Web address:** http://www.switchcraft.com. **Description:** Manufactures electronic components

including switches, connectors, jacks, plugs, cable assemblies, and cords. **NOTE:** See website for job listings. Fax or e-mail resumes. **Positions advertised include:** CAD Operator; Product Engineer. **Corporate headquarters location:** This location.

**SYSTEM SENSOR**
3825 Ohio Avenue, St. Charles IL 60174. 630/377-6580. **Toll-free phone:** 800/736-7672. **Fax:** 630/377-6593. **Contact:** Human Resources. **E-mail address:** careers@systemsensor.com. **World Wide Web address:** http://www.systemsensor.com. **Description:** Manufactures commercial smoke and heat detection devices. **NOTE:** See website for job listings. E-mail resumes or apply online. **Positions advertised include:** Regional Sales Manager; Senior Material Analyst/Planner; Associate Engineer; Electrical Engineer; Director of Marketing. **Corporate headquarters location:** This location. **Parent company:** Pittway Corporation. **Operations at this facility include:** Advertising; Manufacturing; Research and Development; Sales; Service.

**WELLS-GARDNER ELECTRONICS CORPORATION**
9500 West 55th Street, Suite A, McCook IL 60525. 708/290-2100. **Toll-free phone:** 800/336-6630. **Fax:** 708/290-2200. **Contact:** Gene Ahner, Human Resources Director. **E-mail address:** gahner@wellsgardner.com. **World Wide Web address:** http://www.wgec.com. **Description:** Designs and manufactures CRT video monitors for arcade games, and for the leisure and fitness, automotive, intranet, and video wall markets. Founded in 1925. **Corporate headquarters location:** This location. **Operations at this facility include:** Administration; Engineering and Design; Manufacturing; Research and Development.

**WOODHEAD INDUSTRIES, INC.**
3 Parkway North, Suite 550, Deerfield IL 60015. 847/236-9300. **Physical address:** 3411 Woodhead Drive, Northbrook IL 60062. **Fax:** 847/236-0503. **Contact:** Human Resources. **World Wide Web address:** http://www.woodhead.com. **Description:** Manufactures a wide variety of specialty electrical commercial and industrial products including portable lighting and power boxes.

# ENVIRONMENTAL & WASTE MANAGEMENT SERVICES

**You can expect to find the following types of companies in this section:**
Environmental Engineering Firms • Sanitary Services

---

**ATC**
419 Eisenhower Lane South, Lombard IL 60148-5706. 630/916-7272. **Fax:** 630/916-7013. **Contact:** Human Resources. **World Wide Web address:** http://www.atc-enviro.com. **Description:** Provides comprehensive environmental consulting, engineering, and on-site remediation services throughout the United States for clients including federal, state, and local government agencies. ATC's services include assessment of environmental regulations, investigation of contaminated sites, and the design and engineering of methods to correct or prevent contamination. The company addresses hazardous and non-hazardous contaminants in municipal and industrial water supplies; wastewater and storm water from municipal, industrial, and military installations; groundwater, soils, and air space surrounding these types of complexes; and contaminants in buildings and facilities such as asbestos, lead paint, and radioactive contamination. **NOTE:** Apply online. **Positions advertised include:** Project Scientist; Group Leader/Manager.

**ALVORD, BURDICK & HOWSON**
20 North Wacker Drive, Suite 1401, Chicago IL 60606. 312/236-9147. **Fax:** 312/236-0692. **Contact:** Mr. Bon G. Mui, Partner. **E-mail address:** bmui@abhengineers.com. **World Wide Web address:** http://www.abhengineers.com. **Description:** An environmental consulting and engineering firm that is also engaged in mechanical, civil, and structural engineering. **NOTE:** Mail or e-mail resumes to Mr. Mui.

**ARCADIS GERAGHTY & MILLER, INC.**
35 East Wacker Drive, Suite 1000, Chicago IL 60601. 312/263-6703. **Fax:** 317/231-6514. **Contact:** Phil Hutton, Office Administrator. **World Wide Web address:** http://www.arcadis-us.com. **Description:** A consulting firm that provides environmental and engineering services. The company focuses on the environmental, building, and infrastructure markets. Founded in 1888. **NOTE:** Apply online at the company's website. **Positions advertised include:** Principal Scientist; Engineer. **Corporate headquarters location:** Denver CO. **International locations:** Worldwide. **Listed on:** NASDAQ. **Stock exchange symbol:** ARCAF.

**BLOOM ENGINEERING COMPANY, INC.**
18161 Morris Avenue, Homewood IL 60430. 412/760-8737. **Contact:** Human Resources. **E-mail address:** tfennell@bloomeng.com. **World Wide Web address:** http://www.bloomeng.com. **Description:** Provides innovative energy and environmental solutions to industry. **Positions advertised include:** Combustion Technician; Boiler Technician; Controls Technician. **Corporate headquarters location:** Pittsburgh PA.

## CH2M HILL
8501 West Higgins Road, Suite 300,Chicago IL 60631-2801. 773/693-3809. **Contact:** Human Resources. **World Wide Web address:** http://www.ch2m.com. **Description:** CH2M Hill is a group of employee-owned companies operating under the names CH2M Hill, Inc., Industrial Design Corporation, Operations Management International, CH2M Hill International, and CH2M Hill Engineering. The professional staff includes specialists in environmental engineering, waste management, water management, transportation, industrial facilities, and a broad spectrum of infrastructure systems. **NOTE:** This company has offices throughout Chicago, Illinois and the United States. See website for job listings and apply online. **Operations at this facility include:** This location provides transportation and environmental engineering services.

## CLAYTON GROUP SERVICES, INC.
3140 Finley Road, Downers Grove IL 60515. 630/795-3200. **Fax:** 630/795-1130. **Contact:** Human Resources. **E-mail address:** hr@claytongrp.com. **World Wide Web address:** http://www.claytongrp.com. **Description:** An environmental consulting firm that also offers occupational health and safety, strategic environmental management, environmental risk management, and laboratory services. **NOTE:** Resumes may be sent to Human Resources, 45525 Grand River Avenue, Suite 200, Novi, MI 48374; or, they may be faxed to 248/344-0229. Indicate job code in cover letter.

## CLEAN HARBORS, INC.
11800 South Stony Island Avenue, Chicago IL 60617. 773/646-6202. **Fax:** 773/646-6381. **Contact:** Human Resources. **World Wide Web address:** http://www.cleanharbors.com. **Description:** Clean Harbors, Inc., through its subsidiaries, provides comprehensive environmental services in 35 states in the Northeast, Midwest, Central, and Mid-Atlantic regions. Clean Harbors provides a wide range of hazardous waste management and environmental support services to a diversified customer base from over 40 locations. The company's hazardous waste management services include treatment, storage, recycling, transportation, risk analysis, site assessment, laboratory analysis, site closure, and disposal of hazardous materials through environmentally sound methods including incineration. Environmental remediation services include emergency response, surface remediation, groundwater restoration, industrial maintenance, and facility decontamination. **NOTE:** See website for job listings and contact information. **Positions advertised include:** Field Technician. **Corporate headquarters location:** Braintree MA. **Other U.S. locations:** Nationwide.

## CONESTOGA ROVERS & ASSOCIATES
8615 West Bryn Mawr, Chicago IL 60631. 773/380-9933. **Contact:** Human Resources. **World Wide Web address:** http://www.craworld.com. **Description:** An environmental engineering and consulting firm. Founded in 1976. Apply online at this company's website.

## CONSOER TOWNSEND ENVIRODYNE ENGINEERS, INC.
303 East Wacker Drive, Suite 600, Chicago IL 60601. 312/938-0300. **Fax:** 312/938-1109. **Contact:** Director of Human Resources. **E-mail address:** jobs@cte-eng.com. **World Wide Web address:** http://www.cte-eng.com. **Description:** Provides engineering consulting for highways, airports, and waste management projects. **NOTE:** Apply online at the company's website or e-mail resumes.

**FRAMATOME ANP DE&S**
215 Shuman Boulevard, Suite 172, Naperville IL 60563. 630/778-0100. **Fax:** 630/778-4343. **Contact:** Human Resources Department. **World Wide Web address:** http://www.framatome.com. **Description:** Engaged in environmental engineering and consulting with an expertise in nuclear engineering and management. **NOTE:** Entry-level positions are offered. **Special programs:** Internships; Co-ops; Summer Employment.

**GABRIEL ENVIRONMENTAL SERVICES**
1421 North Elston Avenue, Chicago IL 60622. 773/486-2123. **Fax:** 773/486-0004. **Contact:** Human Resources. **World Wide Web address:** http://www.gabrielenvironmental.com. **Description:** Provides environmental consulting, fieldwork, and laboratory services. **Special programs:** Internships. **Corporate headquarters location:** This location.

**GREAT LAKES ANALYTICAL**
1380 Busch Parkway, Buffalo Grove IL 60089. 847/808-7766. **Fax:** 847/808-7772. **Contact:** Human Resources. **World Wide Web address:** http://www.glalabs.com. **Description:** An analytical laboratory that provides a full spectrum of environmental analyses on soil, water, and waste samples. Founded in 1990. **NOTE:** Entry-level positions, part-time jobs, and second and third shifts are offered. **Special programs:** Co-ops; Summer Jobs. **Corporate headquarters location:** This location. **Other U.S. locations:** AZ; CA; CO; HI; NV; OR; PA; TX; WA. **Listed on:** Privately held.

**GREELEY AND HANSEN**
100 South Wacker Drive, Suite 1400, Chicago IL 60606. 312/558-9000. **Contact:** Human Resources. **E-mail address:** careers@greeley-hansen.com. **World Wide Web address:** http://www.greeley-hansen.com. **Description:** A consulting engineering firm specializing in water and wastewater treatment. The company also provides construction management, design engineering, and operations assistance. **Positions advertised include:** Civil Engineer; Management Consultant; Administrative Support. **Listed on:** Privately held.

**HANDEX OF ILLINOIS**
1701 West Quincy Avenue, Naperville IL 60540. 630/527-1666. **Contact:** Human Resources. **World Wide Web address:** http://www.handex.com. **Description:** Provides environmental services including overseeing the installation and removal of underground storage tanks, as well as groundwater and soil sampling. **NOTE:** To apply for a position, contact Paula Griffin, Human Resources Director, Handex Group, Inc., 30914 Suneagle Drive, Mt. Dora FL 32757; 800/989-3753 (phone); 352/735-1904 (fax). **Corporate headquarters location:** Dora FL.

**HARDING ESE**
8901 North Industrial Road, Peoria IL 61615. **Toll-free phone:** 800/373-1999. **Fax:** 309/692-9364. **Contact:** Human Resources. **World Wide Web address:** http://www.mactec.com. **Description:** An engineering and consulting company providing environmental and infrastructure services to commercial and municipal clients, as well as to state and federal government agencies. Founded in 1965. **NOTE:** Send resumes to: Harding ESE, Human Resources, 440 North Cumberland Avenue, Suite 250, Chicago IL 60656. **Positions advertised include:** Lead CADD Operator; Principal Engineer; Senior Bridge Engineer; Senior Civil/Transportation Engineer; Wastewater Treatment Operator. **Special programs:** Internships; Co-ops. **Office hours:** Monday - Friday, 8:00 a.m. - 5:00

p.m. **Other U.S. locations:** Nationwide. **Parent company:** MACTEC, Inc. **Listed on:** Privately held.

## LANDAUER, INC.

2 Science Road, Glenwood IL 60425. 708/755-7000. **Toll-free phone:** 800/323-8830. **Fax:** 708/755-7016. **Contact:** Lana Gowen, Human Resources. **World Wide Web address:** http://www.landauerinc.com. **Description:** Provides environmental testing services that determine exposure to occupational and environmental radiation hazards. The company also provides radiation dosimetry services to a number of industries in which radiation is a threat to employees. Founded in 1954.

## TEST AMERICA

1090 Rock Road Lane, Suite 11, East Dundee IL 60118. 847/783-4960. **Fax:** 847/783-4969. **Contact:** Human Resources. **World Wide Web address:** http://www. testamericainc.com. **Description:** Performs testing of wastewater, hazardous waste, and food. **NOTE:** See website for job listings and contact information. **Operations at this facility include:** Service; Sales.

## WASTE MANAGEMENT, INC.

720 East Butterfield Road, Lombard IL 60148. 630/572-8800. **Contact:** Human Resources Manager. **World Wide Web address:** http://www.wm.com. **Description:** An international provider of comprehensive waste management services as well as engineering, construction, industrial, and related service. **Corporate headquarters location:** Houston TX. **International locations:** Worldwide. **Listed on:** New York Stock Exchange. **Stock exchange symbol:** WMI.

# FABRICATED METAL PRODUCTS AND PRIMARY METALS

## You can expect to find the following types of companies in this section:
Aluminum and Copper Foundries • Die-Castings • Iron and Steel Foundries • Steel Works, Blast Furnaces, and Rolling Mills

---

### ALLIED TUBE & CONDUIT CORPORATION
16100 South Lathrop Avenue, Harvey IL 60426. 708/339-1610. **Toll-free phone:** 800/882-5543. **Fax:** 708/339-2399. **Contact:** Human Resources. **World Wide Web address:** http://www.alliedtube.com. **Description:** Manufactures steel tubing for a variety of commercial and industrial uses. **Parent company:** Tyco International.

### AMSTED INDUSTRIES
205 North Michigan Avenue, 44th Floor, Chicago IL 60601. 312/645-1700. **Fax:** 312/819-8494. **Contact:** Human Resources. **E-mail address:** jobs@amsted.com. **World Wide Web address:** http://www.amsted.com. **Description:** Amsted Industries manufactures steel industrial products for the railroad and construction industries. **Corporate headquarters location:** This location. **Other U.S. locations:** Nationwide. **Operations at this facility include:** This location houses administrative offices. **Listed on:** Privately held.

### BOHLER-UDDEHOLM CORPORATION
4902 Tollview Drive, Rolling Meadows IL 60008. 847/577-2220. **Contact:** Human Resources Manager. **World Wide Web address:** http://www.bohler-uddeholm.com. **Description:** A steel distributor. This location also hires seasonally. **NOTE:** Entry-level positions and part-time jobs are offered. **Special programs:** Internships; Summer Jobs. **Corporate headquarters location:** This location. **Other U.S. locations:** Nationwide. **International locations:** Austria; Canada; Germany; Sweden. **Operations at this facility include:** Administration. **Listed on:** Privately held. **Number of employees worldwide:** 10,000.

### CENTRAL STEEL AND WIRE COMPANY
3000 West 51st Street, Chicago IL 60632. 773/471-3800. **Toll-free phone:** 800/232-9279. **Contact:** Matthews Professional Employment, Inc. **E-mail address:** ppaulmatthews@aol.com. **World Wide Web address:** http://www.centralsteel.com. **Description:** Distributes many types and forms of processed and non-processed, ferrous and nonferrous metals purchased from producing mills and specialty mills. **NOTE:** To apply for positions, contact Matthews Professional Employment via e-mail or fax at 847/249-1133.

### CHICAGO EXTRUDED METALS COMPANY
1601 South 54th Avenue, Cicero IL 60804. 708/656-7900. **Fax:** 708/780-3479. **Contact:** Human Resources. **World Wide Web address:** http://www.cxm.com. **Description:** Manufactures screw machine products, brass wire rods, and other related products. **NOTE:** Apply online. **Corporate headquarters location:** This location.

## COMMERCIAL FORGED PRODUCTS
5757 West 65th Street, Bedford Park IL 60638. 708/458-1220. **Fax:** 708/458-9346. **Contact:** Human Resources. **World Wide Web address:** http://www.commercialforged.com. **Description:** Engaged in upset forging of spindles, axles, drill bits, and tie rods. **Corporate headquarters location:** Oakbrook Terrace IL. **Listed on:** Privately held.

## COPPERWELD
1855 East 122nd Street, Chicago IL 60633. 773/646-4500. **Toll-free phone:** 800/733-5683. **Fax:** 773/646-6128. **Contact:** Human Resources Coordinator. **World Wide Web address:** http://www.copperweld.com. **Description:** Manufactures and sells welded steel tubing. Products are used in low- and medium-rise construction; automotive, railroad and industrial equipment; farm implements and equipment; boat, car, and truck trailers; and industrial storage facilities. **Corporate headquarters location:** Pittsburgh PA. **International locations:** United Kingdom. **Number of employees worldwide:** 2,900.

## A. FINKL & SONS COMPANY
2011 North Southport Avenue, Chicago IL 60614. 773/975-2624. **Fax:** 773/975-2636. **Contact:** Human Resources. **E-mail address:** Jobs@Finkl.com. **World Wide Web address:** http://www.finkl.com. **Description:** A steel forgings manufacturer with domestic and international warehousing operations. A. Finkl & Sons manufactures custom forgings, plastic mold steel, and hot work die steel. **Corporate headquarters location:** This location. **Operations at this facility include:** Administration; Manufacturing; Sales; Service. **Listed on:** Privately held.

## INTERLAKE MATERIAL HANDLING, INC.
1230 East Diehl Road, Suite 400, Naperville IL 60563. 630/245-8800. **Toll-free phone:** 800/468-3752. **Fax:** 630/245-8906. **Contact:** Human Resources. **E-mail address:** career@interlake.com. **World Wide Web address:** http://www.interlake.com. **Description:** Operates through two divisions: Engineered Materials Division manufactures ferrous powders used in aircraft parts; Handling Division produces warehouse storage equipment, conveyor systems, and inventory control systems. **NOTE:** Visit the company's website to review job listings. E-mail resumes indicating desired position. **Positions advertised include:** Designer; Business Development Manager. **Corporate headquarters location:** This location.

## EARLE M. JORGENSEN COMPANY
1900 Mitchell Boulevard, Schaumburg IL 60193. 847/301-6100. **Fax:** 847/301-6114. **Contact:** Human Resources. **World Wide Web address:** http://www.emjmetals.com. **Description:** A full-line steel and aluminum distributor with approximately 40 domestic and international locations. **Corporate headquarters location:** Brea CA. **Other U.S. locations:** Nationwide. **Listed on:** Privately held.

## MACLEAN FASTENERS
## MACLEAN-FOGG COMPANY
1000 Allanson Road, Mundelein IL 60060. 847/566-0010. **Toll-free phone:** 800/323-4536. **Fax:** 847/566-0026. **Contact:** Human Resources. **World Wide Web address:** http://www.maclean-fogg.com. **Description:** Manufactures fasteners including nuts and bolts. Founded in 1925. This is also the location for MacLean Vehicle Systems. **Office hours:** Monday - Friday, 8:00 a.m. - 5:00 p.m.

**Corporate headquarters location:** This location. **Other area locations:** Franklin Park IL; Richmond IL. **Other U.S. locations:** Pocohantas AR; Royal Oak MI. **Listed on:** Privately held.

## MODERN DROP FORGE COMPANY

13810 South Western Avenue, Blue Island IL 60406. 708/388-1806. **Contact:** Human Resources. **World Wide Web address:** http://www.modernforge.com. **Description:** Operates a steel forging plant. **Corporate headquarters location:** This location.

## NATIONAL METALWARES INC.

900 North Russell Avenue, Aurora IL 60506. 630/892-9000. **Fax:** 630/892-2573. **Contact:** Marietta Ryan, Management Recruiter. **E-mail address:** info@nationalmetalwares.com. **World Wide Web address:** http://www.nationalmetalwares.com. **Description:** Manufactures fabricated steel tubing and components. **Corporate headquarters location:** This location. **Parent company:** Varlen Corporation.

## PARKVIEW METAL PRODUCTS

4931 West Armitage Avenue, Chicago IL 60639. 773/622-8414. **Fax:** 73/622-8446. **Contact:** Human Resources. **E-mail address:** HRCHICAGO@parky.com. **World Wide Web address:** http://www.parkviewmetal.com. **Description:** A metal stampings manufacturer servicing metal trades industries nationwide. Parkview Metal Products also builds and maintains progressive dies. **Special programs:** Internships. **Corporate headquarters location:** This location. **Other U.S. locations:** San Marcos TX. **International locations:** Mexico. **Operations at this facility include:** Administration; Manufacturing; Sales.

## PETERSEN ALUMINUM CORPORATION

1005 Tonne Road, Elk Grove Village IL 60007. 847/228-7150. **Contact:** Human Resources. **World Wide Web address:** http://www.pac-clad.com. **Description:** Manufactures and distributes aluminum and steel. Petersen Aluminum also manufactures roofing panels.

## ROCKFORD PRODUCTS CORPORATION

707 Harrison Avenue, Rockford IL 61104-7197. 815/229-4349. **Contact:** Human Resources. **World Wide Web address:** http://www.rpc-usa.com. **Description:** Manufactures metal fasteners. Founded in 1926. **Special programs:** Internships; Training. **Corporate headquarters location:** This location. **Listed on:** Privately held.

## RYERSON TULL

2558 West 16th Street Chicago IL 60608. 773/762-2121. **Fax:** 773/762-0437. **Contact:** Human Resources. **World Wide Web address:** http://www.ryersontull.com. **Description:** Ryerson Tull operates 70 metal service centers and supplies carbon and alloy steel, stainless steel and aluminum, nickel and copper alloys, and a wide range of industrial plastics. Joseph T. Ryerson & Son (also at this location) distributes industrial materials through three divisions: Plastics, Grinding, and Industrial Catalog. Founded in 1842. **Positions advertised include:** Marketing Representative; Corporate Internal Auditor; Inside Sales Professional; Administrative Assistant; Regional Transportation Manager. **Parent company:** Inland Steel Industries, Inc. **Listed on:** New York Stock Exchange. **Stock exchange symbol:** RT.

## RYERSON TULL COILING
720 East 111th Street, Chicago IL 60628. 773/468-2121. **Contact:** Human Resources. **World Wide Web address:** http://www.ryersontull.com. **Description:** A steel works and blast furnace company. **NOTE:** Apply online. **Parent company:** Ryerson Tull. **Listed on:** New York Stock Exchange. **Stock exchange symbol:** RT.

## RYERSON TULL
## JOSEPH T. RYERSON & SON, INC.
P.O. Box 8000, Chicago IL 60680. 773/762-2121. **Physical address:** 2621 West Fifteenth Place, Chicago IL 60608. **Fax:** 773/788-4210. **Contact:** Human Resources. **World Wide Web address:** http://www.ryersontull.com. **Description:** Ryerson Tull operates 70 metal service centers and supplies carbon and alloy steel, stainless steel and aluminum, nickel and copper alloys, and a wide range of industrial plastics. Joseph T. Ryerson & Son (also at this location) distributes industrial materials through three divisions: Plastics, Grinding, and Industrial Catalog. Founded in 1842. **NOTE:** Entry-level positions, part-time jobs, and second and third shifts are offered. **Positions advertised include:** Procurement Specialist; Business Process Improvement Specialist; Direct Sales Representative; Administrative Assistant. **Special programs:** Internships; Training. **Office hours:** Monday - Friday, 8:00 a.m. - 5:00 p.m. **Corporate headquarters location:** This location. **Other U.S. locations:** Nationwide. **Parent company:** Inland Steel Industries, Inc. **Operations at this facility include:** Administration; Manufacturing; Sales; Service. **Listed on:** New York Stock Exchange **Stock exchange symbol:** RT.

## SHEFFIELD STEEL CORPORATION
P.O. Box 727, One Industry Avenue, Joliet IL 60434-0727. 815/723-9335. **Contact:** Human Resources. **World Wide Web address:** http://www.sheffieldsteel.com. **Description:** Operates the largest subsidiary component of Penn Dixie Industries, a multiproduct corporation primarily serving the construction industry. Sheffield Steel Corporation manufactures steel, industrial and welding wire, nails, fencing, welded wire fabric, and other products. Facilities are located in several western and midwestern states. **NOTE:** See website for contact information. **Corporate headquarters location:** Kokomo IN. **Operations at this facility include:** This location manufactures hot-rolled steel merchant bars and lightweight structural steel shapes.

## TEMPEL STEEL COMPANY
5500 North Wolcott, Chicago IL 60640. 773/250-8000. **Fax:** 773/250-8000. **Contact:** Human Resources. **World Wide Web address:** http://www.tempel.com. **Description:** A manufacturer of steel magnetic laminations for electric motors and transformers. **Positions advertised include:** Database Administrator; Programmer Analyst. **Special programs:** Internships. **Corporate headquarters location:** Skokie IL. **Other U.S. locations:** Elk Grove Village IL; Libertyville IL. **Operations at this facility include:** Administration; Divisional Headquarters; Manufacturing. **Listed on:** Privately held.

## TEXTRON FASTENING SYSTEMS
516 18th Avenue, Rockford IL 61104-5181. 815/961-5000. **Fax:** 815/961-5399. **Contact:** Corporate Human Resources Manager. **World Wide Web address:** http://www.camcar.textron.com. **Description:** A world leader in the cold-forming of custom fasteners. **NOTE:** Submit resumes by mail to Textron Fastening Systems – Aerospace, Human Resources Department, 1224 East Warner

Avenue, Santa Ana CA 92707. Resumes may also be faxed to 714/957-2142 or e-mailed to crbrown@tfs.textron.com. **Corporate headquarters location:** Troy MI. **Parent company:** Textron. **Operations at this facility include:** Administration; Manufacturing; Research and Development; Sales; Service. **Number of employees worldwide:** Over 5,000.

## THOMPSON STEEL COMPANY
9470 King Street, Franklin Park IL 60131. 847/678-0400. **Contact:** Human Resources. **World Wide Web address:** http://www.thompsonsteelco.com. **Description:** Engaged in the cold-roll reduction of strip steel. **Corporate headquarters location:** This location.

## U.S. CAN COMPANY
700 East Butterfield, Suite 250, Lombard IL 60148. 630/678-8000. **Contact:** Human Resources. **E-mail address:** humanresources@uscanco.com. **World Wide Web address:** http://www.uscanco.com. **Description:** A manufacturer of metal containers for personal care, household, automotive, paint, and industrial products. In addition, the company manufactures specialty cans. **NOTE:** E-mail resumes and cover letters. **Special programs:** Internships. **Corporate headquarters location:** This location.

## WELLS MANUFACTURING COMPANY
2100 West Lake Shore Drive, Woodstock IL 60098. 815/338-3900. **Contact:** Human Resources. **Description:** National distributor of electric furnace gray and alloyed iron castings, and cast iron bar stock. **Special programs:** Internships. **Corporate headquarters location:** This location.

## WERNER COMPANY
10800 West Belmont Avenue, Franklin Park IL 60131. 847/455-9450. **Contact:** Human Resources. **World Wide Web address:** http://www.wernerco.com. **Description:** Manufactures aluminum extrusions and ladders. **Corporate headquarters location:** Greenville PA.

## FINANCIAL SERVICES

**You can expect to find the following types of companies in this section:**
Consumer Financing and Credit Agencies • Investment Specialists • Mortgage Bankers and Loan Brokers • Security and Commodity Brokers, Dealers, and Exchanges

---

**ABN AMRO PRIVATE EQUITY**
208 South LaSalle Street, 10th Floor, Chicago IL 60604. 312/855-7292. **Fax:** 312/553-6648. **Contact:** Human Resources. **World Wide Web address:** http://www.abnequity.com. **Description:** A venture capital firm that manages more than $300 million of committed capital and is focused on making investments in four broad industries including business services, communications, information technology, and healthcare services. Specific target markets within these broad industry segments include B2B electronic commerce, traditional and e-business services, communications services and infrastructure, Internet applications, and traditional and e-health companies.

**BEAR, STEARNS & COMPANY, INC.**
3 First National Plaza, Chicago IL 60602. 800/753-2327. **Contact:** Human Resources. **World Wide Web address:** http://www.bearstearns.com. **Description:** A leading investment banking and securities trading and brokerage firm serving governments, corporations, institutions, and individuals worldwide. The company offers services in corporate finance, mergers, acquisitions, institutional equities, fixed income sales and trading, derivatives, futures sales and trading, asset management, and custody. **NOTE:** This company provides job listings for all its lo locations on its website. See website and apply online. **Corporate headquarters location:** New York NY. **Other U.S. locations:** Nationwide **International locations:** Worldwide. **Parent company:** The Bear Stearns Companies Inc. **Listed on:** NASDAQ. **Stock exchange symbol:** BSC. **Number of employees nationwide:** 10,500.

**THE CHICAGO BOARD OF TRADE**
141 West Jackson Boulevard, Suite 2080, Chicago IL 60604. 312/435-3494. **Fax:** 312/435-7150. **Contact:** Employment Office. **World Wide Web address:** http://www.cbot.com. **Description:** A commodities, futures, and options exchange. **Positions advertised include:** Trading Systems Analyst; e-CBOT Senior Systems Administrator; Program Office Administrator; Revenue Auditor; Senior Programmer Analyst; Systems Integration Specialist. **Corporate headquarters location:** This location.

**THE CHICAGO BOARD OPTIONS EXCHANGE**
400 South LaSalle Street, Chicago IL 60605. 312/786-7800. **Toll-free phone:** 877/THE-CODE. **Fax:** 312/786-7808. **Contact:** Human Resources. **World Wide Web address:** http://www.cboe.com. **Description:** A nonprofit financial institution engaged in options trading. **NOTE:** Entry-level positions are offered. **Positions advertised include:** Senior Business Analyst; VIP Help Desk Director; Examiner; Investigator; Engineer. **Corporate headquarters location:** This location.

## CHICAGO MERCANTILE EXCHANGE

20 South Wacker Drive, Chicago IL 60606. 312/930-8240. **Fax:** 312/930-2036. **Contact:** Human Resources. **World Wide Web address:** http://www.cme.com. **Description:** One of the world's largest commodities, futures, and options exchanges. **Positions advertised include:** Associate Director of Product Communication; Senior Internal Auditor; Business Analyst; Market Reporter; Assistant General Counsel. **Special programs:** Internships. **Corporate headquarters location:** This location. **Other U.S. locations:** Washington DC; New York NY. **Listed on:** American Stock Exchange. **Stock exchange symbol:** CME.

## CHICAGO STOCK EXCHANGE INC.

440 South LaSalle Street, Chicago IL 60657. 312/663-2526. **Contact:** Human Resources. **E-mail address:** hrrecruiting@chx.com. **World Wide Web address:** http://www.chx.com. **Description:** A stock exchange offering securities trading and depository services. **NOTE:** Send resumes by fax or e-mail only. **Positions advertised include:** Surveillance Investigator; Enforcement Attorney; Senior Programmer Analyst. **Corporate headquarters location:** This location. **Other U.S. locations:** New York NY.

## CODE HENNESSY & SIMMONS LLC

10 South Wacker Drive, Suite 3175, Chicago IL 60606. 312/876-1840. **Fax:** 312/876-3854. **Contact:** Human Resources. **E-mail address:** chs@chsonline.com. **Description:** A private equity investment firm.

## CORNERSTONE CAPITAL HOLDINGS

303 West Madison Street, Suite 1100, Chicago IL 60606. 312/870-5100. **Fax:** 312/673-0239. **Contact:** Human Resources. **World Wide Web address:** http://www.cstonecapital.com. **Description:** A private equity firm investing in manufacturing and industrial service companies with enterprise values ranging from $5 to $30 million. **Other U.S. locations:** Philadelphia PA.

## GLENCOE

222 West Adams Street, Suite 1000, Chicago IL 60606. 312/795-6300. **Contact:** Human Resources. **E-mail address:** info@glencap.com. **World Wide Web address:** http://www.glencap.com. **Description:** Glencoe is a private merchant bank that invests in middle-market companies and provides alternative asset management programs to institutional investors, pension funds, and private investors.

## HOUSEHOLD FINANCE CORPORATION

961 Weigel Drive, Elmhurst IL 60126. 630/617-7000. **Contact:** Human Resources. **World Wide Web address:** http://www.householdfinance.com. **Description:** Household Finance Corporation is one of the oldest and largest independent consumer finance companies in the United States, providing secured and unsecured loans for home improvement, education, bill consolidation, and leisure activities to 1.7 million customers through 400 branches and two regional headquarters. **NOTE:** Apply to job listings found on the company's website. **Positions advertised include:** Underwriter; Sales Assistant Beneficial; Bankruptcy Specialist; Collection Representative; Operations Systems Associate. **Special programs:** Internships. **Other U.S. locations:** San Francisco CA; Wood Dale IL. **Parent company:** Household International (Prospect Heights IL).

## JEFFERIES & COMPANY, INC.
## DERIVATIVES DIRECT
55 West Monroe Street, Suite 3500, Chicago IL 60603. 312/750-4700. **Contact:** Human Resources. **World Wide Web address:** http://www.jefco.com. **Description:** Jefferies & Company is engaged in equity, convertible debt, and taxable fixed income securities brokerage and trading, and corporate finance. Jefferies & Company is one of the leading national firms engaged in the distribution and trading of blocks of equity securities and conducts such activities primarily in the third market. Founded in 1962. **NOTE:** To apply for investment banking positions, contact Dee Dee Bird, Recruiting Coordinator, at dbird@jefco.com or by fax at 310/575-5165. To apply for other positions, contact Mel Locke, Director of People Services at mlocke@jefco.com or via fax at 310/914-1066. **Corporate headquarters location:** Los Angeles CA. **Parent company:** Jefferies Group, Inc. is a holding company that operates several subsidiaries in the securities brokerage and trading, corporate finance, and financial services markets.

## LINCOLN FINANCIAL ADVISORS
8755 West Higgins Road, Suite 550, Chicago IL 60631. 773/380-8518. **Fax:** 773/693-2531. **Contact:** Linda Proskurniak, Vice President of Professional Development. **E-mail address:** Lsproskurniak@LNC.com. **World Wide Web address:** http://www.lfachicago.com. **Description:** Lincoln Financial Advisors markets financial planning, permanent and term life insurance, annuities, disability coverage, and investment products to business owners and professionals. The company also provides complex estate planning and business planning advice. Founded in 1905. **Corporate headquarters location:** Fort Wayne IN. **Other U.S. locations:** Nationwide. **International locations:** Argentina; China; United Kingdom. **Parent company:** Lincoln Financial Group. **Operations at this facility include:** Regional Headquarters; Sales. **Listed on:** New York Stock Exchange. **Stock exchange symbol:** LNC.

## MERRILL LYNCH
33 West Monroe Street, Suite 2200, Chicago IL 60603. 312/269-5100. **Fax:** 312/269-5092. **Contact:** Human Resources. **World Wide Web address:** http://www.ml.com. **Description:** One of the largest securities brokerage firms in the world, Merrill Lynch provides financial services in securities, financial planning, insurance, estate planning, mortgages, and related areas. The company also brokers commodity futures and options, is a major underwriter of new securities issues, and is a dealer in corporate and municipal securities. **NOTE:** This company has other locations throughout Chicago, Illinois and the United States. See website for additional locations and job listings. Apply online. **Special programs:** Internships. **Corporate headquarters location:** New York NY. **Operations at this facility include:** Sales; Service.

## JOHN NUVEEN & COMPANY, INC.
333 West Wacker Drive, 34th Floor, Chicago IL 60606. 312/917-7700. **Toll-free phone:** 800/257-8787. **Fax:** 312/917-8049. **Contact:** Wendy Lindquist, Human Resources Assistant. **World Wide Web address:** http://www.nuveen.com. **Description:** An investment banking company. **Positions advertised include:** Advisor Support Manager; Internal Adviser Services Representative; Data Specialist; Sales; Administrative Assistant.

### STEIN ROE INVESTMENT COUNSEL
One South Wacker Drive, Chicago IL 60606. 312/368-7700. **Fax:** 312/368-8129. **Contact:** Human Resources. **World Wide Web address:** http://www.sric.net. **Description:** An investment counseling firm offering professional advice and services to individuals, institutions, and other organizations. Stein Roe & Farnham also manages 20 no-load mutual funds. **NOTE:** Apply online. **Corporate headquarters location:** This location. **Other U.S. locations:** San Francisco CA; New York NY; Cleveland OH. **International locations:** San Juan, Puerto Rico.

### UNITRIN, INC.
One East Wacker Drive, Chicago IL 60601. 312/661-4600. **Toll-free phone:** 800/999-0546. **Contact:** Personnel. **World Wide Web address:** http://www.unitrin.com. **Description:** A financial services company with subsidiaries engaged in three business areas: life and health insurance, property and casualty insurance, and consumer finance. Founded in 1990. **Positions advertised include:** Actuarial Services Manager; Product Technician; Territory Sales Manager; Regional Claims Manager. **Special programs:** Internships; Summer Jobs. **Office hours:** Monday - Friday, 8:00 a.m. - 4:30 p.m. **Corporate headquarters location:** This location. **Listed on:** NASDAQ. **Stock exchange symbol:** UTR.

### VAN KAMPEN INVESTMENTS
One Parkview Plaza, P.O. Box 5555, Oakbrook Terrace IL 60181. 630/684-6000. **Contact:** Human Resources. **World Wide Web address:** http://www.vankampen.com. **Description:** An investment management firm.

### WASHINGTON MUTUAL HOMELOANS
75 North Fairway Drive, Vernon Hills IL 60061. 847/549-6500. **Fax:** 847/549-2568. **Contact:** Human Resources. **World Wide Web address:** http://www.wamumortgage.com. **Description:** A full-service mortgage banking company that originates, acquires, and services residential mortgage loans. **Operations at this facility include:** Administration; Divisional Headquarters; Service.

### WELLS FARGO HOME MORTGAGE
4800 West Wallbash Road, Springfield IL 62711. 217/547-7500. **Contact:** Human Resources. **World Wide Web address:** http://www.wellsfargo.com. **Description:** Wells Fargo is a diversified financial institution with over $234 billion in assets. Wells Fargo serves over 17 million customers through 5,300 independent locations worldwide. The company also maintains several stand-alone ATMs and branches within retail outlets. Services include community banking, credit and debit cards, home equity and mortgage loans, online banking, student loans, and insurance. Wells Fargo also offers a complete line of commercial and institutional financial services. Founded in 1852. **Corporate headquarters location:** San Francisco CA. **Other U.S. locations:** Nationwide. **International locations:** Worldwide. **Operations at this facility include:** This location offers home equity and mortgage services. **Listed on:** New York Stock Exchange. **Stock exchange symbol:** WFC.

## FOOD AND BEVERAGES/AGRICULTURE

**You can expect to find the following types of companies in this section:**
Crop Services and Farm Supplies • Dairy Farms • Food Manufacturers/Processors and Agricultural Producers • Tobacco Products

---

### ALPHA BAKING COMPANY

4545 West Lyndale Avenue, Chicago IL 60639-3419. 773/489-5400. **Fax:** 773/489-2711. **Contact:** Human Resources. **World Wide Web address:** http://www.alphabaking.com. **Description:** Specializes in preparing and baking breads and rolls. Trucks deliver products east of the Rocky Mountains. An institutional route system delivers products locally. **Corporate headquarters location:** This location. **Operations at this facility include:** Administration; Manufacturing; Sales. **Listed on:** Privately held. **Number of employees nationwide:** 1,000.

### ARCHER DANIELS MIDLAND COMPANY

P.O. Box 1470, Decatur IL 62525. 217/424-5230. **Physical address:** 4666 Faries Parkway, Decatur IL 62526. **Toll-free phone:** 800/637-5843. **Fax:** 217/424-4383. **Contact:** Employment. **World Wide Web address:** http://www.admworld.com. **Description:** A worldwide firm engaged in the procuring, transporting, storing, processing, and merchandising of agricultural commodities. The company processes agricultural products such as corn, soybeans, wheat, rice, cottonseed, and canola and produces a variety of products including vegetable oils, cooking oil, margarine, vitamin E, soy flour, soy isolates, soy protein, soy milk, TVP, high-fructose corn syrup, sorbitol, starch, ethanol, xanthan gum, tryptophan, vitamin C, fermentation products, pasta, and cottonseed flour products. Founded in 1902. **NOTE:** Entry-level positions are offered. Apply online for all positions. **Positions advertised include:** Assistant Building and Grounds; Business Analyst; Clerk; Client Server; Commodity Trader; Construction Superintendent; Control Systems/Automation Specialist. **Corporate headquarters location:** This location. **Other U.S. locations:** Nationwide. **International locations:** Worldwide. **Operations at this facility include:** Administration; Research and Development; Sales. **Listed on:** New York Stock Exchange. **Stock exchange symbol:** ADM. **Number of employees worldwide:** 23,000.

### ARCHER DANIELS MIDLAND COMPANY

One Edmund Street, Peoria IL 61602. 309/673-7828. **Contact:** Human Resources. **World Wide Web address:** http://www.admworld.com. **Description:** Archer Daniels Midland Company is a worldwide firm engaged in the procuring, transporting, storing, processing, and merchandising of agricultural commodities. **NOTE:** Apply online at this company's website. **Corporate headquarters location:** Decatur IL. **Operations at this facility include:** This location produces alcohol.

**BALL HORTICULTURAL COMPANY**
622 Town Road, West Chicago IL 60185-2698. 630/231-3600. **Fax:** 630/231-3605. **Contact:** Human Resources. **E-mail address:** careers@ballhort.com. **World Wide Web address:** http://www.ballhort.com. **Description:** An international horticulture producer and distributor. **Positions advertised include:** Production Research Specialist; Sales Trainee; Technical Manager. **NOTE:** Entry-level positions are offered. **Corporate headquarters location:** This location. **Subsidiaries include:** Ball FloraPlant; Ball Seed Company; Ball Superior Ltd.; ColorLink; PanAmerican Seed Company; Vegmo Plant, BV.

**BUTTERNUT BAKERY**
**CHICAGO BAKING COMPANY**
40 East Garfield Boulevard, Chicago IL 60615. 773/536-7700. **Contact:** Joseph Schulz, Personnel Manager. **Description:** A producer and wholesaler of bread products. **Corporate headquarters location:** Kansas City MO. **Parent company:** Interstate Brands Corporation. **Operations at this facility include:** Manufacturing.

**CANTEEN CORPORATION**
216 West Diversey Avenue, Elmhurst IL 60126. 630/833-3666. **Contact:** Human Resources. **World Wide Web address:** http://www.canteen.com. **Description:** One of the world's largest food and beverage vending companies. Canteen Corporation has over 150,000 vending machines in service. **Positions advertised include:** Branch Manager; Customer Service Manager; Supervisor; Route Driver. **Corporate headquarters location:** This location. **Parent company:** Compass Group plc (London, England).

**CERTIFIED GROCERS MIDWEST, INC.**
One Certified Drive, Hodgkins IL 60525. 708/579-2100. Fax: 708/354-7502. **Contact:** Human Resources. **World Wide Web address:** http://www.certisaver.com. **Description:** A food wholesaler. **Corporate headquarters location:** This location.

**CHEF SOLUTIONS INC.**
20 North Martingale Road, Suite 600, Schaumburg IL 60173. 847/762-8500. **Toll-free phone:** 800/877-1157. **Fax:** 847/762-8605. **Contact:** Human Resources. **E-mail address:** resumes@chefsolutions.com. **World Wide Web address:** http://www.chefsolutions.com. **Description:** Markets a variety of chilled, freshly prepared foods for restaurants, wholesalers, and consumers. **NOTE:** Entry-level positions and second and third shifts are offered. **Special programs:** Internships. **Corporate headquarters location:** This location. **Other area locations:** Wheeling IL (Manufacturing); Northlake IL (Bakery); Mt. Prospect IL (Research and Development). **U.S. locations:** CA; TX; MN; CT; NY; OH; KS; NJ; GA. **International locations:** Mexico. **Parent company:** Questor Management (Southfield MI). **Listed on:** Privately held.

**CLARK NATIONAL, INC.**
**CLARK FOODSERVICE PRODUCTS, INC.**
950 Arthur Avenue, Elk Grove Village IL 60007. 847/956-1730. **Fax:** 847/956-0199. **Contact:** Human Resources. **World Wide Web address:** http://www.clarkfoodservice.com. **Description:** Distributes cleaning supplies, food service disposables, and groceries to the food service industry. **NOTE:** The parent company, Clark National Inc., is located also at this facility. **Positions**

**advertised include:** Corporate Sales Executive. **Operations at this facility include:** Administration; Sales.

## CLAUSSEN PICKLE COMPANY
1300 Claussen Drive, Woodstock IL 60098. 815/338-7000. **Contact:** Human Resources. **World Wide Web address:** http://www.kraftfoods.com/cla. **Description:** A producer and distributor of pickles. **NOTE:** Kraft's corporate website provides job listings for Claussen and its other divisions. To see job listings and to apply, visit http://www.kraftfoods.com/careers. **Parent company:** Kraft Foods. **Operations at this facility include:** Manufacturing. **Listed on:** New York Stock Exchange. **Stock exchange symbol:** KFT.

## CONAGRA REFRIGERATED PREPARED FOODS
215 West Diehl Road, Naperville IL 60563. 630/857-1000. **Fax:** 630/857-1901. **Contact:** Human Resources. **World Wide Web address:** http://www.conagrafoods.com. **Description:** Processes meats such as bacon, ham, fresh smoked and dry sausage, and luncheon meats under the brand names Armour Star, Brown 'N Serve, Butterball, Eckrich, Healthy Choice, and Swift Premium. **NOTE:** Apply online at the parent company's Conagra's, website: http://www.conagrafoods.com. **Corporate headquarters location:** Omaha NE. **Other U.S. locations:** Nationwide. **Parent company:** ConAgra, Inc. **Operations at this facility include:** Administration; Divisional Headquarters; Regional Headquarters; Sales.

## CORN PRODUCTS INTERNATIONAL
5 Westbrook Corporate Center, Westchester IL 60154. 708/551-2600. **Fax:** 708/551-2800. **Contact:** Human Resources. **E-mail address:** hr@cornproducts.com. **World Wide Web address:** http://www.cornproducts.com. **Description:** Supplies sweeteners and starches that come from the corn refining process. Corn Products International serves the brewing, corrugating, food, pharmaceutical, and soft drink industries. **NOTE:** Mail or e-mail resumes. **Listed on:** New York Stock Exchange. **Stock exchange symbol:** CPO.

## DEAN FOODS COMPANY
3600 North River Road, Franklin Park IL 60131. 847/678-1680. **Contact:** Human Resources. **World Wide Web address:** http://www.deanfoods.com. **Description:** A producer and distributor of dairy and specialty food items. Products include milk, cheese, yogurt, sour cream, eggnog, ice cream, vegetables, pickles, salad dressings, pudding, dips, and other condiments. The company also sells and distributes canned meat products to the federal government. **Special programs:** Internships. **Corporate headquarters location:** Dallas TX. **Other U.S. locations:** Nationwide. **Listed on:** New York Stock Exchange. **Stock exchange symbol:** DF.

## F&F FOODS, INC.
3501 West 48th Place, Chicago IL 60632. 773/927-3737. **Contact:** Joe Nelson, Human Resources. **World Wide Web address:** http://www.fffoods.com. **Description:** Manufactures cough drops, dietary supplements, candy, crackers, and a variety of other items under the product names Fast Dry Zinc, F&F Dietary Supplements, Daily C, Smith Brothers Cough Drops, and Foxes.

**FARMLAND FOODS INC.**
1220 North Sixth Street Road, Monmouth IL 61462. 309/734-5353. **Contact:** Human Resources. **World Wide Web address:** http://www.farmland.com. **Description:** A pork processing facility. **Parent company:** Farmland Industries Inc. is one of the largest farmer-owned agricultural food marketing and manufacturing cooperative associations in the United States. The company is engaged in grain marketing, pork and beef processing, and manufacturing of fertilizers, livestock feeds, and petroleum products. Membership includes farmers from Iowa, Kansas, Oklahoma, South Dakota, Illinois, Nebraska, and Mexico.

**GENERAL MILLS, INC.**
704 West Washington Street, West Chicago IL 60185. 630/231-1140. **Fax:** 630/876-4217. **Contact:** Human Resources. **World Wide Web address:** http://www.genmills.com. **Description:** Produces and markets consumer foods including Cheerios, Wheaties, and Total cereals; Betty Crocker desserts, frostings, and baking mixes; Pop Secret microwave popcorn; Gorton's frozen seafood; Yoplait yogurt; Bisquick pancake mix; and Gold Medal flour. Founded in 1866. **NOTE:** This company provides job listings for all its offices throughout the United States. Visit its website and apply online. **Corporate headquarters location:** Minneapolis MN. **Operations at this facility include:** This location is the office for the company's Package Foods Operations Division. **Listed on:** New York Stock Exchange. **Stock exchange symbol:** GIS.

**GONNELLA BAKING CO.**
2002 West Erie Street, Chicago IL 60612. 312/733-2020x376 or x189. **Fax:** 312/733-7670. **Contact:** Lauren Slipkowsky, Human Resources. **World Wide Web address:** http://www.gonnella.com. **Description:** Makers of bread, rolls, frozen dough, garlic bread, and other bakery products. Founded in 1886. **NOTE:** Entry-level positions, part-time jobs, and second and third shifts are offered. This location hires for its corporate offices as well as its plants. Apply online or in person at the Human Resources Office. **Positions advertised include:** Maintenance Mechanic; Route Sales Representative. **Special programs:** Internships; Apprenticeships; Training; Summer Jobs. **Office hours:** Tuesday, 2:00 p.m. – 4:00 p.m.; Thursday, 9:00 a.m. – 11:00 a.m. **Corporate headquarters location:** This location. **Listed on:** Privately held.

**GONNELLA FROZEN PRODUCTS, INC.**
1117 East Wiley Road, Schaumburg, IL 60173. 847/884-8829x5212. **Fax:** 847/884-9469. **Contact:** James Mazukelli, Human Resources and Safety Manager. **World Wide Web address:** http://www.gonnella.com. **Description:** The frozen food division of Gonnella Baking Company. **NOTE:** apply online or in person at the human resources office. **Positions advertised include:** Maintenance Mechanic. **Office hours:** Monday – Friday, 8:00 a.m. – 5:00 p.m.

**GRIFFITH LABORATORIES**
One Griffith Center, Alsip IL 60803. 708/371-0900. **Contact:** Human Resources. **E-mail address:** contactjobsna@griffithlabs.com. **World Wide Web address:** http://www.griffithlabs.com. **Description:** Manufactures food seasonings, coatings, and mixes including soup, gravy, breadcrumbs, batters, sauces, and marinades.

**H.J. HEINZ COMPANY**
2301 Shermer Road, Northbrook IL 60062. 847/291-3900. **Contact:** Human Resources Manager. **World Wide Web address:** http://www.heinz.com

**Description:** Produces bouillon, dry soup, pasta, and pasta sauces. Brand names include Catelli, Creamette, Prince, R&F, Ronco, and Wyler's. **NOTE:** Apply online. **Special programs:** Internships. **Corporate headquarters location:** Pittsburgh PA. **Listed on:** New York Stock Exchange. **Stock exchange symbol:** HNZ.

## HINCKLEY SPRINGS

6155 South Harlem Avenue, Chicago IL 60638. 773/586-8600. **Fax:** 773/586-6542. **Recorded jobline:** 800/329-0835. **Contact:** Judy Archer, Human Resources. **World Wide Web address:** http://www.water.com. **Description:** Hinkley Springs processes and distributes bottled water. Founded in 1888. **NOTE:** Entry-level positions and second and third shifts are offered. **Office hours:** Monday - Friday, 8:15 a.m. - 5:00 p.m. **Corporate headquarters location:** Atlanta GA. **Other U.S. locations:** Indianapolis IN; Kansas City MO. **Parent company:** Suntory Water Group. **Operations at this facility include:** Divisional Headquarters. **Listed on:** Privately held.

## INTERSTATE BRANDS CORPORATION
## HOSTESS BAKERY

9555 West Soreng Avenue, Schiller Park IL 60176. 847/994-9699. **Fax:** 847/678-9651. **Recorded jobline:** 847/994-9690. **Contact:** Russ Hinkle, Human Resources. **Description:** Produces Hostess snack products such as cupcakes and Twinkies. **Special programs:** Apprenticeships; Training. **Corporate headquarters location:** Kansas City MO.

## JEL SERT COMPANY

P.O. Box 261, West Chicago IL 60186. 630/231-7590. **Contact:** Human Resources. **E-mail address:** hr@jelsert.com. **World Wide Web address:** http://www.jelsert.com. **Description:** Manufactures Fla-Vor-Ice, FlavorAid, Mondo, Otter Pops, Pop Ice, and Wyler's products. **NOTE:** Apply online. **Positions advertised include:** Quality Assurance Lab Technician.

## JIM BEAM BRANDS COMPANY

510 Lake Cook Road, Suite 200, Deerfield IL 60015. 847/948-8888. **Contact:** Human Resources. **World Wide Web address:** http://www.jimbeam.com. **Description:** Distills bourbon. **Parent company:** Fortune Brands (Lincolnshire IL).

## KEEBLER COMPANY

545 Lamont Road, Elmhurst IL 60126. 630/833-2900. **Contact:** Human Resources. **World Wide Web address:** http://www.keebler.com. **Description:** A national manufacturer and marketer of cookies, crackers, snack foods, and other consumer food products. Keebler markets its products under the brand names Carr's, Cheez-It, Famous Amos, Murray, Plantation, and Ready Crust. Founded in 1853. **NOTE:** For Keebler job listings, visit Kellogg's website: http://www.careers.kelloggs.com. Apply online. **Corporate headquarters location:** Battle Creek MI. **Other U.S. locations:** Denver CO; Macon GA; Grand Rapids MI; Cincinnati OH. **Subsidiaries include:** Little Brownie's Baker is a licensed supplier of Girl Scout Cookies. **Parent company:** Kellogg Company. **Operations at this facility include:** Administration; Research and Development.

## KRAFT FOODS, INC.

Three Lakes Drive, Northfield IL 60093. 847/646-2000. **Fax:** 847/646-6005. **Contact:** Corporate Staffing. **World Wide Web address:**

http://www.kraft.com/careers. **Description:** One of the largest producers of packaged food in North America. Major brands include Jell-O, Post, Kool-Aid, Crystal Light, Entenmann's, Miracle Whip, Stove Top, and Shake 'n Bake. Kraft Foods markets a number of products under the Kraft brand name including natural and processed cheeses and dry packaged dinners. The Oscar Mayer unit markets processed meats, poultry, lunch combinations, and pickles under the Oscar Mayer, Louis Rich, Lunchables, and Claussen brand names. Kraft is also one of the largest coffee companies with principal brands including Maxwell House, Sanka, Brim, and General Foods International Coffees. **NOTE:** On its website, Kraft provides job listings for its corporate offices and division facilities. Apply online. **Corporate headquarters location:** This location. **Parent company:** Philip Morris Companies (New York) is a holding company whose principal wholly-owned subsidiaries are Philip Morris Inc. (Philip Morris U.S.A.), Philip Morris International Inc., Kraft Foods, Inc., and Philip Morris Capital Corporation. In the tobacco industry, Philip Morris U.S.A. and Philip Morris International together form one of the largest international cigarette operations in the world. U.S. brand names include Marlboro, Parliament, Virginia Slims, Benson & Hedges, and Merit. Philip Morris Capital Corporation is engaged in financial services and real estate. **Listed on:** New York Stock Exchange. **Stock exchange symbol:** KFT.

**LODERS CROKLAAN**
24708 West Durkee Road, Channahon IL 60410. 815/730-5200. **Contact:** Human Resources. **World Wide Web address:** http://www.croklaan.com. **Description:** Loders Croklaan processes, packages, and ships cooking oils. **Operations at this facility include:** This location is a vegetable oil refinery. **Parent company:** Unilever Corporation (New York NY).

**THE MARTIN-BROWER COMPANY**
9500 West Bryn Mawr Avenue, Suite 700, Rosemont IL 60018. 847/227-6500. **Fax:** 847/227-6550. **Contact:** Human Resources. **Description:** An international company that provides food distribution services to the restaurant industry. **Corporate headquarters location:** This location. **Parent company:** Reyes Holdings.

**MONSANTO CORPORATION**
3100 Sycamore Road, De Kalb IL 60115. 815/758-3461. **Fax:** 815/756-2676. **Contact:** Human Resources. **World Wide Web address:** http://www.monsanto.com. **Description:** Manufactures and markets agricultural products, performance chemicals used in consumer products, prescription pharmaceuticals, and food ingredients. **NOTE:** See website for job listings and apply online. **Corporate headquarters location:** Peapack NJ. **Other U.S. locations:** Nationwide. **Operations at this facility include:** This is the DeKalb Genetics Corporation's main office.

**THE MOSAIC COMPANY**
100 South Saunders Street, Lake Forest IL 60045. 847/739-1200. **Fax:** 847/739-1617. **Contact:** Director of Human Resources. **E-mail address:** careers@mosaicco.com. **World Wide Web address:** http://www.mosaicco.com. **Description:** Mosaic mines and manufactures crop nutrients including potash and phosphates; supplies animal feed ingredients necessary for raising livestock; and produces salt for road maintenance. **Corporate headquarters location:** Minneapolis MN. **Listed on:** New York Stock Exchange. **Stock exchange symbol:** MOS. **Number of employees worldwide:** 8,000.

## NK SEEDS

5300 Katrine Avenue, Downers Grove IL 60515-4095. 630/969-6300. **Fax:** 630/969-6373. **Contact:** Human Resources. **World Wide Web address:** http://www.nk-us.com. **Description:** A horticulture broker. **Special programs:** Internships. **Corporate headquarters location:** The Netherlands. **Parent company:** Syngenta. **Operations at this facility include:** Administration; Manufacturing; Research and Development; Sales. **Listed on:** Privately held.

## NABISCO BRANDS, INC.

7300 South Kedzie Avenue, Chicago IL 60629. 773/925-4300. **Contact:** Human Resources. **World Wide Web address:** http://www.kraft.com. **Description:** A producer and distributor of cookies and crackers. **NOTE:** See website for job listings. Apply online. **Other U.S. locations:** Nationwide. **International locations:** Asia; Canada; Europe. **Parent company:** Kraft Foods. **Listed on:** New York Stock Exchange. **Stock exchange symbol:** KFT.

## NABISCO BRANDS, INC.

7777 North Caldwell Avenue, Niles IL 60714. 847/967-6201. **Contact:** Human Resources. **World Wide Web address:** http://www.kraft.com. **Description:** A producer and distributor of cookies and crackers. **NOTE:** See website for job listings. **Parent company:** Kraft Foods. **Operations at this facility include:** This is a manufacturing plant and research and development facility.

## NUTRASWEET COMPANY

200 World Trade Center, Merchandise Mart, Suite 900, Chicago IL 60654. 312/873-5000. **Contact:** Human Resources. **World Wide Web address:** http://www.nutrasweet.com. **Description:** Manufactures and markets agricultural products, performance chemicals used in consumer products, prescription pharmaceuticals, and food ingredients.

## PEPPERIDGE FARM, INC.

230 Second Street, Downers Grove IL 60515. 630/968-4000. **Contact:** Mary Harris, Human Resources Manager. **World Wide Web address:** http://www.pepperidgefarm.com. **Description:** Manufactures and distributes a range of fresh and frozen baked goods and confections including bread, cookies, cakes, pastries, and crackers. **NOTE:** Apply online at Campbell's website: http://www.careers.campbellsoupcompany.com. **Parent company:** Campbells Soup. **Operations at this facility include:** This location is a bakery.

## PEPSIAMERICAS, INC.

3501 Algonquin Road, Rolling Meadows IL 60008. 847/818-5000. **Contact:** Human Resources. **World Wide Web address:** http://www.pepsiamericas.com. **Description:** PepsiAmericas is a holding company for food and beverages. **Corporate headquarters location:** This location. **NOTE:** Apply online. **Positions advertised include:** Sales Specialist; Logistics Analyst; Warehouse Manager. **Operations at this facility include:** This location houses administrative offices.

## PEPSI-COLA BOTTLING COMPANY

1881 Bilter Road, Aurora IL 60504. 630/898-1300. **Fax:** 630/898-1717. **Contact:** Human Resources. **World Wide Web address:** http://www.pepsiamericas.com. **Description:** A bottling facility and a division of Pepsi-Cola Company. **NOTE:** Apply online. **Other U.S. locations:** Nationwide. **Parent company:** PepsiCo,

Inc. (Purchase NY) consists of Frito-Lay Company, Pepsi-Cola Company, Quaker Oats, and Tropicana Products, Inc. **Operations at this facility include:** This location is a bottling plant. **Listed on:** New York Stock Exchange. **Stock exchange symbol:** PEP.

**PFIZER**
5500 Forest Hills Road, Rockford IL 61105. 815/877-8081. **Contact:** Human Resources. **World Wide Web address:** http://www.pfizer.com. **Description:** Pfizer is a leading pharmaceutical company that distributes products concerning cardiovascular health, central nervous system disorders, infectious diseases, and women's health worldwide. The company's brand-name products include Benadryl, Ben Gay, Cortizone, Desitin, Halls, Listerine, Sudafed, and Zantac 75. **NOTE:** This company has other locations in Illinois. See website for job listings and locations. Apply online. **Positions advertised include:** Buyer/Planner; Oncology Sales Consultant. **Corporate headquarters location:** New York NY. **Operations at this facility include:** This location manufactures gum. **Listed on:** New York Stock Exchange. **Stock exchange symbol:** PFE.

**THE QUAKER OATS COMPANY**
555 West Monroe, Suite 16-01, Chicago IL 60604. 312/821-1000. **Contact:** Human Resources. **World Wide Web address:** http://www.quakeroats.com. **Description:** A producer of grain-based foods and sports beverages. Products include Gatorade; Golden Grain pasta and rice; and Quaker Oats hot and ready-to-eat cereals, granola bars, and rice cakes. Founded in 1877. NOTE: Apply online. **Corporate headquarters location:** This location. **Other U.S. locations:** Nationwide. **International locations:** Worldwide. **Parent company:** Pepsico. **Listed on:** New York Stock Exchange. **Stock exchange symbol:** PEP.

**SARA LEE COFFEE AND TEA**
3800 Golf Road, Rolling Meadows IL 60008. 630/860-1400. **Contact:** Human Resources. **World Wide Web address:** http://www.saraleecoffeeandtea.com. **Description:** Produces and sells coffee, tea, salad dressings, syrups, and vending products. **NOTE:** For job listings, visit the Career Section at Sara Lee's website at http://www.saralee.com. Apply online. **Corporate headquarters location:** This location. **Other area locations:** Chicago IL; Elk Grove Village IL.

**SARA LEE CORPORATION**
3 First National Plaza, Chicago IL 60602. 312/726-2600. **Contact:** Human Resources. **World Wide Web address:** http://www.saralee.com. **Description:** This location houses the administrative offices of the international food and consumer products company. **NOTE:** For employment opportunities, see the company's website for job listings and apply online. **Corporate headquarters location:** This location.

**SYSCO FOOD SERVICES**
250 Wieboldt Drive, Des Plaines IL 60016. 847/699-5400. **Fax:** 847/298-3048. **Contact:** Human Resources. **World Wide Web address:** http://www.sysco.com. **Description:** Sells and distributes food service products through more than 65 locations nationwide. **NOTE:** Mail resumes to this location. Entry-level positions and second and third shifts are offered. **Corporate headquarters location:** Houston TX. **Other U.S. locations:** Nationwide.

**TATE & LYLE**
2200 East El Dorado, Decatur IL 62525. 217/423-4411. **Contact:** Human Resources. **World Wide Web address:** http://www.tateandlyle.com. **Description:** A wet mill corn refinery that produces corn products including animal feed, ethanol, starches, and sweeteners. Founded in 1898. **NOTE:** See website for job listings. **Positions advertised include:** Grain Accounting Clerk; Rate Analyst. **Corporate headquarters location:** London.

**TOOTSIE ROLL INDUSTRIES, INC.**
7401 South Cicero Avenue, Chicago IL 60629. 773/838-3400. **Contact:** Human Resources. **World Wide Web address:** http://www.tootsie.com. **Description:** Manufactures and distributes candy, sold primarily under the Tootsie Roll brand name. The company also produces Cella's and Mason candies. Tootsie Roll Industries is one of the largest U.S. confectioners of lollipops sold mainly under the Charms and Blow-Pop brand names. **Corporate headquarters location:** This location.

**U.S. FOODSERVICE**
800 Supreme Drive, Bensenville IL 60106. 630/595-1200. **Fax:** 630/250-4202. **Contact:** Personnel. **World Wide Web address:** http://www.usfoodservice.com. **Description:** A broad-line distributor of food products, equipment and supplies, cleaning chemicals, and disposables to a variety of food service locations such as restaurants, nursing homes, hospitals, and institutional dining facilities. **Parent company:** Royal Ahold. **Listed on:** New York Stock Exchange. **Stock exchange symbol:** AHO. **Number of employees worldwide:** 34,000.

**U.S. FOODSERVICE**
One Sexton Drive, Glendale Heights IL 60139. 630/980-3000. **Fax:** 630/924-2970. **Contact:** Human Resources Department. **World Wide Web address:** http://www.usfoodservice.com. **Description:** An institutional food production and distribution company with clients in the restaurant and health care industries. **Corporate headquarters location:** Columbia MD. **Other U.S. locations:** Nationwide. **Parent company:** Royal Ahold. **Listed on:** New York Stock Exchange. **Stock exchange symbol:** AHO. **Number of employees worldwide:** 34,000.

**U.S. FOODSERVICE**
One Quality Lane, Streator IL 61364. 815/673-3311. **Contact:** Human Resources. **World Wide Web address:** http://www.usfoodservice.com. **Description:** An institutional food production and distribution company with clients in the restaurant and health care industries. **Corporate headquarters location:** Columbia MD. **Other U.S. locations:** Nationwide. **Parent company:** Royal Ahold. **Listed on:** New York Stock Exchange. **Stock exchange symbol:** AHO. **Number of employees worldwide:** 34,000.

**UNITED STATES TOBACCO MANUFACTURING COMPANY**
11601 Copenhagen Court, Franklin Park IL 60131. 847/957-8200. **Contact:** Human Resources. **World Wide Web address:** http://www.ustshareholder.com. **Description:** A manufacturing plant for moist, smokeless tobacco products and a distribution warehouse. Products include Skoal, Copenhagen, and Happy Days smokeless tobaccos. **Corporate headquarters location:** Greenwich CT.

**VIENNA BEEF LTD.**
2501 North Damen Avenue, Chicago IL 60647. 773/278-7800. **Fax:** 773/278-4759. **Contact:** Human Resources. **E-mail address:** jobs@viennabeef.com. **World Wide Web address:** http://www.viennabeef.com. **Description:** Vienna Beef Ltd. is an international distributor and processor of meat and sausage. **Positions advertised include:** Human Resources Clerk. **Corporate headquarters location:** This location. **Operations at this facility include:** This location houses the corporate headquarters as well as a meat-cutting plant.

**GEORGE WESTON BAKERIES**
**ENTENMANN'S**
300 West North Avenue, North Lake IL 60164. 708/562-6311. **Contact:** Human Resources Manager. **World Wide Web address:** http://www.gwbakeries.com. **Description:** George Weston Bakeries operates in two distinct business segments; food processing and food distribution. **Corporate headquarters location:** Bayshore NY. **Operations at this facility include:** This location bakes cakes, cookies, and pies.

**WORLD'S FINEST CHOCOLATE**
4801 South Lawndale Avenue, Chicago IL 60632. 773/847-4600. **Toll-free phone:** 800/366-2462. **Fax:** 773/847-7804. **Contact:** Human Resources. **E-mail address:** humanresources@wfchocolate.com. **World Wide Web address:** http://www.wfchocolate.com. **Description:** An international manufacturer of chocolate and cocoa products. **Corporate headquarters location:** This location.

**WILLIAM WRIGLEY JR. COMPANY**
410 North Michigan Avenue, Chicago IL 60611. 312/644-2121. **Contact:** Human Resources. **World Wide Web address:** http://www.wrigley.com. **Description:** One of the largest producers of chewing gum in the world. Brand name gums include Wrigley's Spearmint, Juicy Fruit, Big Red, Extra, and Freedent. **Positions advertised include:** Chemist; Receptionist; Mechanic; Lab Technician; Machine Operator; Occupational Health Therapist; Sensory Development Scientist. **Corporate headquarters location:** This location. **Other U.S. locations:** GA; NJ. **International locations:** Worldwide. **Subsidiaries include:** Amurol Products Company manufactures and markets novelty chewing gum products; Northwestern Flavors, Inc. produces flavors and mint oil for Wrigley's gums and other food-related products; WRICO Packaging converts raw paper and carton stock into printed packaging materials used by the company; and L.A. Dreyfus manufactures chewing gum base. **Listed on:** New York Stock Exchange. **Stock exchange symbol:** WWY.

# GOVERNMENT

**You can expect to find the following types of companies in this section:**
Courts • Executive, Legislative, and General Government • Public Agencies (Firefighters, Military, Police) • United States Postal Service

## AURORA, CITY OF
44 East Downer Place, Aurora IL 60507. 630/844-3626. **Fax:** 630/892-8837. **Recorded jobline:** 630/906-7415. **Contact:** Human Resources. **World Wide Web address:** http://www.ci.aurora.il.us. **Description:** Houses administrative, municipal, and government offices for the city of Aurora. **NOTE:** Seasonal positions offered. A completed application is required for any position. Apply online. **Office hours:** Monday – Friday, 8:00 a.m. – 5:00 p.m.

## CHICAGO, CITY OF
City Hall, 121 North LaSalle Street, Chicago IL 60602. 312/742-5955. **Recorded jobline:** 312/744-1369. **Contact:** Department of Personnel Service Center. **World Wide Web address:** http://www.cityofchicago.org. **Description:** Administrative offices for the City of Chicago's government departments, agencies and services. **NOTE:** The Department of Personnel only accepts resumes and applications for open positions. Interested jobseekers may call the jobline to hear about current openings; or, they may visit the Department at City Hall in Room 100. An application can be obtained online at the City's website. **Special programs:** Internships. **Office hours:** Monday – Friday, 8:00 a.m. – 5:00 p.m.

## DEPARTMENT OF TRANSPORTATION/CHICAGO
30 North LaSalle Street, Room 600, Chicago IL 60602. 312/744-3674. **Fax:** 312/747-6021. **Recorded jobline:** 312/744-1369. **Contact:** Human Resources. http://www.ci.chi.il.us/transportation. **Description:** Maintains roads and highways and manages transportation infrastructure throughout the city of Chicago. **NOTE:** To apply for a position, visit the City of Chicago's website at http://www.ci.chi.il.us. To apply in person, apply with the City of Chicago's Department of Personnel; City Hall – Room 100, 121 North LaSalle Street, Chicago IL 60602. Office hours: Monday – Friday, 8:00 a.m. – 5:00 p.m.

## DES PLAINES, CITY OF
1420 Miner Street, Des Plaines IL 60016. 847/391-5480. **Contact:** Human Resources. **World Wide Web address:** http://www.desplaines.org. **Description:** This location houses the governmental administrative offices for the City of Des Plaines IL, including its Police Department. **NOTE:** See website for job listings and application procedures. **Positions advertised include:** Police Officer; Director of Community Development.

## NAPERVILLE, CITY OF
Municipal Center, 400 South Eagle Street, Naperville IL 60566-7020. 630/420-6111. **Fax:** 630/305-4048. **Contact:** Human Resources. **E-mail address:** apply@naperville.il.us. **World Wide Web address:** http://www.naperville.il.us. **Description:** The administrative offices for the City of Naperville. **NOTE:** See website for job listings. Mail, fax or e-mail resumes and cover letters. Interested

jobseekers may also apply in person at the Human Resources Office located in the ground floor of the Municipal Center. **Positions advertised include:** Engineering Technician; Community Relations Specialist; Ground Technician.

**SANGAMON, COUNTY OF**
200 South Ninth Street, Springfield IL 62701. 217/753-6650. **Contact:** Human Resources. **World Wide Web address:** http://www.co.sangamon.il.us. **Description:** Houses the administrative and government offices for Sangamon County. **NOTE:** See website for job listings, contact information and application procedures. **Positions advertised include:** Assistant Administrator of Finance; Accounting Technician.

**U.S. BUREAU OF ALCOHOL, TOBACCO, AND FIREARMS**
300 South Riverside Plaza, Suite 350, Chicago IL 60606. 312/353-6935. **Contact:** Human Resources Department. **World Wide Web address:** http://www.atf.treas.gov/jobs/index.htm. **Description:** A government agency responsible for enforcing alcohol, tobacco, and firearms laws. **NOTE:** See website for job listings and application procedures. **Special programs:** Internship; Volunteer. **Operations at this facility include:** This is the Midwest Regional Audit Office.

**U.S. ENVIRONMENTAL PROTECTION AGENCY (EPA)**
77 West Jackson Boulevard, Chicago IL 60604. 312/353-2000. **Contact:** Human Resources. **World Wide Web address:** http://www.epa.gov. **Description:** The EPA is dedicated to improving and preserving the quality of the environment, both nationally and globally, and protecting human health and the productivity of natural resources. The agency is committed to ensuring that federal environmental laws are implemented and enforced effectively; U.S. policy, both foreign and domestic, encourages the integration of economic development and environmental protection so that economic growth can be sustained over the long term; and public and private decisions affecting energy, transportation, agriculture, industry, international trade, and natural resources fully integrate considerations of environmental quality. Founded in 1970. **Special programs:** Internships. **Corporate headquarters location:** Washington DC. **Other U.S. locations:** Nationwide.

**U.S. ENVIRONMENTAL PROTECTION AGENCY (EPA)**
1021 North Grand Avenue East, Springfield IL 62794. 217/782-3397. **Contact:** Human Resources. **World Wide Web address:** http://www.epa.gov. **Description:** The EPA is dedicated to improving and preserving the quality of the environment, both nationally and globally, and protecting human health and the productivity of natural resources. The agency is committed to ensuring that federal environmental laws are implemented and enforced effectively; U.S. policy, both foreign and domestic, encourages the integration of economic development and environmental protection so that economic growth can be sustained over the long term; and public and private decisions affecting energy, transportation, agriculture, industry, international trade, and natural resources fully integrate considerations of environmental quality. Founded in 1970. **Corporate headquarters location:** Washington DC. **Other U.S. locations:** Nationwide.

**U.S. POSTAL SERVICE**
1824 North 25th Avenue, Melrose Park IL 60160. 708/343-2150. **Contact:** Human Resources. **World Wide Web address:** http://www.usps.com. **Description:** A full-service post office serving the Melrose Park area.

# HEALTH CARE SERVICES, EQUIPMENT, AND PRODUCTS

**You can expect to find the following types of companies in this section:**
Dental Labs and Equipment • Home Health Care Agencies • Hospitals and Medical Centers • Medical Equipment Manufacturers and Wholesalers • Offices and Clinics of Health Practitioners • Residential Treatment Centers/Nursing Homes • Veterinary Services

**ADVOCATE ILLINOIS MASONIC MEDICAL CENTER**
836 West Wellington Avenue, Chicago IL 60657. 773/975-1600. Contact: Human Resources. **World Wide Web address:** http://www.advocatehealth.com/immc. **Description:** A hospital specializing in oncology, cardiology and emergency care. **NOTE:** Apply online.

**AKSYS, LTD.**
Two Marriott Drive, Lincolnshire IL 60069. 847/229-2020. **Toll-free phone:** 877/229-5700. Fax: 847/229-2080. **Contact:** Human Resources. **World Wide Web address:** http://www.aksys.com. **Description:** Aksys provides hemodialysis products and services for patients suffering from renal failure. Aksys has developed an automated personal hemodialysis system, which is designed to assist patients in performing hemodialysis in alternate care settings, such as the patient's home, on a more frequent basis than currently practiced. **Positions advertised include:** Area Director, Sales; Principal Engineer; Regional Sales Manager.

**ALEXIAN BROTHERS MEDICAL CENTER**
800 Biesterfield Road, Elk Grove Village IL 60007. 847/437-5500. **Contact:** Human Resources. **World Wide Web address:** http://www.alexian.org. **Description:** A nonprofit, acute care hospital. Alexian Brothers Medical Center offers a wide range of health care services including oncology, radiology, mental health, and obstetrics. Founded in 1972. **NOTE:** This medical center is part of the Alexian Brothers Health System, which includes Alexian Brothers Behavioral Hospital and St. Alexius Medical Center, both in Hoffman Estates IL. Job listings for this hospital and the others can be found at http://www.alexianjobs.org. **Positions advertised include:** Registered Nurse; LPN; Education Coordinator; Critical Care Respiratory Therapist; Staff Chaplains; Administrative Director Perioperative Services, Cardiology Services Director.

**AMERICAN DENTAL ASSOCIATION**
211 East Chicago Avenue, Chicago IL 60611. 312/440-2500. **Contact:** Human Resources. **E-mail address:** jobs@ada.org. **World Wide Web address:** http://www.ada.org. **Description:** A professional association serving the dental community. **Positions advertised include:** Senior Manager, Corporate Relations and Marketing; Marketing Communications Director; Operations Specialist; Editorial/Advertising Assistant; Production Associate, Client Services. **Corporate headquarters location:** This location.

**AMERICAN OSTEOPATHIC ASSOCIATION**
142 East Ontario Street, Chicago IL 60611-2864. 312/202-8000. **Toll-free**

**phone:** 800/621-1773. **Fax:** 312/202-8200. **Contact:** Human Resources. **E-mail address:** recruiter@osteopathic.org. **World Wide Web address:** http://www.osteopathic.org. **Description:** The AOA is a member association representing more than 54,000 osteopathic physicians. The AOA serves as the primary certifying body for osteopathic physicians and is the accrediting agency for all osteopathic medical colleges and health care facilities. The AOA's mission is to advance the philosophy and practice of osteopathic medicine by promoting excellence in education, research, and the delivery of quality, cost-effective healthcare within a distinct, unified profession. **NOTE:** Search for open positions online. **Positions advertised include:** Administrative Assistant; Editorial Assistant; HR Manager; Program Educational Specialist; Research Director. **Corporate headquarters location:** This location.

### BAXTER HEALTHCARE CORPORATION
Route 120 and Wilson Road, Round Lake IL 60073. 847/270-5850. **Contact:** Human Resources. **World Wide Web address:** http://www.baxter.com. **Description:** Baxter Healthcare operates four global businesses: Biotechnology develops therapies and products in transfusion medicine; Cardiovascular Medicine develops products and provides services to treat late-stage cardiovascular disease; Renal Therapy develops products and provides services to improve therapies to fight kidney disease; and Intravenous Systems/Medical Products develops technologies and systems to improve intravenous medication delivery and distributes disposable medical products. **NOTE:** Apply online at the company's website. **Corporate headquarters location:** Deerfield IL. **Operations at this facility include:** This location is a research facility. **Listed on:** New York Stock Exchange. **Stock exchange symbol:** BAX. **Number of employees worldwide:** 48,000.

### BAXTER INTERNATIONAL, INC.
One Baxter Parkway, Deerfield IL 60015. 847/948-2000. **Toll-free phone:** 800/422-9827. **Fax:** 847/948-2964. **Contact:** Human Resources. **World Wide Web address:** http://www.baxter.com. **Description:** A global medical products and services company that is a leader in technologies related to blood and the circulatory system. The company operates four global businesses: Biotechnology develops therapies and products in transfusion medicine; Cardiovascular Medicine develops products and provides services to treat late-stage cardiovascular disease; Renal Therapy develops products and provides services to improve therapies to fight kidney disease; and Intravenous Systems/Medical Products develops technologies and systems to improve intravenous medication delivery and distributes disposable medical products. **NOTE:** Apply online. **Positions advertised include:** Communications Manager; Senior Paralegal; Training and eLearning. . **Special programs:** Internships. **Corporate headquarters location:** This location. **Operations at this facility include:** Administration. **Listed on:** New York Stock Exchange. **Stock exchange symbol:** BAX. **Number of employees worldwide:** 48,000.

### BROMENN REGIONAL MEDICAL CENTER
Franklin & Virginia Streets, Normal IL 61761. 309/268-5717. **Contact:** Human Resources. **World Wide Web address:** http://www.bromenn.org. **Description:** A 244-bed hospital offering a variety of inpatient, outpatient, rehabilitation, acute, and preventive health care services including women's and children's, emergency and trauma, neurological, cardiac, and pulmonary, and orthopedic. **NOTE:** A completed application is required for any position. Apply online. **Positions advertised include:** Cardiovascular Operating Room Technician;

Coder; Cook; Help Desk Operator; Lead Patient Service Representative; Nursing Technician; Physical Therapist. **Parent company:** Bromenn Healthcare. **Operations at this facility include:** Administration; Service.

## CGH MEDICAL CENTER
100 East LeFevre Road, Sterling IL 61081-1279. 815/625-0400. **Contact:** Director of Human Resources. **World Wide Web address:** http://www.cghmc.com. **Description:** An acute care trauma center housing a variety of specialty centers including home nursing, home health, sleep disorder, and speech and hearing. **NOTE:** See website for job listings. An application is required for any position. Download an application from the website and mail it or apply online. **Positions advertised include:** Patient Registration Clerk; RN.

## CARDINAL HEALTH
1430 Waukegan Road, McGraw Park IL 60085. 847/578-9500. **Contact:** Human Resources. **World Wide Web address:** http://www.cardinal.com. **Description:** Cardinal Health is a producer, developer, and distributor of medical products and technologies for use in hospitals and other health care settings. The company operates through two industry segments: medical specialties, and medical/laboratory products and distribution. **NOTE:** Apply online. **Corporate headquarters location:** Dublin OH. **Operations at this facility include:** This location distributes medical supplies to hospitals and government facilities. Number of employees worldwide: 55,000. **Listed on:** New York Stock Exchange. **Stock exchange symbol:** CAH.

## CAREMARK INTERNATIONAL
2211 Sanders Road, Northbrook IL 60062. 847/559-4700. **Contact:** Director of Human Resources. **World Wide Web address:** http://www.caremark.com. **Description:** A leading provider of patient services through health care networks. Divisions include physician practice management and pharmaceutical services, which includes one of the country's largest independent pharmacy benefit management programs, serving approximately 29 million Americans through a mail-order and retail network of pharmacies. AdvancePCS, a mail-order prescription company, is also part of Caremark. Apply online. **International locations:** Worldwide. **Operations at this facility include:** Administration; Operations. **Listed on:** New York Stock Exchange. **Stock exchange symbol:** CMX.

## CARLE FOUNDATION HOSPITAL
611 West Park Street, Urbana IL 61801. 217/383-4000. **Fax:** 217/383-3373. **Contact:** Human Resources. **E-mail address:** Foundation.HR@carle.com. **World Wide Web address:** http://www.carle.com/CFH/about. **Description:** A 295-bed, tertiary care and regional trauma center. Carle Foundation Hospital also includes a 295-bed, long-term care facility, home care agency, retail pharmacy, daycare center, and psychiatric and chemical dependency services. This hospital also provides services for the Carle Medical Clinic, (located in the same building) as well as other healthcare facilities throughout Illinois. **NOTE:** Interested jobseekers may mail or apply online for open positions. Resumes and applications are also accepted in the Human Resources office. **Positions advertised include:** Certified/Registered Coder; Inpatient Coding Coordinator; Therapy Office Coordinator; Health Care Technician; Advanced Practice Nurse; Physical Therapist; Telemedicine and Mobile Clinic Coordinator; Contract Administrator; Physician Services Director. **Office hours:** Monday – Friday, 7:00 a.m. – 5:00 p.m.

## CENTRAL DUPAGE HOSPITAL
## BEHAVIORAL HEALTH SERVICES

25 North Winfield Road, Winfield IL 60190. 630/653-4000. **Fax:** 630/933-2652. **Contact:** Human Resources. **E-mail address:** hr@cdh.org. **World Wide Web address:** http://www.cdh.org. **Description:** A mental health and chemical dependency outpatient and inpatient treatment center. **Positions advertised include:** Purchasing Assistant; Physician Peer Review Clinical Decision Support; RN (Various); Home Health Aide.

## CHICAGO ASSOCIATION FOR RETARDED CITIZENS (CARC)

8 South Michigan Avenue, Suite 1700, Chicago IL 60603. 312/346/6230. **Contact:** Recruiting Manager. **E-mail address:** recruiting@chgoarc.org. **Description:** Provides self-help and vocational training skills to people with physical and mental disabilities. Operates 14 education and vocational centers throughout the Chicago area. **NOTE:** See website for center locations. Send all resumes and cover letters to this address. **Positions advertised include:** Special Education Teacher; QMRP/Counselor.

## DELNOR COMMUNITY HOSPITAL

300 Randall Road, Geneva IL 60134. 630/208-3000. **Contact:** Human Resources. **World Wide Web address:** http://www.delnor.com. **Description:** A 118-bed hospital offering a variety of specialized services including massage therapy, orthopedics, heart care, pediatrics, and cancer care. **NOTE:** Apply online. **Positions advertised include:** RN (Various); Nursing Coordinator; RN Patient Care Coordinator; Special Procedure Anesthetist; Cardiac Ultrasonographer.

## EDWARD HOSPITAL

801 South Washington Street, Naperville IL 60540. 630/527-3401. **Contact:** Human Resources. **World Wide Web address:** http://www.edward.org. **Description:** A 159-bed full-service, nonprofit hospital. Edward Hospital provides a number of health services ranging from preventive education to advanced treatment technology. Its 50-acre campus supports a state-of-the-art, all-private-room inpatient facility; Edward Cardiovascular Institute; Edward Health & Fitness Center; Edward Hospital Cancer Center, affiliated with the Oncology Institute at Loyola University Medical Center; CARE Center, a diagnostic program for sexually abused children; and Linden Oaks Hospital, a private psychiatric facility. The hospital also operates Edward Healthcare Center in Bolingbrook, a satellite health care center with primary and specialty care physicians and a full range of diagnostic services. **NOTE:** Complete the online application located on the hospital's website.

## ELGIN MENTAL HEALTH CENTER

750 South State Street, Elgin IL 60123. 847/742-1040. **Contact:** Director of Employee Services. **Description:** An inpatient, psychiatric hospital serving the metropolitan and suburban Chicago areas. Part of the Illinois Department of Human Services. **NOTE:** Download an application at the Department of Human Service's website: http://www.dhs.state.i.us/careers.

## EVANSTON HOSPITAL CORPORATION

2650 Ridge Avenue, Evanston IL 60201. 847/570-2600. **Fax:** 847/570-1903. **Contact:** Employment Office. **World Wide Web address:** http://www.enh.org. **Description:** Operates Evanston Hospital (also at this location), as well as

Glenbrook Hospital (Glenview IL). **NOTE:** Apply online. **Positions advertised include:** RN (Various); Staff Nurse; Physical Medicine Aide; Research Scientist; Audiologist; Patient Service Representative; Nursing Assistant. **Corporate headquarters location:** This location. **Operations at this facility include:** Administration; Regional Headquarters; Service.

## GALENA-STRAUSS HOSPITAL & NURSING CARE FACILITY

215 Summit Street, Galena IL 61036. 815/777-1340. **Contact:** Melissa Kaiser, Human Resources Manager. **E-mail address:** mjkaiser@galenastauss.org. **World Wide Web address:** http://www.galenahealth.org. **Description:** A 25-bed, nonprofit, acute care hospital and 60-bed nursing home. Founded in 1962. **NOTE:** Entry-level positions and second and third shifts are offered. **Positions advertised include:** Exercise Specialist; Certified Nurses' Assistant; Laboratory Manager; Assistant Director of Nursing. **Office hours:** Monday - Friday, 8:00 a.m. - 4:00 p.m. **Corporate headquarters location:** This location.

## GLENBROOK HOSPITAL

2100 Pfingsten Road, Glenview IL 60026. 847/657-5800. **Contact:** Human Resources. **World Wide Web address:** http://www.enh.org. **Description:** A 136-bed hospital offering a variety of health services including coronary care, plastic surgery, cancer care, and joint replacement. **NOTE:** Apply online. **Positions advertised include:** Medical Secretary; MRI Technologist; EKG Technician; Ophthalmic Technician; Senior Secretary. **Parent company:** Evanston Northwestern Healthcare.

## GLENOAKS HOSPITAL

701 Winthrop Avenue, Glendale Heights IL 60139. 630/545-7300. **Fax:** 630/545-3999. **Contact:** Human Resources. **World Wide Web address:** http://www.ahsmidwest.org. **Description:** A 186-bed, nonprofit, acute care hospital. The hospital is affiliated with the Seventh-Day Adventist Church. Founded in 1980. **NOTE:** Second and third shifts are offered. Apply online. **Positions advertised include:** Case Manager; Certified Nurse Midwife; Charge Nurse; CT Technologist; Quality Management Director. **Special programs:** Training. **Office hours:** Monday - Friday, 7:30 a.m. - 4:30 p.m. **Corporate headquarters location:** Washington DC. **Parent company:** Adventist Health System.

## GOOD SAMARITAN HOSPITAL

3815 Highland Avenue, Downers Grove IL 60515. 630/275-5900. **Contact:** Human Resources. **World Wide Web address:** http://www.advocatehealth.com. **Description:** A 300-bed hospital offering a wide range of health services from emergency care to pediatrics. **NOTE:** Apply online. **Positions advertised include:** Central Outpatient Scheduler; Cleaning and Process Technician; Clinical Education Specialist; RN (Various); Physician (Various).

## GREAT LAKES NAVAL HOSPITAL

3001A Sixth Street, Great Lakes IL 60088. 847/688-4561. **Contact:** Human Resources. **World Wide Web address:** http://www.greatlakes.med.navy.mil. **Description:** A military hospital serving active and retired military personnel and their families in the Midwest region. **NOTE:** This hospital has jobs for military personnel and civilians. Call the regional Human Resources Office at 847/688-2222 to hear job listings and how application procedures.

**HELP AT HOME INC.**
17 North State Street, Suite 1400, Chicago IL 60602. 312/762-9999. **Fax:** 312/704-0022. **Contact:** Human Resources. **World Wide Web address:** http://www.helpathome.com. **Description:** Provides homemaker and nurses aide services for the elderly. **Corporate headquarters location:** This location. **Other area locations:** Danville IL; East Alton IL; Galesburg IL; Joliet IL; Macomb IL; Mount Vernon IL; Oak Forest IL; Ottawa IL; Rock Island IL; Rockford IL; Skokie IL; Springfield IL; St. Charles IL; Waukegan IL. **Other U.S. locations:** IN; MO; MI; AL; MS; TN. **Subsidiaries include:** Oxford Health Care. **Listed on:** NASDAQ. **Stock exchange symbol:** HAHI.

**EDWARD HINES JR. VA HOSPITAL**
P.O. Box 5000, Hines IL 60141. 708/202-8387. **Contact:** Human Resources. **World Wide Web address:** http://www.vagreatlakes.org. **Description:** A medical center operated by the U.S. Department of Veterans Affairs. **NOTE:** For job listings at this facility, visit http://www.vacareers.com. Mail resumes to this location and indicate which center or job you are applying.

**HOLY CROSS HOSPITAL**
2701 West 68th Street, Chicago IL 60629. 773/471-9050. **Fax:** 773/884-8013. **Contact:** Human Resources. **E-mail address:** hrd@holycrosshospital.org. **World Wide Web address:** http://www.holycrosshospital.org. **Description:** A 331-bed, nonprofit, community hospital offering a wide range of inpatient and outpatient health services. **NOTE:** See website for job listings. Resumes may be mailed or faxed. Interested jobseekers may also apply in person at the Human Resources Office. **Office hours:** Monday – Friday, 8:00 a.m. – 4:30 p.m.

**HUDSON RESPIRATORY CARE INC.**
900 West University Drive, Arlington Heights IL 60004. 847/259-7400. **Contact:** Althea J. Schuler, Human Resources Manager. **World Wide Web address:** http://www.hudsonrci.com. **Description:** A specialized manufacturer of sterile disposable products for respiratory therapy. **NOTE:** Apply online or fax resumes for open positions. **Positions advertised include:** Territory Sales Manager; Quality Assurance Compliance Specialist. **Corporate headquarters location:** Temecula CA. **Operations at this facility include:** Administration; Manufacturing. **Listed on:** Privately held.

**INTERIM HEALTHCARE**
3020 West Willow Knolls Drive, Peoria IL 61614. 309/693-7665. **Toll-free phone:** 800/373-0659. **Fax:** 309/693-7664. **Contact:** Human Resources. **World Wide Web address:** http://www.interimhealthcare.com/peoria_il. **Description:** Provides home health care services. **Positions advertised include:** RN; LPN; Physical Therapist; Occupational Therapist; Dental Hygienists; Dental Assistants.

**JACKSON PARK HOSPITAL**
7531 Stony Island Avenue, Chicago IL 60649. 773/947-7512. **Contact:** Human Resources. **World Wide Web address:** http://www.jacksonparkhospital.com. **Description:** A 326-bed hospital offering inpatient and outpatient services. **NOTE:** Apply in person at the hospital's Human Resources Office. **Office hours**: Monday – Friday: 8:00 a.m. – 4:30 p.m. **Operations at this facility include:** Administration; Service.

### KINDRED HOSPITAL/NORTHLAKE

365 East North Avenue, Northlake IL 60164. 708/345-8100. **Contact:** Human Resources. **World Wide Web address:** http://www.kindrednorthlake.com. **Description:** A hospital specializing in wound care; pulmonary medicine; rehabilitative medicine; and vision care. **NOTE:** Apply online. **Positions advertised include:** RN; LPN; Pharmacist; Occupational Therapist; Monitor Technician; Dietary Aide. **Parent company:** Kindred Healthcare.

### LA RABIDA CHILDREN'S HOSPITAL

East 65th Street at Lake Michigan, Chicago IL 60649. 773/363-6700x635. **Fax:** 773/363-7905. **Recorded jobline:** 773/363-6700x500. **Contact:** Recruiter. **E-mail address:** gchurnovic@larabida.org. **World Wide Web address:** http://www.larabida.org. **Description:** A 77-bed pediatric hospital specializing in treating children with chronic illnesses and long-term disabilities. Founded in 1896. **NOTE:** Mail, fax or e-mail resumes or visit the Human Resources Office to fill out an application. **Positions advertised include:** Nutritionist; Senior Physical Therapist; Medical Technologist; Speech Language Pathologist; Respiratory Therapist; RN; LPN; Certified Nurse Assistants.

### LINDEN OAKS HOSPITAL

801 South Washington Street, Naperville IL 60540. 630/305-5500. **Contact:** Human Resources. **World Wide Web address:** http://www.edward.org. **Description:** A full-service behavioral health care system meeting the needs of persons with emotional, behavioral, and substance abuse problems, as well as eating disorders. Linden Oaks Hospital is located on 10 acres of the Edward Hospital medical campus. **NOTE:** Interested jobseekers may apply online at the hospital's website or in person at the Human Resources Office. **Positions advertised include:** File Clerk; Customer Service Specialist; ER Physician Coder; Financial Counselor; Float Unit Secretary; Case Manager; Mammography Technician. **Special programs:** Internships. **Corporate headquarters location:** Macon GA. **Other U.S. locations:** Nationwide. **Operations at this facility include:** Service. **Listed on:** Privately held.

### LITTLE COMPANY OF MARY HOSPITAL

2800 West 95th Street, Evergreen Park IL 60805. 708/422-6200. **Recorded jobline:** 708/229-5050. **Contact:** Human Resources. **World Wide Web address:** http://www.lcmh.org. **Description:** A nonprofit hospital offering a variety of services including oncology, orthopedics, pediatrics, mother/baby care, home care, senior services, and a full-service emergency room. **NOTE:** Jobseekers are encouraged to apply via the website. **Positions advertised include:** Ultrasound Technologist; RN (Various); Surgical Technician; Nurse Manager; Medical Assistant. **Special programs:** Internships; Summer Jobs.

### LOMBART MIDWEST INSTRUMENTS

1312 Marquette Drive, Suite G, Romeoville IL 60446. 630/759-7666. **Toll-free phone:** 800/831-1194. **Fax:** 630/759-1744. **Contact:** Human Resources. **Description:** Lombart Midwest Instruments manufactures nonsurgical, ophthalmic equipment for examinations.

### MACAN ENGINEERING & MANUFACTURING COMPANY

1564 North Damen Avenue, Chicago IL 60622. 773/772-2000. **Toll-free phone:** 866/622-2611. **Fax:** 773/772-2003. **Contact:** Human Resources. **World Wide Web address:** http://www.macanengineering.com. **Description:** Manufactures electorsurgery units for dentists and veterinarians.

## McDONOUGH DISTRICT HOSPITAL
525 East Grant Street, Macomb IL 61455. 309/833-4101. **Fax:** 309/836-1677. **Contact:** Human Resources. **E-mail address:** info@mdh.org. **World Wide Web address:** http://www.mdh.org. **Description:** A 120-bed, nonprofit community hospital. **NOTE:** A completed application is require for any position. See website to download an application and mail or fax it or deliver it in person to the Human Resources Office. **Positions advertised include:** Cardiac Rehabilitation Nurse; Physical Therapist; RN (Various); Staff Dietitian; Nursing Instructor. **Office hours:** Monday – Friday, 7:00 a.m. – 4:30 p.m.

## MEDLINE INDUSTRIES, INC.
One Medline Place, Mundelein IL 60060. 847/949-5500. **Toll-free phone:** 800/MED-LINE. **Fax:** 847/949-2109. **Contact:** Human Resources. **E-mail address:** employment@medline.com. **World Wide Web address:** http://www.medline.net. **Description:** One of the largest privately held manufacturers and distributors of health care products including beds, cots, gowns, and wheelchairs. Founded in 1910. **NOTE:** For sales positions, mail resumes to the Sales Recruiter at this location or send resumes via e-mail to salesrecruiter@medline.com. Entry-level positions and second and third shifts are offered. **Positions advertised include:** Product Manager; Quality Control Inspector; Administrative Assistant; Sales Administration Coordinator; Customer Relations Specialist. **Special programs:** Internships; Co-ops; Summer Jobs. **Office hours:** Monday - Friday, 8:00 a.m. - 5:00 p.m. **Corporate headquarters location:** This location. **Other U.S. locations:** Nationwide. **Operations at this facility include:** Administration; Manufacturing; Sales. **Listed on:** Privately held.

## MELMEDICA CHILDREN'S HEALTHCARE
17600 South Pulaski Road, Country Club Hills IL 60478. 708/335-3331. **Toll-free phone:** 800/387-PEDS. **Fax:** 630/357-4696. **Contact:** Human Resources. **World Wide Web address:** http://www.melmedica.com. **Description:** Provides private, in-home nursing care primarily in pediatrics. The company also offers limited obstetric services. **NOTE:** For all RN positions, call 800/387-7337 or fax resumes to 800/434-7337.

## MERCY HOSPITAL & MEDICAL CENTER
2525 South Michigan Avenue, Chicago IL 60616. 312/567-2011. **Fax:** 312/567-5562. **Contact:** Kay Jensen, Human Resources Director. **E-mail address:** employment@mercy-chicago.org. **World Wide Web address:** http://www.mercy-chicago.org. **Description:** A mid-size teaching hospital that is part of a network of satellite clinic facilities. NOTE: An application is required for any position. See website for job listings and application. Part-time and second and third shifts are offered. **Positions advertised include:** RN (Various); LPN; Patient Care Attendant; Clinical Lab Assistant; Physical Therapist; Clinical Educator; Speech Pathologist; Coding and Data Research Manager; Laboratory Supervisor; Application Business Analyst. **Operations at this facility include:** Administration; Research and Development; Service.

## METHODIST HOSPITAL OF CHICAGO
5015 North Paulina Street, Chicago IL 60640. 773/271-9040. **Contact:** Human Resources. **World Wide Web address:** http://www.bethanymethodist.org. **Description:** A 235-bed, nonprofit, acute care facility that specializes in geriatrics. The hospital is affiliated with a nursing home, retirement community, and immediate care centers. Founded in 1887. **NOTE:** Fax resume or apply in

person at the Human Resources Office. Entry-level positions and second and third shifts are offered. **Positions advertised include:** RN; LPN; Coder; Mental Health Social Worker; Phlebotomist. **Internship information:** Internships in Human Resources are coordinated through area schools. Applications for summer internships must be submitted by mid-April. **Parent company:** Bethany Methodist.

## MIDWEST DENTAL PRODUCTS CORPORATION
901 West Oakton Street, Des Plaines IL 60018. 847/640-4800. **Toll-free phone:** 800/800-2888. **Contact:** Human Resources. **World Wide Web address:** http://www.midwestdental.com. **Description:** Designs, develops, manufactures, and markets a full line of medical and dental X-ray equipment. **Parent company:** DENTSPLY International.

## MIDWESTERN REGIONAL MEDICAL CENTER
2520 Elisha Avenue, Zion IL 60099. 847/872-4561. **Contact:** Human Resources. **World Wide Web address:** http://www.cancercenter.com. **Description:** A community hospital specializing in treating various forms of cancer. **NOTE:** Apply online at http://www.cancercenter.com/employment. **Positions advertised include:** Assistant Director of Imaging; Bone Marrow Transplant; Case Manager; Clinical Manager Assistant; Housekeeper; Medical Technologist.

## MOUNT SINAI HOSPITAL
California Avenue at 15th Street, Chicago IL 60608. 773/542-6236. **Contact:** Human Resources. **World Wide Web address:** http://www.sinai.org. **Description:** A 432-bed, tertiary care hospital. Mount Sinai Hospital also serves as a teaching hospital for The Chicago Medical School. **NOTE:** See website for job listings and contact information. Entry-level, part-time and evening positions offered. Jobseekers interested in nursing positions should call 773/257-6566.

## NORTHWESTERN MEMORIAL HOSPITAL
251 East Huron Street, Chicago IL 60611. 312/908-2000. **Contact:** Human Resources. **World Wide Web address:** http://www.nmh.org. **Description:** A hospital offering a variety of specialized services ranging from preventive medicine to organ transplantation. Northwestern Memorial also serves as the teaching hospital for Northwestern University Medical School. **NOTE:** See website for job listings and contact information. **Special programs:** Internship.

## OTTAWA DENTAL LABORATORY
1304 Starfire Drive, P.O. Box 771, Ottawa IL 61350. **Toll-free phone:** 800/851-8239. **Fax:** 815/434-0760. **Contact:** Joanie Bretag, Human Resources. **E-mail address:** hrodl@ottawadentallab.com. **World Wide Web address:** http://www.ottawadentallab.com. **Description:** A dental lab that manufactures dentures, crowns, bridges, and other dental products. **NOTE:** See website for application.

## OUR LADY OF THE RESURRECTION MEDICAL CENTER
5645 West Addison Street, Chicago IL 60634. 773/282-7000. **Recorded jobline:** 877/737-4636(option 9). **Fax:** 773/794-8467. **Contact:** Human Resources. **World Wide Web address:** http://www.reshealth.org. **Description:** A 288-bed, acute care, community hospital. **NOTE:** The hospital only accepts resumes for open positions. See website for job listings and apply online. Evening and part-time positions offered. **Positions advertised include:** Activities Assistant;

Certified Nursing Assistant; Environmental Service Worker; Nurse Practitioner; Occupational Therapist.

## PALOS COMMUNITY HOSPITAL
12251 South 80th Avenue, Palos Heights IL 60463. 708/923-4880. **Fax:** 708/923-4888. **Recorded jobline:** 708/923-8088. **Contact:** Human Resources. **World Wide Web address:** http://www.paloshospital.org. **Description:** A community hospital. For professional positions, e-mail resumes to holly_brasher@paloscommunityhospital.org. For support staff positions, e-mail resumes to diane_jorgensen@paoloscommunityhospital.org. For nursing positions, e-mail regina_sibley@paloscommunityhospital.org. Part-time jobs and second and third shifts are offered. **Special programs:** Volunteers.

## PEKIN HOSPITAL
600 South 13th Street, Pekin IL 61554. 309/347-1151. **Fax:** 309/347-1249. **Contact:** Human Resources. **E-mail address:** hr@phs1.org. **World Wide Web address:** http://www.pekinhospital.org. **Description:** A hospital engaged in allied health services. **NOTE:** See website for job listings and online application. **Positions advertised include:** Decision Support Analyst; House Supervisor; RN(Various); Surgical Technologist. **Operations at this facility include:** Administration; Service.

## PERKINELMER
2200 Warrenville Road, Downers Grove IL 60515. 630/969-6000. **Toll-free phone:** 800/323-5891. **Fax:** 630/969-6511. **Contact:** Human Resources. **World Wide Web address:** http://www.perkinelmer.com. **Description:** Manufactures biomedical instruments that test blood for disease including the scintillation gamma counter. Primary customers are hospitals and universities located worldwide. **NOTE:** Final Acceptance Testing; Electrical Engineering Manager; Technical Services Manager.

## PROCTOR HOSPITAL
5409 North Knoxville Avenue, Peoria IL 61614. 309/691-1062. **Fax:** 309/689-6062. **Contact:** Human Resources. **World Wide Web address:** http://www.proctor.org. **Description:** A 200-bed general hospital with a specialty addiction recovery clinic. **NOTE:** Entry-level, second- and third- shifts are offered. See website for job listings and application procedures. For nursing opportunities, contact Sheila Johnson at 309/683-6062. **Positions advertised include:** Linen Handler; Medical Lab Technician; Phlebotomist; RN (Various); LPN (Various).

## PROVENA COVENANT MEDICAL CENTER
1400 West Park Street, Urbana IL 61801-2334. 217/337-2224. **Fax:** 217/337-2619. **Contact:** Human Resources. **World Wide Web address:** http://www.provenacovenant.org. **Description:** A 280-bed, nonprofit, acute care hospital. **NOTE:** Apply online. Entry-level positions are offered. **Positions advertised include:** Assistant to the President; Charge RN: Certified Occupational Therapy Assistant; Coder; Communication/Scheduler; Food Service Worker. **Corporate headquarters location:** Mokena IL. **Parent company:** Provena Health.

## PROVENA MERCY CENTER FOR HEALTH CARE
1325 North Highland Avenue, Aurora IL 60506. 630/859-2222. **Contact:** Human Resource. **World Wide Web address:** http://www.provenamercy.com.

**Description:** A 356-bed hospital offering general health and behavioral services. **NOTE:** Apply online. **Positions advertised include:** Central Scheduling; Clinical Coordinator; Intake Counselor; LPN; Physical Therapist; On-Call Social Worker.

**THE REHABILITATION INSTITUTE OF CHICAGO**
345 East Superior Street, Chicago IL 60611. 312/238-6290. **Toll-free phone:** 800/782-7342. **Fax:** 312/238-1263. **Recorded jobline:** 312/238-5600. **Contact:** Human Resources. **World Wide Web address:** http://www.rehabchicago.org. **Description:** A comprehensive rehabilitation facility offering inpatient, outpatient, subacute, and day treatment. The Rehabilitation Institute of Chicago also offers at home rehabilitation services. **NOTE:** Part-time, second and third shifts are offered. **Positions advertised include:** Clinical Instructor; Help Desk Specialist; Nurse Manager; Phlebotomist; Occupational Therapist; Fitness Instructor; Director of Development; Financial Clearance Coordinator. **Corporate headquarters location:** This location.

**ROCKFORD MEMORIAL HOSPITAL**
2400 North Rockton Avenue, Rockford IL 61103. 815/968-6861. **Contact:** Human Resources. **World Wide Web address:** http://www.rhsnet.org. **Description:** A 490-bed hospital. **NOTE:** Apply online at the hospital's website. **Parent company:** Rockford Health System. **Special programs:** Internships.

**RUSH UNIVERSITY MEDICAL CENTER**
1650 West Harrison, Chicago IL 60612. 312/942-5000. **Contact:** Human Resources. **World Wide Web address:** http://www.rush.edu. **Description:** A 825-bed hospital, specializing in children's medicine. It is the teaching hospital for Rush University. **NOTE:** Apply online. **Positions advertised include:** Dosimetrist; Supervisor of Billing; Applications Analyst; Assistant Professor; Staff Pharmacist; Polysomnographic Technician.

**ST. JOHN'S HOSPITAL**
800 East Carpenter Street, Springfield IL 62769. 217/525-5644. **Toll-free phone:** 800/419-2296. **Fax:** 217/525-5601. **Recorded jobline:** 217/525-5600. **Contact:** Human Resources. **World Wide Web address:** http://www.st-johns.org. **Description:** A 750-bed, nonprofit, tertiary care, teaching facility affiliated with Southern Illinois University School of Medicine. **Positions advertised include:** File Clerk; Unit Clerk; RN (Various). **NOTE:** Entry-level positions and second and third shifts are offered. **Corporate headquarters location:** This location. **Other U.S. locations:** WI. **Parent company:** Hospital Sisters Health System.

**ST. JOSEPH MEDICAL CENTER**
77 North Airlite Street, Elgin IL 60123. 847/931-5505. **Contact:** Human Resources. **World Wide Web address:** http://www.provenasaintjoseph.com. **Description:** A 280-bed, acute care hospital with satellite facilities in surrounding communities. **NOTE:** Apply online. **Corporate headquarters location:** Frankfort IL. **Other U.S. locations:** Avilla IN. **Parent company:** Provena Health.

**SHAY HEALTH CARE SERVICES**
5730 West 159th Street, Oak Forest IL 60452. 708/535-4300. **Fax:** 708/535-7520. **Contact:** Karen Carter, Human Resources Coordinator. **Description:** A home health care agency. Founded in 1981. **NOTE:** Entry-level positions and second and third shifts are offered. **Company slogan:** Beyond business as usual. **Positions advertised include:** Certified Nurses Aide; Daycare Worker; Home Health Aide; Licensed Practical Nurse; Registered Nurse. **Office hours:** Monday

- Friday, 8:00 a.m. - 4:00 p.m. **Corporate headquarters location:** Chicago IL. **Listed on:** Privately held.

## SOUTH SHORE HOSPITAL

8012 South Crandon Avenue, Chicago IL 60617. 773/768-0810. **Fax:** 773/468-0749. **Contact:** Joe Perez, Human Resources Director. **E-mail address:** jobs@southshorehospital.com. **World Wide Web address:** http://www.southshorehospital.com. **Description:** A 170-bed, acute care hospital offering a full range of inpatient and outpatient health services. **NOTE:** This company prefers that resumes be mailed or faxed; however, there is an online application form available on its website.

## STERICYCLE, INC.

28161 North Keith Drive, Lake Forest IL 60045. **Toll-free phone:** 800/643-0240. **Fax:** 847/367-9493. **Contact:** Human Resources. **E-mail address:** careers@stericycle.com. **World Wide Web address:** http://www.stericycle.com. **Description:** Provides medical waste management services. Services include regulated medical waste collection, transportation, treatment, disposal, and reduction services. Founded in 1989. **NOTE:** See website for job listings. Entry-level, part-time and temporary positions offered. **Corporate headquarters location:** This location. **Listed on:** NASDAQ. **Stock exchange symbol:** SRCL.

## STREAMWOOD BEHAVIORAL HEALTH CENTER

1400 East Irving Park Road, Streamwood IL 60107. 630/837-9000. **Fax:** 630/540-4290. **Contact:** Mark Paladino, Director of Human Resources. **World Wide Web address:** http://www.streamwoodhospital.com. **Description:** A psychiatric hospital for children and adolescents aged 3 through 18. **NOTE:** Apply online. Entry-level positions and second and third shifts are offered. **Special programs:** Internships. **Listed on:** Privately held.

## THOREK HOSPITAL AND MEDICAL CENTER

850 West Irving Park Road, Chicago IL 60613. 773/525-6780. **Fax:** 773/975-6839. **Contact:** Human Resources. **E-mail address:** humanresources@thorek.org. **World Wide Web address:** http://www.thorek.org. **Description:** A medical center. Thorek also offers The Center for Male Health. **Positions advertised include:** RN; LPN.

## U.S. DEPARTMENT OF VETERANS AFFAIRS
## JESSE BROWN VA MEDICAL CENTER

820 South Damen Avenue, HRMS, Chicago IL 60612. 312/569-8387. **Contact:** Human Resources. **World Wide Web address:** http://www.vagreatlakes.org. **Description:** A medical center operated by the U.S. Department of Veterans Affairs. From 54 hospitals in 1930, the system has grown to include 171 medical centers; more than 364 outpatient, community and outreach clinics; 130 nursing home care units; and 37 domiciliary residences. The VA operates at least one medical center in each of the 48 contiguous states, Puerto Rico, and the District of Columbia. With approximately 76,000 medical center beds, the VA treats nearly 1 million patients in VA hospitals, 75,000 in nursing home care units, and 25,000 in domiciliary residences. The VA's outpatient clinics register approximately 24 million visits a year. The VA is affiliated with 104 medical schools, 48 dental schools, and more than 850 other schools across the country. **NOTE:** For job listings at this facility, visit http://www.vacareers.com. Send resumes and inquiries to Edward Hines Jr. VA Hospital, Human Resources, Chicago Network, HRMS-05, Hines IL 60141. 708/343-7200. Indicate to which

178 /The Chicago JobBank

center or for which job you are applying. **Corporate headquarters location:** Washington DC. **Other U.S. locations:** Nationwide. **Operations at this facility include:** Administration; Research and Development; Service.

## U.S. DEPARTMENT OF VETERANS AFFAIRS
## LAKESIDE CLINIC
333 East Huron Street, Chicago IL 60611. 312/569-8387. **Contact:** Human Resources. **World Wide Web address:** http://www.vagreatlakes.org. **Description:** An outpatient center dedicating to serving veterans and their dependents. The hospital is operated by the U.S. Department of Veterans Affairs. **NOTE:** For job listings at this facility, visit http://www.vacareers.com. Send resumes and inquiries to Edward Hines Jr. VA Hospital, Human Resources, Chicago Network, HRMS-05, Hines IL 60141. 708/343-7200. Indicate to which center or for which job you are applying. **Other U.S. locations:** Nationwide.

## UNIVERSITY OF CHICAGO HOSPITALS & HEALTH SYSTEM
5841 South Maryland Avenue, Chicago IL 60637. 773/702-0198. **Contact:** Human Resources. **World Wide Web address:** http://www.uchospitals.edu. **Description:** A hospital. **NOTE:** Applicants should send resumes to the Employment Office, 800 East 55th Street, Chicago IL 60615. **Positions advertised include:** Certified Nurses Aide; Certified Occupational Therapy Assistant; Dietician/Nutritionist; EEG Technologist; EKG Technician; Emergency Medical Technician; Home Health Aide; Medical Records Technician; Nuclear Medicine Technologist; Occupational Therapist; Pharmacist; Physical Therapist; Physician; Radiological Technologist; Registered Nurse; Respiratory Therapist; Social Worker; Speech-Language Pathologist. **Operations at this facility include:** Administration.

## VICTORY MEMORIAL HOSPITAL
1324 North Sheridan Road, Waukegan IL 60085. 847/360-4170. **Fax:** 847/360-4230. **Contact:** Human Resources. **World Wide Web address:** http://www.vistahealth.com. **Description:** A hospital that provides inpatient, outpatient, and home health care services. **Positions advertised include:** Transcriptionist; Evening & Nights Manager; Medical Technologist; Pharmacist; Senior Environmental Services Aides; Patient Care Technician; Registered Nurse; Transporter. **Other area locations:** Lindenhurst IL. **Parent company:** Vista Health Services.

## VIROTEK LLC / EFOORA, INC.
900 Asbury Drive, Buffalo Grove IL 60089. 847/634-6400. Fax: 847/634-7394. **Contact:** Hiring Manager. **E-mail address:** jobs@virotek.com. **World Wide Web address:** http://www.virotek.com. **Description:** Virotek offers a wide range of products and services, including our own line of rapid diagnostic tests and components, for the clinical, veterinary, industrial, and environmental markets. **Positions advertised include:** Research Associate; Bio-Sensor Associate; Molding Process Technician.

## VISITING NURSE ASSOCIATION
1245 Corporate Boulevard, 5th Floor, Aurora IL 60504. 630/978-2532. **Contact:** Human Resources. **World Wide Web address:** http://www.vnafoxvalley.com. **Description:** Provides home health services to patients. Services include nursing, physical therapy, occupational therapy, speech pathology, nutritional therapy, mental health and enterostomal therapy, medical social services, and hospice care. **Other U.S. locations:** Nationwide.

**VISITING NURSE ASSOCIATION**
720 North Bond Street, Springfield IL 62702. 217/523-4113. **Contact:** Human Resources. **Description:** Provides home health services to patients. Services include nursing, physical therapy, occupational therapy, speech pathology, nutritional therapy, mental health and enterostomal therapy, medical social services, and hospice care.

## HOTELS AND RESTAURANTS

**You can expect to find the following types of companies in this section:**
Casinos • Dinner Theaters • Hotel/Motel Operators • Resorts • Restaurants

---

**ARAMARK**
1801 South Meyers Road, Suite 300, Oak Brook Terrace IL 60181. 630/568-2500. **Contact:** Human Resources. **World Wide Web address:** http://www.aramark.com. **Description:** ARAMARK Correctional Services provides food to more than 125,000 inmates at 175 prisons and jail facilities in 27 states and Puerto Rico. The company also offers facility management services. **Parent company:** ARAMARK is one of the world's leading providers of managed services. The company operates in all 50 states and 15 foreign countries, offering a broad range of services to businesses of all sizes including most *Fortune* 500 companies and thousands of universities, hospitals, and municipal, state, and federal government facilities. The company is employee-owned. With revenues over $7 billion, the company is among the market leaders in all of its businesses. ARAMARK's businesses include Food, Leisure and Support Services including Campus Dining Services, School Nutrition Services, Leisure Services, Business Dining Services, International Services, Healthcare Support Services, Conference Center Management, and Refreshment Services; Facility Services; Correctional Services; Industrial Services; Uniform Services, which includes Uniform Services and Wearguard, a direct marketer of work clothing; Health and Education Services including Spectrum Healthcare Services and Children's World Learning Centers; and Book and Magazine Services. **NOTE:** Apply online.

**CHICAGO MARRIOTT DOWNTOWN**
540 North Michigan Avenue, Chicago IL 60611-3822. 312/836-0100. **Contact:** Human Resources. **World Wide Web address:** http://www.marriott.com. **Description:** A full-service hotel chain offering 1,172 rooms and 20 meeting facilities. **NOTE:** Apply online. **Other U.S. locations:** Nationwide. **Listed on:** New York Stock Exchange. **Stock exchange symbol:** MAR.

**ED DEBEVIC'S RESTAURANT**
640 North Wells, Chicago IL 60610. 312/664-1707. **Fax:** 312/345-85251. **Contact:** Human Resources. **World Wide Web address:** http://www.eddebevics.com. **Description:** A casual dining restaurant chain. Ed Debevic's serves American cuisine and operates a gift shop.

**HOLIDAY INN CHICAGO-CITY CENTRE**
300 East Ohio Street, Chicago IL 60611. 312/787-6100. **Fax:** 312/787-3055. **Contact:** Human Resources. **World Wide Web address:** http://www.chicc.com. **Description:** A 500-room hotel. **Parent company:** TR Streeterville Hotel Corporation.

## HOLIDAY INN CITY CENTRE

500 Hamilton Boulevard, Peoria IL 61602. 309/674-2500. **Fax:** 309/674-8705. **Contact:** Human Resources. **World Wide Web address:** http://www.holidayinnpeoria.com. **Description:** A 300-room hotel. The Holiday Inn City Centre also houses one of Illinois' largest convention centers. **NOTE:** To apply, visit the company's website. Positions advertised include: Bennigan's Bar Manager; Sales Manager; Catering Assistant; Sales Assistant.

## HOLIDAY INN O'HARE INTERNATIONAL

5440 North River Road, Rosemont IL 60018. 847/671-6350. **Contact:** Staffing. **World Wide Web address:** http://chi-ohare.holiday-inn.com. **Description:** A 507-room location of the large hotel chain. **Parent company:** Six Continents Hotels.

## HOLLYWOOD CASINO AURORA

49 North Golino Boulevard, Aurora IL 60506. 630/801-7000. **Contact:** Human Resources. **World Wide Web address:** http://www.pngaming.com. **Description:** Operates a fixed riverboat casino featuring movie memorabilia. **NOTE:** Apply online at the website. **Positions advertised include:** Bartender; Casino Cashier; Casino Scheduler Internal Auditor. **Parent company:** Penn National Gaming.

## HOSTMARK HOSPITALITY GROUP

1111 Plaza Drive, Suite 200, Schaumburg IL 60173. 847/517-9100. **Fax:** 847/517-9797. **Contact:** Human Resources. **World Wide Web address:** http://www.hostmark.com. **Description:** HostMark Hospitality Group is a hotel property management company. **Positions advertised include:** Director of Sales.

## HOTEL 71

71 East Wacker Drive, Chicago IL 60601. 312/346-7100. **Toll-free phone:** 800/621-4005. **Fax:** 312/346-1721. **Contact:** Recruitment Manager. **E-mail address:** jobs@hotel71.com. **World Wide Web address:** http://www.hotel71.com. **Description:** A 417-room full-service hotel. Founded in 1958.

## HYATT REGENCY CHICAGO

151 East Wacker Drive, Chicago IL 60601. 312/565-1234. **Contact:** Human Resources. **World Wide Web address:** http://www.chicagohyatt.com. **Description:** A hotel with over 2,000 rooms. **NOTE:** Apply online at the website. **Positions advertised include:** Deli Attendant; Food Server Assistant; Front Office Supervisor; Master Accounts Coordinator; Off-Premises Catering Driver.

## LETTUCE ENTERTAIN YOU ENTERPRISES INC.

5419 North Sheridan Road, Suite 104, Chicago IL 60640. 773/878-7340. **Fax:** 773/878-0113. **Contact:** Human Resources. **E-mail address:** resumes@leye.com. **World Wide Web address:** http://www.leye.com. **Description:** A restaurant management company operating casual, moderately priced dining establishments. **NOTE:** Call the Recruiting Office at 773/878-5588 for current job listings. Fax or e-mail resumes.

## LUNAN CORPORATION

414 North Orleans Street, Suite 402, Chicago IL 60610. 312/645-9898. **Contact:** Human Resources. **World Wide Web address:** http://www.arbysrestaurants.com. **Description:** The restaurant management

company of the fast food chain Arby's. **Corporate headquarters location:** This location.

### McDONALD'S CORPORATION
2111 McDonald's Drive, Oak Brook IL 60523. 630/623-3000. **Contact:** Human Resources. **World Wide Web address:** http://www.mcdonalds.com. **Description:** McDonald's is one of the largest restaurant chains and food service organizations in the world, operating more than 26,000 restaurants in 119 countries. **NOTE:** For corporate positions, see the website. For restaurant jobs, see http://www.McState.com or apply in person at the nearest location. **Corporate headquarters location:** This location. **Other U.S. locations:** Nationwide. **International locations:** Worldwide. **Listed on:** New York Stock Exchange. **Stock exchange symbol:** MCD.

### PHEASANT RUN RESORT & CONVENTION CENTER
4051 East Main Street, St. Charles IL 60174-5200. 630/584-6300. **Fax:** 630/762-0509. **Contact:** Human Resources. **E-mail address:** lbabusch@pheasantrun.com. **World Wide Web address:** http://www.pheasantrun.com. **Description:** A hotel and convention center. **NOTE:** Fax or e-mail resumes. Interested jobseekers may also apply in person at the Human Resources Office. **Positions advertise include:** Administrative Assistant; Cook; Bartender; Front Desk Agent; Rooms Director; Security. **Office hours:** Monday – Friday, 8:30 a.m. – 5:00 p.m. **Corporate headquarters location:** This location. **Operations at this facility include:** Sales; Service.

### PIZZA HUT OF AMERICA, INC.
4575 Weaver Parkway, Suite 200, Warrenville IL 60555. 630/791-1000. **Fax:** 630/955-0577. **Contact:** Human Resources. **World Wide Web address:** http://www.pizzahut.com. **Description:** Part of the large, worldwide restaurant chain. **NOTE:** Apply in person at this location or online at http://www.yum.com. **Positions advertised include:** Assistant Manager; Management Trainee. **Special programs:** Internships. **Other U.S. locations:** Nationwide. **Parent company:** Yum Brands.

### RAMADA PLAZA HOTEL O'HARE
6600 North Mannheim Road, Rosemont IL 60018. 847/827-5131. **Contact:** Human Resources. **World Wide Web address:** http://www.ramadaplazaohare.com. **Description:** A hotel and conference facility. Ramada has locations nationwide, including Stouffers/Renaissance Hotel Properties. **NOTE:** Entry-level positions are offered. **Special programs:** Internships; Training. **Corporate headquarters location:** Solon OH. **Other U.S. locations:** Nationwide. **Parent company:** Cendant Corporation. **Operations at this facility include:** Sales; Service.

### SPRINGFIELD HILTON
700 East Adams Street, Springfield IL 62701-1601. 217/789-1530. **Fax:** 217/789-0709. **Contact:** Human Resources. **World Wide Web address:** http://www.hilton.com. **Description:** A 30-story hotel with 368 guest rooms. The hotel also offers long-term guest services. **Parent company:** Hilton Hotels Corporation. **Listed on:** New York Stock Exchange. **Stock exchange symbol:** HLT.

**VISTA INTERNATIONAL**
**dba THE DRAKE HOTEL**
140 East Walton Place, Chicago IL 60611. 312/787-2200. **Contact:** Human Resources. **World Wide Web address:** http://www.hilton.com. **Description:** A 535-room hotel and restaurant.

# INSURANCE

## You can expect to find the following types of companies in this section:
Commercial and Industrial Property/Casualty Insurers • Health Maintenance Organizations (HMO's) • Medical/Life Insurance Companies

---

**ALLSTATE CORPORATION**
2775 Sanders Road, Building A1, Northbrook IL 60052. 847/402-5000. **Toll-free phone:** 800/574-3553. **Fax:** 847/402-5000. **Contact:** Employment Manager. **World Wide Web address:** http://www.allstate.com. **Description:** Provides property, liability, life, reinsurance, and commercial lines of insurance. **NOTE:** Apply online at the company's website. **Company slogan:** You're in good hands. **Special programs:** Internships. **Corporate headquarters location:** This location. **Operations at this facility include:** Administration; Service. **Listed on:** New York Stock Exchange. **Stock exchange symbol:** ALL. **Number of employees nationwide:** 37,600.

**ALLSTATE INSURANCE COMPANY**
South Barrington Plaza, 51 West Higgins Road, South Barrington IL 60010-9300. 847/551-2000. **Contact:** Human Resources Manager. **World Wide Web address:** http://www.allstate.com. **Description:** Provides property, liability, life, reinsurance, and commercial lines of insurance. **NOTE:** Apply online at the company's website. **Company slogan:** You're in good hands. **Corporate headquarters location:** Northbrook IL. **Listed on:** New York Stock Exchange. **Stock exchange symbol:** ALL. **Number of employees nationwide:** 37,600.

**AON CORPORATION**
200 East Randolph Street, Suite 900, Chicago IL 60601. 312/381-4800. Fax: 312/381-0240. **Contact:** Human Resources. **World Wide Web address:** http://www.aon.com. **Description:** An insurance holding company. **NOTE:** This company provides job listings for all its Illinois offices. Apply online. **Positions advertised include:** Risk Analyst; Licensing Administrator; Administrative Assistant; Treaty Drafter; Senior Communications Consultant; Production Assistant; Executive Assistant; Vice President; System Administrator. **Corporate headquarters location:** This location. **Subsidiaries include:** Aon Risk Services; Aon Consulting Worldwide; Aon Services Group; Aon Re Worldwide; Aon Warranty Group; Combined Insurance Company; Virginia Surety Company. **Operations at this facility include:** Administration; Sales; Service. **Listed on:** New York Stock Exchange. **Stock exchange symbol:** AOC.

**BANKERS LIFE AND CASUALTY COMPANY**
222 Merchandise Mart Plaza, 19th Floor, Chicago IL 60654. 312/396-7170. **Fax:** 312/396-5969. **Contact:** Human Resources. **World Wide Web address:** http://www.bankerslife.com. **Description:** Offers a variety of health plans including Medicare supplements, long-term care, and managed care, as well as life, annuity, and disability product lines. **NOTE:** Entry-level positions offered. Apply online for all positions. **Positions advertised include:** Actuarial Assistant; Adjuster; Organizational Trainer and Developer; Help Desk Manager; Claims Vice President; Branch Office Sales Managers. **Corporate headquarters**

**location:** This location. **Parent company:** The Conseco Companies. **Operations at this facility include:** Administration; Service.

## BITUMINOUS INSURANCE COMPANY

320 18th Street, Rock Island IL 61201. 309/786-5401. **Toll-free phone:** 800/475-4777. **Fax:** 309/786-4716. **Contact:** Senior Vice President of Administrative Services. **E-mail address:** hr@bituminous.com. **World Wide Web address:** http://www.bituminousinsurance.com. **Description:** Offers a wide variety of individual insurance plans including property and casualty. **NOTE:** Interested jobseekers may apply by sending their resumes via fax, e-mail or mail. An online application may also be completed at the company's website.

## BLUE CROSS AND BLUE SHIELD OF ILLINOIS

300 East Randolph Street, Chicago IL 60601-5099. 312/938-6000. Fax: 312/240-0386. **Contact:** Pat O'Connor, Human Resources. **World Wide Web address:** http://www.bcbsil.com. **Description:** A nonprofit health care insurance organization providing managed health care plans to both individuals and groups. Blue Cross and Blue Shield offers Point-of-Service, individual health, PPO, and HMO plans, as well as vision and dental insurance. **NOTE:** See website for job listings. Fax resume or apply online. **Positions advertised include:** Source Control Technician; Medical Management Program Administrator; Information Systems; Auditor; Senior Internal Auditor; Senior Information Systems Auditor; Financial Analyst; Care Coordinator I; Medical Management Results Coordinator; Senior Project Coordinator. Parent company: Health Care Service Corporation.

## BOND SAFEGUARD INSURANCE COMPANY

1919 South Highland Avenue, Building A, Suite 300, Lombard IL 60148. 630/495-9380. **Toll-free phone:** 800/962-5212. **Fax:** 630/495-9272. **Contact:** Human Resources. **World Wide Web address:** http://www.bondsafeguard.com. **Description:** Offers bond insurance.

## CNA INSURANCE COMPANIES

CNA Plaza, 333 South Wabash Avenue, 31st Floor, Chicago IL 60685. 312/822-5000. **Contact:** Human Resources. **World Wide Web address:** http://www.cna.com. **Description:** An insurance holding company. **NOTE:** Apply online at the company's website. **Corporate headquarters location:** This location. **Subsidiaries include:** American Casualty Company; Continental Assurance Company; National Fire Insurance Company. **Listed on:** New York Stock Exchange. **Stock exchange symbol:** CNA.

## CHICAGO TITLE & TRUST COMPANY

171 North Clark Street, Chicago IL 60601. 312/223-2000. **Toll-free phone:** 800/815-3969. **Contact:** Human Resources. **World Wide Web address:** http://www.ctic.com. **Description:** Provides a variety of insurance related services including credit services, marketing information, flood insurance, field services, and consolidated reconveyance. **Operations at this facility include:** Administration; Sales; Service.

## COUNTRY COMPANIES INSURANCE GROUP

P.O. Box 2020, Bloomington IL 61702-2020. 309/821-3000. **Toll-free phone:** 866/255-7965. **Fax:** 309/821-5160. **Physical address:** 1711 GE Road, Bloomington IL 61702. **Contact:** Human Resources. **E-mail address:** jake.dressler@countryfinancial.com. **World Wide Web address:** http://www.countryfinancial.com. **Description:** Offers a full line of insurance products including auto, home, life, health, disability income, long-term care, farm, ranch, and commercial insurance, as well as annuities, mutual funds, and financial and estate planning. Country Companies include Country Life, Country Mutual, Country Casualty Insurance Companies, and Country Investors Life Assurance Company. Founded in 1925. **NOTE:** Entry-level positions and second and third shifts are offered. Mail, fax or e-mail resumes. **Positions advertised include:** Field Claims Representative. **Special programs:** Internships; Training. **Corporate headquarters location:** This location. **Other U.S. locations:** AK; AZ; CO; KS; MO; NV; OK; OR; WA. **Operations at this facility include:** Administration; Sales; Service. **Listed on:** Privately held.

## FM GLOBAL
300 South Northwest Highway, Park Ridge IL 60068. 847/430-7000. **Contact:** Human Resources. **World Wide Web address:** http://www.fmglobal.com. **Description:** Offers corporate property insurance and risk management services for commercial and industrial organizations. **NOTE:** The company only accepts resumes for current openings. See the website for job listings. **Corporate headquarters location:** Johnston RI. **Other U.S. locations:** Nationwide. **International locations:** Worldwide.

## FARMERS INSURANCE GROUP
P.O. Box 948, Aurora IL 60507. 630/907-0030. **Physical address:** 2245 Sequoia Drive, Aurora IL 60506. **Fax:** 630/907-3498. **Contact:** Joy Brokaw, Human Resources Manager. **World Wide Web address:** http://www.farmersinsurance.com. **Description:** Farmers Insurance Group is one of the nation's largest property and casualty insurance groups. Founded in 1928. **Positions advertised include:** Workman's Compensation Commercial Underwriter; Trial Attorney; Human Resources Operations Specialist. **Corporate headquarters location:** Los Angeles CA. **Operations at this facility include:** This location houses the business support center and commercial operations.

## FIRST HEALTH
3200 Highland Avenue, Downers Grove IL 60515-1223. 630/737-7900. **Contact:** Human Resources. **World Wide Web address:** http://www.firsthealth.com. **Description:** A managed health care company that provides group health benefit programs for employers nationwide. **NOTE:** This company provides jobs listings on its website for all its locations. Apply online.

## FORT DEARBORN LIFE INSURANCE COMPANY
1020 West Thirty-First Street, Downers Grove IL 60515-5591. **Toll-free phone:** 800/633-3696. **Contact:** Human Resources. **World Wide Web address:** http://www.fdl-life.com. **Description:** Provides group life and disability insurance, as well as other financial services. **Corporate headquarters location:** This location.

## ARTHUR J. GALLAGHER & CO.
2 Pierce Place, Itasca IL 60143-3141. 630/773-3800. **Fax:** 630/285-4000. **Contact:** Human Resources. **World Wide Web address:** http://www.ajg.com. **Description:** An insurance brokerage offering property, casualty, and employee benefit plans. Founded in 1927. **NOTE:** Contact this location for job openings and mail or fax resumes. **Special programs:** Internships. **Office hours:** Monday - Friday, 9:00 a.m. - 5:00 p.m. **Corporate headquarters location:** This location. **Listed on:** New York Stock Exchange. **Stock exchange symbol:** AJG.

## THE HORACE MANN COMPANIES

One Horace Mann Plaza, Springfield IL 62715. 217/788-5153. **Fax:** 217/535-7129. **Contact:** Employment Office. **World Wide Web address:** http://www.horacemann.com. **Description:** A multiline insurance company serving the education industry. **NOTE:** See website for job listings and application information. **Positions advertised include:** Programmer Analyst; Assistant Actuary; Home Office Analyst; Director of Planning; Data Input Operator. **Special programs:** Internships. **Operations at this facility include:** Administration; Sales; Service.

## KEMPER INSURANCE COMPANIES

One Kemper Drive, Long Grove IL 60049. 847/320-2000. **Fax:** 847/320-5624. **Contact:** Human Resources. **World Wide Web address:** http://www.kemperinsurance.com. **Description:** Provides property, casualty, and life insurance, reinsurance, and a wide range of diversified financial services operations. Founded in 1912. **NOTE:** Entry-level positions and second and third shifts are offered. **Positions advertised include:** Claim Specialist; Environmental Claims Handler. **Special programs:** Internships; Training; Co-ops; Summer Jobs. **Corporate headquarters location:** This location. **Subsidiaries include:** Eagle Pacific Insurance Company and Pacific Eagle Insurance Company. **Other U.S. locations:** Nationwide.

## LANDAMERICA

10 South LaSalle Street, Suite 2501, Chicago IL 60603. 312/558-5445. **Contact:** Human Resources. **World Wide Web address:** http://www.landam.com. **Description:** Provides title insurance and other real estate services on commercial and residential transactions in the United States, Canada, the Bahamas, Puerto Rico, and the U.S. Virgin Islands. LandAmerica also provides search and examination services, and closing services for a broad-based customer group that includes lenders, developers, real estate brokers, attorneys, and homebuyers. **Corporate headquarters location:** Richmond VA. **NOTE:** This company has locations throughout Illinois. See website for locations, job listings and contact information. **Other area locations:** Statewide. **Other U.S. locations:** Nationwide. **Operations at this facility include:** This location is a regional office. **Listed on:** New York Stock Exchange. **Stock exchange symbol:** LFG.

## LIBERTY MUTUAL INSURANCE GROUP

555 West Pierce Road, Suite 100, Itasca IL 60143. 630/250-7100. **Contact:** Human Resources. **World Wide Web address:** http://www.libertymutual.com. **Description:** A full-line insurance firm offering life, medical, and business insurance, as well as investment and retirement plans. **NOTE:** Apply online at the corporate website. **Corporate headquarters location:** Boston MA. **Other area locations:** Des Plaines IL; Lisle IL; Matteson IL. **Operations at this facility include:** Divisional Headquarters.

## LINCOLN FINANCIAL ADVISORS

8755 West Higgins Road, Suite 550, Chicago IL 60631. 773/380-8518. **Fax:** 773/693-2531. **Contact:** Linda Proskurniak, Vice President of Professional Development. **E-mail address:** Lsproskurniak@LNC.com. **World Wide Web address:** http://www.lfachicago.com. **Description:** Lincoln Financial Advisors markets financial planning, permanent and term life insurance, annuities, disability coverage, and investment products to business owners and professionals. The company also provides complex estate planning and business planning advice. Founded in 1905. **Corporate headquarters location:** Fort Wayne IN. **Other U.S. locations:** Nationwide. **International locations:** Argentina; China; United Kingdom. **Parent company:** Lincoln Financial Group. **Operations at this facility include:** Regional Headquarters; Sales. **Listed on:** New York Stock Exchange. **Stock exchange symbol:** LNC.

## MARSH INC.
500 West Monroe Street, Suite 2100, Chicago IL 60661-3630. 312/627-6000. **Contact:** Human Resources. **World Wide Web address:** http://www.marsh.com. **Description:** Provides advice and services worldwide through an insurance brokerage and risk management firm, reinsurance intermediary facilities, and a consulting and financial services group, to clients concerned with the management of assets and risks. Specific services include insurance and risk management services, reinsurance, consulting and financial services, merchandising, and investment management. The company has subsidiaries and affiliates in 57 countries, with correspondents in 20 other countries. **Corporate headquarters location:** New York NY. **Parent company:** Marsh & McLennan Companies, Inc.

## NORTH AMERICAN COMPANY FOR LIFE AND HEALTH INSURANCE
525 West Van Buren, Chicago IL 60607. 312/648-7600. **Toll-free phone:** 800/733-2524. **Fax:** 312/648-7765. **Contact:** Michael Haley, Vice President of Human Resources. **E-mail address:** mhaley@nacolah.com. **World Wide Web address:** http://www.nacolah.com. **Description:** Provides a variety of annuities and individual life insurance policies. **Positions advertised include:** Agency Services Associate/Consultant; Marketing Communications Specialist. **Corporate headquarters location:** This location. **Other U.S. locations:** Woodland Hills CA; Garden City NY. **Operations at this facility include:** Administration; Sales; Service. **Listed on:** Privately held.

## OLD REPUBLIC INTERNATIONAL CORPORATION
307 North Michigan Avenue, Chicago IL 60601. 312/346-8100. **Fax:** 312/726-0309. **Contact:** Human Resources Director. **World Wide Web address:** http://www.oldrepublic.com. **Description:** An insurance holding company. **Corporate headquarters location:** This location. **International locations:** Canada; Hong Kong; Puerto Rico. **Listed on:** New York Stock Exchange.

## PRUDENTIAL INSURANCE
1901 Butterfield Road, Suite 250, Downers Grove IL 60515. 630/493-0585. **Contact:** Human Resources. **World Wide Web address:** http://www.prudential.com. **Description:** Provides underwriting risk analysis and selection services for 18 midwestern and northeastern states; provides claims services for policyholders in several midwestern states; and provides nonclaims services to policyholders nationwide. Overall, Prudential Property & Casualty Insurance underwrites family automobile and homeowner policies. Founded in 1969. **NOTE:** Apply online. **Parent company:** Prudential Insurance Company of America.

## RLI CORPORATION
9025 North Lindbergh Drive, Peoria IL 61615-1431. 309/692-1000. **Fax:** 309/692-1068. **Contact:** Human Resources. **World Wide Web address:** http://www.rlicorp.com. **Description:** Underwrites property and casualty insurance policies. **NOTE:** Apply online for all positions. Part-time positions are offered. **Positions advertised include:** Graphic Designer; Paralegal;

Applications Analyst; Post Press Technician. **Listed on:** New York Stock Exchange. **Stock exchange symbol:** RLI.

## SAFECO INSURANCE
225 West Washington Street, Suite 1400, Chicago IL 60606. **Fax:** 847/490-2452. **Contact:** Human Resources. **E-mail address:** stehas@safeco.com. **World Wide Web address:** http://www.safeco.com. **Description:** Sells a comprehensive mix of insurance through a network of independent agents, brokers, and financial advisors nationwide. Safeco products include auto, home, and business insurance, and surety bonds. **Corporate headquarters location:** Seattle WA. **Other U.S. locations:** Nationwide.

## SAFECO INSURANCE COMPANIES
2800 West Higgins Road, Suite 1100, Hoffman Estates IL 60195. 847/490-2900. **Fax:** 847/490-2452. **Recorded jobline:** 800/753-5330. **Contact:** Human Resources Manager. **World Wide Web address:** http://www.safeco.com. **Description:** An insurance company offering personal, homeowner's, auto, commercial, property, casualty, life, and health insurance products and services. Founded in 1923. **NOTE:** Apply online. Entry-level positions are offered. **Positions advertised include:** Legal Secretary; Casualty Claims Examiner; Contract Surety Representative; Personal Lines Claims Specialist; Risk Control Specialist; Workers Compensation Claims Examiner. **Special programs:** Internships; Training. **Office hours:** Monday - Friday, 8:00 a.m. - 4:30 p.m. **Corporate headquarters location:** Seattle WA. **Parent company:** Safeco Insurance Corporation. **Operations at this facility include:** Regional Headquarters.

## THE ST. PAUL TRAVELERS COMPANIES, INC.
540 Lake Cook Road, Deerfield IL 60015. 847/374-2400. **Fax:** 847/374-1306. **Contact:** Human Resources. **World Wide Web address:** http://www.stpaultravelers.com. **Description:** Provides property liability and life insurance services. **NOTE:** Apply online. **Corporate headquarters location:** St. Paul MN.

## STATE FARM INSURANCE
P.O. Box 2315, Bloomington IL 61702. 309/766-2311. **Fax:** 309/735-3422. **Contact:** Human Resources. **World Wide Web address:** http://www.statefarm.com. **Description:** Provides homeowner's, health, auto, and life insurance. **NOTE:** See website for job listings and resume submission guidelines. **Positions advertised include:** Collections Representative; Collection Supervisor; Asset/Liability Management Analyst. **Special programs:** Internships. **Corporate headquarters location:** This location. **Operations at this facility include:** Administration.

## STATE LINE INSURANCE COMPANY
P.O. Box 69, Orangeville IL 61060-0069. 815/789-3366. **Contact:** Human Resources. **Description:** Offers a wide variety of insurance to individuals including property and casualty.

## SUNGARD INSURANCE SYSTEMS
321 Susan Drive, Suite C, Normal IL 61761. 309/862-4300. **Fax:** 309/888-2130. **Contact:** Human Resources. **World Wide Web address:** http://www.sungardinsurance.com. **Description:** Develops computer software for the insurance industry. **NOTE:** Apply online. **Special programs:** Internships.

Corporate headquarters location: Atlanta GA. Other U.S. locations: Denver CO. Parent company: SunGard Corporation. Listed on: New York Stock Exchange. Stock exchange symbol: SDS.

**TICOR TITLE INSURANCE**
203 North LaSalle Street, Suite 1390, Chicago IL 60601. 312/621-5000. Fax: 312/621-5033. Contact: Human Resources. World Wide Web address: http://www.ticortitle.com. Description: Specializes in real estate title insurance and escrow services. Corporate headquarters location: Los Angeles CA. Other area locations: Joliet IL; Oaklawn IL; Schaumburg IL.

**TRUSTMARK INSURANCE COMPANY**
400 Field Drive, Lake Forest IL 60045. 847/615-1500. Contact: Human Resources. World Wide Web address: http://www.trustmarkinsurance.com. Description: A legal reserve life insurance company. Trustmark Insurance Company issues a wide variety of individual and group life, disability, annuity, hospital, and medical policies, as well as administrative service-only arrangements for larger groups. Positions advertised include: Actuarial; Direct Sales Manager; Bindery Operator; Investigative Analyst; Senior Staff Assistant; Telecommunications Manager; Underwriter. Corporate headquarters location: This location. Other U.S. locations: Nationwide. Operations at this facility include: Administration; Sales.

**UNITRIN, INC.**
One East Wacker Drive, Chicago IL 60601. 312/661-4600. Toll-free phone: 800/999-0546. Contact: Personnel. World Wide Web address: http://www.unitrin.com. Description: A financial services company with subsidiaries engaged in three business areas: life and health insurance, property and casualty insurance, and consumer finance. Founded in 1990. Positions advertised include: Actuarial Services Manager; Product Technician; Territory Sales Manager; Regional Claims Manager. Special programs: Internships; Summer Jobs. Office hours: Monday - Friday, 8:00 a.m. - 4:30 p.m. Corporate headquarters location: This location. Listed on: NASDAQ. Stock exchange symbol: UTR.

**WPS/MEDICARE**
2108 Cimarron Drive Freeport IL 61032. 815/233-5196. Contact: Human Resources. World Wide Web address: http://www.wpsic.com. Description: A managed health care insurance provider for private industry, government, and non-group subscribers. Corporate headquarters location: Madison WI.

**WAUSAU INSURANCE COMPANIES**
1431 Opus Place, Suite 300, Downers Grove IL 60515. 630/719-0717. Toll-free phone: 800/835-0060. Contact: Human Resources. World Wide Web address: http://www.wausau.com. Description: Offers a full line of business insurance services including casualty, property, and group insurance, through 7 divisional offices and 100 field offices across the United States. Positions advertised include: Account Manager; Underwriter; Claims Case Manager; Associate Business Analyst; Claims Specialist; Property Loss Contents Adjuster; Sales Associate; Law Clerk. Corporate headquarters location: Wausau WI. Other U.S. locations: Nationwide. Operations at this facility include: Divisional Headquarters.

**ZURICH DIRECT**
1400 American Lane, Schaumburg IL 60173. 847/605-6000. **Contact:** Human Resources. **World Wide Web address:** http://www.zurichdirect.com. **Description:** A life insurance company with worldwide operations. **Corporate headquarters location:** This location. **Parent company:** Zurich Kemper Life.

# LEGAL SERVICES

## You can expect to find the following types of companies in this section:
Law Firms • Legal Service Agencies

## AMERICAN BAR ASSOCIATION
321 North Clark Street, Chicago IL 60610. 312/988-5000. **Contact:** Human Resources. **World Wide Web address:** http://www.abanet.org. **Description:** A professional association serving the legal profession. **Corporate headquarters location:** This location.

## ARNSTEIN & LEHR
120 South Riverside Plaza, Suite 1200, Chicago IL 60606. 312/876-7100. **Fax:** 312/876-0288. **Contact:** Denise Simms, Manager of Human Resources. **World Wide Web address:** http://www.arnstein.com. **Description:** A law firm specializing in antitrust, corporate, environmental, insurance, real estate, and tax law. This law firm also has offices in Hoffman Estates IL. **Positions advertised include:** Word Processor; Network Administrator. **Corporate headquarters location:** This location. Other U.S. locations: WI; FL. **Operations at this facility include:** Administration. **Listed on:** Privately held.

## BAKER & McKENZIE
One Prudential Plaza, 130 East Randolph Drive, Chicago IL 60601. 312/861-8800. **Fax:** 312/861-8823. **Contact:** Bethany Phillips, Recruiter. **World Wide Web address:** http://www.bakernet.com. **Description:** A general practice law firm. **Corporate headquarters location:** This location.

## CHAPMAN AND CUTLER
111 West Monroe Street, Chicago IL 60603. 312/845-3898. **Fax:** 312/701-2361. **Contact:** Human Resources. **World Wide Web address:** http://www.chapman.com. **Description:** A law firm specializing in corporate financing, litigation, and tax law. **NOTE:** To apply for attorney positions, contact Stacey Kielbasa, Legal Personnel and Recruitment Manager, at kielbasa@chapman.com. Transcripts must be submitted with cover letters and resumes. For corporate and support positions, send resumes to Kimberly Wongstrom-Torvik via fax at 312/516-1488 or e-mail at legalresumes@chapman.com. **Special programs:** Summer Associates. **Corporate headquarters location:** This location. **Operations at this facility include:** Administration; Service. **Listed on:** Privately held.

## PIPER MARBURY RUDNICK & WOLFE LLP
203 North LaSalle Street, Suite 1400, Chicago IL 60601. 312/368-4000. **Fax:** 312/236-7516. **Contact:** Marguerite E. Strubing, Legal Recruiting Manager. **E-mail address:** marguerite.strubing@piperrudnick.com. **World Wide Web address:** http://www.piperrudnick.com. **Description:** A law firm specializing in bankruptcy, corporate, labor, insurance, and tax law. **Special programs:** Summer employment. **Other U.S. locations:** Nationwide.

**VEDDER, PRICE, KAUFMAN, & KAMMHOLZ**
222 North LaSalle Street, Suite 2600, Chicago IL 60601. 312/609-7500. **Fax:** 312/609-5005. **Contact:** Gina Grunloh, Human Resources. **E-mail address:** ggrunloh@vedderprice.com. **World Wide Web address:** http://www.vedderprice.com. **Description:** A law firm engaged in a variety of legal services including labor, litigation, corporate, health, and pro bono law. **Other U.S. locations:** New York NY; Roseland NJ.

**WILDMAN, HARROLD, ALLEN & DIXON**
2300 Cabot Drive, Suite 455, Lisle IL 60532. 630/955-0555. **Contact:** Human Resources. **World Wide Web address:** http://www.whad.com. **Description:** Wildman, Harrold, Allen & Dixon specialize in corporate, divorce, medical malpractice, real estate, and wills and trusts law. **NOTE:** Resumes should be directed to the corporate headquarters, located at 225 West Wacker Drive, Chicago IL 60606-1229. **Corporate headquarters location:** Chicago IL. **Operations at this facility include:** This location is a satellite office with 12 attorneys.

**WILDMAN, HARROLD, ALLEN & DIXON**
225 West Wacker Drive, Suite 3000, Chicago IL 60606-1229. 312/201-2000. **Contact:** Human Resources. **World Wide Web address:** http://www.whad.com. **Description:** A law firm specializing in corporate, divorce, medical malpractice, real estate, and wills and trusts law. **Special programs:** Summer Internship. **Office hours:** Monday - Friday, 8:00 a.m. - 6:00 p.m. **Corporate headquarters location:** This location.

## MANUFACTURING: MISCELLANEOUS CONSUMER

**You can expect to find the following types of companies in this section:**
Art Supplies • Batteries • Cosmetics and Related Products • Household Appliances and Audio/Video Equipment • Jewelry, Silverware, and Plated Ware • Miscellaneous Household Furniture and Fixtures • Musical Instruments • Tools • Toys and Sporting Goods

---

**ACE HARDWARE CORPORATION**
2200 Kensington Court, Oak Brook IL 60523. 630/990-6600. **Fax:** 630/990-6838. **Contact:** Director of Human Resources. **World Wide Web address:** http://www.acehardware.com. **Description:** A worldwide dealer-owned cooperative operating through 5,100 hardware retailers in 62 countries. Ace Hardware Corporation also produces a line of hand and power tools, plumbing products, lawn and garden products, cleaning supplies, and manufactures a line of paint. **NOTE:** Apply online at the company's website. **Positions advertised include:** Advertising Distribution Analyst; Financial Analyst; Senior Audit Consultant; POR Operator; Network Administrator; Assistant Buyer. **Corporate headquarters location:** This location.

**ALBERTO-CULVER COMPANY**
2525 West Armitage Avenue, Melrose Park IL 60160. 708/450-3000. **Fax:** 708/450-3354. **Contact:** Corporate Human Resources. **World Wide Web address:** http://www.alberto.com. **Description:** Manufactures health and beauty aids and operates a chain of beauty supply stores. Products include shampoos, hair colorings, conditioners, fixatives, deodorants, antistatic sprays, and furniture polish. Brand names include Alberto VO5, Static Guard, TCB, and Kleen Guard. The company also produces consumer food items such as sweeteners, Mrs. Dash seasonings, and the Molly McButter butter substitute. **NOTE:** See website for job postings and contact information. **Positions advertised include:** Executive Secretary; Customer Business Manager; Account Executive; Corporate Auditor; Buyer. **Subsidiaries include:** Cederroth International AB is a manufacturer of bandages, antacid powder, and other consumer goods; Sally Beauty Supply is one of the world's largest chains of beauty supply stores, which operates through 2,000 units in the United States and the United Kingdom. **Listed on:** New York Stock Exchange. **Stock exchange symbol:** ACV.

**BELL SPORTS**
1924 County Road, Rantoul IL 61866. 217/893-9300. **Toll-free phone:** 800-456-2355. **Contact:** Human Resources. **World Wide Web address:** http://www.bellsports.com. **Description:** Manufactures helmets and other safety equipment. **Special programs:** Internships. **Corporate headquarters location:** Scottsdale AZ. **Other U.S. locations:** Los Gatos CA; East Providence RI. **Operations at this facility include:** Manufacturing.

**BLISTEX, INC.**
1800 Swift Drive, Oak Brook IL 60523. 630/571-2870. **Toll-free phone:** 800/837-1800. **Contact:** Human Resources. **World Wide Web address:** http://www.blistex.com. **Description:** Manufactures a line of lip care products

under the Blistex and DCT brand names. **NOTE:** Resumes and cover letters must be mailed. **Corporate headquarters location:** This location.

## ROBERT BOSCH TOOL COMPANY
1800 West Central Road, Mont Prospect IL 60056. 224/232-2000. **Contact:** Human Resources. **World Wide Web address:** http://www.boschtools.com. **Description:** Manufactures hand and power tools. **Other U.S. locations:** Nationwide. **Operations at this facility include:** Administration; Research and Development.

## BOWE BELL & HOWELL COMPANY
760 South Wolf Road, Wheeling IL 60090-6232. 847/675-7600. **Contact:** Human Resources. **World Wide Web address:** http://www.bellhowell.com. **Description:** Bell & Howell is a diversified corporation operating in three major areas: Specialized Business Equipment, which manufactures items including microfilm recorders, readers, and jackets, as well as micropublishing, office collation, and mailing machines; Learning Systems and Materials, which operates technical training schools in electronics and computer science, publishes textbooks, and produces a variety of instructional materials at all levels; and Instrumentation, which manufactures measuring and recording equipment, magnetic tape instrumentation, and a variety of semiconductor compounds, optics equipment, and photoplates for integrated circuits. **NOTE:** See the corporate website for job listings. **Operations at this facility include:** Administrative; Production.

## CPC (CERTIFIED PACKAGING CORPORATION)
3800 Hawthorne Court, Waukegan IL 60087. 888/438-1515. **Contact:** Human Resources. **World Wide Web address:** http://www.cpcpack.com. **Description:** The company is a contract packaging firm offering shrink wrapping, promotional packs, gift set assembly, and compounding/filling services. **Operations at this facility include:** This location manufactures consumer products such as candles and over-the-counter drugs for other companies.

## CHAMBERLAIN GROUP
845 Larch Avenue, Elmhurst IL 60126. 630/530-6752. **Toll-free phone:** 800/528-5880. **Fax:** 630/530-6091. **Contact:** Melanie Ditore, Human Resources. **E-mail address:** mditore@chamberlian.com. **World Wide Web address:** http://www.chamberlaingroup.com. **Description:** Manufactures garage door openers, waxers, and gate openers. **NOTE:** Mail or e-mail resumes and cover letters. **Positions advertised include:** PC Support Specialist; Graphic Design Specialist; Marketing Support Representative; Financial Analyst. **Parent company:** Duchossois Industries, Inc.

## COBRA ELECTRONICS CORPORATION
6500 West Cortland Street, Chicago IL 60707. 773/889-8870. **Fax:** 773/889-4453. **Contact:** Human Resources. **World Wide Web address:** http://www.cobraelec.com. **Description:** Manufactures telephones and consumer electronics products. **NOTE:** Interested jobseekers may mail or fax resumes or apply online at the company's website. **Positions advertised include:** Regional Sales Manager. **Corporate headquarters location:** This location. **Operations at this facility include:** Administration; Manufacturing; Sales; Service. **Listed on:** NASDAQ. **Stock exchange symbol:** COBR.

**CULLIGAN INTERNATIONAL COMPANY**
One Culligan Parkway, Northbrook IL 60062. 847/205-60005902. **Contact:** Manager of Human Resources. **World Wide Web address:** http://www.culligan.com. **Description:** A manufacturer of water filtration equipment and systems. **Positions advertised include:** Accountant; Human Resources Manager. **Corporate headquarters location:** This location. **Parent company:** Astrum, International.

**ELECTROLUX HOME CARE PRODUCTS NA**
807 North Main Street, Bloomington IL 61701. 309/828-2367. **Fax:** 309/823-5203. **Contact:** Denise Younge, Human Resources. **E-mail address:** eureka.hrdept@eureka.com. **World Wide Web address:** http://www.eureka.com. **Description:** A manufacturer of vacuum cleaners. **Positions advertised include:** Controller; National Accounts Sales Director. **Corporate headquarters location:** This location. **Other U.S. locations:** El Paso TX. **Parent company:** WCI, Inc. **Operations at this facility include:** Administration; Divisional Headquarters; Manufacturing; Research and Development; Sales; Service.

**FIRST ALERT**
**BRK BRANDS, INC.**
3901 Liberty Street Road, Aurora IL 60504. 630/851-7330. **Contact:** Human Resources. **World Wide Web address:** http://www.firstalert.com. **Description:** First Alert operates through its subsidiaries to manufacture smoke alarms, fire alarms, carbon monoxide detectors, fire extinguishers, fire escape ladders, rechargeable flashlights, and related home safety products. **Subsidiaries include:** BRK Brands Canada (Ontario, Canada); BRK Brands Europe, Ltd. (Berkshire, England); BRK Brands, Inc. (also at this location); BRK Brands Pty Ltd. (Parramatta, Australia); Electronica RBK de Mexico S.A. de C.V. (Chihuahua, Mexico). **Corporate headquarters location:** This location.

**FLEX-O-GLASS, INC.**
1100 N. Cicero Avenue, Chicago IL 60651. 773/379-7878. **Contact:** Human Resources. **World Wide Web address:** http://www.flexoglass.com. **Description:** Manufacturer of Innovative plastic products. Founded over 81 years ago. Their product lines include, construction and agricultural plastic sheeting, acrylic sheet, lawn and garden products, trash bags, ribbed floor runner and shelf liners, and packaging films. **Positions advertised include:** Plastic Extrusion Setup; Production Leadman. **Other area locations:** Dixon IL.

**GENERAL ELECTRIC COMPANY (GE)**
**CONSUMER PRODUCTS DIVISION**
709 West Wall Street, Morrison IL 61270. 815/772-2131. **Contact:** Human Resources. **World Wide Web address:** http://www.ge.com. **Description:** General Electric operates in the following areas: aircraft engines (jet engines, replacement parts, and repair services for commercial, military, executive, and commuter aircraft); appliances; broadcasting (NBC); industrial (lighting products, electrical distribution and control equipment, transportation systems products, electric motors and related products, a broad range of electrical and electronic industrial automation products, and a network of electrical supply houses); materials (plastics, ABS resins, silicones, superabrasives, and laminates); power systems (products for the generation, transmission, and distribution of electricity); technical products and systems (medical systems and equipment, as well as a full range of computer-based information and data interchange services for both

internal use and external commercial and industrial customers); and capital services (consumer services, financing, and specialty insurance). **NOTE:** Apply online at http://www.gecareers.com. **Company slogan:** We bring good things to life **Corporate headquarters location:** Fairfield CT. **Operations at this facility include:** This location is engaged in quality control for General Electric appliances. **Listed on:** New York Stock Exchange. **Stock exchange symbol:** GE.

**HARRIS MARCUS GROUP**
3757 South Ashland Avenue, Chicago IL 60609. 773/247-7500. **Contact:** Human Resources. **World Wide Web address:** http://www.harris-marcus.com. **Description:** Engaged in the manufacture of lamps, furniture, and accessories for the home. **Corporate headquarters location:** This location. **Operations at this facility include:** Administration; Manufacturing. **Listed on:** Privately held.

**HENRI STUDIO**
1250 Henri Drive, Wauconda IL 60084. 847/526-5200. **Contact:** Diane Walters, Human Resources. **World Wide Web address:** http://www.henristudio.com. **Description:** Manufactures concrete statues, fountains, birdbaths, and planters. **Subsidiaries include:** Henri Studio Edmonton, Ltd.; Henri Studio Europe, Ltd.

**ITW BRANDS**
955 National Parkway, Suite 9500, Schaumburg IL 60173. 847/944-2260. **Contact:** Human Resources. **World Wide Web address:** http://www.itwinc.com. **Description:** A division of Illinois Tool Works, this company manufactures tools and fasteners. It also operates as a warehousing facility.

**MIDWAY GAMES INC.**
2704 West Roscoe Street, Chicago IL 60618. 773/961-1000. **Contact:** Human Resources. **World Wide Web address:** http://www.midway.com. **Description:** Develops a wide variety of coin-operated arcade and home video game entertainment and software products. Midway produces games for Sony, Nintendo, and Saga platforms. **Positions advertised include:** Executive Producer; Financial Planning Analyst. **Special programs:** Internships. **Corporate headquarters location:** This location. **International locations:** Midway Games Limited, London England. **Listed on:** New York Stock Exchange. **Stock exchange symbol:** MWY.

**MITEK CORPORATION**
One Mitek Plaza, Winslow IL 61089. 815/367-3000. **Contact:** Teresa Stamm, Director of Human Resources. **World Wide Web address:** http://www.mitekcorp.com. **Description:** Engaged in the developing, manufacturing, and marketing of automotive, home, and professional loudspeakers. **NOTE:** Apply online. **Corporate headquarters location:** Phoenix AZ. **Other U.S. locations:** Monroe WI. **Operations at this facility include:** Administration; Manufacturing; Research and Development; Sales; Service. **Listed on:** Privately held.

**NEWELL RUBBERMAID**
29 East Stephenson Street, Freeport IL 61032. 815/235-4171. **Contact:** Human Resources. **World Wide Web address:** http://www.newellco.com. **Description:** A manufacturer of housewares, hardware, home furnishings, office products, hair accessories, beauty organizers, picture frames, specialty glass products, and industrial plastics. **NOTE:** This company has facilities throughout Illinois and the

Midwest area. See website for job listings and apply online. **Corporate headquarters location:** This location. **Operations at this facility include:** Administration. **Listed on:** New York Stock Exchange. **Stock exchange symbol:** NWL.

### R.S. OWENS AND COMPANY INC.
5535 North Lynch Avenue, Chicago IL 60630. 773/282-6000. **Contact:** Human Resources. **World Wide Web address:** http://www.rsowens.com. **Description:** Manufactures trophies, plaques, and awards. **Corporate headquarters location:** This location.

### PANASONIC
1707 North Randall Road, Elgin IL 60123. 847/468-4010. **Contact:** Human Resources. **World Wide Web address:** http://www.panasonic.com. **Description:** Manufactures and sells consumer electronic appliances such as televisions, microwave ovens, and videotape machines. **Positions advertised include:** Sales Representative.

### SALTON, INC.
1955 West Field Court, Lake Forest IL 60045. 847/803-4600. **Fax:** 847/803-1186.**Contact:** Human Resources. **World Wide Web address:** http://www.saltoninc.com. **Description:** Designs and markets home appliances, housewares, and beauty care products. Products include the George Foreman grill and the Juiceman juicer. **Corporate headquarters location:** This location. **Listed on:** New York Stock Exchange. **Stock exchange symbol:** SFP. **Annual sales/revenues:** More than $100 million.

### SANFORD CORPORATION
2707 Butterfield Road, Oak Brook IL 60523. 708/547-6650. **Fax:** 708/649-3440. **Contact:** Human Resources. **E-mail address:** recruiter.sanford@sanfordcorp.com. **World Wide Web address:** http://www.sanfordcorp.com. **Description:** Manufactures felt-tip pens and other writing implements. **NOTE:** See website for job listings. Mail or e-mail resumes and cover letters. Entry-level positions, part-time jobs, and second and third shifts are offered. **Corporate headquarters location:** This location. **Other U.S. locations:** TN. **International locations:** Worldwide. **Parent company:** Newell Inc. **Operations at this facility include:** Administration; Divisional Headquarters; Manufacturing; Research and Development; Sales; Service. **Listed on:** New York Stock Exchange. **Stock exchange symbol:** NWL.

### SOLO CUP COMPANY
1501 East 96th Street, Chicago IL 60628. 773/721-3600. **Contact:** Director of Human Resources. **World Wide Web address:** http://www.solocup.com. **Description:** A manufacturer and distributor of paper cups, paper plates, and other disposable products. **NOTE:** See website for job listings. **Corporate headquarters location:** Champaign IL.

### SOLO CUP COMPANY, INC.
7575 South Kostner Avenue, Chicago IL 60652. 773/767-3300. **Contact:** Human Resources Manager. **World Wide Web address:** http://www.solocup.com. **Description:** A manufacturer and distributor of paper cups, paper plates, and other disposable products. **NOTE:** Apply online. **Positions advertised include:** Human Resources Generalist; Quality Manager; Production Supervisor. **Corporate headquarters location:** Champaign IL.

## STROMBECKER CORPORATION
700 North Sacramento Boulevard, Suite 321, Chicago IL 60612. 773/638-1000. **Toll-free phone:** 800/944-8697. **Fax:** 773/638-3679. **Contact:** Robert Knorrek, Director of Human Resources. **E-mail address:** rknorrek@compuserve.com. **World Wide Web address:** http://www.tootsietoy.com. **Description:** Manufactures toys under the Tootsie Toy logo. **NOTE:** Entry-level positions are offered. **Office hours:** Monday - Friday, 8:00 a.m. - 5:00 p.m. **Other U.S. locations:** Nationwide. **International locations:** Worldwide.

## THE SUNSTAR BUTLER COMPANY
4635 W. Foster Avenue, Chicago IL 60630. 800/265-8353. **Fax:** 773/777-9226. **Contact:** R. Varra, Human Resources. **E-mail address:** hr6@jbutler.com. **World Wide Web address:** http://www.jbutler.com. **Description:** Manufactures oral health care products. **Positions advertised include:** Lead Molding Technician. **Corporate headquarters location:** This location. **Other area locations:** Elgin IL. **International locations:** Canada, Germany, and Sweden. **Number of employees worldwide:** 600.

## T&D METAL PRODUCTS INC.
602 East Walnut Street, Watseka IL 60970. 815/432-4938. **Contact:** Human Resources. **World Wide Web address:** http://www.tdmetal.com. **Description:** Manufactures toolboxes, table bases, and go-carts. **Special programs:** Internships. **Corporate headquarters location:** This location. **Other U.S. locations:** Paris IL; Yorkville IL. **Listed on:** Privately held.

## UNILEVER HOME & PERSONAL CARE
205 North Michigan Avenue, Suite 3200, Chicago IL 60601. 312/661-0222. **Contact:** Human Resources. **World Wide Web address:** http://www.unilever.com. **Description:** Develops, manufactures, and sells personal care products including hair and skin care items and deodorants. The company also operates a unit that manufactures and markets similar products for use in beauty salons.

## VAUGHAN & BUSHNELL MANUFACTURING COMPANY
P.O. Box 208, Bushnell IL 61422. 309/772-2131. **Contact:** Human Resources. **World Wide Web address:** http://www.vaughanmfg.com. **Description:** Manufactures hand tools including hammers, saws, hatchets, axes and landscaping tools.

## WEN PRODUCTS, INC.
501 Davis Road, Elgin IL 60123. 847/289-0386. **Fax:** 847/289-0387. **Contact:** Controller. **World Wide Web address:** http://www.wenproducts.com. **Description:** Manufactures a complete line of power tools including electrical soldering guns, sanders, and electric saws. **Other U.S. locations:** Akron IN; Fowler IN. **Parent company:** Great Lakes Tools.

## WILSON SPORTING GOODS COMPANY
8700 West Bryn Mawr Avenue, Chicago IL 60631. 773/714-6400. **Contact:** Human Resources. **World Wide Web address:** http://www.wilsonsports.com. **Description:** Manufactures sporting goods for golf, tennis, and team sports. Wilson has been affiliated with the NFL since 1941, has produced the official baseball of the NCAA championships since 1986, and has produced the official ball of many of professional baseball's minor league teams. Wilson also

manufactures and supplies uniforms to the NFL, MLB, NBA, and many colleges, universities, and high schools throughout the United States. **Corporate headquarters location:** This location. **Parent company:** Amer Group, plc (Helsinki, Finland) is engaged in the marketing of motor vehicles, paper, communications services, and tobacco. **Operations at this facility include:** Administration; Research and Development; Sales; Service.

**WORLD KITCHENS, INC.**
5500 Pearl Street, Suite 400, Rosemont IL 60018. 847/678-8600. **Fax:** 847/678-9424. **Contact:** Human Resources. **Description:** A manufacturer and wholesaler of bakeware and kitchen gadgets.

**ZENITH ELECTRONICS CORPORATION**
2000 Millbrook Drive, Lincolnshire IL 60069. 847/391-7000. **Fax:** 847/941-8200. **Contact:** Human Resources. **E-mail address:** careers@zenith.com. **World Wide Web address:** http://www.zenith.com. **Description:** Designs, manufactures, and markets consumer electronics products including televisions, videocassette recorders, and cable television and network systems. **Special programs:** Internships. **Corporate headquarters location:** This location.

## MANUFACTURING: MISCELLANEOUS INDUSTRIAL

**You can expect to find the following types of companies
in this section:**
Ball and Roller Bearings • Commercial Furniture and Fixtures • Fans,
Blowers, and Purification Equipment • Industrial Machinery and
Equipment • Motors and Generators/Compressors and Engine Parts •
Vending Machines

---

**APV INVENSYS, INC.**
5100 North River Road, 3rd Floor, Schiller Park IL 60176. 847/678-4300.
**Contact:** Human Resources. **World Wide Web address:** http://www.apv.com.
**Description:** Designs, engineers, and installs food and beverage processing
equipment. APV Invensys, Inc. has four regional sales offices, each responsible
for selling processing systems and parts for existing systems. Once a system has
been sold, the sales force submits the engineering work to the Systems
Engineering Group at this location. These engineers design dairy and food
processing systems for APV's customers. After the design phase is complete, the
engineers travel to job sites to supervise the installation of the processing
equipment. They remain on-site until the processing systems are installed and
running and the customer has been fully trained to operate the systems. **NOTE:**
Apply online at this company's website. **Special programs:** Internships. **Other
U.S. locations:** Cerritos CA. **Operations at this facility include:** Sales.
**Number of employees worldwide:** 80,000.

**ACCO USA, INC.**
300 Tower Parkway, Lincolnshire IL 60069. 847/541-9500. **Toll-free phone:**
800/222-6462. **Fax:** 847/484-4492. **Contact:** Human Resources Department.
**World Wide Web address:** http://www.acco.com. **Description:** Manufactures a
wide variety of office supplies and equipment. **NOTE:** Apply online at this
company's website. **Positions advertised include:** Market Development
Manager; Recruiter; Unix/Oracle Manager; Senior System Analyst; Credit Risk
Analyst. **Corporate headquarters location:** This location. **Parent company:**
American Brands, Inc. (New York NY).

**ALCAN PACKAGING**
1731 S. Mont Prospect Road, Des Plaines IL 60018. 847/298-5626. **Fax:**
773/399-3005. **Contact:** Human Resources. **World Wide Web address:**
https://www.alcan.com. **Description:** Provider of aluminum and packaging
solutions to companies worldwide. **Positions advertised include:** Cost
Accountant; HR Assistant; Production Mechanic Technician; Quality Assurance
Manager; Senior Engineer.

**AMERICAN NTN BEARING MANUFACTURING CORPORATION**
1500 Holmes Road, Elgin IL 60123. 847/741-4545. **Contact:** Human Resources.
**World Wide Web address:** http://www.ntnamerica.com. **Description:**
Manufactures bearings. **Corporate headquarters location:** This location. **Other
U.S. locations:** Schiller Park IL. **Parent company:** NTN. **Operations at this
facility include:** Administration; Manufacturing.

## AURORA PUMP

800 Airport Road, North Aurora IL 60542. 630/859-7000. **Contact:** Vicki Swaine, Human Resources. **World Wide Web address:** http://www.aurorapump.com. **Description:** Manufactures water pumps for sprinkler systems.

## AUTOMATION INTERNATIONAL, INC.

1020 Bahls Street, Danville IL 61832. 217/446-9500. **Fax:** 217/446-6855. **Contact:** Mr. Terry Prosser, CEO. **World Wide Web address:** http://www.automation-intl.com. **Description:** Produces custom-designed resistance and arc welding equipment. The company also remanufactures and rebuilds used equipment. Brand names include Swift-Ohio and Federal. Founded in 1991. **Corporate headquarters location:** Quincy IL. **Operations at this facility include:** Manufacturing; Sales; Service. **Number of employees at this location:** 100.

## BELL AND GOSSETT DOMESTIC PUMP
## ITT INDUSTRIES

8200 North Austin Avenue, Morton Grove IL 60053. 847/966-3700. **Contact:** Bill Dempsey, Employee Relations Manager. **World Wide Web address:** http://www.bgasp.ittind.com. **Description:** Produces heat exchangers, plumbing equipment, and pumps. **Corporate headquarters location:** White Plains NY. **Parent company:** ITT Industries is a diversified, global enterprise engaged in four major business areas: Electronic Components; Defense Electronics and Services; Fluid Technology; and Motion and Flow Control. **Listed on:** New York Stock Exchange. **Stock exchange symbol:** ITT.

## BRONSON & BRATTON

220 Shore Drive, Burr Ridge IL 60527. 630/986-1815. **Fax:** 630/655-3801. **Contact:** Human Resources. **World Wide Web address:** http://www.brons.com. **Description:** Manufactures small-lot, specialty tools and dies, specializing in hard-to-machine metals and ceramics.

## CCL CUSTOM MANUFACTURING INC.

One West Hegeler Lane, Danville IL 61832. 217/442-1400. **Contact:** Human Resources Department. **World Wide Web address:** http://www.cclind.com. **Description:** Engaged in the contract filling and packaging of aerosol and liquid containers for a variety of household and automotive purposes. **NOTE:** Apply online. **Corporate headquarters location:** Chicago IL. **Other U.S. locations:** Wixom MI; Cumberland RI; Memphis TN.

## CATERPILLAR INC.

P.O. Box 504, Joliet IL 60434-0504. 815/729-5511. **Contact:** Human Resources. **World Wide Web address:** http://www.cat.com. **Description:** Caterpillar is one of the world's largest manufacturers of construction and mining equipment, natural gas engines, and industrial gas turbines; and a leading global supplier of diesel engines. Products range from track-type tractors to hydraulic excavators, backhoe loaders, motor graders, and off-highway trucks. They are used in the construction, road building, mining, forestry, energy, transportation, and material-handling industries. Caterpillar products and components are manufactured in more than 70 plants worldwide. **NOTE:** Apply online at the corporate website. **Corporate headquarters location:** Peoria IL. **Operations at this facility include:** This location is part of Cat Logistics, a division of Caterpillar. It manufactures hydraulic components and fabrications such as valves, pumps, motors, and cylinders.

**CATERPILLAR INC.**
100 North East Adams Street, Peoria IL 61629-8300. 309/675-5923. **Fax:** 309/675-6476. **Contact:** Corporate Employment Services. **World Wide Web address:** http://www.cat.com. **Description:** Caterpillar is one of the world's largest manufacturers of construction and mining equipment and machine engines. In addition, the company provides a number of business services such as logistics, automation and financial services. **NOTE:** Entry-level positions are offered. This company provides job listings for its corporate office, division offices and manufacturing facilities on its website. See website and apply online. **Special programs:** Internships. **Corporate headquarters location:** This location. **Listed on:** New York Stock Exchange. **Stock exchange symbol:** CAT. **Number of employees worldwide:** 72,000.

**CHICAGO BLOWER CORPORATION**
1675 Glen Ellyn Road, Glendale Heights IL 60139. 630/858-2600. **Fax:** 630/858-7172. **Contact:** Human Resources. **E-mail address:** cbc@fan.net. **World Wide Web address:** http://www.chiblo.com. **Description:** Designs and manufactures industrial fans and blowers. **NOTE:** Interested jobseekers may also apply in person.

**CHICAGO BRIDGE AND IRON COMPANY (CB&I)**
14109 South Route 59, Plainfield IL 60544-8984. 815/439-6000. **Fax:** 815/439-6010. **Contact:** Human Resources. **E-mail address:** employment@CBIepc.com. **World Wide Web address:** http://www.chicago-bridge.com. **Description:** A global engineering and construction company specializing in the engineering, design, fabrication, erection, and repair of petroleum terminals, steel tanks, refinery pressure vessels, low temperature and cryogenic storage facilities, and other steel-plated structures and their associated systems. Founded in 1889. **NOTE:** E-mail resumes and cover letters. **Special programs:** Engineer Training. **Corporate headquarters location:** The Netherlands. **Operations at this facility include:** This location houses the main offices for CB&I Industrial Division and CB&I Water Group. **Listed on:** New York Stock Exchange. **Stock exchange symbol:** CBI. **Number of employees worldwide:** 7,500.

**CHICAGO RAWHIDE**
890 North State Road, Elgin IL 60123. 847/742-7840. **Contact:** Human Resources. **World Wide Web address:** http://www.chicago-rawhide.com. **Description:** Manufactures oil seals, filters, gaskets, and other custom-molded products. **Corporate headquarters location:** This location. **Parent company:** SKF. **Operations at this facility include:** Manufacturing.

**CITATION**
7800 North Austin Avenue, Skokie IL 60077-2675. 847/966-5050. **Fax:** 847/966-9128. **Contact:** Bill Herrmann, Human Resources. **E-mail address:** billh@skokie.citation.net. **World Wide Web address:** http://www.citation.net. **Description:** Citation Corporation is a manufacturer of cast, forged and machined components for the capital and durable goods industries. This location offers four different casting production solutions under one facility. **Positions advertised include:** Casting/Pattern Engineer; Industrial Maintenance Supervisor; Network Administrator; Production Supervisor; Sharepoint Portal Application Developer; Shipping Supervisor. **Corporate headquarters location:** Birmingham AL. **Other area locations:** Lake Zurich IL. **Other U.S. locations:** Berlin WI, Browntown WI, Menomonee Falls WI, Grand Rapids MI, Butler IN,

Lufkin TX, Columbiana AL, Biscoe NC.

**JOHN CRANE INC.**
6400 West Oakton Street, Morton Grove IL 60053. 847/967-2400. **Fax:** 847/967-3040. **Contact:** Employee Relations Department. **E-mail address:** recruiter@johncrane.com. **World Wide Web address:** http://www.johncrane.com. **Description:** Manufactures and markets mechanical seals, packaging, and Teflon products for the industrial, automotive, and marine aftermarkets. John Crane operates over 40 branches throughout the United States including sales, service, and engineering operations. Founded in 1917. **Positions advertised include:** International Documentation Clerk; Mechanical Engineer. **Corporate headquarters location:** This location. **Parent company:** Smiths Group PLC. **Operations at this facility include:** Administration; Manufacturing; Research and Development; Sales; Service.

**DEERE & COMPANY**
One John Deere Place, Moline IL 61265. 309/765-8000. **Contact:** Director of Human Resources. **World Wide Web address:** http://www.deere.com. **Description:** Manufactures, distributes, and finances the sale of heavy equipment and machinery for use in the agricultural and industrial equipment industries. The Agricultural Equipment Sector manufactures tractors, soil, seeding, and harvesting equipment. The Industrial Equipment Segment manufactures a variety of earth moving equipment, tractors, loaders, and excavators. The Consumer Products Division manufactures tractors and products for the homeowner. **NOTE:** On its website, this company provides all of its job listings for all of its locations. Apply online. **Corporate headquarters location:** This location.

**DEVLIEG-BULLARD SERVICES GROUP**
10100 Forest Hills Road, Rockford IL 61115. 815/282-4100. **Toll-free phone:** 800/248-8120. **Fax:** 815/282-4949. **Contact:** Human Resources Manager. **World Wide Web address:** http://www.devliegbullard.com. **Description:** Supplies aftermarket parts and services including rebuilding services to the machine tool industry. **Corporate headquarters location:** Westport CT. **Other U.S. locations:** Cypress CA; Cromwell CT; Twinsburg OH; Abbottstown PA. **Parent company:** DeVlieg-Bullard, Inc. **Operations at this facility include:** Administration; Divisional Headquarters; Sales; Service.

**DUDEK & BOCK SPRING MANUFACTURING**
5100 West Roosevelt Road, Chicago IL 60644. 773/379-4100. **Contact:** Jeff Kopacz, Human Resources. **World Wide Web address:** http://www.dudek-bock.com. **Description:** Manufactures springs, wireforms, and light metal stampings.

**DUO-FAST**
2400 Galvin Drive, Elgin IL 60123. 847/783-5500. **Fax:** 847/783-5705. **Contact:** Human Resources. **E-mail address:** duofastjobs@paslode.com. **World Wide Web address:** http://www.duofast.com. **Description:** A manufacturer of industrial staples and nailing tools. **NOTE:** See website for Fax or e-mail resumes.

**EDSAL MANUFACTURING**
4400 South Packers Avenue, Chicago IL 60609. 773/254-0600. **Fax:** 773/254-1303. **Contact:** Barbara Kazsuk, Director of Human Resources. **World Wide**

**Web address:** http://www.edsalmfg.com. **Description:** Manufactures and markets industrial furniture and steel equipment such as shelves, storage racks, lockers, benches, and shop desks.

**FMC TECHNOLOGIES**
**FMC FOODTECH**
200 East Randolph Drive, Chicago IL 60601. 312/861-6000. **Contact:** Human Resources. **World Wide Web address:** http://www.fmctechnologies.com. **Description:** FMC Technologies is a diversified manufacturer of specialty, industrial, and agricultural chemicals; defense-related systems; industrial machinery. FMC, a subsidiary, creates computerized systems for the food industry. **Corporate headquarters location:** This location is the corporate office for the parent company, FMC Technologies and its subsidiary FMC Foodtech. **Subsidiaries include:** FMC Energy Systems; FMC Airport Systems; FMC Technologies A.G.

**FILTERTEK, INC.**
11411 Price Road, Hebron IL 60034-8936. 815/648-2416. **Fax:** 815/648-1168. **Contact:** Mary Ellen Nilles, Director of Human Resources. **World Wide Web address:** http://www.filtertek.com. **Description:** This location manufactures custom-molded filters. Overall, Filtertek, Inc. manufactures filtration elements used in the automotive, health care, and various other industrial and consumer markets. The company sells its automotive filters directly to automotive manufacturers, automotive suppliers, and companies reselling filters in the automotive aftermarket. Filtertek produces filter products ranging from highly sophisticated disposable medical filters that filter contamination from blood, to a simple air filter used to protect machinery from dust contamination. **NOTE:** Apply online at the company's website. **Corporate headquarters location:** This location. **Parent company:** ESCO Electronics Corporation is a diversified producer of commercial products that are sold to a variety of customers worldwide. ESCO's products include electronic equipment, valves and filters, filtration and fluid flow components, automatic test equipment, utility load management equipment, and anechoic/shielding systems. ESCO's other operating subsidiaries include PTI Technologies, Inc.; VACCO Industries; Distribution Control Systems, Inc.; Rantec Microwave & Electronics; Lindgren RF Enclosures; Comtrak Technologies, Inc.; and EMC Test Systems, L.P. **Operations at this facility include:** Administration; Divisional Headquarters; Research and Development; Sales.

**FOOTE-JONES/ILLINOIS GEAR**
2102 North Natchez Avenue, Chicago IL 60707. 773/622-8000. **Fax:** 773/622-8176. **Contact:** Human Resources Manager. **World Wide Web address:** http://www.footejones.com. **Description:** Manufactures precision gears, gearboxes, and other machine parts.

**GNB TECHNOLOGIES, INC.**
2475 West Station Street, Kankakee IL 60901. 815/937-6925. **Contact:** Human Resources. **World Wide Web address:** http://www.gnb.com. **Description:** Manufactures and recycles lead-acid batteries for a wide range of consumer and industrial uses. **Corporate headquarters location:** Princeton NJ.

**GENERAL BINDING CORPORATION**
One GBC Plaza, Northbrook IL 60062-4195. 847/272-3700. **Contact:** Human Resources. **World Wide Web address:** http://www.generalbinding.com.

**Description:** An international manufacturer and distributor of office binding and laminating systems and supplies. **NOTE:** Apply online at this company's website. **Positions advertised Include:** Mechanical Engineer; Print Estimator. **Operations at this facility include:** Administration; Manufacturing; Research and Development.

### GREIF BROTHERS CORPORATION
P.O. Box 248, Oreana IL 62554. 800/468-2396. **Fax:** 217/468-2264. **Contact:** Human Resources. **World Wide Web address:** http://www.gbcdecatur.com. **Description:** Produces and sells shipping containers and materials including fiber, steel and plastic drums, multiwall bags, and other related items. The company also produces and sells containerboard and related products including corrugated paper, and corrugated containers. **NOTE:** For career opportunities, see Greif Inc's website, http://www.greif.com/careers/. Resumes may also be mailed or faxed to the corporate Human Resources Manager at Greif Inc., 425 Winter Road, Delaware, OH 433015 or fax, 740/549-6100. **Positions advertised include:** Account Manager; Lead/Set-up Person Molding Department.

### HOLLYMATIC CORPORATION
600 East Plainfield Road, Countryside IL 60525. 708/579-3700. **Fax:** 708/579-1057. **Contact:** Human Resources. **World Wide Web address:** http://www.hollymatic.com. **Description:** Manufactures food processing machines and parts, and paper products. **Corporate headquarters location:** This location.

### HYDAC TECHNOLOGY CORPORATION
445 Windy Point Drive, Glendale Heights IL 60139. 630/545-0800. **Fax:** 630/545-0033. **Contact:** Human Resources. **World Wide Web address:** http://www.hydacusa.com. **Description:** Provides fluid power solutions intended to increase the efficiency, longevity, and safety of fluid power systems. **Positions advertised include:** Computer Network Support Specialist; Product Manager; Regional Sales Manager. **Corporate headquarters location:** Bethlehem PA. **Other U.S. locations:** Nationwide.

### HYDRO GEAR
1411 S. Hamilton Street Sullivan IL 61951. 217/728-7665. **Fax:** 866/207-7512. **Contact:** Christina O'Brien. **E-mail address:** careers@hydro-gear.com. **World Wide Web address:** http://hydro-gear.com. **Description:** Hydro Gear designs, manufactures, sells, and services hydrostatic drive systems for the lawn and garden industry. They produce high-performance hydrostatic transmissions, gear reduction drives, piston pumps, wheel motors, and accessories for both the consumer and commercial markets. **NOTE:** Search for open positions online. **Positions advertised include:** Buyer; Market Development Manager; Model Shop Technician; Production Supervisor. **Operations at this facility include:** Administrative; Production.

### ITW INDUSTRIAL FINISHING
195 International Boulevard, Glendale Heights IL 60139. 630/237-5000. **Fax:** 630/237-5011. **Contact:** Human Resources. **Description:** A manufacturer of spray finishing and coating application equipment.

### ITW SIGNODE CORPORATION
3650 West Lake Avenue, Glenview IL 60025. 800/531-1022. **Contact:** Human Resources. **World Wide Web address:** http://www.signode.com. **Description:**

ITW Signode manufactures and distributes strapping systems for use in packaging and materials handling by a broad range of industries. **Parent company:** Illinois Tool Works Inc. (Glenview IL) develops, produces, and markets various highly-engineered components, fasteners, assemblies, and packaging systems for clients in the industrial and construction markets. Products of the company include metal components, construction products and polymers, consumer packaging products and systems, industrial packaging systems, and finishing systems. Illinois Tool Works has over 250 operating facilities in 33 countries.

## ILLINOIS TOOL WORKS INC. (ITW)
3600 West Lake Avenue, Glenview IL 60025. 847/724-7500. **Contact:** Barbara Morris, Manager of Human Resources. **World Wide Web address:** http://www.itwinc.com. **Description:** Illinois Tool Works develops, produces, and markets various components, fasteners, assemblies, and packaging systems for clients in the industrial and construction markets. Products include metal components, construction products and polymers, consumer packaging products and systems, industrial packaging systems, and finishing systems. The company has over 250 operating facilities worldwide. **Corporate headquarters location:** This location. **Listed on:** New York Stock Exchange. **Stock exchange symbol:** ITW. **Number of employees worldwide:** 52,000.

## INGERSOLL MILLING MACHINE COMPANY
707 Fulton Avenue, Rockford IL 61103. 815/987-6000. **Fax:** 815/987-6725. **Contact:** Human Resources. **World Wide Web address:** http://www.ingersoll.com. **Description:** Manufactures industrial machinery including dicmaking and various types of milling machines. **NOTE:** Call the company's Human Resources Office to hear bout employment opportunities. **Subsidiaries include:** Ingersoll Milling Machines (Rockford IL); Ingersoll Production Systems (Rockland IL); Ingersoll Rapid Response (Rockford IL); Ingersoll Contract Manufacturing Company; Ingersoll Automation (Machesney Park, IL).

## INTERLAKE MATERIAL HANDLING, INC.
1230 East Diehl Road, Suite 400, Naperville IL 60563. 630/245-8800. **Toll-free phone:** 800/468-3752. **Fax:** 630/245-8906. **Contact:** Human Resources. **E-mail address:** career@interlake.com. **World Wide Web address:** http://www.interlake.com. **Description:** Operates through two divisions: Engineered Materials Division manufactures ferrous powders used in aircraft parts; Handling Division produces warehouse storage equipment, conveyor systems, and inventory control systems. **NOTE:** Visit the company's website to review job listings. E-mail resumes indicating desired position. **Positions advertised include:** Designer; Business Development Manager. **Corporate headquarters location:** This location.

## JOSLYN MANUFACTURING COMPANY
3700 South Morgan Street, Chicago IL 60609. 773/927-1420. **Contact:** Human Resources. **World Wide Web address:** http://www.joslynmfg.com. **Description:** Manufactures a variety of products associated with power utility distribution and transmission lines and communication systems. This company has two plants in the Chicago area and one in Franklin Park, IL.

**KOMATSU AMERICA**
440 North Fairway Drive, Vernon Hills IL 60061. 847/970-4100. **Fax:** 847/970-5737. **Contact:** Human Resources. **World Wide Web address:** http://www.komatsuamerica.com. **Description:** Manufactures mining trucks, excavators, and haulers. The company also offers mining equipment repair services. **NOTE:** This company's website provides job listings for all its Illinois locations. Apply online. **Corporate headquarters location:** This location. **Other area locations:** Peoria IL (Manufacturing); Downers Grove IL (Financial Facility). **Parent company:** Komatsu Global (Japan). **Operations at this facility include:** Manufacturing.

**LAKEWOOD ENGINEERING & MANUFACTURING COMPANY**
501 North Sacramento Boulevard, Chicago IL 60612. 773/722-4300. **Toll-free phone:** 800/621-4277. **Fax:** 773/722-1541. **Contact:** Human Resources. **World Wide Web address:** http://www.lakewoodeng.com. **Description:** Manufactures ventilating fans, electric heaters, and other products.

**LASER PRECISION**
1755 Butterfield Road, Suite B, Libertyville IL 60048. 847/367-0282. **Fax:** 847/367-0236. **Contact:** Human Resources. **E-mail address:** brake@laserprecision.com. **World Wide Web address:** http://www.laserprecision.com. **Description:** Laser Precision utilizes lasers and turret punching to manufacture parts for the food, medical, transportation and agricultural industries. **Positions advertised include:** Machinist, Press Brake Set-Up, Quality Control Inspector, Sheet Metal Estimator, Welder. **Operations at this facility include:** Administration; Production.

**LYON METAL PRODUCTS LLC**
P.O. Box 671, Aurora IL 60507-0671. 630/892-8941. **Fax:** 630/264-4548. **Contact:** Carol Stathis, Human Resources Manager. **World Wide Web address:** http://www.lyonworkspace.com. **Description:** Manufactures metal storage products including lockers, cabinets, shelving, office products, and ergonomic furniture. Founded in 1901.

**MCDONNELL AND MILLER**
**ITT INDUSTRIES**
3500 North Spaulding Avenue, Chicago IL 60618. 773/267-1600. **Contact:** Kathy Stone, Director of Human Resources. **World Wide Web address:** http://www.mcdonnellmiller.com. **Description:** Produces water control valves and boiler equipment for heating and air conditioning systems. **Corporate headquarters location:** White Plains NY. **Parent company:** ITT Industries is a diversified, global enterprise engaged in four major business areas: Electronic Components; Defense Electronics and Services; Fluid Technology; and Motion and Flow Control. **Listed on:** New York Stock Exchange. **Stock exchange symbol:** ITT.

**MILLER FLUID POWER CORPORATION**
800 North York Road, Bensenville IL 60106. 630/766-3400. **Fax:** 630/766-2013. **Contact:** Human Resources. **E-mail address:** employment@millerfp.com. **World Wide Web address:** http://www.millerfluidpower.com. **Description:** A manufacturer of pneumatic and hydraulic cylinders and components. **Corporate headquarters location:** This location. **Operations at this facility include:** Administration; Manufacturing; Research and Development; Sales; Service.

## NTN-BOWER
711 North Bower Road, Macomb IL 61455. 309/833-4541. **Contact:** Human Resources. **World Wide Web address:** http://www.ntnamerica.com. **Description:** Manufactures bearings and joints for the automotive, airline, and industrial fields. **NOTE:** This company also has offices in Illinois. See website for addresses.

## NISSAN FORKLIFT CORPORATION, NORTH AMERICA
240 North Prospect Street, Marengo IL 60152-3298. 815/568-0061. **Toll-free phone:** 800/871-LIFT. **Fax:** 815/568-0181. **Contact:** Human Resources Manager. **E-mail address:** careers@nfcna.com. **World Wide Web address:** http://www.nissanforklift.com. **Description:** Manufactures forklifts including electric-powered and internal combustion engines. Founded in 1988. **NOTE:** Cover letters and resumes may be mailed, faxed or e-mailed. Entry-level positions, part-time jobs, and second shifts are offered. **Positions advertised include:** Parts Marketing Manager; Product Service Specialist; Design/Product Engineer; Electrical Project Engineer. **Special programs:** Internships; Summer Jobs. **Office hours:** Monday - Friday, 8:00 a.m. - 5:00 p.m. **Corporate headquarters location:** This location. **International locations:** Japan; Spain. **Parent company:** Nissan Motor Company, Ltd. **Operations at this facility include:** Administration; Manufacturing; Research and Development; Sales; Service. **Listed on:** Privately held.

## NUARC COMPANY INC.
One North 372 Main Street, Glen Ellyn IL 60137. 847/967-4400. **Toll-free phone:** 800/962-8883. **Contact:** Human Resources. **World Wide Web address:** http://www.mrprint.com/nuarc. **Description:** Manufactures graphic arts equipment such as exposure systems. **Corporate headquarters location:** This location.

## OCE-USA, INC.
1800 Bruning Drive West, Itasca IL 60143. 630/351-2900. **Toll-free phone:** 800/445-3526. **Contact:** Human Resources. **World Wide Web address:** http://www.oceusa.com. **Description:** The company manufactures office printers, high-speed printing systems, copy machines, and scanners. **NOTE:** Resumes should be directed to Jim Sunberg, Director of Staffing and Organizational Development, 5450 North Cumberland, Chicago IL 60656. Interested jobseekers may also apply online at the company's website. **Positions advertised include:** Staffing Specialist; Customer Delivery Coordinator Manager; Inventory Analyst; Display Graphics Sales Executive. **Corporate headquarters location:** Chicago IL. **Operations at this facility include:** This location is a sales office. **Number of employees at this location:** 3,000.

## OTIS ELEVATOR COMPANY
651 West Washington Boulevard, Suite 1-N, Chicago IL 60661. 312/454-1616. **Fax:** 312/454-0217. **Contact:** Gretchen E. Simpson, Human Resources Manager. **World Wide Web address:** http://www.otis.com. **Description:** One of the world's largest manufacturers of elevators and escalators. Founded in 1853. **NOTE:** This company has offices throughout the Greater Chicago area and Illinois. See website for job listings and contact information. **Positions advertised include:** Sales Representative; Project Manager. **Corporate headquarters location:** Farmington CT. **Parent company:** United Technologies.

## PARKER HANNIFIN CORPORATION
595 Schelter Road, Lincolnshire IL 60069. 847/821-1500. **Fax:** 847/821-7600. **Contact:** Human Resources. **World Wide Web address:** http://www.parker.com. **Description:** An international fluid power firm that manufactures components and replacement parts for hydraulic and pneumatic power systems that are used by the automotive, aviation, industrial, and marine industries. Parker Hannifin has also entered the biomedical market to research and help produce equipment and products for treating chronic illnesses. **Operations at this facility include:** This location manufactures truck hydraulic parts and systems.

## PARKER HANNIFIN CORPORATION
500 South Wolf Road, Des Plaines IL 60016. 847/298-2400. **Contact:** Lou Ford, Human Resources Manager. **E-mail address:** cylmktg@parker.com. **World Wide Web address:** http://www.parker.com. **Description:** Parker Hannifin Corporation is an international fluid power firm that manufactures components and replacement parts for hydraulic and pneumatic power systems that are used by the automotive, aviation, industrial, and marine industries. Parker Hannifin has also entered the biomedical market to research and help produce equipment and products for treating chronic illnesses. **NOTE:** To apply, visit the company's website. **Positions advertised include:** Senior Design Engineer. **Corporate headquarters location:** Cleveland OH. **Other U.S. locations:** Nationwide. **Operations at this facility include:** This location is a sales office for the Cylinder Division.

## PAYMASTER TECHNOLOGIES, INC.
900 Pratt Boulevard, Elk Grove Village IL 60007. 773/878-9200. **Toll-free phone:** 800/462-4477. **Fax:** 847/758-0123. **Contact:** Human Resources. **E-mail address:** paymaster@paymastertech.com. **World Wide Web address:** http://www.paymastertech.com. **Description:** Manufactures and sells check-writing machines and check protectors. **Corporate headquarters location:** This location.

## PRECISION TWIST DRILL COMPANY
One Precision Plaza, P.O. Box 9000, Crystal Lake IL 60039. 815/459-2040. **Contact:** Human Resources Director. **World Wide Web address:** http://www.precisiontwistdrill.com. **Description:** Manufactures drills and cutting tools for the aerospace, automotive, and construction industries. **Corporate headquarters location:** This location. **Subsidiaries include:** Triumph Twist Drill Company. **Operations at this facility include:** Administration; Manufacturing; Research and Development; Sales. **Listed on:** Privately held.

## QUINCY COMPRESSOR
3501 Wismann Lane, Quincy IL 62301. 217/222-7700. **Contact:** Tina Engelmeyer, Human Resources. **E-mail address:** Tina.Engelmeyer@quincycompressor.com. **World Wide Web address:** http://www.quincycompressor.com. **Description:** Manufactures and sells air compressors and vacuum pumps. Their products are used around the world in manufacturing plants, hospitals, and climate control systems. **Positions advertised include:** Customer Service Manager; Manufacturing Engineer; Market Specialist; Packaging Engineer. **Corporate headquarters location:** This location. **Other U.S. locations:** Bay Minette AL.

## RHC SPACEMASTER

1400 North 25th Avenue, Melrose Park IL 60160. 708/345-2500. **Contact:** Linda Atkinson, Personnel Director. **World Wide Web address:** http://www.rhcspacemaster.com. **Description:** Manufactures store fixtures, office furniture, and library equipment. **Corporate headquarters location:** This location.

## RADIAN CORPORATION

6718 West Plank Road, Peoria IL 61604. 309/697-4400. **Contact:** Human Resources. **E-mail address:** careers@radiancorp.com. **World Wide Web address:** http://www.radiancorp.com. **Description:** Rohn Industries manufactures cabinets for housing electrical equipment; steel and concrete fencing; prefabricated concrete units; and cattle handling equipment, stalls, and corrals. **Operations at this facility include:** This location is the primary plant for the manufacturing of tower and pole products used to mount transmitting devices.

## REVCOR, INC.

251 Edwards Avenue, Carpentersville IL 60110. 847/428-4411. **Fax:** 847/426-0589. **Contact:** Human Resources. **World Wide Web address:** http://www.revcor.com. **Description:** Manufactures fans and blowers for computerized electronic systems. **Corporate headquarters location:** This location. **Other U.S. locations:** Fort Worth TX. **Operations at this facility include:** Administration; Manufacturing; Research and Development; Sales; Service.

## REXAM BEVERAGE CAN COMPANY

8770 West Bryn Mawr Avenue, Chicago IL 60631. 773/399-3000. **Contact:** Director of Human Resources. **World Wide Web address:** http://www.rexam.com. **Description:** Manufactures a variety of container and packaging products. **Corporate headquarters location:** This location.

## REXAM BEVERAGE CAN COMPANY

2250 Lively Boulevard, Elk Grove Village IL 60007. 847/734-5500. **Contact:** Human Resources. **World Wide Web address:** http://www.rexam.com. **Description:** Manufactures a variety of container and packaging products. **NOTE:** Human Resources is located at 8770 West Bryn Mawr Avenue, Chicago IL 60631. 773-399-3000. **Corporate headquarters location:** Chicago IL. **Operations at this facility include:** This location is a research and development facility.

## RICHARDS-WILCOX, INC.

600 South Lake Street, Aurora IL 60506. 630/897-6951. **Fax:** 630/897-4011. **Contact:** Human Resources. **E-mail address:** RWHR@richrdswilcox.com. **World Wide Web address:** http://www.richards-wilcox.com. **Description:** Engaged in the manufacture and distribution of materials handling equipment and office systems products. Products include overhead chain conveyors, horizontal and vertical carousels, general hardware, Aurora shelving, Timer 2, and mobile base. **Corporate headquarters location:** This location. **Operations at this facility include:** Administration; Manufacturing; Research and Development; Sales.

## ROHM & HAAS COMPANY
123 North Wacker Drive, Chicago IL 60606. 312/807-2000. **Contact:** Human Resources. **World Wide Web address:** http://www.rohmhaas.com. **Description:** A diverse manufacturer of industrial and consumer items including Morton brand salt. The company is also a large producer of inflatable air bags for the automotive industry, adhesives for the packaging industry, liquid plastic coatings for automobiles, electronic products used in printed circuit boards and semiconductor wafers, and dyes used by the printing industry. **International locations:** Bahamas; Canada; Europe; Mexico. **Listed on:** New York Stock Exchange. **Stock exchange symbol:** ROH.

## ROHM & HAAS COMPANY
5005 Barnard Mill Road, Ringwood IL 60072. 815/653-2411. **Contact:** Human Resources. **World Wide Web address:** http://www.rohmhaas.com. **Description:** A location of Rohm and Haas company.

## ROHM & HAAS COMPANY
2701 East 170th Street, Lansing IL 60438. 708/868-7270. **Contact:** Human Resources. **Description:** A location of Rohm & Haas Company.

## ROTADYNE
2512 West 24th Street, Chicago IL 60608. 800/621-8521. **Contact:** Human Resources. **World Wide Web address:** http://www.rotadyne.com. **Description:** Manufactures roller manufacturing equipment and rollers used in the graphic arts industry. **Corporate headquarters location:** Hinsdale IL. **Operations at this facility include:** Divisional Headquarters; Manufacturing; Research and Development; Service.

## SCHAFER GEAR & MACHINE, INC.
5876 Sandy Hollow Road, Rockford IL 61109. 815/874-4327. **Contact:** Human Resources. **World Wide Web address:** http://www.schafergear.com. **Description:** Manufactures gears.

## SCIAKY INC.
4915 West 67th Street, Bedford Park IL 60638. 708/594-3800. **Fax:** 708/496-6191. **Contact:** Comptroller. **World Wide Web address:** http://www.sciaky.com. **Description:** A manufacturer of precision-integrated welding systems. The company engineers and manufactures systems for resistance, advanced arc, electron beam, and laser welding. **NOTE:** See website for job listings. Fax resumes and cover letters to the attention of the Comptroller. **Positions advertised include:** Lathe Operator; Gear Cutter; Senior Mechanical Engineer; Proposal Engineer; Machinist; Machine Builder. **Parent company:** Phillips Service Industries. **Operations at this facility include:** Administration; Divisional Headquarters; Manufacturing; Research and Development; Sales; Service.

## SCULLY-JONES CORPORATION
1901 South Rockwell Street, Chicago IL 60608. 773/247-5900. **Contact:** Gerald Walton, Human Resources. **World Wide Web address:** http://www.scullyjones.com. **Description:** A manufacturer of precision tool holders for machine tools. **Corporate headquarters location:** This location. **Operations at this facility include:** Administration; Manufacturing. **Listed on:** Privately held.

## SEAQUISTPERFECT DISPENSING
1160 North Silver Lake Road, Cary IL 60013. 847/639-2124. **Contact:** Rob Revak, Human Resources. **World Wide Web address:** http://www.seaqperf.com. **Description:** Manufactures aerosol valves and spray pumps. **Special programs:** Internships. **Corporate headquarters location:** This location. **Parent company:** Aptar Group. **Operations at this facility include:** Administration; Manufacturing; Research and Development.

## SLOAN VALVE COMPANY
10500 Seymour Avenue, Franklin Park IL 60131. 847/671-4300. **Contact:** Human Resources. **World Wide Web address:** http://www.sloanvalve.com. **Description:** An international manufacturer of valves for toilets, railroad cars, air brakes, and faucets. Brand names include Slimline, Flushmate, Act-O-Matic, and Optima. **Corporate headquarters location:** This location. **Other U.S. locations:** AR. **Listed on:** Privately held.

## SPRAYING SYSTEMS COMPANY
P.O. Box 7900, Wheaton IL 60189. 630/665-5000. **Fax:** 630/260-0842. **Contact:** Jim Yehling, Director of Human Resources. **World Wide Web address:** http://www.spray.com. **Description:** Manufactures spraying components for industrial use. Products include air atomizing, tank wash, air control, spray/dry, and gas conditioning nozzles; spray guns; and portable spray systems. **Corporate headquarters location:** This location.

## STENOGRAPH CORPORATION
1500 Bishop Court, Mount Prospect IL 60056. **Toll-free phone:** 800/323-4247. **Contact:** Human Resources. **World Wide Web address:** http://www.stenograph.com. **Description:** Manufactures court reporting equipment.

## STEVENS INDUSTRIES INC.
704 West Main Street, Teutopolis IL 62467. 217/857-6411. **Fax:** 217/540-3101. **Contact:** Human Resources. **E-mail address:** joant@stevensind.com. **World Wide Web address:** http://www.stevensind.com. **Description:** A manufacturer of laminated case goods, integrated component parts, and panels. **NOTE:** See website for job listings. E-mail resumes or apply in person in the Human Resources Office. Second- and third-shift positions are offered. **Positions advertised include:** Team Leader; Estimator; Inventory Clerk; Machine Operator, Supervisor. **Office hours:** Monday – Friday, 8:00 a.m. – 4:00 p.m. **Corporate headquarters location:** This location. **Operations at this facility include:** Administration; Manufacturing; Research and Development; Sales; Service. **Listed on:** Privately held.

## SYMONS CORPORATION
200 East Touhy Avenue, Des Plaines IL 60018. 847/298-3200. **Fax:** 847/635-9287. **Contact:** Human Resources. **E-mail address:** jobs@symons.com. **World Wide Web address:** http://www.symons.com. **Description:** An international manufacturer of standard, custom, and fiberglass concrete-forming equipment. The company also manufactures chemical systems including acrylic sealers, bonding agents, construction grouts, and curing compounds. **NOTE:** See website for job listings. Fax resumes or apply online. **Positions advertised include:** Customer Service Coordinator; Senior Account Manager; Senior Form Designer; Administrative Assistant; Corporate Health and Safety Specialist. **Corporate headquarters location:** This location.

**TAYLOR COMPANY**
750 North Blackhawk Boulevard, Rockton IL 61072. 815/624-8333. **Contact:** Human Resources. **World Wide Web address:** http://www.taylor-company.com. **Description:** Manufactures soft-serve ice cream freezers and other food preparation equipment.

**TEMPLETON, KENLY & COMPANY, INC.**
2525 Gardner Road, Broadview IL 60155. 708/865-1500. **Toll-free phone:** 800/275-5225. **Fax:** 708/865-0894. **Contact:** Human Resources. **World Wide Web address:** http://www.tksimplex.com. **Description:** Manufactures hydraulic and mechanical jacks under the brand name Simplex. **Corporate headquarters location:** This location.

**TETRA PAK INC.**
101 Corporate Woods Parkway, Vernon Hills IL 60061. 847/955-6000. **Contact:** Human Resources. **E-mail address:** tpincjobs@tetrapak.com. **World Wide Web address:** http://www.tetrapakusa.com. **Description:** Manufactures food processing equipment. **NOTE:** See the corporate website for job listings – http://www.tetrapak.com. Apply online or e-mail resumes. **Operations at this facility:** Sales.

**3M**
22614 Route 84 North Cordova, IL 61242-9779. 309/654-2291. **Contact:** Human Resources. **World Wide Web address:** http://www.3m.com. **Description:** 3M manufactures products in three sectors. The Industrial and Consumer sector includes a variety of products under brand names including 3M, Scotch, Post-it, Scotch-Brite, and Scotchgard. The Information, Imaging, and Electronic sector is a leader in several high-growth, global industries including telecommunications, electronics, electrical, imaging, and memory media. The Life Science sector serves two broad market categories: health care, and traffic and personal safety. In the health care market, 3M is a leading provider of medical and surgical supplies, drug delivery systems, and dental products; in traffic and personal safety, 3M is a leader in products for transportation safety, worker protection, vehicle and sign graphics, and out-of-home advertising. **NOTE:** Apply online. **Corporate headquarters location:** St. Paul MN. **International locations:** Worldwide. **Operations at this facility include:** Manufacturing plant.

**TUTHILL CORPORATION**
12500 South Pulaski Road, Alsip IL 60805. 708/389-2500. **Contact:** Human Resources. **E-mail address:** jobs@tuthill.com. **World Wide Web address:** http://www.tuthill.com. **Description:** An international distributor and manufacturer of rotary pumps, positive displacement gear, test plugs, and tube connectors. **NOTE:** See website for job listings. **Corporate headquarters location:** Burr Ridge IL. **Operations at this facility include:** Manufacturing.

**USFILTER/ HPD**
23562 West Main Street, Plainfield IL 60544. 815/436-3013. **Contact:** Human Resources. **World Wide Web address:** http://www.usfilter.com. **Description:** USFilter is engaged in the manufacture and servicing of water purification and treatment equipment. Primary customers include the electronics industry, utilities, pharmaceutical companies, and other entities with the need for highly purified water. **Operations at this facility include:** This location is a research and

development facility for pollution control products. **Parent company:** Veolia Environment.

**USFILTER**
55 Shuman Boulevard, Naperville IL 60563. 630/357-7330. **Contact:** Janice Slawinski, Human Resources Manager. **World Wide Web address:** http://www.usfilter.com. **Description:** USFilter is engaged in the manufacture and servicing of water purification and treatment equipment. Primary customers include the electronics industry, utilities, pharmaceutical companies, and other entities with the need for highly purified water. **Operations at this facility include:** This location is a design facility for the company's water purification and treatment technologies. **Parent company:** Veolia Environment.

**USFILTER**
1501 East Woodfield Road, Suite 200 West, Schaumburg IL 60173. 847/706-6900. **Contact:** Human Resources. **World Wide Web address:** http://www.usfilter.com. **Description:** USFilter is engaged in the manufacture and servicing of water purification and treatment equipment. Primary customers include the electronics industry, utilities, pharmaceutical companies, and other entities with the need for highly purified water. **Operations at this facility include:** This location engineers and manufactures air pollution control equipment. **Parent company:** Veolia Environment.

**VIDEOJET TECHNOLOGIES**
1500 North Mittel Boulevard, Wood Dale IL 60191-1073. 630/860-7300. **Fax:** 630/616-3678. **Contact:** Human Resources. **World Wide Web address:** http://www.videojet.com. **Description:** Provides development, manufacturing, sales, and service of nonimpact ink-jet coding and marking equipment. **Positions advertised include:** International Customer Service Representative; Buyer/Planner; Procurement Buyer; Strategic Account Manager.

**WAREHOUSE EQUIPMENT, INC.**
2500 York Road, Elk Grove Village IL 60007. 847/595-9400. **Fax:** 847/595-2126. **Contact:** General Manager. **World Wide Web address:** http://www.weinet.com. **Description:** Manufactures and distributes material handling products, provides engineering services for product handling systems, and designs storage and retrieval equipment. Founded in 1971. **NOTE:** Jobseekers may apply for open positions online. **Corporate headquarters location:** This location.

**WHITING CORPORATION**
26000 Whiting Way, Monee IL 60449. 708/587-4000. **Fax:** 708/587-2041. **Contact:** Human Resources. **World Wide Web address:** http://www.whitingcorp.com. **Description:** A manufacturer of heavy overhead gantry cranes, metallurgical process equipment, and transportation maintenance and repair equipment. **Corporate headquarters location:** This location. **Operations at this facility include:** Manufacturing; Sales; Service.

**WICKS ORGAN COMPANY**
1100 5$^{th}$ Street, Highland IL 62249. 618/654-2191. **Fax:** 618/654-3770. **Contact:** Scott Wick, Vice President. **World Wide Web address:** http://www.wicks.com. **Description:** A manufacturer of church pipe organs. **Positions advertised include:** Sales Representative. **Corporate headquarters location:** This location. **Operations at this facility include:** Manufacturing; Sales; Service.

**WOODS EQUIPMENT COMPANY**
2606 South Illinois Route 2, P.O. Box 1000, Oregon IL 61061. 815/732-2141.
**Fax:** 815/732-7580. **Contact:** Human Resources. **World Wide Web address:**
http://www.woodsequipment.com. **Description:** Manufacturer of farm equipment,
and lawn and garden products. **Positions advertised include:** Agriculture & Turf
Sales Specialist; Construction Equipment Sales Specialist; General Manager;
Operations Manager; Manufacturing Engineer. **Corporate headquarters
location:** This location. **Other U.S. locations:** Nationwide.

**ZEBRA TECHNOLOGIES CORPORATION**
333 Corporate Woods Parkway, Vernon Hills IL 60061. 847/634-6700. **Fax:**
847/913-8766. **Contact:** Human Resource Director. **World Wide Web address:**
http://www.zebra.com. **Description:** Designs, manufactures, sells, and supports
a broad line of computerized label and ticket printing systems and related
specialty supplies. The company provides barcode labeling solutions to
manufacturing customers and government entities worldwide for use in automatic
identification and data collection systems. **Positions advertised include:**
Administrative Assistant; Billing Specialist; Corporate Reservation Agent; Data
Entry Specialist; IP Counsel; Claims Coordinator; Cost Accountant; Credit
Coordinator; Staff Accountant.

## MINING, GAS, PETROLEUM, ENERGY RELATED

### You can expect to find the following types of companies in this section:

Anthracite, Coal, and Ore Mining • Mining Machinery and Equipment • Oil and Gas Field Services • Petroleum and Natural Gas

---

**AIR LIQUIDE AMERICA CORPORATION**
5230 South East Avenue, Countryside IL 60525. 708/482-8400. **Fax:** 708/579-7702. **Contact:** Ronald J. Nowak, Manager of Administration. **World Wide Web address:** http://www.airliquide.com. **Description:** Air Liquide America Corporation is a diversified manufacturer engaged in the recovery and sale of atmospheric industrial gases, the manufacture and sale of oil field equipment and supplies, and the distribution of welding and industrial equipment and supplies. The company operates several business segments. The Gas Group produces and sells oxygen, nitrogen, and argon in liquid and gaseous forms through approximately 20 locations, operating more than 2,200 miles of pipeline; The Energy Group operates under two names, Bowen Tools and Dia-Log Companies, and manufactures and sells equipment to petroleum and natural gas companies; The Welding Group distributes electric arc welding equipment and supplies. **NOTE:** Apply online. **Special programs:** Internships. **Corporate headquarters location:** Houston TX. **Other U.S. locations:** CA; FL; HI; LA. **Operations at this facility include:** This location is a technology center involved in the engineering and research of industrial gases and related equipment. **Parent company:** L'Air Liquide. **Number of employees worldwide:** 30,000.

**BP AMOCO**
28100 Torch Parkway, Warrenville IL 60555-3938. 630/420-5111. **Contact:** Human Resources. **World Wide Web address:** http://www.bp.com. **Description:** Engaged in the energy business, principally domestic oil and natural gas. The firm is a major holder of domestic crude oil reserves and is also involved in the refining and marketing of petroleum products. **NOTE:** This company provides job listings for all its Illinois, United States and international locations. See website and apply online. **Corporate headquarters location:** This location. **Parent company:** BP (United Kingdom). **Listed on:** New York Stock Exchange. **Stock exchange symbol:** BP. **Number of employees worldwide:** 104,000.

**CITGO PETROLEUM CORPORATION**
3737 South Cicero Avenue, Cicero IL 60804. 708/780-5700. **Contact:** Human Resources. **World Wide Web address:** http://www.citgo.com. **Description:** Citgo Petroleum wholesales gasoline that is then sold to gas stations by a distributor. **Corporate headquarters location:** Tulsa OK. **Operations at this facility include:** This location manufactures lubricants.

**CITGO PETROLEUM CORPORATION**
135th Street & New Avenue, Lemont IL 60439. 630/257-7761. **Contact:** Personnel. **World Wide Web address:** http://www.citgo.com. **Description:** Citgo Petroleum wholesales gasoline that is then sold to gas stations by a distributor. **Positions advertised include:** Chemical Engineer; Electrical Engineer;

Mechanical Engineer. **Corporate headquarters location:** Tulsa OK. **Operations at this facility include:** This location is a refinery.

### ELGIN NATIONAL INDUSTRIES
2001 Butterfield Road, Suite 1020, Downers Grove IL 60515-1050. 630/434-7200. **Fax:** 630/434-7272. **Contact:** Harry Chase, Human Resources. **World Wide Web address:** http://www.eni.com. **Description:** A diversified company engaged in coal engineering and manufacturing. **NOTE:** See website for companies that operate under the Elgin name.

### EXXONMOBIL CORPORATION
P.O. Box 874, Joliet IL 60410. 815/423-5571. **Contact:** Employee Relations Manager. **World Wide Web address:** http://www.exxon.mobil.com. **Description:** ExxonMobil is an integrated oil company engaged in petroleum and chemical products marketing, refining, manufacturing, exploration, production, transportation, and research and development worldwide. **NOTE:** For administrative positions, visit the nearest ExxonMobil office location. For technician positions, apply online at the corporate website. **Corporate headquarters location:** Irving TX. **Operations at this facility include:** This location is the Midwest regional office and also houses a refinery. **Listed on:** New York Stock Exchange. **Stock exchange symbol:** XON.

### GATX CORPORATION
500 West Monroe Street, 42nd Floor, Chicago IL 60661. 312/621-6200. **Fax:** 312/621-8062. **Contact:** Human Resources. **E-mail address:** jobs@gatx.com. **World Wide Web address:** http://www.gatx.com. **Description:** A holding company engaged in the lease and sale of rail cars and storage tanks for petroleum transport; equipment and capital asset financing and related services; the operation of tank storage terminals, pipelines, and related facilities; the operation of warehouses; and distribution and logistics support. Founded in 1898. **NOTE:** Entry-level positions are offered. **Positions advertised include:** Payroll Specialist; Senior Financial Analyst. **Special programs:** Internships. **Office hours:** Monday - Friday, 8:30 a.m. - 4:45 p.m. **Corporate headquarters location:** This location. **Other U.S. locations:** Nationwide. **International locations:** Worldwide. **Subsidiaries include:** American Steamship Company; GATX Capital Corporation; GATX Logistics; GATX Terminals Corporation; General American Trans. **Operations at this facility include:** Administration. **Listed on:** New York Stock Exchange. **Stock exchange symbol:** GMT.

### MARTIN ENGINEERING
One Martin Place, Neponset IL 61345. 309/594-2384. **Contact:** Human Resources. **World Wide Web address:** http://www.martinengineering.com. **Description:** Manufactures and markets products designed to make the handling of bulk materials safer, cleaner, and more expedient. The company serves the coal, metallic and nonmetallic mineral, pulp and paper, aggregate, and cement industries among many others. Founded in 1944. **Positions advertised include:** Customer Development Representative; International Operations Engineer; Distribution Supervisor.

### PREMCOR INC.
201 East Hawthorne Street, Hartford IL 62048. 618/254-7301. **Fax:** 618/254-4661. Christine Carnicelli, Human Resources. **E-mail address:** christine.carnicelli@premcor.com. **World Wide Web address:** http://www.premcorinc.com. **Description:** Manufactures petroleum products.

**NOTE:** Contact Ms. Carnicelli at 1700 East Putnam, Suite 400, Old Greenwich CT 06870, or via phone at 203/698-5649. **Positions advertised include:** Senior Safety Specialist; Electrician; Process Engineer. **Operations at this facility include:** This location is a terminal facility.

**UOP, INC.**
25 East Algonquin Road, Des Plaines IL 60017. 847/391-2000. **Fax:** 847/391-2253. **Contact:** Human Resources. **World Wide Web address:** http://www.uop.com. **Description:** Provides research, development, engineering, and manufacturing services relating to process technology and products for the petroleum and petrochemical industries. **NOTE:** Apply online. Part-time positions offered. **Positions advertised include:** Project Engineer; MRO Buyer; Web Coordinator; Development Chemist; Research Technician; Field Technical Advisor. **Special programs:** Internships. **Corporate headquarters location:** This location. **Listed on:** Privately held.

**UOP, INC.**
P.O. Box 163, Riverside IL 60546. 708/442-7400. **Contact:** Human Resources. **World Wide Web address:** http://www.uop.com. **Description:** UOP provides research, development, engineering, and manufacturing services relating to process technology and products for the petroleum and petrochemical industries. **NOTE:** Apply online. **Operations at this facility include:** This location is a research center.

# PAPER AND WOOD PRODUCTS

## You can expect to find the following types of companies in this section:

Forest and Wood Products and Services • Lumber and Wood Wholesalers • Millwork, Plywood, and Structural Members • Paper and Wood Mills

---

**BEMIS COMPANY INC.**
P.O. Box 568, Peoria IL 61651. 309/682-5406. **Physical address:** One Sloan Street, Peoria IL 61603. **Contact:** Human Resources. **World Wide Web address:** http://www.bemis.com. **Description**: Bemis Company is a diversified producer of consumer and industrial packaging materials, film products, and business products. Packaging products include tapes and paper bags for pharmaceuticals, candy, toilet paper, and detergents. The company also produces sheetprint stock, roll labels, laminates, and adhesive products. **NOTE:** Apply online at the company's website. **Corporate headquarters location:** Minneapolis MN. **Operations at this facility include:** : This location manufactures paper bags. **Listed on:** New York Stock Exchange. **Stock exchange symbol:** BMS.

**CENVEO**
3001 North Rockwell Street, Chicago IL 60618. 773/267-3600. **Contact:** Human Resources. **World Wide Web address:** http://www.mail-wellenvelope.com. **Description:** An envelope manufacturer. **Corporate headquarters location:** Englewood CO. **Operations at this facility include:** This is a manufacturing plant. **Other area locations:** DeKalb IL; Kankakee IL. **Other U.S. locations:** Nationwide. **Listed on:** New York Stock Exchange. **Stock exchange symbol:** CVO.

**FELLOWES MANUFACTURING COMPANY**
1789 Norwood Avenue, Itasca IL 60143. 630/893-1600. **Contact:** Director of Human Resources. **World Wide Web address:** http://www.fellowes.com. **Description:** Manufactures corrugated boxes. Fellowes Manufacturing also manufactures, markets, and sells a variety of office equipment and supplies. **NOTE:** Apply online for open job positions at this company's website.

**INTERNATIONAL PAPER FOOD SERVICE**
500 Dacey Drive, Shelbyville IL 62565. 217/774-2176. **Contact:** Human Resources. **World Wide Web address:** http://www.ipfoodservice.com. **Description:** Manufactures cartons and containers for the food service industry. **NOTE:** Apply online at the parent company's website: http://www.internationalpaper.com. **Parent company:** International Paper Company (Purchase NY). **Listed on:** New York Stock Exchange. **Stock exchange symbol:** IP.

**IVEX PACKAGING CORPORATION**
100 Tri-State International, Suite 200, Lincolnshire IL 60069. 847/945-9100. **Contact:** Human Resources. **World Wide Web address:** http://www.ivexpackaging.com. **Description:** Manufactures paper and plastic

packaging products including dessert trays, containers, and toilet tissue overwraps. **Corporate headquarters location:** This location. **Operations at this facility include:** Administration.

## IVEX PACKAGING CORPORATION

8100 South 77th Avenue, Bridgeview IL 60455. 708/458-8084. **Contact:** Shelly Dentzman, Human Resources. **World Wide Web address:** http://www.ivexpackaging.com. **Description:** Manufactures corrugated packaging and mailers. **Corporate headquarters location:** Lincolnshire IL.

## MASONITE

1955 Powis Road, West Chicago IL 60185. 630/584-6330. **Contact:** Human Resources Manager. **World Wide Web address:** http://www.masonite.com. **Description:** Masonite manufactures doors. **Other U.S. locations:** Nationwide. **International locations:** Worldwide. **Operations at this facility include:** Sales.

## PACTIV CORPORATION

1900 West Field Court, Lake Forest IL 60045. 847/482-2000. **Toll-free phone:** 888/828-2850. **Fax:** 847/482-4738. **Contact:** Human Resources. **World Wide Web address:** http://www.pactiv.com. **Description:** A worldwide manufacturer of paper, corrugated paper, paperboard, aluminum, and plastic packaging material. Products are used in the packaging of food, paper and paper products, metal products, rubber and plastics, automotive products, point-of-purchase displays, soap, detergent, and food products, as well as residential construction. Brands include Hefty paper and plastic products. **Special programs:** Internships. **Corporate headquarters location:** This location. **Listed on:** New York Stock Exchange. **Stock exchange symbol:** PTV.

## SMURFIT-STONE CONTAINER CORPORATION

150 North Michigan Avenue, Chicago IL 60601. 312/346-6600. **Contact:** Recruiting Specialist. **World Wide Web address:** http://www.smurfit-stone.com. **Description:** One of the world's leading paper-based packaging companies. Smurfit-Stone Container Corporation's main products include corrugated containers, folding cartons, and multiwall industrial bags. The company is also one of the world's largest collectors and processors of recycled products. Smurfit-Stone Container Corporation also operates several paper tube, market pulp, and newsprint production facilities. **Corporate headquarters location:** This location. **Other U.S. locations:** Nationwide. **Listed on:** NASDAQ. **Stock exchange symbol:** SSCC.

## WEYERHAEUSER COMPANY

4160 Campus Drive, Aurora IL 60504. 630/585-3400. **Contact:** Human Resources. **World Wide Web address:** http://www.weyerhaeuser.com. **Description:** A forest management and manufacturing company. Weyerhauser recycles pulp, paper, and packaging products; manufactures wood products; manages timberland; and develops real estate. **Positions advertised include:** Automation Representative; Outside Sales Representative; Customer Service Manager; Human Resources Manager. **Corporate headquarters location:** Tacoma WA. **Other U.S. locations:** Nationwide.

## PRINTING AND PUBLISHING

**You can expect to find the following types of companies in this section:**
Book, Newspaper, and Periodical Publishers • Commercial Photographers • Commercial Printing Services • Graphic Designers

**AMERICAN LIBRARY ASSOCIATION**
50 East Huron Street, Chicago IL 60611. 312/944-6780. **Fax:** 314/944-6763. **Contact:** Human Resources. **World Wide Web address:** http://www.ala.org. **Description:** A membership association focusing on library information science. The association works with legislators to obtain federal support for libraries; engages in public educational programs; maintains a library and research center; presents over 100 awards, scholarships, and grants including the Newbury and Caldecott Medals for children's literature; publishes journals, monographs, and reference works; and holds two conferences each year for its members. **NOTE:** See website for job listings and contact information. **Corporate headquarters location:** This location. **Other U.S. locations:** Washington DC.

**BANTA DIRECT MARKETING GROUP**
2075 Busse Road, Elk Grove Village IL 60007-5791. 847/593-1200. **Contact:** Human Resources. **E-mail address:** apply@Banta.com. **World Wide Web address:** http://www.banta.com. **Description:** Produces direct mail products including brochures, publication and package inserts, coupons, reply cards, return envelopes, and specialty booklets for national advertisers, direct marketers, publishers, and ad agencies. **NOTE:** Apply online to open positions. For general employment inquiries, e-mail the company. **Positions advertised include:** Customer Service Representative; Executive Assistant; Marketing Assistant/Database Coordinator; Sales and Marketing Assistant. **Parent company:** Banta Corporation (Menasha WI) is a technology and market leader in printing and digital imaging. The corporation serves publishers of educational and general books, special-interest magazines, consumer and business catalogs, and direct marketing materials. In addition to printing and digital imaging, Banta offers multimedia and software packages, interactive media, point-of-purchase materials, and single-use products. Banta operates through the following groups: Banta Book Group; Banta Catalog Group; Banta Digital Group; Banta Direct Marketing Group; Banta Information Services Group; Banta Publications Group; Signs, Displays, Labels & Stamps; and Single-Use Products. **Listed on:** New York Stock Exchange. **Stock exchange symbol:** BN.

**THE BEACON NEWS**
101 South River Street, Aurora IL 60506. 630/844-5811. **Contact:** Human Resources. **World Wide Web address:** http://www.suburbanchicagonews.com. **Description:** A daily newspaper serving De Kalb, DuPage, Kane, and Kendall Counties. The paper has a daily circulation of approximately 90,000. Founded in 1846. **Parent company:** The Copley Press (La Jolla CA) publishes 45 newspapers nationwide.

## BROWN PRINTING
11595 McConnell Road, Woodstock IL 60098. 815/338-6750. **Contact:** Ed Davis, Human Resources Manager. **E-mail address:** ed.davis@bpc.com. **World Wide Web address:** http://www.bpc.com. **Description:** Provides color printing, binding, and related services to the publishers of trade and special-interest magazines. Services include selective binding, ink-jet technology, carrier-route sorting, and bar coding of customers' subscriber lists.

## CHICAGO SUN-TIMES INC.
350 North Orleans, Chicago IL 60604. 312/321-3000. **Contact:** Employment Manager. **World Wide Web address:** http://www.suntimes.com. **Description:** Publishes one of the largest daily newspapers in the United States. **Special programs:** Internships. **Corporate headquarters location:** This location. **Parent company:** American Publishing Company. **Operations at this facility include:** Administration; Manufacturing; Sales; Service.

## CHRISTIANITY TODAY, INC. (CTI)
465 Gundersen Drive, Carol Stream IL 60188. 630/260-6200. **Fax:** 630/260-0114. **Contact:** Jaime Patrick, Human Resources. **World Wide Web address:** http://www.christianitytoday.com. **Description:** A publisher of evangelical magazines. **Special programs:** Internships. **Corporate headquarters location:** This location.

## COMMERCE CLEARING HOUSE, INC. (CCH, INC.)
4025 West Peterson, Chicago IL 60646. 773/583-8500. **Contact:** Human Resources. **World Wide Web address:** http://www. cch.com. **Description:** Provides business law information to the legal and accounting professions by publishing loose-leaf news reports and books primarily on tax and business law. The company also provides corporate services to lawyers and offers computer services for processing income tax returns. It also provides information to the healthcare and human resources industries. **NOTE:** See website for job listings and apply online. **Corporate headquarters location:** Riverwoods IL. **Other U.S. locations:** Quail Hill CA; Washington DC; St. Petersburg FL; Clark NJ; New York NY. **Operations at this facility include:** Administration; Manufacturing; Service.

## COOK COMMUNICATIONS MINISTRIES
850 North Grove Avenue, Elgin IL 60120. 847/741-2400. **Contact:** Human Resources. **World Wide Web address:** http://www.cookministries.com. **Description:** Creates, designs, produces, prints, publishes, markets, and distributes evangelical material. **Positions advertised include:** Internet Product Coordinator; Clerical Assistant; Marketing Specialist; Publicist; Senior Accountant; Sales Representative; Marketing Brand Manager. **Corporate headquarters location:** This location. **Operations at this facility include:** Administration; Manufacturing; Research and Development; Sales; Service.

## THE COURIER NEWS
P.O. Box 351, Elgin IL 60121. 847/888-7800. **Physical address:** 300 Lake Street, Elgin IL 60120. **Contact:** Human Resources. **World Wide Web address:** http://www.suburbanchicagonews.com. **Description:** A daily newspaper with a circulation of approximately 30,000.

## CRABAR/GBF
200 West Railroad Avenue, Princeton IL 61356. **Toll-free phone:** 800/423-4569. **Contact:** Human Resources. **World Wide Web address:**

http://www.crabargbf.com. **Description:** A full-service commercial printer specializing in customized business forms and direct mail printing. Founded in 1952. **Corporate headquarters location:** Dayton OH. **Other U.S. locations:** Nationwide. **Listed on:** Privately held.

## CRAIN COMMUNICATIONS
360 North Michigan Avenue, Chicago IL 60601. 312/649-5200. **Fax:** 312/649-5331. **Contact:** Human Resources. **E-mail address:** chicago_jobs@crain.com. **World Wide Web address:** http://www.craincommunications.com. **Description:** Publishes health, trade, and business magazines and newspapers.

## DAILY HERALD
## PADDOCK PUBLICATIONS, INC.
P.O. Box 280, Arlington Heights IL 60006-0280. 847/427-4300. **Fax:** 847/427-1270. **Recorded jobline:** 847/427-4398. **Contact:** Employment Recruiter. **E-mail address:** staffing@dailyherald.com. **World Wide Web address:** http://www.dailyherald.com. **Description:** Publishes a daily newspaper. Founded in 1872. **NOTE:** Entry-level positions, part-time jobs, and second and third shifts are offered. **NOTE:** See website or call the recorded job line for open positions. Fax or e-mail resumes. **Special programs:** Internships; Training; Co-ops. **Corporate headquarters location:** This location. **Listed on:** Privately held.

## THE DAILY SOUTHTOWN
6901 West 159th Street, Tinley Park IL 60477. 708/633-6700. **Contact:** Human Resources. **World Wide Web address:** http://www.dailysouthtown.com. **Description:** A daily newspaper serving the Chicago metropolitan area. **Corporate headquarters location:** This location.

## DEARBORN FINANCIAL PUBLISHING
30 South Wacker Drive, Suite 2500, Chicago IL 60606. 312/836-4400. **Toll-free phone:** 800/824-8742. **Contact:** Human Resources. **World Wide Web address:** http://www.dearborn.com. **Description:** A publisher of financial, educational, and trade materials.

## R.R. DONNELLEY & SONS COMPANY
77 West Wacker Drive, Chicago IL 60601-1696. 312/326-8000. **Fax:** 312/326-8543. **Contact:** Human Resources. **World Wide Web address:** http://www.rrdonnelley.com. **Description:** A world leader in managing, reproducing, and distributing print and digital information for publishing, merchandising, and information technology customers. The company is one of the largest commercial printers in the world, producing catalogs, inserts, magazines, books, directories, computer documentation, and financial printing. R.R. Donnelley has more than 180 sales offices and production facilities. Principal services offered by the company are conventional and digital prepress operations; computerized printing and binding; sophisticated pool shipping and distribution services for printed products; information repackaging into multiple formats including print, magnetic, and optical media; database management, list rental, list enhancement, and direct mail production services; turnkey computer documentation services including outsourcing, translation, printing, binding, diskette replication, kitting, licensing, republishing, and fulfillment; reprographics and facilities management; creative design and communication services; and digital and conventional map creation and related services. Founded in 1864. **NOTE:** This company has offices throughout Chicago, Illinois, and the world. See website for job listings and apply online. **Corporate headquarters location:** This

location. **Other U.S. locations:** Nationwide. **International locations:** Worldwide. **Listed on:** New York Stock Exchange. **Stock exchange symbol:** RRD.

### ENCYCLOPAEDIA BRITANNICA
310 South Michigan Avenue, Chicago IL 60604. 312/347-7000. **Fax:** 312/294-2135. **Contact:** Human Resources. **E-mail address:** staffing@eb.com. **World Wide Web address:** http://www.britannica.com. **Description:** An international publisher of reference books and other educational materials. **Corporate headquarters location:** This location.

### FOLLETT CORPORATION
2233 West Street, River Grove IL 60171. 708/583-2000. **Toll-free phone:** 800/621-4345. **Fax:** 708/452-9347. **Contact:** Rene Collier, Director of Human Resources. **World Wide Web address:** http://www.follett.com. **Description:** Distributes educational textbooks, library books, and software systems for library management. Follett is also engaged in the nationwide operation of college bookstores. **NOTE:** Temporary and part-time positions offered. This company has other positions throughout the state of Illinois. See its website for additional locations and job listings. **Positions advertised include:** Plant Operator, Facility Maintenance; Marketing Specialist; Operational Auditor; Financial Analyst; Gold Planner; Inside Sales Representatives.

### GENERAL LEARNING CORPORATION
### CAREER WORLD
900 Skokie Boulevard, Suite 200, Northbrook IL 60062-4028. 847/205-3000. **Toll-free phone:** 800/641-3912. **Fax:** 847/564-8197. **Contact:** Human Resources. **World Wide Web address:** http://www.glcomm.com. **Description:** Publishes *Career World,* a career guidance magazine with a circulation of approximately 85,000.

### GOSS GRAPHIC SYSTEMS, INC.
3 Territorial Court, Bolingbrook IL 60440-3557. 630/755-9300. **Fax:** 630/755-9301. **Contact:** Human Resources. **World Wide Web address:** http://www.gossgraphic.com. **Description:** A world leader in color offset printing, press manufacturing, and development. The company offers color printing services for newspapers and magazines. **Office hours:** Monday - Friday, 8:00 a.m. - 5:00 p.m. **Corporate headquarters location:** This location. **International locations:** Japan; United Kingdom; France; China.

### JOHNSON PUBLISHING COMPANY, INC.
820 South Michigan Avenue, Chicago IL 60605. 312/322-9200. **Contact:** LaDoris Foster, Personnel Director. **World Wide Web address:** http://www.ebony.com. **Description:** Publishes Ebony and Jet magazines. The company also markets the Fashion Fair cosmetics line. **Corporate headquarters location:** This location.

### MANUFACTURERS' NEWS, INC.
1633 Central Street, Evanston IL 60201. 847/864-7000. **Fax:** 847/332-1100. **Contact:** Human Resources. **World Wide Web address:** http://www.mninfo.com. **Description:** Compiles and publishes directories and databases of U.S. manufacturers. Founded in 1912. **NOTE:** Part-time jobs are offered. **Office hours:** Monday – Friday, 8:30 a.m. – 4:30 p.m.

**MCGRAW-HILL CONTEMPORARY PUBLISHING**
10 NE Prudential Plaza, Chicago IL 60601. 312/233-6500. **Fax:** 847/679-2494.
**Contact:** Human Resources Manager. **World Wide Web address:**
http://www.mhcontemporary.com. **Description:** A division of McGraw-Hill that
publishes career, foreign language, travel, reference, business, and children's
books. **NOTE:** Apply online at the parent company's website:
http://www.mcgraw-hill.com/careers. **Special programs:** Internships. **Corporate
headquarters location:** Columbus OH. **International locations:** Markham,
Ontario.

**MOORE WALLACE**
1200 South Lakeside Drive, Bannockburn IL 60015. 847/607-6000. **Contact:**
Human Resources. **World Wide Web address:** http://www.rrdonnelley.com.
**Description:** A manufacturer of business systems, forms, and equipment. The
company has more than 280 locations in 39 countries. **NOTE:** Apply online at the
corporate website for open positions. **Special programs:** Internships. **Corporate
headquarters location:** This location. **Parent company:** RR Donnelley.

**THE NEWS SUN**
2383 North Delany Road, Waukegan, IL 60087. 847/336-7000. **Fax:** 847/249-
7254. **Contact:** Chris Cashman, Managing Editor. **World Wide Web address:**
http://www.suburbanchicagonews.com. **Description:** A daily newspaper that
serves Waukegan and Lake counties. **Corporate headquarters location:** This
location. **Other U.S. locations:** Lake Villa IL; Libertyville IL. **Parent company:**
The Copley Press (La Jolla CA) publishes 45 newspapers nationwide.
**Operations at this facility include:** Administration.

**NYSTROM COMPANY**
3333 Elston Avenue, Chicago IL 60618. 773/463-1144. **Toll-free phone:**
800/621-8086. **Fax:** 773/463-0515. **Contact:** Paige Johnson, Human Resources
Director. **World Wide Web address:** http://www.nystromnet.com. **Description:**
Manufactures and publishes charts, maps, globes, and other visual learning
instruments. **Parent company:** Herff Jones, Inc. **Operations at this facility
include:** This location is the main office for Herff Jones Education Division.

**J.S. PALUCH COMPANY, INC.**
3708 River Road, Suite 400, Franklin Park IL 60131. 847/678-9300. **Contact:**
Linda Kaup, Manager of Human Resources. **World Wide Web address:**
http://www.jspaluch.com. **Description:** Publishes and prints religious material
such as computer software, educational bulletins, Sunday bulletins, and worship
aids.

**PEORIA JOURNAL STAR, INC.**
One News Plaza, Peoria IL 61643. 309/686-3125. **Fax:** 309/686-3297. **Contact:**
Julie O'Donnnell, Human Resources Manager. **E-mail address:**
jodonnell@pjstar.com. **World Wide Web address:** http://www.pjstar.com.
**Description:** Publishes a daily newspaper with a circulation of 72,000.

**PLAYBOY ENTERPRISES**
680 North Lake Shore Drive, 15th Floor, Chicago IL 60611. 312/751-8000.
**Contact:** Human Resources. **World Wide Web address:**
http://www.playboy.com. **Description:** Publishes and markets products in almost
200 countries through six business groups. The Casino Gaming Group has plans
to open a club in London, England. The Catalog Group markets print and online

versions of Critic's Choice Video and Collector's Choice Music Catalogs. The Entertainment Group operates Playboy TV networks and home video markets. Playboy.com INC. operates the company's Website. The Product Marketing Group markets accessories and apparel. The Publishing Group publishes *Playboy* magazine and books. **NOTE:** Apply online. **Listed on:** New York Stock Exchange. **Stock exchange symbol:** PLA.

## PUBLICATIONS INTERNATIONAL LTD.
7373 North Cicero Avenue, Lincolnwood IL 60712. 847/676-3470. **Contact:** Human Resources. **World Wide Web address:** http://www.pubint.com. **Description:** A publisher of fiction, nonfiction, and consumer guides.

## RAND McNALLY & COMPANY
8255 North Central Park Avenue, Skokie IL 60076. 847/329-8100. **Toll-free phone:** 800/333-0136. **Fax:** 847/329-6361. **Contact:** Human Resources. **World Wide Web address:** http://www.randmcnally.com. **Description:** A book, map, and road atlas publisher. **NOTE:** Apply online. **Corporate headquarters location:** This location. **Positions advertised include:** Customer Service Representative; Senior Category Manager; National Account Manager; Internet Marketing Manager.

## REED BUSINESS INFORMATION
2000 Clearwater Drive, Oak Brook IL 60523. 847/635-8800. **Contact:** Human Resources. **World Wide Web address:** http://www.reedbusiness.com. **Description:** Publishes travel information guides. **Positions advertised include:** Sale Representative; Human Resources Manager; Data Enhancer; Senior Editor. **Operations at this facility include:** Administration; Sales.

## SCHAWK, INC.
1695 River Road, Des Plaines IL 60018. 847/827-9494. **Fax:** 847/827-1264. **Contact:** Human Resources. **E-mail address:** recruit@schawk.com. **World Wide Web address:** http://www.schawk.com. **Description:** Schawk offers an entire range of creative and prepress capabilities for books, magazines, directories, retail and catalog advertising, and corporate communications. Services include design, copywriting, editorial development, photography, electronic composition, color separations, and data management. **NOTE:** See website for job listings. E-mail resumes and cover letters. **Corporate headquarters location:** This location. **Other U.S. locations:** GA; MI; MN; NJ; NY. **Operations at this facility include:** Administration; Service.

## SCHAWK, INC.
6115 Official Road, Crystal Lake IL 60014. 815/459-8520. **Fax:** 815/459-7259. **Contact:** Human Resources. **World Wide Web address:** http://www.schawk.com. **Description:** Schawk offers an entire range of creative and prepress capabilities for books, magazines, directories, retail and catalog advertising, and corporate communications. Services include design, copywriting, editorial development, photography, electronic composition, color separations, and data management. **Corporate headquarters location:** Des Plaines IL. **Other U.S. locations:** GA; MI; MN; NJ; NY. **Operations at this facility include:** Administration; Service.

## SCOTT FORESMAN
1900 East Lake Avenue, Glenview IL 60025. 847/729-3000. **Fax:** 847/486-3968. **Recorded jobline:** 847/657-3920. **Contact:** Human Resources. **World Wide**

**Web address:** http://www.scottforesman.com. **Description:** One of the largest educational publishers in the United States. The company publishes teaching materials including textbooks, computer software, video, and CD-ROM products for elementary and high school students in all major disciplines. **Special programs:** Internships. **Corporate headquarters location:** This location. **Listed on:** Privately held.

**SEVEN WORLDWIDE, INC.**
225 West Superior Street, Chicago IL 60610. 312/616-7777. **Contact:** Human Resources. **World Wide Web address:** http://www.sevenww.com. **Description:** A commercial graphic arts company providing digital imaging prepress services. Founded in 1953.

**STANDARD EDUCATIONAL COMPANY**
900 North Shore Drive, Suite 252, Lake Bluff IL 60044. 847/283-0301. **Contact:** Human Resources Manager. **World Wide Web address:** http://www.fergpubco.com. **Description:** Publishers of the *Careers in Focus* series and numerous other career and training-related books and CD-ROMs.

**STAR PUBLICATIONS, INC.**
6901 West 159th Street, Tinley Park IL 60477. 708/802-8800. **Contact:** Human Resources. **World Wide Web address:** http://www.starnewspapers.com. **Description:** Publishes biweekly community newspapers. **NOTE:** Entry-level positions are offered. **Special programs:** Internships. **Corporate headquarters location:** West Frankfort IL. **Parent company:** American Publishing Company. **Operations at this facility include:** Administration; Manufacturing; Sales; Service.

**THE STATE JOURNAL-REGISTER**
One Copley Plaza, Springfield IL 62701. 217/788-1330. **Contact:** Elaine Kerhlikar, Human Resources. **World Wide Web address:** http://www.sj-r.com. **Description:** Publishes a morning, daily newspaper covering 11 central Illinois counties. **NOTE:** Part-time positions offered. **Parent company:** The Copley Press (La Jolla CA) publishes 45 newspapers nationwide.

**THIRD WORLD PRESS**
7822 South Dobson, Chicago IL 60619. 773/651-0700. **Contact:** Human Resources. **World Wide Web address:** http://www.thirdworldpressinc.com. **Description:** A publisher of fiction, nonfiction, and children's stories by African-American authors. Third World Press also publishes titles on audio and produces some videos. **Corporate headquarters location:** This location.

**TRADER PUBLISHING COMPANY**
840 Oak Creek Drive, Lombard IL 60148. 630/620-7355. **Contact:** Human Resources. **World Wide Web address:** http://www.traderonline.com. **Description:** Publishes classified advertising magazines that feature used vehicles along with parts and accessories. **NOTE:** Submit resumes by mail indicating department of interest.

**THE TRIBUNE COMPANY**
435 North Michigan Avenue, Chicago IL 60611. 312/222-9100. **Contact:** Human Resources. **World Wide Web address:** http://www.tribune.com. **Description:** Publishes daily newspapers including the *Chicago Tribune, Fort Lauderdale Sun-Sentinel, Los Angeles Times, Baltimore Sun, Hartford Courant, Orlando Sentinel,*

and *Daily Press.* The company also owns eight independent TV stations in Illinois, New York, Colorado, Pennsylvania, California, Massachusetts, Georgia, and Louisiana; six radio stations in Illinois, New York, Colorado, and California; and the Chicago Cubs baseball team. **NOTE:** See website for job listings and contact information. Mail resumes to this location. **Special programs:** Internships. **Corporate headquarters location:** This location. **Subsidiaries include:** Independent Network News; The Wright Group; Tribune Entertainment Company. **Listed on:** New York Stock Exchange. **Stock exchange symbol:** TRB.

**TYNDALE HOUSE PUBLISHERS, INC.**
P.O. Box 80, Wheaton IL 60189. 630/668-8300. **Contact:** Human Resources. **World Wide Web address:** http://www.tyndalebooksellers.com. **Description:** Publishes *The Living Bible,* as well as other religious products including books, movies, calendars, audio books, and Bible reference products. Founded in 1962. **Office hours:** Monday - Friday, 8:00 a.m. - 4:30 p.m. **Corporate headquarters location:** This location. **Listed on:** Privately held.

**UNIVERSITY OF CHICAGO PRESS**
1427 East 60th Street, Chicago IL 60637. 773/702-7700. **Contact:** Human Resources. **World Wide Web address:** http://www.press.uchicago.edu. **Description:** A nonfiction book and periodical publisher. **Positions advertised include:** Advertising Clerk. **Parent company:** University of Chicago. **Operations at this facility include:** Administration.

**WORLD BOOK INTERNATIONAL**
233 North Michigan Avenue, Suite 2000, Chicago IL 60601. 312/729-5800. **Fax:** 312/729-5600. **Contact:** Director of Human Resources. **World Wide Web address:** http://www.worldbook.com. **Description:** An encyclopedia publisher.

# REAL ESTATE

**You can expect to find the following types of companies in this section:**
Land Subdividers and Developers • Real Estate Agents, Managers, and Operators • Real Estate Investment Trusts

---

**BAIRD & WARNER**
120 South LaSalle Street, Suite 2000, Chicago IL 60603. 312/368-1855. **Toll-free phone:** 800/644-1855. **Fax:** 302/368-1490. **Contact:** Wendy Adametz, Human Resources Director. **World Wide Web address:** http://www.bairdwarner.com. **Description:** A full-service, residential real estate broker operating 30 offices in the Chicago area. **NOTE:** Part-time positions offered. See website for all job listings. **Positions advertised include:** Mortgage Underwriter; Loan Officer. **Corporate headquarters location:** This location.

**COLDWELL BANKER RESIDENTIAL BROKERAGE**
875 North Michigan Avenue, Suite 3500, Chicago IL 60611. 312/751-9100. **Fax:** 312/751-9293. **Contact:** Human Resources. **World Wide Web address:** http://www.coldwellbanker.com. **Description:** One of the largest residential real estate companies in the United States and Canada. **Corporate headquarters location:** Parsippany NJ.

**GENERAL GROWTH PROPERTIES, INC.**
110 North Wacker Drive, Chicago IL 60606. 312/960-5000. **Fax:** 312/960-5475. **Contact:** Human Resources. **E-mail address:** careers@generalgrowth.com. **World Wide Web address:** http://www.generalgrowth.com. **Description:** Owns, operates, develops, and renovates shopping malls. Mail or e-mail resume and cover letters, stating interest in a specific type of position. Special programs: Internships. **Positions advertised include:** CAD Specialist; Director of Grocery Store Leasing; Director of Operations; Group Vice President of Marketing. **Corporate headquarters location:** This location. **Parent company:** Sears, Roebuck & Co. **Listed on:** New York Stock Exchange. **Stock exchange symbol:** GGP.

**GRUBB & ELLIS COMPANY**
2215 Sanders Road, Suite 400, Northbrook IL 60062. 847/753-9010. **Contact:** Human Resources. **World Wide Web address:** http://www.grubb-ellis.com. **Description:** A commercial and residential real estate brokerage firm. **Corporate headquarters location:** This location.

**JMB REALTY CORPORATION**
**J&V URBAN RETAIL PROPERTIES COMPANY**
900 North Michigan Avenue, Chicago IL 60611. 312/440-4800. **Fax:** 312/915-2310. **Contact:** Human Resources. **Description:** Owns and manages shopping malls and strip malls nationwide. **Corporate headquarters location:** This location. **Other U.S. locations:** Nationwide. **Listed on:** Privately held.

**MERCHANDISE MART PROPERTIES, INC.**
200 World Trade Center, Suite 470, Chicago IL 60654. 312/527-7792. **Fax:** 312/527-7905. **Contact:** Tom Fitzpatrick, Director of Human Resources. **E-mail address:** careers@mmart.com. **World Wide Web address:** http://www.merchandisemart.com. **Description:** The management and leasing agent for prominent wholesale showroom facilities, which include the Merchandise Mart and Apparel Center (Chicago), the Decorators and Designers Building (New York), and the Washington Design Center (Washington DC). **Positions advertised include:** Concierge; Administrative Assistant. **Special programs:** Internships. **Corporate headquarters location:** This location. **Other U.S. locations:** Washington DC; High Point NC. **Parent company:** Vornado Realty Trust. **Operations at this facility include:** Administration; Research and Development; Sales; Service. **Listed on:** Privately held.

**RE/MAX TEAM 2000**
7130 West 127th Street, Palos Heights IL 60463. 708/361-5950. **Contact:** Human Resources. **World Wide Web address:** http://www.chicago-area-homes.com. **Description:** A residential and commercial real estate agency.

# RETAIL

**You can expect to find the following types of companies in this section:**
Catalog Retailers • Department Stores, Specialty Stores • Retail Bakeries • Supermarkets

---

## ACE HARDWARE CORPORATION
2200 Kensington Court, Oak Brook IL 60523. 630/990-6600. **Fax:** 630/990-6838. **Contact:** Director of Human Resources. **World Wide Web address:** http://www.acehardware.com. **Description:** A worldwide dealer-owned cooperative operating through 5,100 hardware retailers in 62 countries. Ace Hardware Corporation also produces a line of hand and power tools, plumbing products, lawn and garden products, cleaning supplies, and manufactures a line of paint. **NOTE:** Apply online at the company's website. **Positions advertised include:** Advertising Distribution Analyst; Financial Analyst; Senior Audit Consultant; POR Operator; Network Administrator; Assistant Buyer. **Corporate headquarters location:** This location.

## ALBERTSON'S INC.
3030 Cullerton Drive, Franklin Park IL 60131. **Toll-free phone:** 800/964-1434. **Fax:** 888/541-5793. **Contact:** Director of Recruiting. **World Wide Web address:** http://www.albertsons.com. **Description:** One of the largest retail food-drug chains in the United States. The company operates approximately 2,300 stores in 33 states. **NOTE:** Entry-level positions and part-time jobs are offered. **Positions advertised include:** Programmer Analyst; Computer Programmer; Management Trainee; Pharmacist; Systems Analyst. **Corporate headquarters location:** Boise ID. **Listed on:** New York Stock Exchange. **Stock exchange symbol:** ABS.

## ALDI INC.
2080 West Main Street, Batavia IL 60510. 630/879-8100. **Contact:** Human Resources. **World Wide Web address:** http://www.aldifoods.com. **Description:** Operates a chain of discount grocery stores throughout the Midwest. **Corporate headquarters location:** This location.

## AVON PRODUCTS INC.
6901 Golf Road, Morton Grove IL 60053. 847/966-0200. **Contact:** Human Resources. **World Wide Web address:** http://www.avoncareers.com. **Description:** A direct seller of beauty care products, fashion jewelry, gifts, fragrances, and decorative products. Avon, a *Fortune* 500 company, markets its products through a network of 2.8 million independent sales representatives in 135 countries worldwide. Founded in 1886. **NOTE:** For corporate positions, see job listings on the website. Salespeople are considered independent contractors or dealers and most work part-time. If you are interested in becoming a sales representative, please call 800/FOR-AVON, or visit the company's website for more information. **Positions advertised include:** Order Fulfillment Supervisor; Order Fulfillment Supervisor; Packaging Advisor; Customer Service Specialist. **Corporate headquarters location:** New York NY. **Other U.S. locations:** Pasadena CA; Newark DE; Atlanta GA; Suffern NY; Springdale OH. **Operations**

at this facility include: Manufacturing. Listed on: New York Stock Exchange. Stock exchange symbol: AVP. CEO/President: Andrea Jung. Number of employees nationwide: 40,000.

## BARNES & NOBLE BOOKSTORES
1550 West 75th Street, Downers Grove IL 60516. 630/663-0181. Fax: 630/663-0188. Contact: Manager. World Wide Web address: http://www.barnesandnobleinc.com. Description: One location of the nationwide bookstore chain. This location has a cafe in addition to its book departments. NOTE: Apply online or at the nearest retail location. Positions advertised include: Book Seller; Music Seller; Café Attendant; Department Manager; Community Relations Manager. Corporate headquarters location: New York NY. Other U.S. locations: Nationwide. Listed on: NASDAQ. Stock exchange symbol: BNBN.

## BARNES & NOBLE BOOKSTORES
47 East Chicago Avenue, Suite 132, Naperville IL 60540. 630/579-0200. Fax: 630/579-6921. Contact: Manager. World Wide Web address: http://www.barnesandnobleinc.com. Description: One location of the nationwide bookstore chain. NOTE: Apply online or at the nearest retail location. Positions advertised include: Book Seller; Music Seller; Café Attendant; Department Manager; Community Relations Manager. Corporate headquarters location: New York NY. Listed on: NASDAQ. Other U.S. locations: Nationwide. Stock exchange symbol: BNBN.

## BRIDGESTONE/FIRESTONE, INC.
## RETAIL AND COMMERCIAL DIVISION
333 East Lake Street Bloomingdale IL 60108. 630/259-9000. Fax: 630/259-9158. Contact: Human Resources. World Wide Web address: http://www.mastercareusa.com. Description: This location is the support center and headquarters for the Bridgestone/Firestone, Inc. retail stores, MasterCare. Founded in 1900. NOTE: Entry-level positions and part-time jobs are offered. Apply online at the website. Office hours: Monday - Friday, 8:00 a.m. - 5:00 p.m. Corporate headquarters location: Nashville TN. Other U.S. locations: Nationwide. International locations: Worldwide. Parent company: Bridgestone. Operations at this facility include: Administration; Divisional Headquarters; Service.

## CARSON PIRIE SCOTT & COMPANY
One South State Street, Chicago IL 60603. 312/641-7000. Fax: 312/641-7088. Contact: Hiring Manager. World Wide Web address: http://www.carsons.com. Description: The department store chain's flagship store in downtown Chicago. Overall, Carson Pirie Scott & Company operates a department store chain with more than 50 Midwest locations. Parent company: Saks Incorporated operates a number of retail stores offering fashion apparel, accessories, cosmetics, and home furnishings. Saks Incorporated operates more than 350 stores in 38 states. Stores include: Proffitt's, McRae's, Younkers, and Saks Fifth Avenue. The company also operates two direct mail companies, Folio and Bullock & James. NOTE: This chain has several locations throughout the Chicago area and Illinois and the Midwest. To apply, see the corporate website for open positions; or visit the nearest store location. Listed on: New York Stock Exchange. Stock exchange symbol: SKS.

**CARSON PIRIE SCOTT & COMPANY/BERGNERS DISTRIBUTION CENTER**
4650 Shepherd Trail, Rockford IL 61103. 815/654-5420. **Contact:** Human Resources. **World Wide Web address:** http://www.carsons.com. **Description:** Carson Pirie Scott & Company Bergner's Company operate department store chains with more than 100 Midwest locations. **Parent company:** Saks Incorporated operates a number of retail stores offering fashion apparel, accessories, cosmetics, and home furnishings. Saks Incorporated operates more than 350 stores in 38 states. Other stores include: Proffitt's, McRae's, Younkers, and Saks Fifth Avenue. The company also operates two direct mail companies, Folio and Bullock & James. **NOTE:** Interested jobseekers must visit this facility's Human Resources Office. **Office hours:** Monday – Thursday, 7:00 a.m. – 4:30 p.m.; Friday, 8:00 a.m. to noon. **Operations at this facility include:** This location is the distribution center for Carson Pirie Scott and Bergner's. **Listed on:** New York Stock Exchange. **Stock exchange symbol:** SKS.

**CREATIVE COMPUTERS INTEGRATED TECHNOLOGIES**
1155 West Dundee Road, Suite 100, Arlington Heights IL 60004. 224/625-8800. **Toll-free phone:** 800/700-1000. **Contact:** Human Resources. **World Wide Web address:** http://www.cc-inc.com. **Description:** Owns and operates a chain of retail stores that sell computers and related accessories. This company also sells computers on the Internet. **NOTE:** Entry-level positions are offered. **Corporate headquarters location:** This location. **Other U.S. locations:** CO; IN; KS. **Parent company:** PC Mall (Torrance CA).

**DOMINICK'S FINER FOODS**
711 Jorie Boulevard, Oak Brook IL 60523. 888/723-3929. **Contact:** Human Resources. **World Wide Web address:** http://www.dominicks.com. **Description:** Operates a chain of retail grocery stores. **NOTE:** Apply online at this company's website. **Corporate headquarters location:** This location. **Operations at this facility include:** Administration.

**FORTUNE BRANDS INC.**
300 Tower Parkway, Lincolnshire IL 60069. 847/484-4400. **Contact:** Human Resources. **World Wide Web address:** http://www.fortunebrands.com. **Description:** A consumer products company offering home and office products, golf equipment, and spirits and wine. **Brand names include:** Jim Beam, Master Lock, Moen, El Tesoro, Acco, Dekuyper, Titlelist; Footjoy. **NOTE:** For positions with a specific Fortune Brand company, see its corporate website for links to the its subsidiaries' websites. **Corporate headquarters location:** This location. **Listed on:** New York Stock Exchange. **Stock exchange symbol:** FO.

**JC PENNEY COMPANY, INC.**
3 Woodfield Mall, Schaumburg IL 60173. 847/240-5000. **Contact:** Human Resources. **World Wide Web address:** http://www.jcpenney.net. **Description:** A national retail service corporation with department stores in most major American cities. JC Penney sells apparel, home furnishings, and leisure lines in catalogs and 1,900 retail stores. Other operations include JC Penney Life Insurance Company, which sells life, health, and credit insurance; and JC Penney National Bank. **Corporate headquarters location:** Dallas TX. **Other U.S. locations:** Ford City IL; Lombard IL; North Riverside IL. **Operations at this facility include:** Regional Headquarters. **Listed on:** New York Stock Exchange. **Stock exchange symbol:** JCP.

## JEWEL OSCO

1955 West North Avenue, Melrose Park IL 60160. 708/531-6000. **Fax:** 708/531-6047. **Contact:** Employment Manager. **E-mail address:** JJ.JobsAtJEWELCO@ALBERTSONS.COM. **World Wide Web address:** http://www.jewelosco.com. **Description:** Operates a chain of retail food stores. **NOTE:** For store management positions, e-mail resumes. For retail positions, apply at the nearest Jewel Osco location. For pharmacy employment, send resume to Recruiting Department, 3030 Cullerton, Franklin Park, IL 60130; fax: 888/541-5793; or e-mail: pharmacyrecruiting@Albertsons.com. When sending a resume, please indicate department of interest. Special programs: Internships; Store Management Training. **Corporate headquarters location:** This location.

## K'S MERCHANDISE

3103 North Charles Street, Decatur IL 62526. 217/875-1440. **Fax:** 217/875-6978. **Contact:** Human Resources. **World Wide Web address:** http://www.catalog.ksmerchandise.com. **Description:** A retail catalog showroom chain. **Positions advertised include:** Store Manager Trainee; Jewelry Assistant; Jewelry Manager; Jeweler Promotional Coordinator; Jeweler. **Corporate headquarters location:** This location. **Operations at this facility include:** Administration; Manufacturing; Sales; Service.

## NEW YORK & COMPANY

4190-E North Harlem Avenue, Chicago IL 60634. 773/625-9684. **Contact:** Human Resources. **E-mail address:** recruiting@nyandcompany.com. **World Wide Web address:** http://www.nyandcompany.com. **Description:** New York & Company sells moderately priced women's fashions through a chain of retail stores. **NOTE:** See website for corporate job listings. To apply for retail positions, visit the nearest store location. **Operations at this facility include:** This location houses administrative offices. **Parent company:** The Limited, Inc.

## SAKS FIFTH AVENUE

700 North Michigan Avenue, Chicago IL 60611. 312/944-6500. **Contact:** Human Resources. **World Wide Web address:** http://www.saksincorporated.com. **Description:** Saks Fifth Avenue is a 62-store chain emphasizing soft-goods products, primarily apparel for men, women, and children. **NOTE:** See website for job listings and apply online. **Parent company:** Saks Incorporated is a department store holding company that operates approximately 360 stores in 36 states. The company's stores include Saks Fifth Avenue, Parisian, Proffit's, Younker's, Herberger's, Carson Pirie Scott, Boston Store, Bergner's, and Off 5th, the company's outlet store. Saks Incorporated also operates two retail catalogs and several retail Internet sites. **Operations at this facility include:** This location is a part of the nationwide specialty department store chain. **Listed on:** New York Stock Exchange. **Stock exchange symbol:** SKS.

## SEARS, ROEBUCK & CO.

3333 Beverly Road, Hoffman Estates IL 60179. 847/286-2500. **Contact:** Director of Human Resources. **World Wide Web address:** http://www.sears.com. **Description:** Operates a chain of department stores. **Corporate headquarters location:** This location. **Subsidiaries include:** Advantis, a partnership formed by Sears and IBM, is a networking technology company that provides businesses with data, voice, and multimedia services; Allstate Insurance Group is one of the nation's largest publicly held property and casualty insurance companies, with more than 20 million customers and approximately 14,600 full-time agents in the United States and Canada. Allstate offers automobile insurance, homeowners insurance, life insurance, annuity and pension products, business insurance (insurance for small and mid-size businesses, as well as reinsurance for other insurers), and mortgage guaranty insurance (through Allstate's wholly-owned subsidiary, PMI Mortgage Insurance Company); Homart is one of the country's leading developers, owners, and managers of regional shopping malls and community centers; Prodigy, a Sears/IBM partnership, is a home computer network providing a wide variety of personal Internet services including news, shopping, bulletin boards, travel ticketing, brokerage, banking, and e-mail services; and Sears Merchandise Group is a leading retailer of apparel, home, and automotive products and related services for families throughout North America. **Listed on:** New York Stock Exchange. **NOTE:** For corporate positions, apply online. For retail positions, visit the nearest retail location. **Stock exchange symbol:** S.

**THE SHERWIN-WILLIAMS COMPANY**
619 Howard Street, Evanston IL 60202. 847/869-9030. **Contact:** Human Resources. **World Wide Web address:** http://www.sherwin.com. **Description:** Sherwin-Williams Company manufactures, sells, and distributes coatings and related products. Coatings are produced for original equipment manufacturers in various industries, as well as for the automotive aftermarket, the industrial maintenance market, and the traffic paint market. Sherwin-Williams labeled architectural and industrial coatings are sold through company-owned specialty paint and wallcovering stores. The Sherwin-Williams Company also manufactures paint under the Acme, Dutch Boy, Kem-Tone, Lucas, Martin-Senour, Minwax, Pratt & Lambert, Rogers, and Thompson brand names, as well as private labels, and markets its products to independent dealers, mass merchandisers, and home improvement centers. **NOTE:** Apply in person at this location. See website for corporate job listings. **Corporate headquarters location:** Cleveland OH. **Operations at this facility include:** This location is a retail and wholesale outlet.

**SPIEGEL, INC.**
3500 Lacey Road, Downers Grove IL 60515. 630/986-8800. **Fax:** 630/769-2012. **Contact:** Human Resources. **E-mail address:** careers@spgl.com. **World Wide Web address:** http://www.spiegel.com. **Description:** A retailer of goods and services for the home, as well as current fashions for women, men, and children. **NOTE:** See website for job listings and apply online. **Positions advertised include:** Recruiter. **Corporate headquarters location:** This location. **Subsidiaries include:** Eddie Bauer, Inc.

**STRATFORD HALL**
6253 West 74th Street, Box 2001, Bedford Park IL 60499-2001. 800/258-4084. **Contact:** Human Resources. **World Wide Web address:** http://www.stratfordhall.com. **Description:** Engaged in the catalog sale of personalized holiday cards for businesses. **Corporate headquarters location:** This location.

**TRUE VALUE COMPANY**
8600 West Bryn Mawr Avenue, Chicago IL 60631-3505. 773/695-5000. **Contact:** Human Resources. **E-mail address:** jobs@truevalue.com. **World Wide Web address:** http://www.truevaluecompany.com. **Description:** A *Fortune* 500 company that operates the True Value, Home & Garden Showplace, and Taylor Rental national retail chains. **NOTE:** Apply online. **Positions advertised include:** Import Logistics Manager; Import Coordinator; Inventory Analyst; Field

Marketing Manager; Retail Project Supervisor; Accounts Payable Manager; Transportation Compliance Analyst. **Corporate headquarters location:** This location.

## VALUE CITY FURNITURE
15770 S. La Grange Road, Orland Park IL 60462. 708/226-8121. **Fax:** 708/226-8177. **Contact:** John Jacobe, General Manager. **E-mail address:** John.Jacobe@vcf.com. **World Wide Web address:** http://www.vcf.com. **Description:** A furniture retailer with over 100 stores throughout the Midwestern, Eastern, and Southern United States. **Positions advertised include:** Delivery Driver; General Warehouse Worker; Sales Professional; Service Technician; Visual Merchandiser. **Other U.S. locations:** Nationwide.

## WALGREEN COMPANY
200 Wilmot Road, Deerfield IL 60015. 847/940-2500. **Contact:** Personnel Recruiting. **World Wide Web address:** http://www.walgreens.com. **Description:** Walgreen operates one of the largest retail drug store chains in the United States, which sells prescription and nonprescription drugs, cosmetics, toiletries, liquor and beverages, tobacco, and general merchandise. **Corporate headquarters location:** This location.

## XPEDX
3555 North Kimball Avenue, Chicago IL 60618. 773/463-0822. **Fax:** 773/463-4862. **Contact:** Human Resources. **World Wide Web address:** http://www.xpedx.com. **Description:** A retailer of paper and office products. **NOTE:** For corporate positions, send resumes and cover letters to Bill Alexander, Human Resources Manager, at this location. For retail positions, contact Tom Phillips at 773/463-6423. **Corporate headquarters location:** This location. **Parent company:** International Paper Company. **Operations at this facility include:** Administration; Sales; Service. **Listed on:** New York Stock Exchange. **Stock exchange symbol:** IP.

## STONE, CLAY, GLASS, AND CONCRETE PRODUCTS

### You can expect to find the following types of companies in this section:
Cement, Tile, Sand, and Gravel • Crushed and Broken Stone • Glass and Glass Products • Mineral Products

---

**AMERICAN COLLOID COMPANY**
1500 West Shure Drive, Arlington Heights IL 60004. 847/392-4600. **Fax:** 847/506-6199. **Contact:** Human Resources. **World Wide Web address:** http://www.colloid.com. **Description:** American Colloid mines bentonite clay. The company's Volclay sodium bentonite is used in oil well drilling and foundry forming applications.

**CARDINAL GLASS COMPANY**
1087 Research Parkway, Rockford IL 61109. 815/394-1400. **Contact:** Human Resources. **Description:** Replaces automobile glass, distributes flat glass, and performs commercial and residential glazing.

**OZINGA BROTHERS**
2255 South Lumber Street, Chicago IL 606016. 312/432-8100. **Fax:** 312/432-8101. **Contact:** Human Resources. **World Wide Web address:** http://www.ozinga.com. **Description:** Manufactures concrete and plaster materials for use in construction. Founded in 1928. **NOTE:** See website for job listings, contact information and application forms. Fax or e-mail resumes. **Positions advertised include:** Quality Control Technician; Driver.

**PILKINGTON COMPANY**
20th and Center Streets, Ottawa IL 61350. 815/433-0932. **Fax:** 815/434-8088. **Contact:** Human Resources. **World Wide Web address:** http://www.pilkington.com. **Description:** Pilkington-Libby-Owens-Ford Company is a diversified manufacturer of fluid power and fluid systems components, automotive glass, flat and tinted glass products, decorative laminates, and molded plastics. **NOTE:** See website for job listings. **Listed on:** Privately held.

**U.S. PRECISION GLASS COMPANY**
1900 Holmes Road, Elgin IL 60123. 847/931-1200. **Fax:** 847/931-4144. **Contact:** Lynn M. Sprangers, Human Resources Manager. **World Wide Web address:** http://www.uspg.com. **Description:** Fabricates precision glass for appliance, commercial, industrial, and technical applications. **Special programs:** Internships. **Corporate headquarters location:** This location. **Other U.S. locations:** Lewisburg OH; Jefferson TX. **Operations at this facility include:** Administration; Manufacturing; Research and Development; Sales; Service.

**USG CORPORATION**
**UNITED STATES GYPSUM COMPANY**
125 South Franklin Street, Chicago IL 60606. 312/606-4390. **Contact:** Greg Puchalski, Vice President of Human Resources. **World Wide Web address:** http://www.usgcorp.com. **Description:** Manufacturers a wide range of products for use in building construction, repair, and remodeling, and in many industry

processes. Products include wallboard, plasters, and agricultural gypsum. The company operates more than 100 plants. **Positions advertised include:** Plant Manager; Production Engineer; Project Engineer; Services Manager; Lab Director; Senior Development Associate; Accountant; Corporate Auditor; Financial Analyst. **Corporate headquarters location:** This location. **International locations:** Canada; Europe; Mexico. **Operations at this facility include:** Administration.

## TRANSPORTATION AND TRAVEL

**You can expect to find the following types of companies in this section:**
Air, Railroad, and Water Transportation Services • Courier Services • Local and Interurban Passenger Transit • Ship Building and Repair • Transportation Equipment • Travel Agencies • Trucking • Warehousing and Storage

---

### ABF FREIGHT SYSTEM, INC.
1970 Weisbrook Drive, Oswego IL 60543. 630/966-0606. **Toll-free phone:** 800/610-5544. **Fax:** 800/599-2810 **Contact:** Branch Manager. **World Wide Web address:** http://www.abfs.com. **Description:** One of the nation's largest motor carriers. **NOTE:** Apply online at website. Special programs: Management Training. **Positions advertised include:** Drivers; Office Clerk; Operations Supervisor; Quotation Analyst; Industrial Engineer. **Corporate headquarters location:** Fort Smith, AK.

### ACE DORAN HAULING & RIGGING COMPANY
5529 Dial Drive, Granite City IL 62040. 618/797-0047. **Contact:** Human Resources. **World Wide Web address:** http://www.acedoran.com. **Description:** Provides truck transportation of heavy and specialized commodities such as steel, aluminum, self-propelled vehicles in excess of 15,000 pounds, and construction equipment. **NOTE:** For driver positions, apply online. For all other positions, send resumes to: Ace Doran Hauling & Rigging Company, Human Resources, 1601 Blue Rock Street, Cincinnati OH 45223.

### A1 TRAVEL
1506 Wabash Avenue, Springfield IL 62704. 217/546-1090. **Contact:** Hiring Manager. **Description:** A travel agency. A1 Travel also offers classes for individuals who are considering becoming travel consultants. **Corporate headquarters location:** This location.

### ALLIANCE SHIPPERS, INC.
15515 South 70th Court, Orland Park IL 60462. 708/802-7000. **Contact:** Manager. **World Wide Web address:** http://www.alliance.com. **Description:** Transports packages for businesses and consumers throughout the world. **Corporate headquarters location:** This location. **International locations:** Worldwide.

### ALLIED VAN LINES
700 Oakmont Lane, Westmont IL 60559. 630/570-3000. **Fax:** 630/570-3606. **Contact:** Human Resources. **World Wide Web address:** http://www.alliedvan.com. **Description:** A moving company whose major markets are household goods moving and specialized transportation services. **NOTE:** To see job listings and to apply, visit the corporate website at http://www.careers.sirva.com. **Positions advertised include:** Customer Service Manager; Transportation Manager; IT Quality Assurance Analyst; Claims Adjustor. **Corporate headquarters location:** This location. **Parent company:** SIRVA. **Number of employees at this location:** 690.

**BEKINS VAN LINES**
330 South Mannheim Road, Hillside IL 60162. 708/547-2000. **Fax:** 708/547-3228. **Contact:** Human Resources. **World Wide Web address:** http://www.bekins.com. **Description:** A moving and storage company. **Positions advertised include:** Driver. **Corporate headquarters location:** This location. **Parent company:** The Bekins Company. **Operations at this facility include:** Service. **Listed on:** Privately held.

**CH2M HILL**
8501 West Higgins Road, Suite 300,Chicago IL 60631-2801. 773/693-3809. **Contact:** Human Resources. **World Wide Web address:** http://www.ch2m.com. **Description:** CH2M Hill is a group of employee-owned companies operating under the names CH2M Hill, Inc., Industrial Design Corporation, Operations Management International, CH2M Hill International, and CH2M Hill Engineering. The professional staff includes specialists in environmental engineering, waste management, water management, transportation, industrial facilities, and a broad spectrum of infrastructure systems. **NOTE:** This company has offices throughout Chicago, Illinois and the United States. See website for job listings and apply online. **Operations at this facility include:** This location provides transportation and environmental engineering services.

**CARRY TRANSIT**
7830 West 71st Street, Bridgeview IL 60455. 800/777-2288. **Fax:** 708-594-5110. **Contact:** Neil Desmond, Human Resources. **E-mail address:** ndesmond@carrytransit.com. **World Wide Web address:** http://www.carrytransit.com. **Description:** Operates one of the nation's largest fleets of stainless steel food grade tankers, serving as a liquid and dry bulk distribution partner to various food products manufacturers. **Positions advertised include:** Local Truck Driver; Truck Driver CDL; Trucking Terminal Manager. **Corporate headquarters location:** This location.

**CONSOER TOWNSEND ENVIRODYNE ENGINEERS, INC.**
303 East Wacker Drive, Suite 600, Chicago IL 60601. 312/938-0300. **Fax:** 312/938-1109. **Contact:** Director of Human Resources. **E-mail address:** jobs@cte-eng.com. **World Wide Web address:** http://www.cte-eng.com. **Description:** Provides engineering consulting for highways, airports, and waste management projects. **NOTE:** Apply online at the company's website or e-mail resumes.

**ELGIN, JOLIET & EASTERN RAILWAY COMPANY**
1141 Maple Road, Joliet IL 60432. 815/740-6760. **Fax:** 815/740-6757. **Contact:** Human Resources. **World Wide Web address:** http://www.tstarinc.com. **Description:** A common carrier freight line. **NOTE:** Resumes only accepted for open positions. The company's website provides job listings. Apply online or fax or e-mail resumes. **Positions advertised include:** Motor Car Repairman; Trainman/Remote Control/Locomotive Engineer Trainee. **Other U.S. locations:** IN. **Parent company:** Transtar (Monroeville PA). **Operations at this facility include:** Service.

**FEDERAL EXPRESS CORPORATION (FEDEX)**
500 Commerce Street, Aurora IL 60504. 630/820-1061. **Toll-free phone:** 800/463-3339. **Contact:** Human Resources. **World Wide Web address:** http://www.fedex.com. **Description:** One of the world's largest express transportation companies serving 212 countries worldwide. FedEx ships

approximately 3.2 million packages daily. FedEx operates more than 45,000 drop-off locations, and has a fleet that consists of more than 640 aircraft and 44,5000 vehicles. **NOTE:** Apply online at the company's website. **Corporate headquarters location:** Memphis TN. **Other U.S. locations:** Nationwide. **Operations at this facility include:** This location is a World Service Center.

## GATX CORPORATION
500 West Monroe Street, 42nd Floor, Chicago IL 60661. 312/621-6200. **Fax:** 312/621-8062. **Contact:** Human Resources. **E-mail address:** jobs@gatx.com. **World Wide Web address:** http://www.gatx.com. **Description:** A holding company engaged in the lease and sale of rail cars and storage tanks for petroleum transport; equipment and capital asset financing and related services; the operation of tank storage terminals, pipelines, and related facilities; the operation of warehouses; and distribution and logistics support. Founded in 1898. **NOTE:** Entry-level positions are offered. **Positions advertised include:** Payroll Specialist; Senior Financial Analyst. **Special programs:** Internships. **Office hours:** Monday - Friday, 8:30 a.m. - 4:45 p.m. **Corporate headquarters location:** This location. **Other U.S. locations:** Nationwide. **International locations:** Worldwide. **Subsidiaries include:** American Steamship Company; GATX Capital Corporation; GATX Logistics; GATX Terminals Corporation; General American Trans. **Operations at this facility include:** Administration. **Listed on:** New York Stock Exchange. **Stock exchange symbol:** GMT.

## GE CAPITAL CORPORATION
540 West Northwest Highway, Barrington IL 60010. 847/277-4000. **Contact:** Human Resources. **World Wide Web address:** http://www.gecareers.com. **Description:** GE Capital Corporation is one of the largest vehicle leasing and financing companies in the United States and Canada, providing fleet and related management services to corporate clients. **Parent company:** General Electric Company operates in the following areas: aircraft engines (jet engines, replacement parts, and repair services for commercial, military, executive, and commuter aircraft); appliances; broadcasting (NBC); industrial (lighting products, electrical distribution and control equipment, transportation systems products, electric motors and related products, a broad range of electrical and electronic industrial automation products, and a network of electrical supply houses); materials (plastics, ABS resins, silicones, superabrasives, and laminates); power systems (products for the generation, transmission, and distribution of electricity); technical products and systems (medical systems and equipment, as well as a full range of computer-based information and data interchange services for both internal use and external commercial and industrial customers); and capital services (consumer services, financing, and specialty insurance). **Operations at this facility include:** This location provides automobile leasing and financing. **Listed on:** New York Stock Exchange. **Stock exchange symbol:** GE.

## GE CAPITAL CORPORATION
500 West Monroe Street, Chicago IL 60661. 312/441-7000. **Fax:** 305/476-6550. **Contact:** Human Resources. **World Wide Web address:** http://www.gecas.com. **Description:** Provides financing and leasing services to small and mid-sized businesses including equipment, real estate, and capital loans. **Parent company:** General Electric Company.

## GE CAPITAL RAILCAR SERVICES
161 North Clark Street, Chicago IL 60601. 312/853-5000. **Contact:** Employment Manager. **World Wide Web address:** http://www.gecareers.com. **Description:**

A major lessor of railcars in North America. The company's primary areas of business are: leasing and managing railcar equipment, financing, car repair and maintenance, and wheel services. The company's fleet includes covered hoppers, tank cars, boxcars, intermodal cars, pressure differential cars, coal cars, and other specialty cars. The company offers a full variety of lease types and equipment management services. **Special programs:** Internships. **Other U.S. locations:** El Cerrito CA; Englewood CO; Atlanta GA; Oak Brook IL; Albany NY; Bala-Cynwyd PA; Houston TX. **Parent company:** General Electric Company.

## GARRETT AVIATION SERVICES
1200 North Airport Drive, Springfield IL 62707-8417. 217/544-3431. **Toll-free phone:** 800/731-7371. **Fax:** 217/544-8911. **Contact:** Steve Fox, Human Resources. **World Wide Web address:** http://www.garrettaviation.com. **Description:** Provides a comprehensive group of services to the general aviation industry. Garrett performs airframe, engine, and modification services at its six domestic locations. **NOTE:** Second and third shifts are offered. **Office hours:** Monday - Friday, 8:00 a.m. - 5:00 p.m. **Corporate headquarters location:** Annapolis MD. **Other U.S. locations:** Los Angeles CA; Van Nuys CA; Augusta GA; Ronkonkoma NY; Houston TX. **Parent company:** General Electric Company. **Operations at this facility include:** Administration; Sales; Service. **Listed on:** New York Stock Exchange. **Stock exchange symbol:** GE.

## ILLINOIS CENTRAL RAILROAD COMPANY
455 North Cityfront Plaza Drive, Chicago IL 60611-5317. 312/755-7500. **Contact:** Human Resources. **World Wide Web address:** http://www.cn.ca. **Description:** Operates one of the largest rail networks in the United States. The company's network includes 2,700 miles of main lines; 1,700 miles of passing, yard, and switching track; and 300 miles of secondary main lines. The company serves land shippers in Illinois, Louisiana, Michigan, Alabama, Kentucky, and Tennessee. Illinois Central's equipment consists of locomotives; freight cars; work equipment; and highway trailers and tractors. **NOTE:** Apply online. **Positions advertised include:** Communication Technician. **Corporate headquarters location:** This location. **Parent company:** Canadian National Railway.

## LAIDLAW TRANSIT, INC.
## SCHOOL BUS DIVISION
1240 East Diehl Road, Suite 100, Naperville IL 60563. 630/955-0003. **Fax:** 630/955-0653. **Contact:** Human Resources. **World Wide Web address:** http://www.laidlawschoolbus.com. **Description:** Provides busing services. **NOTE:** Apply online. **Positions advertised include:** School Bus Driver; Dispatcher; Mechanic; Safety Supervisor; Location Manager. **Parent company:** Laidlaw, Inc. provides solid waste collection, compaction, transportation, treatment, transfer and disposal services; provides hazardous waste services; operates hazardous waste facilities and wastewater treatment plants; and operates passenger and school buses, transit system buses, and tour and charter buses.

## LANDSTAR EXPRESS AMERICA, INC.
2136 12th Street, Suite 106, Rockford IL 61104. 815/226-2170. **Contact:** Human Resources. **World Wide Web address:** http://www.landstar.com. **Description:** Performs expedited and emergency air and truck freight services. **Corporate headquarters location:** Jacksonville FL. **Parent company:** Landstar System,

Inc. is divided into specialized freight transportation segments: Landstar Carrier Group and Landstar Logistics. **Listed on:** NASDAQ. **Stock exchange symbol:** LSTR.

### LANDSTAR CARRIER GROUP

P.O. Box 7013, Rockford IL 61125-7013. 815/972-5000. **Physical address:** 1000 Simpson Road, Rockford IL 61102. **Contact:** Human Resources. **World Wide Web address:** http://www.landstar.com. **Description:** Provides truckload transportation services through independent contractors and commission sales agents. **Corporate headquarters location:** Jacksonville FL.

### MERIDIAN RAIL

1545 State Street, Chicago Heights IL 60411. 708/757-8223. **Contact:** Human Resources. **World Wide Web address:** http://www.meridianrail.com. **Description:** Manufactures and markets replacement and original equipment products for the railroad industry. Products include railroad tracks, wheels, brake shoes, and signals. **Other area locations:** Cicero IL (Manufacturing).

### MESSENGER MOUSE

7818 Forest Hills Road, Loves Park IL 61111. 815/877-2224. **Contact:** Human Resources. **Description:** Offers package delivery services to companies and individual consumers throughout Illinois and Wisconsin.

### SPRINGFIELD AIRPORT AUTHORITY

1200 Capital Airport Drive, Springfield IL 62707-8419. 217/788-1060. **Contact:** Human Resources. **World Wide Web address:** http://www.flyspi.com. **Description:** Operates the Capital Airport. Founded in 1947. **Corporate headquarters location:** This location.

### TTX COMPANY

101 North Wacker Drive, Chicago IL 60606. 312/853-3223. **Contact:** Human Resources. **World Wide Web address:** http://www.ttx.com. **Description:** A rail transportation company.

### TRANSX

720 Greenleaf Avenue, Elk Grove Village IL 60007. 630/458-1310. **Contact:** Human Resources. **World Wide Web address:** http://www.transx.com. **Description:** A trucking and air freight company. **NOTE:** To apply, visit the website and complete the online application. Interested jobseekers may also contact the Recruiter by phone at 800/385-5005 or via e-mail at jnesbitt@transx.com.

### U.S. FREIGHTWAYS

8550 West Bryn Mawr Avenue, Suite 700, Chicago IL 60631. 773/824-1000. **Contact:** Human Resources. **World Wide Web address:** http://www.usfreightways.com. **Description:** U.S. Freightways offers assembly and distribution, domestic and international freight forwarding, and logistics. **Positions advertised include:** Director of Carrier Systems; EDI Coordinator; Senior Programmer/Analyst; Systems Engineer; Systems Support Administrator. **NOTE:** Applicants should indicate the department in which they are interested.

### UNITED AIRLINES, INC. (UAL)

P.O. Box 66100, Chicago IL 60666. 847/700-4000. **Physical address:** 1200 East Algonquin Road, Elk Grove Township IL 60007. **Fax:** 847/700-5287.

**Contact:** Human Resources. **World Wide Web address:** http://www.ual.com. **Description:** United Airlines services 159 airports in the United States and 32 foreign countries in Europe, North and South America, and Asia. Domestic hubs are located in Chicago, Denver, San Francisco, and Washington DC. International hubs are located in Japan and England. **Special programs:** Internships. **Corporate headquarters location:** This location. **Operations at this facility include:** Administration; Sales.

**VAPOR BUS INTERNATIONAL**
1010 Johnson Drive, Buffalo Grove IL 60089. 847/777-6429. **Fax:** 847/520-2225. **Contact:** Dennis E. Huebner, Director Human resources. **Description:** Manufactures transit, shuttle, commuter, and tour coach bus doors. **Corporate headquarters location:** This location.

246 /The Chicago JobBank

# UTILITIES: ELECTRIC, GAS, AND WATER

**You can expect to find the following types of companies in this section:**
Gas, Electric, and Fuel Companies • Other Energy-Producing Companies • Public Utility Holding Companies • Water Utilities

**AMERENCIPS**
**CENTRAL ILLINOIS PUBLIC SERVICE**
607 East Adams Street, Springfield IL 62739. 217/523-3600. **Fax:** 877/226-3736. **Contact:** Employee Development Supervisor. **World Wide Web address:** http://www.ameren.com. **Description:** An electric and gas utility company serving central and southern Illinois. **NOTE:** This company's website provides job listings. Apply online **Parent company:** Ameren Corporation. **Listed on:** New York Stock Exchange. **Stock exchange symbol:** AEE.

**AMERENIP**
500 South 27th Street, Decatur IL 62521. 217/424-6600. **Toll-free phone:** 800/755-5000. **Contact:** Human Resources. **World Wide Web address:** http://www.amerenip.com. **Description:** An electric and gas utility serving 1.4 million customers in Illinois. **Listed on:** New York Stock Exchange. **Stock exchange symbol:** AEE.

**EXELON CORPORATION**
P.O. Box 805379, Chicago IL 60680. 312/394-7398. **Contact:** Human Resources. **E-mail address:** ccresumes@exeloncorp.com. **World Wide Web address:** http://www.exeloncorp.com. **Description:** A holding company. **NOTE:** See website for job listings. E-mail resumes. **Positions advertised include:** Testing Group Supervisor; Communications Manager; Senior Planning Analyst; Corporate Crisis Management; **Corporate headquarters location:** This location. **Subsidiaries include:** Commonwealth Edison is a utility company that provides electricity to northern Illinois.

**GTI**
1700 South Mount Prospect Road, Des Plaines IL 60018. 847/768-0500. **Fax:** 847/468-0501. **Contact:** Human Resources. **E-mail address:** hr@gastechnology.org. **World Wide Web address:** http://www.gastechnology.org. **Description:** A nonprofit research and development institution serving the energy field including gas companies and the Department of Energy. **NOTE:** See website for job listings. Mail, fax or e-mail resumes. Temporary positions are offered. **Positions advertised include:** Research and Development; Administrative; Non-Technical. **Special programs:** Internships.

**NICOR GAS**
1844 West Ferry Road, Naperville IL 60563. 630/983-8676. **Contact:** Human Resources. **E-mail address:** nigashr@nigas.com. **World Wide Web address:** http://www.nicorinc.com. **Description:** One of the nation's largest gas distribution companies. NICOR Gas delivers natural gas to more than 1.8 million customers including transportation service, gas storage, and gas supply backup to

approximately 18,000 commercial and industrial customers. **NOTE:** Apply online. Entry-level positions are offered. **Positions advertised include:** Meter Reader; General Clerk Legal Secretary; HVAC Install Helper; Accountant; Credit Analyst; Mapping Analyst; Risk Analyst; Sourcing Specialist; Staff Manager. **Special programs:** Internships. **Corporate headquarters location:** This location. **Other area locations:** Bellwood IL; Crystal Lake IL; Glen Ellyn IL; Glenview IL; Glenwood IL; Joliet IL; Rockford IL. **Parent company:** NICOR Inc. (also at this location). **Operations at this facility include:** Administration; Regional Headquarters; Research and Development; Sales. **Listed on:** New York Stock Exchange. **Stock exchange symbol:** GAS.

## MISCELLANEOUS WHOLESALING

**You can expect to find the following types of companies in this section:**
Exporters and Importers • General Wholesale Distribution Companies

---

**BOISE OFFICE SOLUTIONS**
**CORPORATE HEADQUARTERS**
150 East Pierce Road, Itasca IL 60143. **Toll-Free phone:** 800-47BOISE. **Fax:** 800/57BOISE. **Contact:** Human Resources. **World Wide Web address:** http://www.bcop.com. **Description:** A business-to-business distributor of office and computer supplies, furniture, paper products, and promotional products. Founded in 1964. **NOTE:** Apply online. **International locations:** Australia; Canada; England; France; Germany; Spain. **Subsidiaries include:** Boise Marketing Services, Inc.; Grande Toy; JPG; Neat Ideas; Reliable. **Parent company:** Boise Cascade Corporation. **Listed on:** New York Stock Exchange. **Stock exchange symbol:** BCC.

**BOISE OFFICE SOLUTIONS**
**CHICAGO DISTRIBUTION CENTER**
800 West Bryn Mawr Avenue, Itasca IL 60143-1594. **Toll-Free phone:** 800-47BOISE. **Fax:** 800/57BOISE. **Contact:** Human Resources. **World Wide Web address:** http://www.bcop.com. **Description:** The company's main distribution office. **Parent company:** Boise Cascade Corporation. **Listed on:** New York Stock Exchange. **Stock exchange symbol:** BCC.

**THE DO-ALL COMPANY**
254 North Laurel Avenue, Des Plaines IL 60016. 847/824-1122. **Fax:** 847/699-7524. **Contact:** Human Resources. **World Wide Web address:** http://www.doall.com. **Description:** Distributes machine tools and other supplies primarily for the metalworking and industrial markets. **NOTE:** Apply online.

**EDWARD DON & COMPANY**
2500 South Harlem Avenue, North Riverside IL 60546. 708/442-9400. **Toll-free phone:** 800/777-4366. **Fax:** 708/883-8268. **Contact:** Bill Doucette, Human Resources Manager. **World Wide Web address:** http://www.don.com. **Description:** Distributes food service equipment and supplies. **NOTE:** Apply online. **Positions advertised include:** Customer Service Representative; Credit Representative; Sales Representative. **Special programs:** Internships. **Corporate headquarters location:** This location. **Listed on:** Privately held.

**W.W. GRAINGER**
100 Grainger Parkway, Lake Forest IL 60045. 847/535-1000. **Contact:** Human Resources. **World Wide Web address:** http://www.grainger.com. **Description:** Distributes a variety of equipment and components to the industrial, commercial, contracting, and institutional markets nationwide. The company operates 337 branches in all 50 states and Puerto Rico. Products include equipment and components for motors, air tools, hydraulic products, refrigeration items, power and hand tools, office equipment, computer supplies, storage equipment, replacement parts, industrial products, safety items, cold weather clothing, and

sanitary supplies. **NOTE:** This company provides job listings for this location and its other locations on its website. Apply online. **Corporate headquarters location:** This location.

## GRAINGER PARTS
1657 Shermer Road, Northbrook IL 60062. 847/498-5900. **Fax:** 847/559-6192. **Contact:** Human Resources. **World Wide Web address:** http://www.grainger.com. **Description:** Distributes repair and replacement parts to industrial and commercial markets. **Corporate headquarters location:** Skokie IL. **Parent company:** W.W. Grainger, Inc. (Skokie IL). **Operations at this facility include:** Administration; Divisional Headquarters; Sales; Service.

## LAWSON PRODUCTS, INC.
1666 East Touhy Avenue, Des Plaines IL 60018. 847/827-9666. **Toll-free phone:** 800/448-8985. **Fax:** 847/827-0083. **Contact:** Human Resources. **World Wide Web address:** http://www.lawsonproducts.com. **Description:** Distributes a variety of industrial parts and fasteners for machinery, automobiles, and other industrial products. **NOTE:** Apply online.

## CHARLES LEVY CIRCULATING COMPANY
1140 N. North Branch Street, Chicago IL 60622. 312/440-4400. **Contact:** Steve Damiani, Human Resources. **World Wide Web address:** http://www.chaslevy.com. **Description:** A wholesale distributor of magazines, books, videos, cassettes, CDs, and other consumer products. **Corporate headquarters location:** Melrose Park IL. **Other U.S. locations:** Grand Rapids MI; Philadelphia PA. **Operations at this facility include:** Sales; Service. **Listed on:** Privately held.

## MCMASTER-CARR SUPPLY
600 County Line Road, Elmhurst IL 60126. 630/833-0300. **Fax:** 630/993-3008. **Contact:** Human Resources. **E-mail address:** rita.lally@mcmaster.com. **World Wide Web address:** http://www.mcmaster.com. **Description:** Publishes a catalog of more than 420,000 industrial supplies used in a multitude of different fields. McMaster keeps 98% of that merchandise on their own warehouse shelves and ready to ship as soon as orders are placed. **Positions advertised include:** Accountant; Customer Service; Data Entry; Marketing Research Assistant; Proofreader; Warehouse Distribution Specialist. **Other U.S. locations:** Atlanta GA, Cleveland OH, Los Angeles CA, Dayton NJ.

## NEW HOLLAND CONSTRUCTION
245 East North Avenue, Carol Stream IL 60188. 630/260-4000. **Contact:** Human Resources. **World Wide Web address:** http://www.newholland.com. **Description:** Distributes parts for industrial equipment including tractors and backhoes.

## THE RELIABLE CORPORATION
1501 East Woodfield Road, Suite 300 West, Schaumburg IL 60173. 847/413-1300. **Contact:** Human Resources. **World Wide Web address:** http://www.reliable.com. **Description:** A wholesaler of a wide variety of office supplies sold primarily through a mail-order catalog. **Corporate headquarters location:** This location. **Parent company:** Boise Cascade. **Operations at this facility include:** Administration.

## ROSCOR CORPORATION
1061 Feehanville Drive, Mount Prospect IL 60056. 847/299-8080. **Fax:** 847/803-8089. **Contact:** Human Resources. **E-mail address:** opportunities@roscor.com. **World Wide Web address:** http://www.roscor.com. **Description:** Distributes industrial video equipment.

## UNITED STATIONERS SUPPLY COMPANY
2200 East Golf Road, Des Plaines IL 60016. 847/699-5000. **Fax:** 847/699-8046. **Contact:** Personnel. **World Wide Web address:** http://www.unitedstationers.com. **Description:** A wholesale distributor of office supplies, furniture, and machines. **Corporate headquarters location:** This location. **Other U.S. locations:** Nationwide. **Operations at this facility include:** Administration; Sales; Service.

## WEBER MARKING SYSTEMS, INC.
711 West Algonquin Road, Arlington Heights IL 60005. 847/364-8570. **Fax:** 847/364-8572. **Contact:** Shirley Hurley, Vice President of Human Resources. **E-mail address:** hrdept@webermarketing.com. **World Wide Web address:** http://www.webermarking.com. **Description:** An international distributor of product identification addressing, labeling, industrial, and marking machines and devices. Weber Marking Systems also operates several sales locations. **Corporate headquarters location:** This location.

# INDUSTRY ASSOCIATIONS

## ACCOUNTING AND MANAGEMENT CONSULTING

**AMERICAN ACCOUNTING ASSOCIATION**
5717 Bessie Drive, Sarasota FL 34233-2399. 941/921-7747. **Fax:** 941/923-4093. **E-mail address:** Office@aaahq.org. **World Wide Web address:** http://aaahq.org. **Description:** A voluntary organization founded in 1916 to promote excellence in accounting education, research and practice.

**AMERICAN INSTITUTE OF CERTIFIED PUBLIC ACCOUNTANTS**
1211 Avenue of the Americas, New York NY 10036. 212/596-6200. **Toll-free phone:** 888/777-7077. **Fax:** 212/596-6213. **World Wide Web address:** http://www.aicpa.org. **Description:** A non-profit organization providing resources, information, and leadership to its members.

**AMERICAN MANAGEMENT ASSOCIATION**
1601 Broadway, New York NY 10019. 212/586-8100. **Fax:** 212/903-8168. **Toll-free phone:** 800/262-9699. **E-mail address:** info@amanet.org. **World Wide Web address:** http://www.amanet.org. **Description:** A non-profit association providing its members with management development and educational services.

**ASSOCIATION OF GOVERNMENT ACCOUNTANTS**
2208 Mount Vernon Avenue, Alexandria VA 22301. 703/684-6931. **Toll-free phone:** 800/AGA-7211. **Fax:** 703/548-9367. **World Wide Web address:** http://www.agacgfm.org. **Description:** A public financial management organization catering to the professional interests of financial managers at the local, state and federal governments and public accounting firms.

**ASSOCIATION OF MANAGEMENT CONSULTING FIRMS**
380 Lexington Avenue, Suite 1700, New York NY 10168. 212/551-7887. **Fax:** 212/551-7934. **E-mail address:** info@amcf.org. **World Wide Web address:** http://www.amcf.org. **Description:** Founded in 1929 to provide a forum for confronting common challenges; increasing the collective knowledge of members and their clients; and establishing a professional code conduct.

**CONNECTICUT SOCIETY OF CERTIFIED PUBLIC ACCOUNTANTS**
845 Brook Street, Building Two, Rocky Hill CT 06067-3405. 860/258-4800. **Fax:** 860/258-4859. **E-mail address:** info@cs-cpa.org. **World Wide Web address:** http://www.cs-cpa.org. **Description:** A statewide professional membership organization catering to CPAs.

**INSTITUTE OF INTERNAL AUDITORS**
247 Maitland Avenue, Altamonte Springs FL 32701-4201. 407-937-1100. **Fax:** 407-937-1101. **E-mail address:** iia@theiia.org. **World Wide Web address:** http://www.theiia.org. **Description:** Founded in 1941 to serves members in internal auditing, governance and internal control, IT audit, education, and security worldwide.

**INSTITUTE OF MANAGEMENT ACCOUNTANTS**
10 Paragon Drive, Montvale NJ 07645-1718. 201/573-9000. **Fax:** 201/474-1600. **Toll-free phone:** 800/638-4427. **E-mail address**: ima@imanet.org. **World Wide Web address:** http://www.imanet.org. **Description:** Provides members personal and professional development opportunities in management accounting, financial management and information management through education and association

with business professionals and certification in management accounting and financial management.

**INSTITUTE OF MANAGEMENT CONSULTANTS**
2025 M Street, NW, Suite 800, Washington DC 20036-3309. 202/367-1134. **Toll-free phone:** 800/221-2557. **Fax:** 202/367-2134. **E-mail address:** office@imcusa.org. **World Wide Web address:** http://www.imcusa.org. **Description** Founded in 1968 as the national professional association representing management consultants and awarding the CMC (Certified Management Consultant) certification mark.

**NATIONAL ASSOCIATION OF TAX PROFESSIONALS**
720 Association Drive, PO Box 8002, Appleton WI 54912-8002. 800/558-3402. **Fax:** 800/747-0001. **E-Mail address:** natp@natptax.com. **World Wide Web address:** http://www.natptax.com. **Description:** Founded in 1979 as a nonprofit professional association dedicated to excellence in taxation with a mission to serve professionals who work in all areas of tax practice.

**NATIONAL SOCIETY OF PUBLIC ACCOUNTANTS**
1010 North Fairfax Street, Alexandria VA 22314. 703/549-6400. **Toll-free phone:** 800/966-6679. **Fax:** 703/549-2984. **Email address:** members@nsacct.org. **World Wide Web address:** http://www.nsacct.org. **Description:** For more than 50 years, NSA has supported its members with resources and representation to protect their right to practice, build credibility and grow the profession. NSA protects the public by requiring its members to adhere to a strict Code of Ethics.

## ADVERTISING, MARKETING, AND PUBLIC RELATIONS

**ADVERTISING RESEARCH FOUNDATION**
641 Lexington Avenue, New York NY 10022. 212/751-5656. **World Wide Web address:** http://www.thearf.com. **Description:** Founded in 1936 by the Association of National Advertisers and the American Association of Advertising Agencies, the Advertising Research Foundation (ARF) is a nonprofit corporate-membership association, which is today the preeminent professional organization in the field of advertising, marketing and media research. Its combined membership represents more than 400 advertisers, advertising agencies, research firms, media companies, educational institutions and international organizations.

**AMERICAN ASSOCIATION OF ADVERTISING AGENCIES**
405 Lexington Avenue, 18th Floor, New York NY 10174-1801. 212/682-2500. **Fax:** 212/682-8391. **World Wide Web address:** http://www.aaaa.org. **Description:** Founded in 1917 as the national trade association representing the advertising agency business in the United States.

**AMERICAN MARKETING ASSOCIATION**
311 South Wacker Drive, Suite 5800, Chicago IL 60606. 312/542-9000. **Fax:** 312/542-9001. **Toll-free phone:** 800/AMA-1150. **E-mail address:** info@ama.org. **World Wide Web address:** http://www.marketingpower.com. **Description:** A professional associations for marketers providing relevant marketing information that experienced marketers turn to everyday.

**DIRECT MARKETING ASSOCIATION**
1120 Avenue of the Americas, New York NY 10036-6700. 212/768-7277. **Fax:** 212/302-6714. **E-mail address:** info@the-dma.org. **World Wide Web address:** http://www.the-dma.org. **Description:** Founded in 1917 as a non-profit organization representing professionals working in all areas of direct marketing.

**INTERNATIONAL ADVERTISING ASSOCIATION**
521 Fifth Avenue, Suite 1807, New York NY 10175. 212/557-1133. **Fax:** 212/983-0455. **E-mail address:** iaa@iaaglobal.org. **World Wide Web address:** http://www.iaaglobal.org. **Description:** A strategic partnership that addresses the common interests of all the marketing communications disciplines ranging from advertisers to media companies to agencies to direct marketing firms to individual practitioners.

**MARKETING RESEARCH ASSOCIATION**
1344 Silas Deane Highway, Suite 306, PO Box 230, Rocky Hill CT 06067-0230. 860/257-4008. **Fax:** 860/257-3990. **E-mail address:** email@mra-net.org. **World Wide Web address:** http://www.mra-net.org. **Description:** MRA promotes excellence in the opinion and marketing research industry by providing members with a variety of opportunities for advancing and expanding their marketing research and related business skills. To protect the marketing research environment, we will act as an advocate with appropriate government entities, other associations, and the public.

**PUBLIC RELATIONS SOCIETY OF AMERICA**
33 Maiden Lane, 11th Floor, New York NY 10038-5150. 212/460-1400. **Fax:** 212/995-0757. **E-mail address:** info@prsa.org. **World Wide Web address:** http://www.prsa.org. **Description:** A professional organization for public relations

practitioners. Comprised of nearly 20,000 members organized into 116 Chapters represent business and industry, counseling firms, government, associations, hospitals, schools, professional services firms and nonprofit organizations.

## AEROSPACE

**AMERICAN INSTITUTE OF AERONAUTICS AND ASTRONAUTICS**
1801 Alexander Bell Drive, Suite 500, Reston VA 20191-4344. 703/264-7500. **Toll-free phone:** 800/639-AIAA. **Fax:** 703/264-7551. **E-mail address:** info@aiaa.org. **World Wide Web address:** http://www.aiaa.org. **Description:** The principal society of the aerospace engineer and scientist.

**NATIONAL AERONAUTIC ASSOCIATION OF USA**
1815 N. Fort Myer Drive, Suite 500, Arlington VA 22209. 703/527-0226. **Fax:** 703/527-0229. **E-mail address:** naa@naa-usa.org. **World Wide Web address:** http://www.naa-usa.org. **Description:** A non-parochial, charitable organization serving all segments of American aviation whose membership encompass all areas of flight including skydiving, models, commercial airlines, and military fighters.

**PROFESSIONAL AVIATION MAINTENANCE ASSOCIATION**
717 Princess Street, Alexandria VA 22314. 703/683-3171. **Toll-free phone:** 866/865-PAMA. **Fax:** 703/683-0018. **E-mail address:** hq@pama.org. **World Wide Web address:** http://www.pama.org. **Description:** A non-profit organization concerned with promoting professionalism among aviation maintenance personnel; fostering and improving methods, skills, learning, and achievement in aviation maintenance. The association also conducts regular industry meetings and seminars.

## APPAREL, FASHION, AND TEXTILES

**AMERICAN APPAREL AND FOOTWEAR ASSOCIATION**
1601 North Kent Street, Suite 1200, Arlington VA 22209. 703/524-1864. **Fax:** 703/522-6741. **World Wide Web address:** http://apparelandfootwear.org. **Description:** The national trade association representing apparel, footwear and other sewn products companies, and their suppliers. Promotes and enhances its members' competitiveness, productivity and profitability in the global market.

**THE FASHION GROUP**
8 West 40th Street, 7th Floor, New York NY 10018. 212/302-5511. **Fax:** 212/302-5533. **E-mail address:** info@fgi.org. **World Wide Web address:** http://www.fgi.org. **Description:** A non-profit association representing all areas of the fashion, apparel, accessories, beauty and home industries.

**INTERNATIONAL ASSOCIATION OF CLOTHING DESIGNERS AND EXECUTIVES**
124 West 93rd Street, Suite 3E, New York NY 10025. 603/672-4065. **Fax:** 603/672-4064. **World Wide Web address:** http://www.iacde.com. **Description:** Founded in 1911, with the mission to serve as a global network for the sharing of information by its members on design direction and developments, fashion and fiber trends, and technical innovations affecting tailored apparel, designers, their suppliers, retailers, manufacturing executives and educational institutions for the purpose of enhancing their professional standing and interests.

**NATIONAL COUNCIL OF TEXTILE ORGANIZATIONS**
1776 I Street, NW, Suite 900, Washington DC 20006. 202/756-4878. **Fax:** 202/756-1520. **World Wide Web address:** http://www.ncto.org. **Description:** The national trade association for the domestic textile industry with members operating in more than 30 states and the industry employs approximately 450,000 people.

# ARCHITECTURE, CONSTRUCTION, AND ENGINEERING

**AACE INTERNATIONAL: THE ASSOCIATION FOR TOTAL COST MANAGEMENT**
209 Prairie Avenue, Suite 100, Morgantown WV 26501. 304/296-8444. **Fax:** 304/291-5728. **E-mail address:** info@aacei.org. **World Wide Web address:** http://www.aacei.org. **Description:** Founded 1956 to provide its approximately 5,500 worldwide members with the resources to enhance their performance and ensure continued growth and success. Members include cost management professionals: cost managers and engineers, project managers, planners and schedulers, estimators and bidders, and value engineers.

**AMERICAN ASSOCIATION OF ENGINEERING SOCIETIES**
1828 L Street, NW, Suite 906, Washington DC 20036. 202/296-2237. **Fax:** 202/296-1151. **World Wide Web address:** http://www.aaes.org. **Description:** A multidisciplinary organization of engineering societies dedicated to advancing the knowledge, understanding, and practice of engineering.

**AMERICAN CONSULTING ENGINEERS COMPANIES**
1015 15$^{th}$ Street, 8$^{th}$ Floor, NW, Washington DC, 20005-2605. 202/347-7474. **Fax:** 202/898-0068. **E-mail address:** acec@acec.org. **World Wide Web address:** http://www.acec.org. **Description:** Engaged in a wide range of engineering works that propel the nation's economy, and enhance and safeguard America's quality of life. These works allow Americans to drink clean water, enjoy a healthy life, take advantage of new technologies, and travel safely and efficiently. The Council's mission is to contribute to America's prosperity and welfare by advancing the business interests of member firms.

**AMERICAN INSTITUTE OF ARCHITECTS**
1735 New York Avenue, NW, Washington DC 20006. 202/626-7300. **Fax:** 202/626-7547. **Toll-free phone:** 800/AIA-3837. **E-mail address:** infocentral@aia.org. **World Wide Web address:** http://www.aia.org. **Description:** A non-profit organization for the architecture profession dedicated to: Serving its members, advancing their value, improving the quality of the built environment. Vision Statement: Through a culture of innovation, The American Institute of Architects empowers its members and inspires creation of a better-built environment.

**AMERICAN INSTITUTE OF CONSTRUCTORS**
P.O. Box 26334, Alexandria VA 22314. 703/683-4999. **Fax:** 703/683-5480. **E-mail address:** admin@aicnet.org. **World Wide Web address:** http://www.aicnet.org. **Description:** Founded to help individual construction practitioners achieve the professional status they deserve and serves as the national qualifying body of professional constructor. The Institute AIC membership identifies the individual as a true professional. The Institute is the constructor's counterpart of professional organizations found in architecture, engineering, law and other fields.

**AMERICAN SOCIETY FOR ENGINEERING EDUCATION**
1818 N Street, NW, Suite 600, Washington DC, 20036-2479. 202/331-3500. **Fax:** 202/265-8504. **World Wide Web address:** http://www.asee.org. **Description:** A nonprofit member association, founded in 1893, dedicated to promoting and improving engineering and technology education.

## AMERICAN SOCIETY OF CIVIL ENGINEERS
1801 Alexander Bell Drive, Reston VA 20191-4400. 703/295-6300. **Fax:** 703/295-6222. **Toll-free phone:** 800/548-2723. **World Wide Web address:** http://www.asce.org. **Description:** Founded to provide essential value to its members, their careers, partners and the public by developing leadership, advancing technology, advocating lifelong learning and promoting the profession.

## AMERICAN SOCIETY OF HEATING, REFRIGERATION, AND AIR CONDITIONING ENGINEERS
1791 Tullie Circle, NE, Atlanta GA 30329. 404/636-8400. **Fax:** 404/321-5478. **Toll-free phone:** 800/527-4723. **E-mail address:** ashrae@ashrae.org. **World Wide Web address:** http://www.ashrae.org. **Description:** Founded with a mission to advance the arts and sciences of heating, ventilation, air conditioning, refrigeration and related human factors and to serve the evolving needs of the public and ASHRAE members.

## AMERICAN SOCIETY OF MECHANICAL ENGINEERS
Three Park Avenue, New York, NY 10016-5990. 973-882-1167. **Toll-free phone:** 800/843-2763. **E-mail address:** infocentral@asme.org. **World Wide Web address:** http://www.asme.org. **Description:** Founded in 1880 as the American Society of Mechanical Engineers, today ASME International is a nonprofit educational and technical organization serving a worldwide membership of 125,000.

## AMERICAN SOCIETY OF NAVAL ENGINEERS
1452 Duke Street, Alexandria VA 22314-3458. 703/836-6727. **Fax:** 703/836-7491. **E-mail address:** asnehq@navalengineers.org. **World Wide Web address:** http://www.navalengineers.org. **Description:** Mission is to advance the knowledge and practice of naval engineering in public and private applications and operations, to enhance the professionalism and well being of members, and to promote naval engineering as a career field.

## AMERICAN SOCIETY OF PLUMBING ENGINEERS
8614 Catalpa Avenue, Suite 1007, Chicago IL 60656-1116. 773/693-2773. **Fax:** 773/695-9007. **E-mail address:** info@aspe.org. **World Wide Web address:** http://www.aspe.org. **Description:** The international organization for professionals skilled in the design, specification and inspection of plumbing systems. ASPE is dedicated to the advancement of the science of plumbing engineering, to the professional growth and advancement of its members and the health, welfare and safety of the public.

## AMERICAN SOCIETY OF SAFETY ENGINEERS
1800 E Oakton Street, Des Plaines IL 60018. 847/699-2929. **Fax:** 847/768-3434. **E-mail address:** customerservice@asse.org. **World Wide Web address:** http://www.asse.org. **Description:** A non-profit organization promoting the concerns of safety engineers.

## ASSOCIATED BUILDERS AND CONTRACTORS
4250 N. Fairfax Drive, 9th Floor, Arlington VA 22203-1607. 703/812-2000. **E-mail address:** gotquestions@abc.org. **World Wide Web address:** http://www.abc.org. **Description:** A national trade association representing more than 23,000 merit shop contractors, subcontractors, material suppliers and related firms in 80 chapters across the United States. Membership represents all specialties within the U.S. construction industry and is comprised primarily of firms that perform work in the industrial and commercial sectors of the industry.

## ASSOCIATED GENERAL CONTRACTORS OF AMERICA, INC.
333 John Carlyle Street, Suite 200, Alexandria VA 22314. 703/548-3118. **Fax:** 703/548-3119. **E-mail address:** info@agc.org. **World Wide Web address:** http://www.agc.org. **Description:** A construction trade association, founded in 1918 on a request by President Woodrow Wilson.

## THE ENGINEERING CENTER (TEC)
One Walnut Street, Boston MA 02108-3616. 617/227-5551. **Fax:** 617/227-6783. **E-mail address:** tec@engineers.org. **World Wide Web address:** http://www.engineers.org. **Description:** Founded with a mission to increase public awareness of the value of the engineering profession; to provide current information affecting the profession; to offer administrative facilities and services to engineering organizations in New England; and to provide a forum for discussion and resolution of professional issues.

## ILLUMINATING ENGINEERING SOCIETY OF NORTH AMERICA
120 Wall Street, Floor 17, New York NY 10005. 212/248-5000. **Fax:** 212/248-5017(18). **E-mail address:** iesna@iesna.org. **World Wide Web address:** http://www.iesna.org. **Description:** To advance knowledge and to disseminate information for the improvement of the lighted environment to the benefit of society.

## JUNIOR ENGINEERING TECHNICAL SOCIETY
1420 King Street, Suite 405, Alexandria VA 22314. 703/548-5387. **Fax:** 703/548-0769. **E-mail address:** info@jets.org. **World Wide Web address:** http://www.jets.org. **Description:** JETS is a national non-profit education organization that has served the pre-college engineering community for over 50 years. Through competitions and programs, JETS serves over 30,000 students and 2,000 teachers, and holds programs on 150 college campuses each year.

## NATIONAL ACTION COUNCIL FOR MINORITIES IN ENGINEERING
440 Hamilton Avenue, Suite 302, White Plains NY 10601-1813. 914/539-4010. **Fax:** 914/539-4032. **E-mail address:** webmaster@nacme.org. **World Wide Web address:** http://www.nacme.org. **Description:** Founded in 1974 to provide leadership and support for the national effort to increase the representation of successful African American, American Indian and Latino women and men in engineering and technology, math- and science-based careers.

## NATIONAL ASSOCIATION OF BLACK ENGINEERS
1454 Duke Street, Alexandria VA 22314. 703/549-2207. **Fax:** 703/683-5312. **E-mail address:** info@nsbe.org. **World Wide Web address:** http://www.nsbe.org. **Description:** A non-profit organization dedicated to increasing the number of culturally responsible Black engineers who excel academically, succeed professionally and positively impact the community.

## NATIONAL ASSOCIATION OF HOME BUILDERS
1201 15th Street, NW, Washington DC 20005. 202/266-8200. **Toll-free phone:** 800/368-5242. **World Wide Web address:** http://www.nahb.org. **Description:** Founded in 1942, NAHB has been serving its members, the housing industry, and the public at large. A trade association that promotes the policies that make housing a national priority.

## NATIONAL ASSOCIATION OF MINORITY ENGINEERING PROGRAM ADMINISTRATORS
1133 West Morse Boulevard, Suite 201, Winter Park FL 32789. 407/647-8839. **Fax:** 407/629-2502. **E-mail address:** namepa@namepa.org **World Wide Web**

**address:** http://www.namepa.org. **Description:** Provides services, information, and tools to produce a diverse group of engineers and scientists, and achieve equity and parity in the nation's workforce.

**NATIONAL ELECTRICAL CONTRACTORS ASSOCIATION**
3 Bethesda Metro Center, Suite 1100, Bethesda MD 20814. 301/657-3110. **Fax:** 301/215-4500. **World Wide Web address:** http://www.necanet.org. **Description:** Founded in 1901 as representative segment of the construction market comprised of over 70,000 electrical contracting firms.

**NATIONAL SOCIETY OF PROFESSIONAL ENGINEERS**
1420 King Street, Alexandria VA 22314-2794. 703/684-2800. **Fax:** 703/836-4875. **World Wide Web address:** http://www.nspe.org. **Description:** An engineering society that represents engineering professionals and licensed engineers (PEs) across all disciplines. Founded in 1934 to promote engineering licensure and ethics, enhance the engineer image, advocate and protect legal rights, publish industry news, and provide continuing education.

**SOCIETY OF FIRE PROTECTION ENGINEERS**
7315 Wisconsin Avenue, Suite 620E, Bethesda MD 20814. 301/718-2910. **Fax:** 301/718-2242. **E-mail address:** sfpehqtrs@sfpe.org. **World Wide Web address:** http://www.sfpe.org. **Description:** Founded in 1950 and incorporated as in independent organization in 1971, the professional society represents professionals in the field of fire protection engineering. The Society has approximately 3500 members in the United States and abroad, and 51 regional chapters, 10 of which are outside the US.

## ARTS, ENTERTAINMENT, SPORTS, AND RECREATION

**AMERICAN ASSOCIATION OF MUSEUMS**
1575 Eye Street NW, Suite 400, Washington DC 20005. 202/289-1818. **Fax:** 202/289-6578. **World Wide Web address:** http://www.aam-us.org. **Description:** Founded in 1906, the association promotes excellence within the museum community. Services include advocacy, professional education, information exchange, accreditation, and guidance on current professional standards of performance.

**AMERICAN FEDERATION OF MUSICIANS**
1501 Broadway, Suite 600, New York NY 10036. 212/869-1330. **Fax:** 212/764-6134. **World Wide Web address:** http://www.afm.org. **Description:** Represents the interests of professional musicians. Services include negotiating agreements, protecting ownership of recorded music, securing benefits such as health care and pension, or lobbying our legislators. The AFM is committed to raising industry standards and placing the professional musician in the foreground of the cultural landscape.

**AMERICAN MUSIC CENTER**
30 West 26$^{th}$ Street, Suite 1001, New York NY 10010. 212/366-5260. **Fax:** 212/366-5265. **World Wide Web address:** http://www.amc.net. **Description:** Dedicated to fostering and composition, production, publication, and distribution of contemporary (American) music.

**AMERICAN SOCIETY OF COMPOSERS, AUTHORS, AND PUBLISHERS (ASCAP)**
One Lincoln Plaza, New York NY 10023. 212/621-6000. **Fax:** 212/724-9064. **E-mail address:** info@ascap.com. **World Wide Web address:** http://www.ascap.com. **Description:** A membership based association comprised of composers, songwriters, lyricists, and music publishers across all genres of music.

**AMERICAN SYMPHONY ORCHESTRA LEAGUE**
33 West 60th Street, 5th Floor, New York NY 10023-7905. 212/262-5161. **Fax:** 212/262-5198. **E-mail address:** league@symphony.org. **World Wide Web address:** http://www.symphony.org. **Description:** Founded in 1942 to exchange information and ideas with other orchestra leaders. The league also publishes the bimonthly magazine.

**AMERICAN ZOO AND AQUARIUM ASSOCIATION**
8403 Colesville Road, Suite 710, Silver Spring MD 20910-3314. 301/562-0777. **Fax:** 301/562-0888. **World Wide Web address:** http://www.aza.org. **Description:** Dedicated to establishing and maintaining excellent professional standards in all AZA Institutions through its accreditation program; establishing and promoting high standards of animal care and welfare; promoting and facilitating collaborative conservation and research programs; advocating effective governmental policies for our members; strengthening and promoting conservation education programs for our public and professional development for our members, and; raising awareness of the collective impact of its members and their programs.

**ASSOCIATION OF INDEPENDENT VIDEO AND FILMMAKERS**

304 Hudson Street, 6th floor, New York NY 10013. 212/807-1400. **Fax:** 212/463-8519. **E-mail address:** info@aivf.org. **World Wide Web address:** http://www.aivf.org. **Description:** A membership organization serving local and international film and videomakers including documentarians, experimental artists, and makers of narrative features.

**NATIONAL ENDOWMENT FOR THE ARTS**
1100 Pennsylvania Avenue, NW, Washington DC 20506. 202/682-5400. **E-mail address:** webmgr@arts.endow.com. **World Wide Web address:** http://www.nea.gov. **Description:** Founded in 1965 to foster, preserve, and promote excellence in the arts, to bring art to all Americans, and to provide leadership in arts education.

**NATIONAL RECREATION AND PARK ASSOCIATION**
22377 Belmont Ridge Road, Ashburn VA 20148-4150. 703/858-0784. **Fax:** 703/858-0794. **E-mail address:** info@nrpa.org. **World Wide Web address:** http://www.nrpa.org. **Description:** Works "to advance parks, recreation and environmental conservation efforts that enhance the quality of life for all people."

**WOMEN'S CAUCUS FOR ART**
P.O. Box 1498, Canal Street Station, New York NY 10013. 212/634-0007. **E-mail address:** info@nationalwca.com. **World Wide Web address:** http://www.nationalwca.com. **Description:** Founded in 1972 in connection with the College Art Association (CAA), as a national organization unique in its multi-disciplinary, multicultural membership of artists, art historians, students /educators, museum professionals and galleries in the visual arts.

## AUTOMOTIVE

### NATIONAL AUTOMOBILE DEALERS ASSOCIATION
8400 Westpark Drive, McLean VA 22102. 703/821-7000. **Toll-free phone:** 800/252-6232. **E-mail address:** nadainfo@nada.org. **World Wide Web address:** http://www.nada.org. **Description:** NADA represents America's franchised new-car and -truck dealers. Today there are more than 19,700 franchised new-car and -truck dealer members holding nearly 49,300 separate new-car and light-, medium-, and heavy-duty truck franchises, domestic and import. Founded in 1917.

### NATIONAL INSTITUTE FOR AUTOMOTIVE SERVICE EXCELLENCE
101 Blue Seal Drive, SE, Suite 101, Leesburg VA 20175. 703/669-6600. **Toll-free phone:** 877/ASE-TECH. **World Wide Web address:** http://www.ase.com. **Description:** An independent, non-profit organization established in 1972 to improve the quality of vehicle repair and service through the testing and certification of repair and service professionals. More than 420,000 professionals hold current ASE credentials.

### SOCIETY OF AUTOMOTIVE ENGINEERS
400 Commonwealth Drive, Warrendale PA 15096-0001. 724/776-4841. **E-mail address:** customerservice@sae.org. **World Wide Web address:** http://www.sae.org. **Description:** An organization with more than 84,000 members from 97 countries who share information and exchange ideas for advancing the engineering of mobility systems.

# BANKING

**AMERICA'S COMMUNITY BANKERS**
900 Nineteenth Street, NW, Suite 400, Washington DC 20006. 202/857-3100.
**Fax:** 202/296-8716. **World Wide Web address:** http://www.acbankers.org.
**Description:** Represents the nation's community banks of all charter types and
sizes providing a broad range of advocacy and service strategies to enhance
their members' presence and contribution to the marketplace.

**AMERICAN BANKERS ASSOCIATION**
1120 Connecticut Avenue, NW, Washington DC 20036. 800/BANKERS. **World
Wide Web address:** http://www.aba.com. **Description:** Founded in 1875 and
represents banks on issues of national importance for financial institutions and
their customers. Members include all categories of banking institutions, including
community, regional and money center banks and holding companies, as well as
savings associations, trust companies and savings banks.

## BIOTECHNOLOGY, PHARMACEUTICALS, AND SCIENTIFIC R&D

**AMERICAN ASSOCIATION FOR CLINICAL CHEMISTRY**
2101 L Street, NW, Suite 202, Washington DC 20037-1558. 202/857-0717. **Fax:** 202/887-5093. **Toll-free phone:** 800/892-1400. **World Wide Web address:** http://www.aacc.org. **Description:** Founded in 1948 as an international scientific/medical society of clinical laboratory professionals, physicians, research scientists and other individuals involved with clinical chemistry and other clinical laboratory science-related disciplines. The society has 10,000 members.

**AMERICAN ASSOCIATION OF COLLEGES OF PHARMACY**
1426 Prince Street, Alexandria VA 22314. 703/739-2330. **Fax:** 703/836-8982. **E-mail address:** mail@aacp.org. **World Wide Web address:** http://www.aacp.org. **Description:** Founded in 1900 as the national organization representing the interests of pharmaceutical education and educators. Comprising all 89 U.S. pharmacy colleges and schools including more than 4,000 faculty, 36,000 students enrolled in professional programs, and 3,600 individuals pursuing graduate study, AACP is committed to excellence in pharmaceutical education.

**AMERICAN ASSOCIATION OF PHARMACEUTICAL SCIENTISTS**
2107 Wilson Boulevard, Suite 700, Arlington VA 22201-3042. 703/243-2800. **Fax:** 703/243-9650. **E-mail address:** aaps@aaps.org. **World Wide Web address:** http://www.aaps.org. **Description:** Founded in 1986 as professional, scientific society of more than 10,000 members employed in academia, industry, government and other research institutes worldwide. The association advances science through the open exchange of scientific knowledge; serves as an information resource; and contributes to human health through pharmaceutical research and development.

**AMERICAN COLLEGE OF CLINICAL PHARMACY (ACCP)**
3101 Broadway, Suite 650, Kansas City MO 64111. 816/531-2177. **Fax:** 816/531-4990. **E-mail address:** accp@accp.com **World Wide Web address:** http://www.accp.com. **Description:** A professional and scientific society providing leadership, education, advocacy, and resources enabling clinical pharmacists to achieve excellence in practice and research.

**AMERICAN PHARMACISTS ASSOCIATION**
2215 Constitution Avenue, NW, Washington DC 20037-2985. 202/628-4410. **Fax:** 202/783-2351. **E-mail address:** info@aphanet.org. **World Wide Web address:** http://www.aphanet.org. **Description:** Founded in 1852 as the national professional society of pharmacists. Members include practicing pharmacists, pharmaceutical scientists, pharmacy students, pharmacy technicians, and others interested in advancing the profession.

**AMERICAN SOCIETY FOR BIOCHEMISTRY AND MOLECULAR BIOLOGY**
9650 Rockville Pike, Bethesda MD 20814-3996. 301/634-7145. **Fax:** 301/634-7126. **E-mail address:** asbmb@asbmb.faseb.org. **World Wide Web address:** http://www.asbmb.org. **Description:** A nonprofit scientific and educational organization with over 11,900 members. Most members teach and conduct research at colleges and universities. Others conduct research in various government laboratories, nonprofit research institutions and industry. The Society's student members attend undergraduate or graduate institutions.

**AMERICAN SOCIETY OF HEALTH-SYSTEM PHARMACISTS**
7272 Wisconsin Avenue, Bethesda MD 20814. 301/657-3000. **Toll-free phone:** 866/279-0681. **World Wide Web address:** http://www.ashp.org. **Description:** A national professional association representing pharmacists who practice in hospitals, health maintenance organizations, long-term care facilities, home care, and other components of health care systems.

**NATIONAL PHARMACEUTICAL COUNCIL**
1894 Preston White Drive, Reston VA 20191-5433. 703/620-6390. **Fax:** 703/476-0904. **E-mail address:** main@npcnow.com. **World Wide Web address:** http://www.npcnow.org. **Description:** Conducts research and education programs geared towards demonstrating that the appropriate use of pharmaceuticals improves both patient treatment outcomes and the cost effective delivery of overall health care services.

**NATIONAL SPACE BIOMEDICAL RESEARCH INSTITUTE**
One Baylor Plaza, NA-425, Houston TX 77030. 713/798-7412. **Fax:** 713/798-7413. **E-mail address:** info@www.nsbri.org. **World Wide Web address:** http://www.nsbri.org. **Description:** Conducts research into health concerns facing astronauts on long missions.

## BUSINESS SERVICES & NON-SCIENTIFIC RESEARCH

**AMERICAN SOCIETY OF APPRAISERS**
555 Herndon Parkway, Suite 125, Herndon VA 20170. 703/478-2228. **Fax:** 703/742-8471. **E-mail address:** asainfo@appraisers.org. **World Wide Web address:** http://www.appraisers.org. **Description:** Fosters professional excellence through education, accreditation, publication and other services. Its goal is to contribute to the growth of its membership and to the appraisal profession.

**EQUIPMENT LEASING ASSOCIATION OF AMERICA**
4301 North Fairfax Drive, Suite 550, Arlington VA 22203-1627. 703/527-8655. **Fax:** 703/527-2649. **World Wide Web address:** http://www.elaonline.com. **Description:** Promotes and serves the general interests of the equipment leasing and finance industry.

**NATIONAL ASSOCIATION OF PERSONNEL SERVICES**
The Village at Banner Elk, Suite 108, P.O. Box 2128, Banner Elk NC 28604. 828/898-4929. **Fax:** 828/898-8098. **World Wide Web address:** http://www.napsweb.org. **Description**: Serves, protects, informs, and represents all facets of the personnel services industry regarding federal legislation and regulatory issues by providing education, certification, and member services which enhance the ability to conduct business with integrity and competence.

# CHARITIES AND SOCIAL SERVICES

**AMERICAN COUNCIL FOR THE BLIND**
1155 15th Street, NW, Suite 1004, Washington DC 20005. 202/467-5081. **Fax:** 202/467-5085. **Toll-free phone:** 800/424-8666. **World Wide Web address:** http://www.acb.org. **Description:** The nation's leading membership organization of blind and visually impaired people. It was founded in 1961.

**CATHOLIC CHARITIES USA**
1731 King Street, Alexandria VA 22314. 703/549-1390. **Fax:** 703/549-1656. **World Wide Web address:** http://www.catholiccharitiesusa.org. **Description:** A membership association of social service networks providing social services to people in need.

**NATIONAL ASSOCIATION OF SOCIAL WORKERS**
750 First Street, NE, Suite 700, Washington DC 20002-4241. 202/408-8600. **E-mail address:** membership@naswdc.org. **World Wide Web address:** http://www.naswdc.org. **Description:** A membership organization comprised of professional social workers working to enhance the professional growth and development of its members, to create and maintain professional standards, and to advance sound social policies.

**NATIONAL COUNCIL ON FAMILY RELATIONS**
3989 Central Avenue, NE, #550, Minneapolis MN 55421. 763/781-9331. **Fax:** 763/781-9348. **Toll-free phone:** 888/781-9331. **E-mail address:** info@ncfr.org. **World Wide Web address:** http://www.ncfr.org. **Description:** Provides a forum for family researchers, educators, and practitioners to share in the development and dissemination of knowledge about families and family relationships, establishes professional standards, and works to promote family well-being.

**NATIONAL FEDERATION OF THE BLIND**
1800 Johnson Street, Baltimore MD 21230-4998. 410/659-9314. **Fax:** 410/685-5653. **World Wide Web address:** http://www.nfb.org. **Description:** Founded in 1940, the National Federation of the Blind (NFB) is the nation's largest membership organization of blind persons. With fifty thousand members, the NFB has affiliates in all fifty states plus Washington D.C. and Puerto Rico, and over seven hundred local chapters. As a consumer and advocacy organization, the NFB is a leading force in the blindness field today.

**NATIONAL MULTIPLE SCLEROSIS SOCIETY**
733 Third Avenue, New York NY 10017. **Toll-free phone:** 800/344-4867. **World Wide Web address:** http://www.nmss.org. **Description:** Provides accurate, up-to-date information to individuals with MS, their families, and healthcare providers is central to our mission.

## CHEMICALS, RUBBER, AND PLASTICS

**AMERICAN CHEMICAL SOCIETY**
1155 Sixteenth Street, NW, Washington DC 20036. 202/872-4600. **Fax:** 202/872-6067. **Toll-free phone:** 800/227-5558. **E-mail address:** help@acs.org. **World Wide Web address:** http://www.acs.org. **Description:** A self-governed individual membership organization consisting of more than 159,000 members at all degree levels and in all fields of chemistry. The organization provides a broad range of opportunities for peer interaction and career development, regardless of professional or scientific interests. The Society was founded in 1876.

**AMERICAN INSTITUTE OF CHEMICAL ENGINEERS**
3 Park Avenue, New York NY 10016-5991. 212/591-8100. **Toll-free phone:** 800/242-4363. **Fax:** 212/591-8888. **E-mail address:** xpress@aiche.org. **World Wide Web address:** http://www.aiche.org. **Description:** Founded in 1908 and provides leadership in advancing the chemical engineering profession; fosters and disseminates chemical engineering knowledge, supports the professional and personal growth of its members, and applies the expertise of its members to address societal needs throughout the world.

**THE ELECTROCHEMICAL SOCIETY**
65 South Main Street, Building D, Pennington NJ 08534-2839. 609/737-1902. **Fax:** 609/737-2743. **World Wide Web address:** http://www.electrochem.org. **Description:** Founded in 1902, The Electrochemical Society has become the leading society for solid-state and electrochemical science and technology. ECS has 8,000 scientists and engineers in over 75 countries worldwide who hold individual membership, as well as roughly 100 corporate members.

**SOCIETY OF PLASTICS ENGINEERS**
14 Fairfield Drive, PO Box 403, Brookfield CT 06804-0403. 203/775-0471. **Fax:** 203/775-8490. **E-mail address:** info@4spe.org. **World Wide Web address:** http://www.4spe.org. **Description:** A 25,000-member organization promoting scientific and engineering knowledge relating to plastics. Founded in 1942.

**THE SOCIETY OF THE PLASTICS INDUSTRY, INC.**
1667 K Street, NW, Suite 1000, Washington DC 20006. 202/974-5200. **Fax:** 202/296-7005. **World Wide Web address:** http://www.socplas.org. **Description:** Founded in 1937, The Society of the Plastics Industry, Inc., is the trade association representing one of the largest manufacturing industries in the United States. SPI's members represent the entire plastics industry supply chain, including processors, machinery and equipment manufacturers and raw materials suppliers. The U.S. plastics industry employs 1.4 million workers and provides more than $310 billion in annual shipments.

## COMMUNICATIONS:TELECOMMUNICATIONS AND BROADCASTING

**ACADEMY OF TELEVISION ARTS & SCIENCES**
5220 Lankershim Boulevard, North Hollywood CA 91601-3109. 818/754-2800. **Fax:** 818/761-2827. **World Wide Web address:** http://www.emmys.com. **Description:** Promotes creativity, diversity, innovation and excellence though recognition, education and leadership in the advancement of the telecommunications arts and sciences.

**AMERICAN DISC JOCKEY ASSOCIATION**
20118 North 67$^{th}$ Avenue, Suite 300-605, Glendale AZ 85308. 888/723-5776. **E-mail address:** office@adja.org. **World Wide Web address:** http://www.adja.org. **Description:** Promotes ethical behavior, industry standards and continuing education for its members.

**AMERICAN WOMEN IN RADIO AND TELEVISION, INC.**
8405 Greensboro Drive, Suite 800, McLean VA 22102. 703/506-3290. **Fax:** 703/506-3266. **E-mail address:** info@awrt.org. **World Wide Web address:** http://www.awrt.org. **Description:** A non-profit, professional organization of women and men who work in the electronic media and allied fields.

**COMPTEL/ASCENT**
1900 M Street, NW, Suite 800, Washington DC 20036. 202/296-6650. **Fax:** 202/296-7585. **World Wide Web address:** http://www.comptelascent.org. **Description:** An association representing competitive telecommunications companies in virtually every sector of the marketplace: competitive local exchange carriers, long-distance carriers of every size, wireless service providers, Internet service providers, equipment manufacturers, and software suppliers.

**MEDIA COMMUNICATIONS ASSOCIATION-INTERNATIONAL**
7600 Terrace Avenue, Suite 203, Middleton WI 53562. 608/827-5034. **Fax:** 608/831-5122. **E-mail address:** info@mca-i.org. **World Wide Web address:** http://www.itva.org. **Description:** A not-for-profit, member-driven organization that provides opportunities for networking, forums for education and the resources for information to media communications professionals.

**NATIONAL ASSOCIATION OF BROADCASTERS**
1771 N Street, NW, Washington DC 20036. 202/429-5300. **Fax:** 202/429-4199. **E-mail address:** nab@nab.org. **World Wide Web address:** http://www.nab.org. **Description:** A trade association that represents the interests of free, over-the-air radio and television broadcasters.

**NATIONAL CABLE & TELECOMMUNICATIONS ASSOCIATION**
1724 Massachusetts Avenue, NW, Washington DC 20036. 202/775-3550. **E-mail address:** webmaster@ncta.com. **World Wide Web address:** http://www.ncta.com. **Description:** The National Cable and Telecommunications Association is the principal trade association of the cable and telecommunications industry. Founded in 1952, NCTA's primary mission is to provide its members with a strong national presence by providing a single, unified voice on issues affecting the cable and telecommunications industry.

**PROMAX & BDA**
9000 West Sunset Boulevard, Suite 900, Los Angeles CA 90069. 310/788-7600.
**Fax:** 310/788-7616. **World Wide Web address:** http://www.promax.org.
**Description:** A non-profit association dedicated to advancing the role and effectiveness of promotion, marketing, and broadcast design professionals in the electronic media.

**U.S. TELECOM ASSOCIATION**
1401 H Street, NW, Suite 600, Washington DC 20005-2164. 202/326-7300. **Fax:** 202/326-7333. **E-mail address:** membership@usta.org. **World Wide Web address:** http://www.usta.org. **Description:** A trade association representing service providers and suppliers for the telecom industry. Member companies offer a wide range of services, including local exchange, long distance, wireless, Internet and cable television service.

# COMPUTER HARDWARE, SOFTWARE, AND SERVICES

**ASSOCIATION FOR COMPUTING MACHINERY**
1515 Broadway, New York NY, 10036. 212/626-0500. 212/626-0500. **Toll-free phone:** 800/342-6626. **World Wide Web address:** http://www.acm.org. **Description:** A 75-000-member organization founded in 1947 to advance the skills of information technology professionals and students worldwide.

**ASSOCIATION FOR MULTIMEDIA COMMUNICATIONS**
PO Box 10645, Chicago IL 60610. 773/276-9320. **E-mail address:** info@amcomm.org. **World Wide Web address:** http://www.amcomm.org. **Description:** A networking and professional organization for people who create New Media, including the Web, CD-ROMs and DVDs, interactive kiosks, streaming media, and other digital forms. The association promotes understanding of technology, e-learning, and e-business.

**ASSOCIATION FOR WOMEN IN COMPUTING**
41 Sutter Street, Suite 1006, San Francisco CA 94104. 415/905-4663. **Fax:** 415/358-4667. **E-mail address:** info@awc-hq.org. **World Wide Web address:** http://www.awc-hq.org. **Description:** A not-for-profit, professional organization for individuals with an interest in information technology. The association is dedicated to the advancement of women in the computing fields, in business, industry, science, education, government, and the military.

**BLACK DATA PROCESSING ASSOCIATES**
6301 Ivy Lane, Suite 700, Greenbelt MD 20770. 301/220-2180. **Fax:** 301/220-2185. **Toll-free phone:** 800/727-BDPA. **World Wide Web address:** http://www.bdpa.org. **Description:** A member-focused organization that positions its members at the forefront of the IT industry. BDPA is committed to delivering IT excellence to our members, strategic partners, and community.

**INFORMATION TECHNOLOGY ASSOCIATION OF AMERICA**
1401 Wilson Boulevard, Suite 1100, Arlington VA 22209. 703/522-5055. **Fax:** 703/525-2279. **Wide Web address:** http://www.itaa.org. **Description:** A trade association representing the U.S. IT industry and providing information about its issues, association programs, publications, meetings, and seminars.

**INTERNATIONAL WEBMASTER'S ASSOCIATION- HTML WRITERS GUILD**
119 E. Union Street, Suite F, Pasadena CA 91030. **World Wide Web address:** http://www.hwg.org. **Description:** Provides online web design training to individuals interested in web design and development.

**NETWORK PROFESSIONAL ASSOCIATION**
17 South High Street, Suite 200, Columbus OH 43215. 614/221-1900. **Fax:** 614/221-1989. **E-mail address:** npa@npa.org. **World Wide Web address:** http://www.npa.org. **Description:** A non-profit association for professionals in Network Computing.

**SOCIETY FOR INFORMATION MANAGEMENT**
401 North Michigan Avenue, Chicago IL 60611. 312/527-6734. **E-mail address:** sim@simnet.org **World Wide Web address:** http://www.simnet.org. **Description:** With 3,000 members, SIM is a network for IT leaders including CIOs, senior IT executives, prominent academicians, consultants, and others. SIM is a community of thought leaders who share experiences and knowledge, and who explore future IT direction. Founded in 1968.

**SOCIETY FOR TECHNICAL COMMUNICATION**
901 North Stuart Street, Suite 904, Arlington VA 22203-1822. 703/522-4114. **Fax:** 703/522-2075. **World Wide Web address:** http://www.stc.org. **Description:** A 25,000-member organization dedicated to advancing the arts and sciences of technical communication

**SOFTWARE & INFORMATION INDUSTRY ASSOCIATION**
1090 Vermont Avenue, NW, Sixth Floor, Washington DC 20005-4095. 202/289-7442. **Fax:** 202/289-7097. **World Wide Web address:** http://www.siia.net. **Description:** The SIIA is the principal trade association for the software and digital content industry. SIIA provides services in government relations, business development, corporate education and intellectual property protection to leading companies.

**USENIX ASSOCIATION**
2560 Ninth Street, Suite 215, Berkeley CA, 94710. 510/528-8649. **Fax:** 510/548-5738. **E-mail address:** office@usenix.org. **World Wide Web address:** http://www.usenix.org. **Description:** Founded in 1975 the association fosters technical excellence and innovation, supports and disseminates practical research, provides a neutral forum for discussion of technical issues, and encourages computing outreach to the community. USENIX brings together engineers, system administrators, scientists, and technicians working on the cutting edge of the computing world.

# EDUCATIONAL SERVICES

**AMERICAN ASSOCIATION OF SCHOOL ADMINISTRATORS**
801 North Quincy Street, Suite 700, Arlington VA 22203-1730. 703/528-0700.
**Fax:** 703/841-1543. **E-mail address:** info@aasa.org. **World Wide Web
address:** http://www.aasa.org. **Description:** The professional organization for
more than 14,000 educational leaders in the U.S. and other countries. The
association supports and develops effective school system leaders who are
dedicated to the highest quality public education for all children.

**AMERICAN ASSOCIATION FOR HIGHER EDUCATION**
One Dupont Circle, Suite 360, Washington DC 20036-1143. 202/293-6440. **Fax:**
202/293-0073. **E-mail address:** info@aahe.org. **World Wide Web address:**
http://www.aahe.org. **Description:** An independent, membership-based,
nonprofit organization dedicated to building human capital for higher education.

**AMERICAN FEDERATION OF TEACHERS**
555 New Jersey Avenue, NW, Washington DC 20001. 202/879-4400. **E-mail
address:** online@aft.org. **World Wide Web address:** http://www.aft.org.
**Description:** Improves the lives of its members and their families, gives voice to
their professional, economic and social aspirations, brings together members to
assist and support one another and to promote democracy, human rights and
freedom.

**COLLEGE AND UNIVERSITY PROFESSIONAL ASSOCIATION FOR HUMAN
RESOURCES**
Tyson Place, 2607 Kingston Pike, Suite 250, Knoxville TN 37919. 865/637-7673.
**Fax:** 865/637-7674. **World Wide Web address:** http://www.cupa.org.
**Description:** Promotes the effective management and development of human
resources in higher education and offers many professional development
opportunities.

**NATIONAL ASSOCIATION FOR COLLEGE ADMISSION COUNSELING**
1631 Prince Street, Alexandria VA 22314-2818. 703/836-2222. **Fax:** 703/836-
8015. **World Wide Web address:** http://www.nacac.com. **Description:** Founded
in 1937, NACAC is an organization of 8,000 professionals dedicated to serving
students as they make choices about pursuing postsecondary education.
NACAC supports and advances the work of college admission counseling
professionals.

**NATIONAL ASSOCIATION OF COLLEGE AND UNIVERSITY BUSINESS
OFFICERS**
2501 M Street, NW, Suite 400, Washington DC 20037. 202/861-2500. **Fax:**
202/861-2583. **World Wide Web address:** http://www.nacubo.org. **Description:**
A nonprofit professional organization representing chief administrative and
financial officers at more than 2,100 colleges and universities across the country.

**NATIONAL SCIENCE TEACHERS ASSOCIATION**
1840 Wilson Boulevard, Arlington VA 22201-3000. 703/243-7100. **World Wide
Web address:** http://www.nsta.org. **Description:** Promotes excellence and
innovation in science teaching and learning.

## ELECTRONIC/INDUSTRIAL ELECTRICAL EQUIPMENT AND COMPONENTS

**AMERICAN CERAMIC SOCIETY**
P.O. Box 6136, Westerville OH 43086-6136. 614/890-4700. **Fax:** 614/899-6109. **E-mail address:** info@ceramics.org. **World Wide Web address:** http://www.acers.org. **Description:** Provides technical, scientific and educational information to its members and others in the ceramics and related materials field, structures its services, staff and capabilities to meet the needs of the ceramics community, related fields, and the general public.

**ELECTRONIC INDUSTRIES ALLIANCE**
2500 Wilson Boulevard, Arlington VA 22201. 703/907-7500. **World Wide Web address:** http://www.eia.org. **Description:** A national trade organization including 2,500 U.S. manufacturers. The Alliance is a partnership of electronic and high-tech associations and companies whose mission is promoting the market development and competitiveness of the U.S. high-tech industry through domestic and international policy efforts.

**ELECTRONICS TECHNICIANS ASSOCIATION, INTERNATIONAL**
5 Depot Street, Greencastle IN 46135. 765/653-8262. **Fax:** 765/653-4287. **Toll-free phone:** 800/288-3824. **E-mail address:** eta@tds.net. **World Wide Web address:** http://www.eta-sda.org. **Description:** A not-for-profit, worldwide professional association founded by electronics technicians and servicing dealers in 1978. Provides professional credentials based on an individual's skills and knowledge in a particular area of study.

**FABLESS SEMICONDUCTOR ASSOCIATION**
Three Lincoln Center, 5430 LBJ Freeway, Suite 280, Dallas TX 75240. 972/866-7579. **Fax:** 972/239-2292. **World Wide Web address:** http://www.fsa.org. **Description:** An industry organization aimed at achieving an optimal balance between wafer supply and demand.

**INSTITUTE OF ELECTRICAL AND ELECTRONICS ENGINEER (IEEE)**
3 Park Avenue, 17th Floor, New York NY 10016-5997. 212/419-7900. **Fax:** 212/752-4929. **E-mail address:** ieeeusa@ieee.org. **World Wide Web address:** http://www.ieee.org. **Description:** Advances the theory and application of electrotechnology and allied sciences, serves as a catalyst for technological innovation and supports the needs of its members through a wide variety of programs and services.

**INTERNATIONAL SOCIETY OF CERTIFIED ELECTRONICS TECHNICIANS**
3608 Pershing Avenue, Fort Worth TX 76107-4527. 817/921-9101. **Fax:** 817/921-3741 **Toll-free phone:** 800/946-0201 **E-mail address:** info@iscet.org **World Wide Web address:** http://www.iscet.org. **Description:** Prepares and tests technicians in the electronics and appliance service industry. Designed to measure the degree of theoretical knowledge and technical proficiency of practicing technicians.

**NATIONAL ELECTRONICS SERVICE DEALERS ASSOCIATION**
3608 Pershing Avenue, Fort Worth TX 76107-4527. 817/921-9061. **Fax:** 817/921-3741. **World Wide Web address:** http://www.nesda.com. **Description:** A trade organization for professionals in the business of repairing consumer electronic equipment, appliances, or computers.

# ENVIRONMENTAL & WASTE MANAGEMENT SERVICES

**AIR & WASTE MANAGEMENT ASSOCIATION**
One Gateway Center, 3rd Floor, 420 Fort Duquesne Boulevard, Pittsburgh PA 15222-1435. 412/232-3444. **Fax:** 412/232-3450. **E-mail address:** info@awma.org. **World Wide Web address:** http://www.awma.org. **Description:** A nonprofit, nonpartisan professional organization providing training, information, and networking opportunities to thousands of environmental professionals in 65 countries.

**AMERICAN ACADEMY OF ENVIRONMENTAL ENGINEERS**
130 Holiday Court, Suite 100, Annapolis MD 21401. 410/266-3311. **Fax:** 410/266-7653. **World Wide Web address:** http://www.aaee.net. **Description:** AAEE was founded in 1955 for the principal purpose of serving the public by improving the practice, elevating the standards, and advancing public recognition of environmental engineering through a program of specialty certification of qualified engineers.

**INSTITUTE OF CLEAN AIR COMPANIES**
1660 L Street, NW, Suite 1100, Washington DC 20036. 202/457-0911. **Fax:** 202/331-1388. **World Wide Web address:** http://www.icac.com. **Description:** The nonprofit national association of companies that supply air pollution monitoring and control systems, equipment, and services for stationary sources.

**NATIONAL SOLID WASTES MANAGEMENT ASSOCIATION**
4301 Connecticut Avenue, NW, Suite 300, Washington DC 20008-2304. 202/244-4700. **Fax:** 202/364-3792. **Toll-free phone:** 800/424-2869. **World Wide Web address:** http://www.nswma.org. **Description:** A non-profit, trade association that represents the interests of the North American waste services industry.

**WATER ENVIRONMENT FEDERATION**
601 Wythe Street, Alexandria VA 22314-1994. 703/684-2452. **Fax:** 703/684-2492. **Toll-free phone:** 800/666-0206. **World Wide Web address:** http://www.wef.org. **Description:** A not-for-profit technical and educational organization, founded in 1928, with members from varied disciplines. The federation's mission is to preserve and enhance the global water environment. The WEF network includes water quality professionals from 79 Member Associations in over 30 countries.

## FABRICATED METAL PRODUCTS AND PRIMARY METALS

**ASM INTERNATIONAL: THE MATERIALS INFORMATION SOCIETY**
9639 Kinsman Road, Materials Park OH 44073-0002. 440/338-5151. **Fax:** 440/338-4634. **Toll-free phone:** 800/336-5152. **E-mail address:** cust-srv@asminternational.org. **World Wide Web address:** http://www.asm-intl.org. **Description:** An organization for materials engineers and scientists, dedicated to advancing industry, technology and applications of metals and materials.

**AMERICAN FOUNDRYMEN'S SOCIETY**
1695 Penny Lane, Schaumburg IL 60173-4555. 847/824-0181. **Fax:** 847/824-7848. **Toll-free phone:** 800/537-4237. **World Wide Web address:** http://www.afsinc.org. **Description:** An international organization dedicated to provide and promote knowledge and services that strengthen the metalcasting industry. AFS was founded in 1896 and has approximately 10,000 members in 47 countries.

**AMERICAN WELDING SOCIETY**
550 NW LeJeune Road, Miami FL 33126. 305/443-9353. **Toll-free phone:** 800/443-9353. **E-mail address:** info@aws.org. **World Wide Web address:** http://www.aws.org. **Description:** Founded in 1919 as a multifaceted, nonprofit organization with a goal to advance the science, technology and application of welding and related joining disciplines.

## FINANCIAL SERVICES

**THE BOND MARKET ASSOCIATION**
360 Madison Avenue, New York NY 10017-7111. 646/637-9200. **Fax:** 646/637-9126. **World Wide Web address:** http://www.bondmarkets.com. **Description:** The trade association representing the largest securities markets in the world. The Association speaks for the bond industry, advocating its positions and representing its interests in New York; Washington, D.C.; London; Frankfurt; Brussels and Tokyo; and with issuer and investor groups worldwide. The Association represents a diverse mix of securities firms and banks, whether they are large, multi-product firms or companies with special market niches.

**FINANCIAL EXECUTIVES INSTITUTE**
200 Campus Drive, PO Box 674, Florham Park NJ 07932-0674. 973/765-1000. **Fax:** 973/765-1018. **E-mail address:** conf@fei.org. **World Wide Web address:** http://www.fei.org. **Description:** An association for financial executives working to alert members to emerging issues, develop the professional and management skills of members, provide forums for peer networking, advocate the views of financial executives, and promote ethical conduct.

**NATIONAL ASSOCIATION FOR BUSINESS ECONOMICS**
1233 20th Street, NW, #505, Washington DC 20036. 202/463-6223. **Fax:** 202/463-6239. **E-mail address:** nabe@nabe.com. **World Wide Web address:** http://www.nabe.com. **Description:** An association of professionals who have an interest in business economics and who want to use the latest economic data and trends to enhance their ability to make sound business decisions. Founded in 1959.

**NATIONAL ASSOCIATION OF CREDIT MANAGEMENT**
8840 Columbia 100 Parkway, Columbia MD 21045. 410/740-5560. **Fax:** 410/740-5574. **E-mail address:** nacm_info@nacm.org. **World Wide Web address:** http://www.nacm.org. **Description:** Founded in 1896 to promote good laws for sound credit, protect businesses against fraudulent debtors, improve the interchange of credit information, develop better credit practices and methods, and establish a code of ethics.

**NATIONAL ASSOCIATION OF REAL ESTATE INVESTMENT TRUSTS**
1875 Eye Street, NW, Washington DC 20006. 202/739-9400. **Fax:** 202/739-9401. **E-mail address:** info@nareit.org. **World Wide Web address:** http://www.nareit.com. **Description:** NAREIT is the national trade association for REITs and publicly traded real estate companies. Members are real estate investment trusts (REITs) and other businesses that own, operate and finance income-producing real estate, as well as those firms and individuals who advise, study and service these businesses.

**SECURITIES INDUSTRY ASSOCIATION**
120 Broadway, 35th Floor, New York NY 10271-0080. 212/608-1500. **Fax:** 212/968-0703. **E-mail address:** info@sia.com. **World Wide Web address:** http://www.sia.com. **Description:** The Securities Industry Association (SIA) was established in 1972 through the merger of the Association of Stock Exchange Firms (1913) and the Investment Banker's Association (1912). The Securities Industry Association brings together the shared interests of more than 600 securities firms to accomplish common goals. SIA member-firms (including

investment banks, broker-dealers, and mutual fund companies) are active in all U.S. and foreign markets and in all phases of corporate and public finance.

**WOMEN'S INSTITUTE OF FINANCIAL EDUCATION**
PO Box 910014, San Diego CA 92191. 760/736-1660. **E-mail address:** info@wife.org. **World Wide Web address:** http://www.wife.org. **Description:** A non-profit organization dedicated to providing financial education to women in their quest for financial independence.

## FOOD AND BEVERAGES/AGRICULTURE

**AMERICAN ASSOCIATION OF CEREAL CHEMISTS (AACC)**
3340 Pilot Knob Road, St. Paul MN 55121-2097. 651/454-7250. **Fax:** 651/454-0766. **World Wide Web address:** http://www.aaccnet.org. **Description:** A non-profit international organization of nearly 4,000 members who are specialists in the use of cereal grains in foods. The association gathers and disseminates scientific and technical information to professionals in the grain-based foods industry worldwide for over 85 years.

**AMERICAN BEVERAGE ASSOCIATION**
1101 16th Street, NW, Washington DC 20036. 202/463-6732. **Fax:** 202/659-5349. **World Wide Web address:** http://www.ameribev.org. **Description:** An association for America's non-alcoholic beverage industry, serving the public and its members for more than 75 years.

**AMERICAN FROZEN FOOD INSTITUTE**
2000 Corporate Ridge, Suite 1000, McLean VA 22102. 703/821-0770. **Fax:** 703/821-1350. **E-mail address:** info@affi.com. **World Wide Web address:** http://www.affi.com. **Description:** A national trade association representing all aspects of the frozen food industry supply chain, from manufacturers to distributors to suppliers to packagers; the Institute is industry's voice on issues crucial to future growth and progress.

**AMERICAN SOCIETY OF AGRICULTURAL ENGINEERS**
2950 Niles Road, St. Joseph MI 49085. 269/429-0300. **Fax:** 269/429-3852. **World Wide Web address:** http://www.asae.org. **Description:** An educational and scientific organization dedicated to the advancement of engineering applicable to agricultural, food, and biological systems.

**AMERICAN SOCIETY OF BREWING CHEMISTS**
3340 Pilot Knob Road, St. Paul MN 55121-2097. 651/454-7250. **Fax:** 651/454-0766. **World Wide Web address:** http://www.asbcnet.org. **Description:** Founded in 1934 to improve and bring uniformity to the brewing industry on a technical level.

**CIES – THE FOOD BUSINESS FORUM**
8455 Colesville Road, Suite 705, Silver Spring MD 20910. 301/563-3383. **Fax:** 301/563-3386. **E-mail address:** us.office@ciesnet.com. **World Wide Web address:** http://www.ciesnet.com. **Description:** An independent global food business network. Membership in CIES is on a company basis and includes more than two thirds of the world's largest food retailers and their suppliers.

**CROPLIFE AMERICA**
1156 15th Street, NW, Suite 400, Washington DC 20005. 202/296-1585. **Fax:** 202/463-0474. **World Wide Web address:** http://www.croplifeamerica.org. **Description:** Fosters the interests of the general public and member companies by promoting innovation and the environmentally sound manufacture, distribution, and use of crop protection and production technologies for safe, high-quality, affordable and abundant food, fiber and other crops.

**INTERNATIONAL DAIRY FOODS ASSOCIATION**
1250 H Street, NW, Suite 900, Washington DC 20005. 202/737-4332. **Fax:** 202/331-7820. **E-mail address:** membership@idfa.org. **World Wide Web**

**address:** http://www.idfa.org. **Description:** IDFA represents more than 500 dairy food manufacturers, marketers, distributors and industry suppliers in the U.S. and 20 other countries, and encourages the formation of favorable domestic and international dairy policies.

## NATIONAL BEER WHOLESALERS' ASSOCIATION
1101 King Street, Suite 600, Alexandria VA 22314-2944. 703/683-4300. **Fax:** 703/683-8965. **E-mail address:** info@nbwa.org. **World Wide Web address:** http://www.nbwa.org. **Description:** Founded in 1938 as a trade association for the nations' beer wholesalers. NBWA provides leadership which enhances the independent malt beverage wholesale industry; advocates before government and the public on behalf of its members; encourages the responsible consumption of beer; and provides programs and services that will enhance members' efficiency and effectiveness.

## NATIONAL FOOD PROCESSORS ASSOCIATION
1350 I Street, NW, Suite 300, Washington DC 20005. 202/639.5900. **E-mail address:** nfpa@nfpa-food.org. **World Wide Web address:** http://www.nfpa-food.org. **Description:** NFPA is the voice of the $500 billion food processing industry on scientific and public policy issues involving food safety, nutrition, technical and regulatory matters and consumer affairs.

## HEALTH CARE SERVICES, EQUIPMENT, AND PRODUCTS

**ACCREDITING COMMISSION ON EDUCATION FOR HEALTH SERVICES ADMINISTRATION**
2000 14th Street North, Arlington VA 22201. 703/894-0960. **Fax:** 703/894-0941. **World Wide Web address:** http://www.acehsa.org. **Description:** An association of educational, professional, clinical, and commercial organizations devoted to accountability and quality improvement in the education of health care management and administration professionals.

**AMERICAN ACADEMY OF ALLERGY, ASTHMA, AND IMMUNOLOGY**
555 East Wells Street, Suite 1100, Milwaukee WI 53202-3823. 414/272-6071. **E-mail address:** info@aaaai.org. **World Wide Web address:** http://www.aaaai.org. **Description:** A professional medical specialty organization representing allergists, asthma specialists, clinical immunologists, allied health professionals, and other physicians with a special interest in allergy. Established in 1943.

**AMERICAN ACADEMY OF FAMILY PHYSICIANS**
11400 Tomahawk Creek Parkway, Leawood KS 66211-2672. 913/906-6000. **Toll-free phone:** 800/274-2237. **E-mail address:** fp@aafp.org. **World Wide Web address:** http://www.aafp.org. **Description:** Founded in 1947, the Academy represents family physicians, family practice residents and medical students nationwide. AAFP's mission is to preserve and promote the science and art of family medicine and to ensure high quality, cost-effective health care for patients of all ages.

**AMERICAN ACADEMY OF PEDIATRIC DENTISTRY**
211 East Chicago Avenue, Suite 700, Chicago IL 60611-2663. 312/337-2169. **Fax:** 312/337-6329. **World Wide Web address:** http://www.aapd.org. **Description:** A membership organization representing the specialty of pediatric dentistry.

**AMERICAN ACADEMY OF PERIODONTOLOGY**
737 North Michigan Avenue, Suite 800, Chicago IL 60611-2690. 312/787-5518. **Fax:** 312/787-3670. **World Wide Web address:** http://www.perio.org. **Description: A** 7,900-member association of dental professionals specializing in the prevention, diagnosis and treatment of diseases affecting the gums and supporting structures of the teeth and in the placement and maintenance of dental implants. The Academy's purpose is to advocate, educate, and set standards for advancing the periodontal and general health of the public and promoting excellence in the practice of periodontics.

**AMERICAN ACADEMY OF PHYSICIANS ASSISTANTS**
950 North Washington Street, Alexandria VA 22314-1552. 703/836-2272. **Fax:** 703/684-1924. **E-mail address:** aapa@aapa.org. **World Wide Web address:** http://www.aapa.org. **Description:** Promotes quality, cost-effective, accessible health care, and the professional and personal development of physician assistants.

**AMERICAN ASSOCIATION FOR CLINICAL CHEMISTRY**
2101 L Street, NW, Suite 202, Washington DC 20037-1558. 202/857-0717. **Fax:** 202/887-5093. **Toll-free phone:** 800/892-1400. **World Wide Web address:**

http://www.aacc.org. **Description:** Founded in 1948 as an international scientific/medical society of clinical laboratory professionals, physicians, research scientists and other individuals involved with clinical chemistry and other clinical laboratory science-related disciplines. The society has 10,000 members.

## AMERICAN ASSOCIATION FOR ORAL AND MAXILLOFACIAL SURGEONS
9700 West Bryn Mawr Avenue, Rosemont IL 60018-5701. 847/678-6200. **E-mail address:** inquiries@aaoms.org. **World Wide Web address:** http://www.aaoms.org. **Description:** The American Association of Oral and Maxillofacial Surgeons (AAOMS), is a not-for-profit professional association serving the professional and public needs of the specialty of oral and maxillofacial surgery.

## AMERICAN ASSOCIATION FOR RESPIRATORY CARE
9425 North MacArthur Boulevard, Suite 100, Irving TX 75063-4706. 972/243-2272. **Fax:** 972/484-2720. **E-mail address:** info@aarc.org. **World Wide Web address:** http://www.aarc.org. **Description:** Advances the science, technology, ethics, and art of respiratory care through research and education for its members and teaches the general public about pulmonary health and disease prevention.

## AMERICAN ASSOCIATION OF COLLEGES OF OSTEOPATHIC MEDICINE
5550 Friendship Boulevard, Suite 310, Chevy Chase MD 20815-7231. 301/968-4100. **Fax:** 301/968-4101. **World Wide Web address:** http://www.aacom.org. **Description:** Promotes excellence in osteopathic medical education throughout the educational continuum, in research and in service; to enhance the strength and quality of the member colleges; and to improve the health of the American public.

## AMERICAN ASSOCIATION OF COLLEGES OF PODIATRIC MEDICINE
15850 Crabbs Branch Way, Suite 320, Rockville MD 20855. **Fax:** 301/948-1928. **Toll-free phone:** 800/922-9266. **E-mail address:** aacpmas@aacpm.org. **World Wide Web address:** http://www.aacpm.org. **Description:** An organization advancing podiatric medicine and its education system.

## AMERICAN ASSOCIATION OF HEALTHCARE CONSULTANTS
5938 North Drake Avenue, Chicago IL 60659. **Fax:** 773/463-3552. **Toll-free phone:** 888/350-2242. **E-mail address:** info@aahc.net. **World Wide Web address:** http://www.aahc.net. **Description:** Founded in 1949 as the professional membership society for leading healthcare consultants and consulting firms.

## AMERICAN ASSOCIATION OF HOMES AND SERVICES FOR THE AGING
2519 Connecticut Avenue, NW, Washington DC 20008. 202/783.2242. **Fax:** 202/783-2255. **World Wide Web address:** http://www.aahsa.org. **Description:** The American Association of Homes and Services for the Aging (AAHSA) is committed to advancing the vision of healthy, affordable, ethical aging services for America. The association represents 5,600 not-for-profit nursing homes, continuing care retirement communities, assisted living and senior housing facilities, and home and community-based service providers.

## AMERICAN ASSOCIATION OF MEDICAL ASSISTANTS
20 North Wacker Drive, Suite 1575, Chicago IL 60606. 312/899-1500. **World Wide Web address:** http://www.aama-ntl.org. **Description:** The mission of the American Association of Medical Assistants is to enable medical assisting professionals to enhance and demonstrate the knowledge, skills and

professionalism required by employers and patients; protect medical assistants' right to practice; and promote effective, efficient health care delivery through optimal use of multiskilled Certified Medical Assistants (CMAs).

### AMERICAN ASSOCIATION OF NURSE ANESTHETISTS

222 South Prospect Avenue, Park Ridge IL 60068. 847/692-7050. **World Wide Web address:** http://www.aana.com. **Description:** Founded in 1931 as the professional association representing more than 30,000 Certified Registered Nurse Anesthetists (CRNAs) nationwide. The AANA promulgates education, and practice standards and guidelines, and affords consultation to both private and governmental entities regarding nurse anesthetists and their practice.

### AMERICAN CHIROPRACTIC ASSOCIATION

1701 Clarendon Boulevard, Arlington VA 22209. **Fax:** 703/243-2593. **Toll-free phone:** 800/986-4636. **E-mail address:** memberinfo@amerchiro.org. **World Wide Web address:** http://www.americhiro.org. **Description:** A professional association representing doctors of chiropractic that provides lobbying, public relations, professional and educational opportunities for doctors of chiropractic, funds research regarding chiropractic and health issues, and offers leadership for the advancement of the profession.

### AMERICAN COLLEGE OF HEALTH CARE ADMINISTRATORS

300 North Lee Street, Suite 301, Alexandria VA 22314. 703/739-7900. **Fax:** 703/739-7901. **Toll-free phone:** 888/882-2422. **E-mail address:** membership@achca.org. **World Wide Web address:** http://www.achca.org. **Description:** A non-profit membership organization that provides educational programming, certification in a variety of positions, and career development for its members. Founded in 1962.

### AMERICAN COLLEGE OF HEALTHCARE EXECUTIVES

One North Franklin Street, Suite 1700, Chicago IL 60606-4425. 312/424-2800. **Fax:** 312/424-0023. **World Wide Web address:** http://www.ache.org. **Description:** An international professional society of nearly 30,000 healthcare executives who lead our nation's hospitals, healthcare systems, and other healthcare organizations.

### AMERICAN COLLEGE OF MEDICAL PRACTICE EXECUTIVES

104 Inverness Terrace East, Englewood CO 80112-5306. 303/799-1111. **Fax:** 303/643-4439. **Toll-free phone:** 877/275-6462. **E-mail address:** acmpe@mgma.com. **World Wide Web address:** http://www.mgma.com/acmpe. **Description:** Established in 1956, the ACMPE offers board certification, self-assessment and leadership development for medical practice executives.

### AMERICAN COLLEGE OF OBSTETRICIANS AND GYNECOLOGISTS

409 12th Street, SW, PO Box 96920, Washington DC 20090-6920. **World Wide Web address:** http://www.acog.org. **Description:** Founded in 1951, the 46,000-member organization is the nation's leading group of professionals providing health care for women.

### AMERICAN COLLEGE OF PHYSICIAN EXECUTIVES

4890 West Kennedy Boulevard, Suite 200, Tampa FL 33609. 813/287-2000. **Fax:** 813/287-8993. **Toll-free phone:** 800/562-8088. **E-mail address:** acpe@acpe.org. **World Wide Web address:** http://www.acpe.org. **Description:** A specialty society representing physicians in health care leadership. Provides educational and career development programs.

## AMERICAN DENTAL ASSOCIATION
211 East Chicago Avenue, Chicago IL 60611-2678. 312/440-2500. **World Wide Web address:** http://www.ada.org. **Description:** A dental association serving both public and private physicians. Founded in 1859.

## AMERICAN DENTAL EDUCATION ASSOCIATION
1400 K Street, NW Suite 1100, Washington DC 20005. 202/289-7201. **Fax:** 202/289-7204. **World Wide Web address:** http://www.adea.org. **Description:** A national organization for dental education. Members include all U.S. and Canadian dental schools, advanced dental education programs, hospital dental education programs, allied dental education programs, corporations, faculty, and students.

## AMERICAN DENTAL HYGIENISTS ASSOCIATION
444 North Michigan Avenue, Suite 3400, Chicago IL 60611. 312/440-8900. **E-mail address:** mail@adha.net. **World Wide Web address:** http://www.adha.org. **Description:** Founded in 1923, the association develops communication and mutual cooperation among dental hygienists and represents the professional interests of the more than 120,000 registered dental hygienists (RDHs) in the United States.

## AMERICAN HEALTH INFORMATION MANAGEMENT ASSOCIATION
233 North Michigan Avenue, Suite 2150, Chicago IL 60601-5800. 312/233-1100. **Fax:** 312/233-1090. **E-mail address:** info@ahima.org. **World Wide Web address:** http://www.ahima.org. **Description:** Represents more than 46,000 specially educated health information management professionals who work throughout the healthcare industry. Health information management professionals serve the healthcare industry and the public by managing, analyzing, and utilizing data vital for patient care -- and making it accessible to healthcare providers when it is needed most.

## AMERICAN HOSPITAL ASSOCIATION
One North Franklin, Chicago IL 60606-3421. 312/422-3000. **Fax:** 312/422-4796. **World Wide Web address:** http://www.aha.org. **Description:** A national organization that represents and serves all types of hospitals, health care networks, and their patients and communities. Approximately 5,000 institutional, 600 associate, and 27,000 personal members belong to the AHA.

## AMERICAN MEDICAL ASSOCIATION
515 North State Street, Chicago IL 60610. **Toll-free phone:** 800/621-8335. **World Wide Web address:** http://www.ama-assn.org. **Description:** American Medical Association speaks out on issues important to patients and the nation's health. AMA policy on such issues is decided through its democratic policy-making process, in the AMA House of Delegates, which meets twice a year.

## AMERICAN MEDICAL INFORMATICS ASSOCIATION
4915 St. Elmo Avenue, Suite 401, Bethesda MD 20814. 301/657-1291. **Fax:** 301/657-1296. **World Wide Web address:** http://www.amia.org. **Description:** The American Medical Informatics Association is a nonprofit membership organization of individuals, institutions, and corporations dedicated to developing and using information technologies to improve health care. Founded in 1990.

## AMERICAN MEDICAL TECHNOLOGISTS
710 Higgins Road, Park Ridge IL 60068. 847/823-5169. **Fax:** 847/823-0458. **Toll-free phone:** 800/275-1268. **World Wide Web address:** http://www.amt1.com. **Description:** A nonprofit certification agency and

professional membership association representing nearly 27,000 individuals in allied health care. Provides allied health professionals with professional certification services and membership programs to enhance their professional and personal growth.

## AMERICAN MEDICAL WOMEN'S ASSOCIATION
801 North Fairfax Street, Suite 400, Alexandria VA 22314. 703/838-0500. **Fax:** 703/549-3864. **E-mail address:** info@amwa-doc.org. **World Wide Web address:** http://www.amwa-doc.org. **Description:** An organization of 10,000 women physicians and medical students dedicated to serving as the unique voice for women's health and the advancement of women in medicine.

## AMERICAN NURSES ASSOCIATION
8515 Georgia Avenue, Suite 400 West, Silver Spring MD 20910. 301/628-5000. **Fax:** 301//628-5001. **Toll-free phone:** 800/274-4ANA. **World Wide Web address:** http://www.nursingworld.org. **Description:** A professional organization representing the nation's 2.6 million Registered Nurses through its 54 constituent state associations and 13 organizational affiliate members. Fosters high standards of nursing practice, promotes the economic and general welfare of nurses in the workplace, projects a positive and realistic view of nursing, and by lobbies Congress and regulatory agencies on health care issues affecting nurses and the public.

## AMERICAN OCCUPATIONAL THERAPY ASSOCIATION
4720 Montgomery Lane, PO Box 31220, Bethesda MD 20824-1220. 301/652-2682. **Fax:** 301/652-7711. **Toll-free phone:** 800/377- 8555. **World Wide Web address:** http://www.aota.org. **Description:** A professional association of approximately 40,000 occupational therapists, occupational therapy assistants, and students of occupational therapy.

## AMERICAN OPTOMETRIC ASSOCIATION
243 North Lindbergh Boulevard, St. Louis MO 63141. 314/991-4100. **Fax:** 314/991-4101. **World Wide Web address:** http://www.aoanet.org. **Description:** The American Optometric Association is the acknowledged leader and recognized authority for primary eye and vision care in the world.

## AMERICAN ORGANIZATION OF NURSE EXECUTIVES
325 Seventh Street, NW, Washington DC 20004. 202/626-2240. **Fax:** 202/638-5499. **E-mail address:** aone@aha.org. **World Wide Web address:** http://www.aone.org. **Description:** Founded in 1967, the American Organization of Nurse Executives (AONE), a subsidiary of the American Hospital Association, is a national organization of nearly 4,000 nurses who design, facilitate, and manage care. Its mission is to represent nurse leaders who improve healthcare.

## AMERICAN ORTHOPAEDIC ASSOCIATION
6300 North River Road, Suite 505, Rosemont IL 60018-4263. 847/318-7330. **Fax:** 847/318-7339. **E-mail address:** info@aoassn.org **World Wide Web address:** http://www.aoassn.org. **Description:** Founded in 1887, The American Orthopaedic Association is the oldest orthopaedic association in the world.

## AMERICAN PHYSICAL THERAPY ASSOCIATION
1111 North Fairfax Street, Alexandria VA 22314-1488. 703/684-2782. **Fax:** 703/684-7343. **Toll-free phone:** 800/999-2782. **World Wide Web address:** http://www.apta.org. **Description:** The American Physical Therapy Association (APTA) is a national professional organization representing more than 63,000

members. Its goal is to foster advancements in physical therapy practice, research, and education.

## AMERICAN PODIATRIC MEDICAL ASSOCIATION

9312 Old Georgetown Road, Bethesda MD 20814. 301/571-9200. **Fax:** 301/530-2752. **Toll-free phone:** 800/FOOTCARE. **World Wide Web address:** http://www.apma.org. **Description:** The American Podiatric Medical Association is the premier professional organization representing the nation's Doctors of Podiatric Medicine (podiatrists). The APMA represents approximately 80 percent of the podiatrists in the country. APMA includes 53 component societies in states and other jurisdictions, as well as 22 affiliated and related societies.

## AMERICAN PSYCHIATRIC ASSOCIATION

1000 Wilson Boulevard, Suite 1825, Arlington VA.22209-3901. 703/907-7300. **E-mail address:** apa@psych.org **World Wide Web address:** http://www.psych.org. **Description:** With 35,000 members, the American Psychiatric Association is a medical specialty society recognized worldwide.

## AMERICAN PUBLIC HEALTH ASSOCIATION

800 I Street, NW, Washington DC 20001. 202/777-2742. **Fax:** 202/777-2534. **E-mail address:** comments@apha.org. **World Wide Web address:** http://www.apha.org. **Description:** The American Public Health Association (APHA) is the oldest and largest organization of public health professionals in the world, representing more than 50,000 members from over 50 occupations of public health.

## AMERICAN SOCIETY OF ANESTHESIOLOGISTS

520 N. Northwest Highway, Park Ridge IL 60068-2573. 847/825-5586. **Fax:** 847/825-1692. **E-mail address:** mail@asahq.org. **World Wide Web address:** http://www.asahq.org. **Description:** An educational, research and scientific association of physicians organized to raise and maintain the standards of the medical practice of anesthesiology and improve the care of the patient. Founded in 1905.

## AMERICAN SPEECH-LANGUAGE-HEARING ASSOCIATION

10801 Rockville Pike, Rockville MD 20852-3226. **Toll-free phone:** 800/638-8255. **E-mail address:** actioncenter@asha.org. **World Wide Web address:** http://www.asha.org. **Description:** The professional, scientific, and credentialing association for more than 110,000 audiologists, speech-language pathologists, and speech, language, and hearing scientists with a mission to ensure that all people with speech, language, and hearing disorders have access to quality services to help them communicate more effectively.

## AMERICAN VETERINARY MEDICAL ASSOCIATION

1931 North Meacham Road, Suite 100, Schaumburg IL 60173. 847/925-8070. **Fax:** 847/925-1329. **E-mail address:** avmainfo@avma.org. **World Wide Web address:** http://www.avma.org. **Description:** A not-for-profit association founded in 1863 representing more than 69,000 veterinarians working in private and corporate practice, government, industry, academia, and uniformed services.

## ASSOCIATION OF AMERICAN MEDICAL COLLEGES

2450 N Street, NW, Washington DC 20037-1126. 202/828-0400. **Fax:** 202/828-1125. **World Wide Web address:** http://www.aamc.org. **Description:** A non-profit association founded in 1876 to work for reform in medical education. The association represents the nation's 126 accredited medical schools, nearly 400 major teaching hospitals, more than 105,000 faculty in 96 academic and scientific societies, and the nation's 66,000 medical students and 97,000 residents.

**ASSOCIATION OF UNIVERSITY PROGRAMS IN HEALTH ADMINISTRATION**
2000 North 14th Street, Suite 780, Arlington VA 22201. 703/894-0940. **Fax:** 703/894-0941. **E-mail address:** aupha@aupha.org. **World Wide Web address:** http://www.aupha.org. **Description:** A not-for-profit association of university-based educational programs, faculty, practitioners, and provider organizations. Its members are dedicated to continuously improving the field of health management and practice. It is the only non-profit entity of its kind that works to improve the delivery of health services throughout the world - and thus the health of citizens - by educating professional managers.

**HEALTH INFORMATION AND MANAGEMENT SYSTEMS SOCIETY**
230 East Ohio Street, Suite 500, Chicago IL 60611-3269. 312/664-4467. **Fax:** 312/664-6143. **World Wide Web address:** http://www.himss.org. **Description:** Founded in 1961 and provides leadership for the optimal use of healthcare information technology and management systems for the betterment of human health.

**HEALTHCARE FINANCIAL MANAGEMENT ASSOCIATION**
2 Westbrook Corporate Center, Suite 700, Westchester IL 60154-5700. 708/531-9600. **Fax:** 708/531-0032. **Toll-free phone:** 800/252-4362. **World Wide Web address:** http://www.hfma.org. **Description:** A membership organization for healthcare financial management professionals with 32,000 members.

**NATIONAL ASSOCIATION FOR CHIROPRACTIC MEDICINE**
15427 Baybrook Drive, Houston TX 77062. 281/280-8262. **Fax:** 281/280-8262. **World Wide Web address:** http://www.chiromed.org. **Description:** A consumer advocacy association of chiropractors striving to make legitimate the utilization of professional manipulative procedures in mainstream health care delivery.

**NATIONAL MEDICAL ASSOCIATION**
1012 Tenth Street, NW, Washington DC 20001. 202/347-1895. **Fax:** 202/898-2510. **World Wide Web address:** http://www.nmanet.org. **Description:** Promotes the collective interests of physicians and patients of African descent with a mission to serve as the collective voice of physicians of African descent and a leading force for parity in medicine, elimination of health disparities and promotion of optimal health.

## HOTELS AND RESTAURANTS

**AMERICAN HOTEL AND LODGING ASSOCIATION**
1201 New York Avenue, NW, #600, Washington DC 20005-3931. 202/289-3100.
**Fax:** 202/289-3199. **World Wide Web address:** http://www.ahla.com.
**Description:** Provides its members with assistance in operations, education, and communications, and lobbies on Capitol Hill to provide a business climate in which the industry can continue to prosper. Individual state associations provide representation at the state level and offer many additional cost-saving benefits.

**THE EDUCATIONAL FOUNDATION OF THE NATIONAL RESTAURANT ASSOCIATION**
175 West Jackson Boulevard, Suite 1500, Chicago IL 60604-2702. 312/715-1010. **Toll-free phone:** 800/765-2122. **E-mail address:** info@nraef.org. **World Wide Web address:** http://www.nraef.org. **Description:** A not-for-profit organization dedicated to fulfilling the educational mission of the National Restaurant Association. Focusing on three key strategies of risk management, recruitment, and retention, the NRAEF is the premier provider of educational resources, materials, and programs, which address attracting, developing and retaining the industry's workforce.

**NATIONAL RESTAURANT ASSOCIATION**
1200 17th Street, NW, Washington DC 20036. 202/331-5900. 202/331-5900.
**Fax:** 202/331-2429. **Toll-free phone:** 800/424-5156. **World Wide Web address:** http://www.restaurant.org. **Description:** Founded in 1919 as a business association for the restaurant industry with a mission to represent, educate and promote a rapidly growing industry that is comprised of 878,000 restaurant and foodservice outlets employing 12 million people.

## INSURANCE

### AMERICA'S HEALTH INSURANCE PLANS
601 Pennsylvania Avenue, NW, SOuth Building, Suite 500, Washington DC 20004. 202/778-3200. **Fax:** 202/331-7487. **World Wide Web address:** http://www.ahip.org. **Description:** A national association representing nearly 1,300 member companies providing health insurance coverage to more than 200 million Americans.

### INSURANCE INFORMATION INSTITUTE
110 William Street, New York NY 10038. 212/346-5500. **World Wide Web address:** http://www.iii.org. **Description:** Provides definitive insurance information. Recognized by the media, governments, regulatory organizations, universities and the public as a primary source of information, analysis and referral concerning insurance.

### NATIONAL ASSOCIATION OF PROFESSIONAL INSURANCE AGENTS
400 North Washington Street, Alexandria VA 22314. 703/836-9340. **Fax:** 703/836-1279. **E-mail address:** piaweb@pianet.org. **World Wide Web address:** http://www.pianet.com. **Description:** Represents independent agents in all 50 states, Puerto Rico and the District of Columbia. Founded in 1931.

### PROPERTY CASUALTY INSURERS ASSOCIATION OF AMERICA
2600 South River Road, Des Plaines IL 60018-3286. 847/297-7800. **Fax:** 847/297-5064. **World Wide Web address:** http://www.pciaa.net. **Description:** A property/casualty trade association representing more than 1,000 member companies, PCI advocates its members' public policy positions at the federal and state levels and to the public.

## LEGAL SERVICES

### AMERICAN BAR ASSOCIATION
321 North Clark Street, Chicago IL 60610. 312/988-5000. **E-mail address:** askaba@abanet.org. **World Wide Web address:** http://www.abanet.org. **Description:** A voluntary professional association with more than 400,000 members, the ABA provides law school accreditation, continuing legal education, information about the law, programs to assist lawyers and judges in their work, and initiatives to improve the legal system for the public.

### FEDERAL BAR ASSOCIATION
2215 M Street, NW, Washington DC 20037. 202/785-1614. **Fax:** 202/785-1568. **E-mail address:** fba@fedbar.org. **World Wide Web address:** http://www.fedbar.org. **Description:** The professional organization for private and government lawyers and judges involved in federal practice.

### NATIONAL ASSOCIATION OF LEGAL ASSISTANTS
1516 South Boston, #200, Tulsa OK 74119. 918/587-6828. **World Wide Web address:** http://www.nala.org. **Description:** A professional association for legal assistants and paralegals, providing continuing education and professional development programs. Founded in 1975.

### NATIONAL FEDERATION OF PARALEGAL ASSOCIATIONS
2517 Eastlake Avenue East, Suite 200, Seattle WA 98102. 206/652-4120. **Fax:** 206/652-4122. **E-mail address:** info@paralegals.org. **World Wide Web address:** http://www.paralegals.org. **Description:** A non-profit professional organization representing more than 15,000 paralegals in the United States and Canada. NFPA is the national voice and the standard for excellence for the paralegal profession through its work on the issues of regulation, ethics and education.

## MANUFACTURING: MISCELLANEOUS CONSUMER

**ASSOCIATION FOR MANUFACTURING EXCELLENCE**
380 Palantine Road West, Wheeling IL 60090-5863. 847/520-3282. **Fax:** 847/520-0163. **World Wide Web address:** http://www.ame.org. **Description:** A not-for-profit organization founded in 1985 consisting of 6000 executives, senior and middle managers who wish to improve the competitiveness of their organizations.

**ASSOCIATION FOR MANUFACTURING TECHNOLOGY**
7901 Westpark Drive, McLean VA 22102-4206. 703/893-2900. **Fax:** 703/893-1151. **Toll-free phone:** 703/893-2900. **World Wide Web address:** http://www.amtonline.org. **Description:** Supports and promotes American manufacturers of machine tools and manufacturing technology. Provides members with industry expertise and assistance on critical industry concerns.

**ASSOCIATION OF HOME APPLIANCE MANUFACTURERS**
1111 19th Street, NW, Suite 402, Washington DC 20036. 202/872-5955. **Fax:** 202/872-9354. **World Wide Web address:** http://www.aham.org. **Description:** Represents the manufacturers of household appliances and products/services associated with household appliances.

**SOCIETY OF MANUFACTURING ENGINEERS**
One SME Drive, Dearborn MI 48121. 313/271-1500. **Fax:** 313/425-3401. **Toll-free phone:** 800/733-4763. **World Wide Web address:** http://www.sme.org. **Description:** Promotes an increased awareness of manufacturing engineering and helps keep manufacturing professionals up to date on leading trends and technologies. Founded in 1932.

## MANUFACTURING: MISCELLANEOUS INDUSTRIAL

### ASSOCIATION FOR MANUFACTURING EXCELLENCE
380 Palantine Road West, Wheeling IL 60090-5863. 847/520-3282. **Fax:** 847/520-0163. **World Wide Web address:** http://www.ame.org. **Description:** A not-for-profit organization founded in 1985 consisting of 6000 executives, senior and middle managers who wish to improve the competitiveness of their organizations.

### INSTITUTE OF INDUSTRIAL ENGINEERS
3577 Parkway Lane, Suite 200, Norcross GA 30092. 770/449-0460. **Fax:** 770/441-3295. **Toll-free phone:** 800/494-0460. **World Wide Web address:** http://www.iienet.org. **Description:** A non-profit professional society dedicated to the support of the industrial engineering profession and individuals involved with improving quality and productivity. Founded in 1948.

### NATIONAL ASSOCIATION OF MANUFACTURERS
1331 Pennsylvania Avenue, NW, Washington DC 20004-1790. 202/637-3000. **Fax:** 202/637-3182. **E-mail address:** manufacturing@nam.org. **World Wide Web address:** http://www.nam.org. **Description:** With 14,000 members, NAM's mission is to enhance the competitiveness of manufacturers and to improve American living standards by shaping a legislative and regulatory environment conducive to U.S. economic growth, and to increase understanding among policymakers, the media and the public about the importance of manufacturing to America's economic strength.

### NATIONAL TOOLING AND MACHINING ASSOCIATION
9300 Livingston Road, Fort Washington MD 20744-4998. 800/248-6862. **Fax:** 301/248-7104. **World Wide Web address:** http://www.ntma.org. **Description:** A trade organization representing the precision custom manufacturing industry throughout the United States.

### SOCIETY OF MANUFACTURING ENGINEERS
One SME Drive, Dearborn MI 48121. 313/271-1500. **Fax:** 313/425-3401. **Toll-free phone:** 800/733-4763. **World Wide Web address:** http://www.sme.org. **Description:** Promotes an increased awareness of manufacturing engineering and helps keep manufacturing professionals up to date on leading trends and technologies. Founded in 1932.

## MINING, GAS, PETROLEUM, ENERGY RELATED

**AMERICAN ASSOCIATION OF PETROLEUM GEOLOGISTS**
P.O. Box 979, Tulsa OK 74101-0979. 918/584-2555. **Physical address:** 1444 South Boulder, Tulsa OK 74119. **Fax:** 918/560-2665. **Toll-free phone:** 800/364-2274. **E-mail address:** postmaster@aapg.org. **World Wide Web address:** http://www.aapg.org. **Description:** Founded in 1917, the AAPG's purpose is to foster scientific research, advance the science of geology, promote technology, and inspire high professional conduct. The AAPG has over 30,000 members.

**AMERICAN GEOLOGICAL INSTITUTE**
4220 King Street, Alexandria VA 22302-1502. 703/379-2480. **Fax:** 703/379-7563. **World Wide Web address:** http://www.agiweb.org. **Description:** A nonprofit federation of 42 geoscientific and professional associations that represents more than 100,000 geologists, geophysicists, and other earth scientists. Provides information services to geoscientists, serves as a voice of shared interests in the profession, plays a major role in strengthening geoscience education, and strives to increase public awareness of the vital role the geosciences play in society's use of resources and interaction with the environment.

**AMERICAN NUCLEAR SOCIETY**
555 North Kensington Avenue, La Grange Park IL 60526. 708/352-6611. **Fax:** 708/352-0499. **World Wide Web address:** http://www.ans.org. **Description:** A not-for-profit, international, scientific and educational organization with a membership of 10,500 engineers, scientists, administrators, and educators representing 1,600 corporations, educational institutions, and government agencies.

**AMERICAN PETROLEUM INSTITUTE**
1220 L Street, NW, Washington DC 20005-4070. 202/682-8000. **World Wide Web address:** http://www.api.org. **Description:** Functions to insure a strong, viable U.S. oil and natural gas industry capable of meeting the energy needs of our Nation in an efficient and environmentally responsible manner.

**GEOLOGICAL SOCIETY OF AMERICA**
3300 Penrose Place, P.O. Box 9140, Boulder CO 80301. 303/447-2020. **Fax:** 303/357-1070. **Toll-free phone:** 888/443-4472. **E-mail address:** gsaservice@geosociety.org. **World Wide Web address:** http://www.geosociety.org. **Description:** The mission of GSA is to advance the geosciences, to enhance the professional growth of its members, and to promote the geosciences in the service of humankind.

**SOCIETY FOR MINING, METALLURGY, AND EXPLORATION**
8307 Shaffer Parkway, Littleton CO 80127-4102. 303/973-9550. **Fax:** 303/973-3845. **Toll-free phone:** 800/763-3132. **E-mail address:** sme@smenet.org. **World Wide Web address:** http://www.smenet.org. **Description:** An international society of professionals in the mining and minerals industry.

**SOCIETY OF PETROLEUM ENGINEERS**
P.O. Box 833836, Richardson TX 75083-3836. 972/952-9393. **Physical address:** 222 palisades Creek Drive, Richardson TX 75080. **Fax:** 972/952-9435. **E-mail address:** spedal@spe.org. **World Wide Web address:** http://www.spe.org. **Description:** SPE is a professional association whose

60,000-plus members worldwide are engaged in energy resources development and production. SPE is a key resource for technical information related to oil and gas exploration and production and provides services through its publications, meetings, and online.

# PAPER AND WOOD PRODUCTS

### AMERICAN FOREST AND PAPER ASSOCIATION
1111 Nineteenth Street, NW, Suite 800, Washington DC 20036. **Toll-free phone:** 800/878-8878. **E-mail address:** info@afandpa.org. **World Wide Web address:** http://www.afandpa.org. **Description:** The national trade association of the forest, pulp, paper, paperboard and wood products industry.

### FOREST PRODUCTS SOCIETY
2801 Marshall Court, Madison WI 53705-2295. 608/231-1361. **Fax:** 608/231-2152. **E-mail address:** info@forestprod.org. **World Wide Web address:** http://www.forestprod.org. **Description:** An international not-for-profit technical association founded in 1947 to provide an information network for all segments of the forest products industry.

### NPTA ALLIANCE
500 Bi-County Boulevard, Suite 200E, Farmingdale NY 11735. 631/777-2223. **Fax:** 631/777-2224. **Toll-free phone:** 800/355-NPTA. **World Wide Web address:** http://www.gonpta.com. **Description:** An association for the $60 billion paper, packaging, and supplies distribution industry.

### PAPERBOARD PACKAGING COUNCIL
201 North Union Street, Suite 220, Alexandria VA 22314. 703/836-3300. **Fax:** 703/836-3290. **E-mail address:** http://www.ppcnet.org. **World Wide Web address:** http://www.ppcnet.org. **Description:** A trade association representing the manufacturers of paperboard packaging in the United States.

### TECHNICAL ASSOCIATION OF THE PULP AND PAPER INDUSTRY
15 Technology Parkway South, Norcross GA 30092. 770/446-1400. **Fax:** 770/446-6947. **Toll-free phone:** 800/332-8686. **World Wide Web address:** http://www.tappi.org. **Description:** The leading technical association for the worldwide pulp, paper, and converting industry.

## PRINTING AND PUBLISHING

### AMERICAN BOOKSELLERS ASSOCIATION
828 South Broadway, Tarrytown NY 10591. 914/591-2665. **Fax:** 914/591-2720. **Toll-free phone:** 800/637-0037. **E-mail address:** info@bookweb.org. **World Wide Web address:** http://www.bookweb.org. **Description:** A not-for-profit organization founded in 1900 devoted to meeting the needs of its core members of independently owned bookstores with retail storefront locations through advocacy, education, research, and information dissemination.

### AMERICAN INSTITUTE OF GRAPHIC ARTS
164 Fifth Avenue, New York NY 10010. 212/807-1990. **Fax:** 212/807-1799. **E-mail address:** comments@aiga.org. **World Wide Web address:** http://www.aiga.org. **Description:** Furthers excellence in communication design as a broadly defined discipline, strategic tool for business and cultural force. AIGA is the place design professionals turn to first to exchange ideas and information, participate in critical analysis and research and advance education and ethical practice. Founded in 1914.

### AMERICAN SOCIETY OF NEWSPAPER EDITORS
11690B Sunrise Valley Drive, Reston VA 20191-1409. 703/453-1122. **Fax:** 703/453-1133. **E-mail address:** asne@asne.org. **World Wide Web address:** http://www.asne.org. **Description:** A membership organization for daily newspaper editors, people who serve the editorial needs of daily newspapers and certain distinguished individuals who have worked on behalf of editors through the years.

### ASSOCIATION OF AMERICAN PUBLISHERS, INC.
71 Fifth Avenue, 2$^{nd}$ Floor, New York NY 10003. 212/255-0200. **Fax:** 212/255-7007. **World Wide Web address:** http://www.publishers.org. **Description:** Representing publishers of all sizes and types located throughout the U.S., the AAP is the principal trade association of the book publishing industry.

### ASSOCIATION OF GRAPHIC COMMUNICATIONS
330 Seventh Avenue, 9$^{th}$ Floor, New York NY 10001-5010. 212/279-2100. **Fax:** 212/279-5381. **E-mail address:** info@agcomm.org. **World Wide Web address:** http://www.agcomm.org. **Description:** The AGC serves as a network for industry information and idea exchange, provides graphic arts education and training, promotes and markets the industry, and advocates legislative and environmental issues.

### BINDING INDUSTRIES OF AMERICA
100 Daingerfield Road, Alexandria VA 22314. 703/519-8137. **Fax:** 703/548-3227. **World Wide Web address:** http://www.bindingindustries.org. **Description:** A trade association representing Graphic Finishers, Loose-Leaf Manufacturers, and suppliers to these industries throughout the United States, Canada, and Europe.

### THE DOW JONES NEWSPAPER FUND
P.O. Box 300, Princeton NJ 08543-0300. 609/452-2820. **Fax:** 609/520-5804. **E-mail address:** newsfund@wsj.dowjones.com. **World Wide Web address:** http://djnewspaperfund.dowjones.com. **Description:** Founded in 1958 by editors of The Wall Street Journal to improve the quality of journalism education and the pool of applicants for jobs in the newspaper business. It provides internships and scholarships to college students, career literature, fellowships for high school

journalism teachers and publications' advisers and training for college journalism instructors. The Fund is a nonprofit foundation supported by the Dow Jones Foundation, Dow Jones & Company, Inc. and other newspaper companies.

**GRAPHIC ARTISTS GUILD**
90 John Street, Suite 403, New York NY 10038-3202. 212/791-3400. **World Wide Web address:** http://www.gag.org. **Description:** A national union of illustrators, designers, web creators, production artists, surface designers and other creatives who have come together to pursue common goals, share their experience, raise industry standards, and improve the ability of visual creators to achieve satisfying and rewarding careers.

**INTERNATIONAL GRAPHIC ARTS EDUCATION ASSOCIATION**
1899 Preston White Drive, Reston VA 20191-4367. 703/758-0595. **World Wide Web address:** http://www.igaea.org. **Description:** An association of educators in partnership with industry, dedicated to sharing theories, principles, techniques and processes relating to graphic communications and imaging technology.

**MAGAZINE PUBLISHERS OF AMERICA**
810 Seventh Avenue, 24th Floor, New York NY 10019. 212/872-3746. **E-mail address:** infocenter@magazine.org. **World Wide Web address:** http://www.magazine.org. **Description:** An industry association for consumer magazines representing more than 240 domestic publishing companies with approximately 1,400 titles, more than 80 international companies and more than 100 associate members.

**NATIONAL ASSOCIATION FOR PRINTING LEADERSHIP**
75 West Century Road, Paramus NJ 07652-1408. 201/634-9600. **Fax:** 201/986-2976. **E-mail address:** information@napl.org. **World Wide Web address:** http://www.napl.org. **Description:** A not-for-profit trade association founded in 1933 for commercial printers and related members of the Graphic Arts Industry.

**NATIONAL NEWSPAPER ASSOCIATION**
P.O. Box 7540,, Columbia MO 65205-7540. 573/882-5800. **Fax:** 573/884-5490. **Toll-free phone:** 800/829-4662. **World Wide Web address:** http://www.nna.org. **Description:** A non-profit association promoting the common interests of newspapers.

**NATIONAL PRESS CLUB**
529 14th Street, NW, Washington DC 20045. 202/662-7500. **Fax:** 202/662-7512. **World Wide Web address:** http://npc.press.org. **Description:** Provides people who gather and disseminate news a center for the advancement of their professional standards and skills, the promotion of free expression, mutual support and social fellowship. Founded in 1908.

**NEWSPAPER ASSOCIATION OF AMERICA**
1921 Gallows Road, Suite 600, Vienna VA 22182-3900. 703/902-1600. **Fax:** 703/917-0636. **World Wide Web address:** http://www.naa.org. **Description:** A nonprofit organization representing the $55 billion newspaper industry.

**THE NEWSPAPER GUILD**
501 Third Street, NW, Suite 250, Washington DC 20001. 202/434-7177. **Fax:** 202/434-1472. **E-mail address:** guild@cwa-union.org. **World Wide Web address:** http://www.newsguild.org. **Description:** Founded as a print journalists' union, the Guild today is primarily a media union whose members are diverse in their occupations, but who share the view that the best working conditions are achieved by people who have a say in their workplace.

## TECHNICAL ASSOCIATION OF THE GRAPHIC ARTS
200 Deer Run Road, Sewickley PA 15213. 412/259-1813. **Fax:** 412/741-2311. **E-mail address:** jallen@piagatf.org. **World Wide Web address:** http://www.taga.org. **Description:** A professional technical association founded in 1948 for the graphic arts industries.

## WRITERS GUILD OF AMERICA WEST
7000 West Third Street, Los Angeles CA 90048. 323/951-4000. **Fax:** 323/782-4800. **Toll-free phone:** 800/548-4532. **E-mail address: World Wide Web address:** http://www.wga.org. **Description:** Represents writers in the motion picture, broadcast, cable and new technologies industries.

## REAL ESTATE

**INSTITUTE OF REAL ESTATE MANAGEMENT**
430 North Michigan Avenue, Chicago IL 60611-4090. 312/329-6000. **Fax:** 800/338-4736. **Toll-free phone:** 800/837-0706. **E-mail address:** custserv@irem.org. **World Wide Web address:** http://www.irem.org. **Description:** IREM, an affiliate of the National Association of Realtors, is an association of professional property and asset managers who have met strict criteria in the areas of education, experience, and a commitment to a code of ethics.

**INTERNATIONAL REAL ESTATE INSTITUTE**
1224 North Nokomis, NE, Alexandria MN 56308. 320/763-4648. **Fax:** 320/763-9290. **E-mail address:** irei@iami.org. **World Wide Web address:** http://www.iami.org/irei. **Description:** A real estate association with members in more than 100 countries, providing media to communicate on an international basis.

**NATIONAL ASSOCIATION OF REALTORS**
30700 Russell Ranch Road, Westlake Village CA 91362. 805/557-2300. **Fax:** 805/557-2680. **World Wide Web address:** http://www.realtor.com. **Description:** An industry advocate of the right to own, use, and transfer real property; the acknowledged leader in developing standards for efficient, effective, and ethical real estate business practices; and valued by highly skilled real estate professionals and viewed by them as crucial to their success.

## RETAIL

### INTERNATIONAL COUNCIL OF SHOPPING CENTERS
1221 Avenue of the Americas, 41st floor, New York NY 10020-1099. 646/728-3800. **Fax:** 732/694-1755. **E-mail address:** icsc@icsc.org. **World Wide Web address:** http://www.icsc.org. **Description:** A trade association of the shopping center industry founded in 1957.

### NATIONAL ASSOCIATION OF CHAIN DRUG STORES
413 North Lee Street, PO Box 1417-D49, Alexandria VA 22313-1480. 703/549-3001. **Fax:** 703/836-4869. **World Wide Web address:** http://www.nacds.org. **Description:** Represents the views and policy positions of member chain drug companies accomplished through the programs and services provided by the association.

### NATIONAL RETAIL FEDERATION
325 7th Street, NW, Suite 1100, Washington DC 20004. 202/783-7971. **Fax:** 202/737-2849. **Toll-free phone:** 800/NRF-HOW2. **World Wide Web address:** http://www.nrf.com. **Description:** A retail trade association, with membership that comprises all retail formats and channels of distribution including department, specialty, discount, catalog, Internet and independent stores as well as the industry's key trading partners of retail goods and services. NRF represents an industry with more than 1.4 million U.S. retail establishments, more than 20 million employees - about one in five American workers - and 2003 sales of $3.8 trillion.

## STONE, CLAY, GLASS, AND CONCRETE PRODUCTS

**THE AMERICAN CERAMIC SOCIETY**
PO Box 6136, Westerville OH 43086-6136. 614/890-4700. **Fax:** 614/899-6109.
**E-mail address:** info@ceramics.org. **World Wide Web address:**
http://www.acers.org. **Description:** An organization dedicated to the
advancement of ceramics.

**NATIONAL GLASS ASSOCIATION**
8200 Greensboro Drive, Suite 302, McLean VA 22102-3881. 866/342-5642. **Fax:**
703/442-0630. **World Wide Web address:** http://www.glass.org. **Description:** A
trade association founded in 1948 representing the flat (architectural and
automotive) glass industry. The association represents nearly 5,000 member
companies and locations, and produces the industry events and publications.

## TRANSPORTATION AND TRAVEL

### AIR TRANSPORT ASSOCIATION OF AMERICA
1301 Pennsylvania Avenue, NW, Suite 1100, Washington DC 20004-1707. 202/626-4000. **Fax:** 301/206-9789. **Toll-free phone:** 800/497-3326. **E-mail address:** ata@airlines.org. **World Wide Web address:** http://www.air-transport.org. **Description:** A trade organization for the principal U.S. airlines.

### AMERICAN SOCIETY OF TRAVEL AGENTS
1101 King Street, Suite 200, Alexandria VA 22314. 703/739-2782. **Fax:** 703/684-8319. **World Wide Web address:** http://www.astanet.com. **Description:** An association of travel professionals whose members include travel agents and the companies whose products they sell such as tours, cruises, hotels, car rentals, etc.

### AMERICAN TRUCKING ASSOCIATIONS
2200 Mill Road, Alexandria VA 22314. 703/838-1700. **Toll-free phone:** 888/333-1759. **World Wide Web address:** http://www.trucking.org. **Description:** Serves and represents the interests of the trucking industry with one united voice; positively influences Federal and State governmental actions; advances the trucking industry's image, efficiency, competitiveness, and profitability; provides educational programs and industry research; promotes highway and driver safety; and strives for a healthy business environment.

### ASSOCIATION OF AMERICAN RAILROADS
50 Γ Street, NW, Washington DC 20001-1564. 202/639-2100. **World Wide Web address:** http://www.aar.org. **Description:** A trade associations representing the major freight railroads of the United States, Canada and Mexico.

### INSTITUTE OF TRANSPORTATION ENGINEERS
1099 14th Street, NW, Suite 300 West, Washington DC 20005-3438. 202/289-0222. **Fax:** 202/289-7722. **E-mail address:** ite_staff@ite.org. **World Wide Web address:** http://www.ite.org. **Description:** An international individual member educational and scientific association whose members are traffic engineers, transportation planners and other professionals who are responsible for meeting society's needs for safe and efficient surface transportation through planning, designing, implementing, operating and maintaining surface transportation systems worldwide.

### MARINE TECHNOLOGY SOCIETY
5565 Sterrett Place, Suite 108, Columbia MD 21044. 410/884-5330. **Fax:** 410/884-9060. **E-mail address:** mtsmbrship@erols.com. **World Wide Web address:** http://www.mtsociety.org. **Description:** A member-based society supporting all the components of the ocean community: marine sciences, engineering, academia, industry and government. The society is dedicated to the development, sharing and education of information and ideas.

### NATIONAL TANK TRUCK CARRIERS
2200 Mill Road, Alexandria VA 22314. 703/838-1960. **Fax:** 703/684-5753. **E-mail address:** inquiries@tanktruck.org. **World Wide Web address:** http://www.tanktruck.net. **Description:** A trade association founded in 1945 and composed of approximately 180 trucking companies, which specialize in the nationwide distribution of bulk liquids, industrial gases and dry products in cargo tank motor vehicles.

## UTILITIES: ELECTRIC, GAS, AND WATER

**AMERICAN PUBLIC GAS ASSOCIATION**
201 Massachusetts Avenue, NE, Suite C-4 Washington DC 20002. 202/464-2742. **Fax:** 202/464-0246. **E-mail address:** website@apga.org. **World Wide Web address:** http://www.apga.org. **Description:** A nonprofit trade organization representing publicly owned natural gas local distribution companies (LDCs). APGA represents the interests of public gas before Congress, federal agencies and other energy-related stakeholders by developing regulatory and legislative policies that further the goals of our members. In addition, APGA organizes meetings, seminars, and workshops with a specific goal to improve the reliability, operational efficiency, and regulatory environment in which public gas systems operate.

**AMERICAN PUBLIC POWER ASSOCIATION (APPA)**
2301 M Street, NW, Washington DC 20037-1484. 202/467-2900. **Fax:** 202/467-2910. **World Wide Web address:** http://www.appanet.org. **Description:** The service organization for the nation's more than 2,000 community-owned electric utilities that serve more than 40 million Americans. Its purpose is to advance the public policy interests of its members and their consumers, and provide member services to ensure adequate, reliable electricity at a reasonable price with the proper protection of the environment.

**AMERICAN WATER WORKS ASSOCIATION**
6666 West Quincy Avenue, Denver CO 80235. 303/794-7711. **Fax:** 303/347-0804. **Toll-free phone:** 800/926-7337. **World Wide Web address:** http://www.awwa.org. **Description:** A resource for knowledge, information, and advocacy to improve the quality and supply of drinking water in North America. The association advances public health, safety and welfare by uniting the efforts of the full spectrum of the drinking water community.

**NATIONAL RURAL ELECTRIC COOPERATIVE ASSOCIATION**
4301 Wilson Boulevard, Arlington VA 22203. 703/907-5500. **E-mail address:** nreca@nreca.coop. **World Wide Web address:** http://www.nreca.org. **Description:** A national organization representing the national interests of cooperative electric utilities and the consumers they serve. Founded in 1942.

## MISCELLANEOUS WHOLESALING

**NATIONAL ASSOCIATION OF WHOLESALER-DISTRIBUTORS (NAW)**
1725 K Street, NW, Washington DC 20006-1419. 202/872-0885. **Fax:** 202/785-0586. **World Wide Web address:** http://www.naw.org. **Description:** A trade association that represents the wholesale distribution industry active in government relations and political action; research and education; and group purchasing.

# INDEX OF PRIMARY EMPLOYERS